Family and Community in Ireland

Family and Community in Ireland

Conrad M. Arensberg / Solon T. Kimball

Second Edition

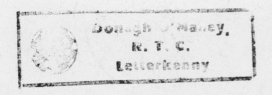
Harvard University Press

Cambridge, Massachusetts

1968

To EARNEST ALBERT HOOTON

Note on the Second Edition

The issuance of a new edition of *Family and Community in Ireland* more than a quarter of a century after its original appearance offers an opportunity and imposes an obligation upon its authors to comment upon their original efforts. The plan and intention had been to publish a second book — an analysis of the organization and life of Irish townsmen complementary to our report on family and community among the countrymen. Very considerable progress was made toward realizing this goal. Great segments of our data had been analyzed, and that part which described the family system of the town's shopkeepers and of the connections between town and country had been presented as a dissertation by one of the authors. We were also well along in describing the ecological setting, demography, occupation, and social class. Perhaps with a little more time the project would have come to fruition, but unfortunately, the time was not to be. The urgencies of World War II swept us, like so many others, away from the routines of civilian life. When the war was over, new interests and their demands carried us ever farther from any expectation that a report on Irish townsmen would be completed.

We were faced with the same problem which all ethnographers encounter. The intrinsic value of the field notes gathered some years earlier may not decline with age, but awareness that changes have occurred in the field situation and that new concepts and methods of research date one's earlier efforts produces a serious reluctance to exhume the past. The alternatives seem to be either to abandon any hope of publication or to return to the field for a new look. The latter alternative appeared to be the desirable solution, but many considerations have made it impossible up to the present moment. Without the materials for an updating of the original, we felt that that analysis should stand as it is — a document expressing a point-of-time in the social life of rural Ireland and a distinctive methodological approach. Furthermore there are other more recent studies of rural Ireland, now issued or in preparation, which describe the contemporary situation and specify the changes that have occurred since our own earlier period of field study. (Among these we wish to mention the work of Robert Cresswell, of Father Alexander Humphreys, and of Art Gallaher.) Their efforts have produced a rich yield.

This new edition, however, gives us a welcome opportunity to present some relevant portions of our already completed analyses of town life. We are fully aware that such a procedure is somewhat less than we would wish for, but we also hope that the new chapters will deepen understanding of Irish society and culture. We feel too that they can discharge some of our obligation to those who planned the study initially, to our friends in Ireland who contributed so much to the success of our field efforts, and to our colleagues for whom this new material may be of some value. In addition, we hope that our results may stimulate new research built upon the bench mark which had been set in an earlier period.

Therefore, to the original book we have added six new chapters on the behavior of townsmen as we learned it in the early

1930's. Our substantive focus reflects the two main concerns with which we were then preoccupied. First, we wanted to make explicit the relationships between the institutional arrangements and the behavior and values of those participating in them. We were eager to discover whether the central position occupied by family among the countrymen was duplicated in the town setting. We also wanted to trace the connections between family and the greatly elaborated economic, religious, educational, and political institutions of the town. We also sought to delineate the patterns of social class and its reflection in institution and behavior.

Our second major concern was the connection between town and country. Some of this relation had been examined in the original book's description of markets and fairs. Although the social arrangements by which products were assembled and distributed showed great stability and historical antiquity, there was no necessary social continuity in the dealings between buyers and sellers. If we were to uncover ties of a less ephemeral sort we must do so in tracing the regularities which tied townsman and countryman together in other ways. It should be no surprise that these emerged from an analysis of the process by which rural youths were incorporated into the town's setting and into the social and economic activity of shopkeepers. These young men and women, a small portion of the stream of rural youth dispersed in the great familial reformation associated with the restructuring of the Irish rural family at the point of marriage, carried with them into the towns the reciprocal obligations of kin. From family they drew that strength which gave them entrance and ensured their survival as they encountered the new values of the urban world and its social class divisions. Although there are other aspects of town life to be examined if we are to see it whole, we hope that our selective study will give a real sense of the distinctions separating urban life from life in the countryside even as the two remain intimately linked.

Conrad M. Arensberg

Solon T. Kimball

June 1967

Preface

Until very recently the study of modern social life has been neglected by social anthropologists. In their zeal to understand human social behavior they have not hesitated to study such complex and populous communities as those of India and China or such simple groups as those of New Guinea and Australia. Their failure to study our own society has not been mere oversight, and not entirely because the subject attracted young men who found in it an excuse for faraway adventure among exotic peoples.

Anthropology has been defined by many ethnologists as "the science of man and his works." Yet they themselves have stubbornly refused to accept the validity of this definition. Physical anthropologists have studied men of the modern world as well as those of other races and societies. Archaeologists have done research on the prehistories of both modern and primitive man. But ethnologists have separated modern and primitive society and declared our own social life to be outside the "science of man." This limitation is the result, in part, of the development of anthropology out of the interests of early travelers, who came back from other lands with accounts of customs far different from our own; in part, of academic conservatism and timidity. But probably the most important influence is the uselessness of the methods and theories of the older ethnologists — historical rather than analytical — for the investigation of modern life.

Most older anthropologists, and many contemporary ones as well, insist that anthropology is and should be only a form of history, a study of historical origins and development. All else, including much of the discipline calling itself social anthropology, is illegitimate. With the increase of Émile Durkheim's influence upon modern European and American anthropology, however, social anthropology has become a social science investigating the nature of social behavior with hypotheses tested inductively by comparative research upon societies of diverse types. Already ethnographic descriptions of several hundred tribes and communities from all parts of the world have led to the making of simple generalizations about these groups, their institutions, and their means of solving the problems of human existence. Some modern anthropologists have come to realize that the diverse communities of the world can be classified in a range of varying degrees of simplicity and complexity, much as animal organisms have been classified, and that our understanding of each group will be greatly enhanced by our knowledge of its comparative position among the social systems of the world.

Once a comparative sociology seems possible, the next step is to include modern society in the scheme of classification. Euro-American society is one of a few highly differentiated cultures which lie at the extreme pole of complexity. Obviously, if we are to study properly variations in human behavior and arrive at adequate generalizations, it is necessary to examine the most complex groups along with the simplest ones. Inevitably, we must bring our own society into such a study. For example, any examination of simple societies demonstrates that most of them have fully developed family and kinship systems, which pervade their whole community life, but simple, undifferentiated economic orders. In more complex societies — as in China and India — economic institutions have grown in importance, and those of family life have decreased. Yet the latter are still of great influence, and much is to be learned from the interdependence of the two. When our own society is added to the range of complexity, our understanding of the connections of these two kinds of social behavior is greatly increased. Our family life has declined, and our economic life has grown immensely in scope, and the mechanism of the change can be compared with that in more simple societies.

It is plain that, if we are to develop a full-grown comparative social science of man, the communities of modern life must be included among those studied by anthropologists. If this means that the subject matter of ethnology is the same as that of sociology, so much the better. Anthropologists may then make effective use of sociological methods, sociologists of anthropological ones.

In accordance with these tendencies, when the Department of Anthropology at Harvard began a study of Ireland under the general direction of Professor Earnest A. Hooton, it was decided to send three types of investigators into the field: physical anthropologists, archaeologists, and social anthropologists. As I was at Harvard at that time, I had the pleasure of acting as director of the work of the social anthropologists, Dr. Kimball and Dr. Arensberg. In the summer of 1931 I made a preliminary survey of the twenty-six counties of the Irish Free State and chose County Clare as most likely to fulfill our needs — a county in which there was a blending of older Gaelic and modern British influences, and one that was neither entirely Gaelic nor entirely English in speech. Dr. Arensberg and I settled in Clare in the summer of 1932 and began the task of collecting the necessary ethnographic data. At the end of the summer I returned to Harvard. Dr. Arensberg remained in Clare, where he was later

Preface

joined by Dr. Kimball, and the two men continued their field work for a period of almost two years. The book that has grown out of their experience there is an excellent contribution to our ever-growing body of knowledge of the communities of the world. From such knowledge we may sometime expect a comparative science of the social life of man.

University of Chicago   W. Lloyd Warner
November, 1939

Acknowledgments

It befits the science of man that its practitioners should depend entirely upon human support and human kindness. The number of persons to whom the two authors have repaired, severally and collectively, is larger than can appear here. We can only hope that the many whom we cannot name will know, as we do, how impossible the production of this book would have been without the help they gave.

To the Department of Anthropology at Harvard University we owe the original project, much of its support, and constant stimulation and encouragement over the years during and after our connections there. Dr. Earnest A. Hooton begat the project out of a fertile imagination and a wide vision of mankind, nourished it, and kept a fatherly eye upon it to the end. Mr. William Lloyd Warner, now of the University of Chicago, taught us social science by precept and field work by example, combining roles of teacher and friend that continue to this day. Dr. Alfred M. Tozzer aided and encouraged us. Dr. Carleton Coon and Dr. Eliot Chapple helped us retain the perspective of ethnology. The Society of Fellows of Harvard University made it possible for one of us to bring the work to completion, with generous provision of freedom for research and allowance for travel. The Sheldon Fund gave the other of us a year and more of field work. Generous friends of Irish scholarship in Boston contributed to the project of which our work was a small part. Dr. Lawrence J. Henderson and Dr. Carle C. Zimmerman helped us to fuller views of social and rural study. Dr. Elton Mayo and Dr. Fritz Roethlisberger gave us criticisms and comparisons of interest. The staff of the Peabody Museum, under Mr. Donald Scott, and our archaeological colleagues, Dr. Hugh O'Neill Hencken, Dr. Hallam Movius, and Mr. John Otis Brew, made our way easy and pleasant both at home and abroad.

Without the gracious aid of many people in Ireland, our task would have been an impossibility. Dr. Eoin MacNeill and Dr. George O'Brien introduced us to the past and present of their country. Dr. Henry Kennedy set us upon the study of agriculture. Dr. Seamus O Duilearga paved our way among the country people. Mr. Patrick Meghen, then Commissioner for Ennis, Mr. Dermot Gleeson, District Justice, Dr. Daniel Coghlan, of the Land Commission, Mr. Michael J. Carey, Secretary of the County Council, Mr. Edward J. Kerin, County Councillor, Dr. Donough MacNamara, Colonel O'Callaghan-Westrupp, the Right Reverend Dr. Fogarty, Bishop of Killaloe, were only a few among our hosts and benefactors in County Clare, too many to name in full. We owe our gratitude to the members, officials, and employees of the Ennis Urban Council; the clergy of the Diocese and in particular of the Diocesan College; the officials of the local branch of the Irish Land Commission; the teachers of both National and Christian Brothers schools; the officers and men of the Garda Siochana; and the members of the legal and medical professions. The people of both town and country in County Clare deserve only praise and gratitude for the warmth of their traditional hospitality and the intelligence of their sympathy with our inquiry. Chief among them are the kind and generous folk among whom we lived in the country districts.

In preparing our materials for publication we had the assistance of Mrs. Grace Senders Dane, Mrs. Frances Mattison Hill, Miss Josephine Thompson, and, particularly with proofs and style, Mrs. Margaret Arensberg. Mrs. Arensberg's labor has made possible whatever grace the book may have.

The material for the figures was prepared by Miss Helen Mitchell. Permission to reprint certain matter copyrighted by Macmillan and Company, Ltd., is acknowledged elsewhere.

C.M.A.
S.T.K.

Cambridge, Massachusetts
December, 1939

Contents

Figures, Tables, and Maps

Figures

Tables

Maps

Family and Community in Ireland

Introduction

Objective study of contemporary social behavior has already begun, in recent years, to yield a new field of inquiry into human relations and human activity. Community studies, social surveys, industrial descriptions, and collections of folk culture and folk custom are beginning to put the investigation of modern Euro-American social life on a par with the ethnology of non-European peoples. The company of such reports is still very small, but it has a healthy growth. There is as yet no common name for them, and the scientific interest behind them has ranged very widely, from psychology to population study or economic history. Nevertheless, the basis for a comparative sociology, or social anthropology if you will, of all the world's peoples, both modern and "primitive," is gradually emerging. The present work is a small attempt to place rural southern Ireland on the roster. It submits a description of certain aspects of contemporary Irish "folk culture."

Ireland really has no need of people to represent her. Her

writers, statesmen, and emigrants have carried her story far beyond the limits of the English-speaking world. The history of her agrarian movements and reforms and the renascence of her autonomy in political and cultural life have been amply documented. Yet the major social and economic conditions of her existence have been presented only through literary or political commentary and controversy. Consequently, an inquiry into sociological matters in the rural hinterland of the country, aiming at a description of the social matrix out of which her rich tradition springs, breaks new ground. The following report of inquiry into the several aspects of rural life in the south and west, carried on in a limited area by two foreigners, is offered to the Irish people as a merest beginning in a task they themselves are best equipped to carry on. The country that has taken a place once again among the free nations of the world deserves to be thoroughly known. It deserves to be put forward among students of human affairs as an example of human life and human achievement unique in respect to history and tradition but similar to others the world over in respect to human relations and organization.

Yet the book that follows studies only a very few of the many aspects of contemporary Irish social life. In the course of field work the problem of the influence of family structure and kinship early forced itself into the center of the stage. The form of the community and the lives of its members could not be understood apart from the kind of relations among persons bound by blood and marriage which the country people exhibited. That influence, therefore, became the principal area of investigation. For this reason this report upon field work is a descriptive account of the connection between several aspects of community life among the small farmers of County Clare, which was the region visited, and the system of ordering family relationships to be found among them.

Though the work deals with rural communities, the authors do not intend it to be in any sense a community study or social survey. Intensive observation brought the authors into intimate contact with three small communities, whose names will appear very often. But their field work was not directed toward discovering what was particular to these. It was aimed at a larger problem. It was based on an assumption fundamental to anthropological theory today. It assumed that the chief determinant factor in human society may well be human activity itself. The question behind the authors' inquiries was couched in terms of this hypothesis. What could they learn to help them to an explanation of the uniformities of human action by following the influence of one kind of activity of human culture upon another? Their results have thus always the same general form: men do these things because they do those others. The nature of the causality remains another question, but the connections observed must first be stated.

Consequently the book deals with indices, particularly statistical ones, describing all the Irish rural folk. It treats the Irish countrymen and countrywomen actually observed and interviewed as instances of a general condition to which such indices might refer. The instance illuminates the index; two knowns thus forecast the unknown generality. Whether the procedure is legitimate, the authors do not argue here; they merely make use of it. The three communities that appear from time to time in the following pages are thus samples, just as County Clare itself is a sample, a fairly representative mean among the major social and economic conditions in Ireland upon which there was documentation in the year 1932.

A good deal of the material presented here has been presented before, though rather differently. Several passages will be familiar to those who have read *The Irish Countryman* by one of the authors, Conrad M. Arensberg. Chapter 10 is in great part a reprint from that work. The authors are deeply indebted to the publishers, the Macmillan Company of London, for permission to include such materials here. They make the inclusion in order to put the behavior described in its perspective in relation to the other topics discussed here. Without it, the present story of mutual dependence and functional interconnection between kinds of activity among the small farmers of southern Ireland would be incomplete. For the theoretical problem that is involved in a discussion of the sociology of subsistence in rural Ireland is of far wider importance than any description of things Irish.

The nature of a social system and the nature of cause and effect in human affairs in social life becomes with each decade more and more important a problem for the increasingly self-conscious nations of the age. In its practical applications, the problem pushes beyond the confines of the sociological and anthropological inquiries which fostered it originally. Legislative changes, attempts at reform and planning, essays in propaganda and persuasion, campaigns for solidarity or defense, forecasts of development, all come to depend for practical success more and more upon a knowledge of how the complex social organism of a modern nation or culture will react. The Irish situation is thus merely an instance. It is an essay in the interconnectedness of the conditions of human social life. Whether one wishes to destroy, change, or preserve, the fact of interconnection exists and must be reckoned with.

As an academic problem, the form of the connection between the parts of the social organism, better stated as the effect of some events of human social life upon others, has been largely the concern of a few theoretical sociologists and a single school of anthropologists. The sociologists have dealt principally with its theoretical aspects, formulating abstract forecasts of the necessary connections. The anthropologists, of the "functional" school, have had to face the problem as a concrete requirement of description. Their tribes and native cultures have presented them with whole situations in which each part was foreign to them and in which each part had no other reference than the situation itself could give. Alert readers will detect the influence of both approaches in this book. Yet the emphasis throughout will be placed on the concrete necessities of description. The behavior of the Irish country people and the indices which report it are specific matters of observation and record. The internal connections they may have are equally specific matters.

Yet the authors do not wish to be thought in any sense experts on the Irish scene or to be motivated primarily by a desire to explain things Irish to the world. Much as they desire to understand and give proper value to the nation which so kindly and courteously received them, they do not feel themselves qualified in any way to characterize or evaluate the culture, tradition, or social life of the communities in which they made their study. Therefore, they present the results of their examination of the data they gathered in Ireland in answer to quite another set of problems. If they by chance and inadvertence happen to bring the light of a fresh foreign point of view into matters which are of much more than theoretical interest to Irishmen in the Free State, or to students of Ireland and her problems, they will count themselves lucky indeed.

The purpose of the study is not so much to characterize the communities described as it is to examine the behavior of the persons living in them. The data upon which the argument of the book rests are the data of events, biographies, and situations in which the members of the communities took their parts. But the conclusions which advance the argument and which the authors draw from these data are not primarily intended as characterizations of the behavior involved. They are steps in the elaboration of a view of human behavior in social life to which they impel the authors and toward which it is hoped the reader will likewise find himself drawn.

That this should be the case involves the earliest history of the present research. It was begun in 1932 as an intensive field research in social anthropology as it had grown up in the ethnological work of Malinowski and through the theoretical formulations of Radcliffe-Brown. Neither of the authors of this book had done firsthand work among primitive peoples. They had served apprenticeships in field work under Professor William Lloyd

meet that reader's disapproval, we are afraid, if he is not an Irishman, or win his enthusiastic support, if he is. Against that sort of interpretation the authors must protect themselves as best they can. Only the development of further studies of similar nature and the growth of understanding of what mechanisms are universal and what are particular in social structure will resolve such controversy.

But the reader must remember that, even though the book draws upon details of the most minute and personal kind, taken out of the most distinctively Irish situations, the use they are put to is not characterizing or descriptive. The authors use the observation of personal relations, individual and group activities, expressions of sentiment and emotion of every kind, as expository matter in the presentation of the general process by which individuals are united, groups are formed, joined, opposed, and in which the cohesion of the community is created, maintained, defended, and lost.

What is here attempted, then, is a work of inductive social analysis. Perhaps the adjectives "analytic" and "interpretive" describe the purpose of the authors best. Detail, local color, dramatic incident, and specific quotation are offered not for themselves, or for the picture they make, but in answer to questions of how and why human beings come to act upon one another in certain ways, to govern their lives in particular fashions, and to accept sentiments and beliefs of the kinds recorded.

The book works toward the problem of the individual as well, particularly so because its data are individual acts, events, expressions of opinion and attitude. For the problem of how science is to deal with individual life and individual behavior is inseparable, as we shall see, from the inquiry here pursued. The authors certainly do not intend any study of Irish psychology *per se,* or attempt psychoanalysis of the Irish mind. Rather they work toward the view of the problem of the individual in society which their inductions force upon them. In fact, it is another reason for the authors' adherence to anthropological

nologist's point of view. They seek to describe a culture, taking that word in its anthropological sense. And they seek to do so as observers of the minutiae of social life.

Naturally the culture so to be described need not have been that of Ireland, as far as the larger purpose of the study was concerned. But Ireland has many advantages for just such an inquiry, and in the authors' view, well warranted choice as a scene of operations.

In the first place, Ireland presented a distinctive and characteristic variant of western European civilization and a long, relatively unbroken tradition dating back to pre-Christian and pre-Roman times. Yet this distinctiveness is comprised within what is, after all, a small compass. Ireland is by no means a large country, and, however its people may be conscious of their own internal differences, it is very homogeneous indeed. Any acquaintance with Ireland at all soon establishes the fact that, far from being on the retreat, the distinctive culture of Ireland is increasing in strength and autonomy, however much it has learned to assimilate the technological and other developments of the modern age.

Nor is the anthropologist abashed by the arguments of those who deny any autonomy to national and ethnic cultures because, after all, they are part and parcel of a larger whole — that of the general occidental civilization. For all classifications of this sort are relative, and need be accepted only for the purpose one wishes to put them to. Just as one can speak of Iroquois culture in contradistinction to Algonquin, though both are eastern woodland American Indians, so one can speak of English and Irish cultures or national groups. The two are distinguishable by differences of behavior and outlook and products of quite different ways of life, even though in many aspects they are comparable and similarly derived historically.

Thus in many cases the data will be distinctly Irish and the conclusions may seem to some readers applicable only to Irish conditions. This will be the case particularly where the data meet that reader's disapproval, we are afraid, if he is not an Irishman, or win his enthusiastic support, if he is. Against that sort of interpretation the authors must protect themselves as best they can. Only the development of further studies of similar nature and the growth of understanding of what mechanisms are universal and what are particular in social structure will resolve such controversy.

But the reader must remember that, even though the book draws upon details of the most minute and personal kind, taken out of the most distinctively Irish situations, the use they are put to is not characterizing or descriptive. The authors use the observation of personal relations, individual and group activities, expressions of sentiment and emotion of every kind, as expository matter in the presentation of the general process by which individuals are united, groups are formed, joined, opposed, and in which the cohesion of the community is created, maintained, defended, and lost.

What is here attempted, then, is a work of inductive social analysis. Perhaps the adjectives "analytic" and "interpretive" describe the purpose of the authors best. Detail, local color, dramatic incident, and specific quotation are offered not for themselves, or for the picture they make, but in answer to questions of how and why human beings come to act upon one another in certain ways, to govern their lives in particular fashions, and to accept sentiments and beliefs of the kinds recorded.

The book works toward the problem of the individual as well, particularly so because its data are individual acts, events, expressions of opinion and attitude. For the problem of how science is to deal with individual life and individual behavior is inseparable, as we shall see, from the inquiry here pursued. The authors certainly do not intend any study of Irish psychology *per se*, or attempt psychoanalysis of the Irish mind. Rather they work toward the view of the problem of the individual in society which their inductions force upon them. In fact, it is another reason for the authors' adherence to anthropological

havior of the Irish country people and the indices which report it are specific matters of observation and record. The internal connections they may have are equally specific matters.

Yet the authors do not wish to be thought in any sense experts on the Irish scene or to be motivated primarily by a desire to explain things Irish to the world. Much as they desire to understand and give proper value to the nation which so kindly and courteously received them, they do not feel themselves qualified in any way to characterize or evaluate the culture, tradition, or social life of the communities in which they made their study. Therefore, they present the results of their examination of the data they gathered in Ireland in answer to quite another set of problems. If they by chance and inadvertence happen to bring the light of a fresh foreign point of view into matters which are of much more than theoretical interest to Irishmen in the Free State, or to students of Ireland and her problems, they will count themselves lucky indeed.

The purpose of the study is not so much to characterize the communities described as it is to examine the behavior of the persons living in them. The data upon which the argument of the book rests are the data of events, biographies, and situations in which the members of the communities took their parts. But the conclusions which advance the argument and which the authors draw from these data are not primarily intended as characterizations of the behavior involved. They are steps in the elaboration of a view of human behavior in social life to which they impel the authors and toward which it is hoped the reader will likewise find himself drawn.

That this should be the case involves the earliest history of the present research. It was begun in 1932 as an intensive field research in social anthropology as it had grown up in the ethnological work of Malinowski and through the theoretical formulations of Radcliffe-Brown. Neither of the authors of this book had done firsthand work among primitive peoples. They had served apprenticeships in field work under Professor William Lloyd

Warner, then of Harvard University, in a study of a contemporary New England city and were thoroughly devoted to social anthropology as a technique for study of modern civilized communities.

Thus the conclusions of the book are in the nature of answers to the questions originally responsible for setting about the research. Experience in Yankee City in New England had led the authors to the point of view which is the central hypothesis of functional anthropology. The more they worked, the more it grew certain for them that to a certain approximation it is useful to regard society as an integrated system of mutually interrelated and functionally interdependent parts. A study in Ireland, then, should be a study to test this hypothesis. In a setting far different but still in some ways closely comparable to the American scene which the authors already knew, they would try to give it a greater precision.

The pooled experience of the authors, in so far as they themselves can judge it, did not involve a rigid insistence upon or acceptance of any one anthropological view within the broad confines of the functionalist approach. It also carried them far beyond the confines of anthropology, as the reader will soon learn.

For the most part the Irish communities the authors undertook to examine and in which they had a brief but enjoyable participation were, in a sense, laboratories and workshops. They exemplified concretely the problems contained in the concepts, social structure, social system, and organization of human behavior.

That is why, then, even though the authors found themselves becoming, as far as their halting steps would take them, economists, political scientists, folklorists, students of religion and whatnot, they found the general role of ethnologist and social anthropologist most congenial to their task. Even where their data, in part at least, necessitate the formulation of a general sociology, they are still confirmed in what is essentially the eth-

method and anthropological outlook that the study confirms them in an original view. That is that there is no sociology which is not equally a psychology, nor any psychology which is not equally a sociology. In one aspect, the book will be a treatise on the necessity for abandoning distinctions between the fields and an attempt to force the realization of this identity.

If there is any single conclusion to which the authors wish to point with greatest emphasis, it is this: that social life and society must be understood not in terms of any hypostatization either of *the individual* or of *society*. There is no such thing as *the* society or *the* individual. Both concepts are conclusions of relative and limited validity. There are only persons behaving in various ways.

But this view is not the purpose of the book. It is the conclusion to which the authors were led in pursuance of their purpose. Nevertheless, it bears statement here at the outset, because it is so simple. Yet the whole course of the book is necessary to establish it and to show it to be the base upon which objective and inductive social science, still only a distant goal, can be built.

The final purpose of the book is to reach this base. It is an attempt to clear away in a concrete case the manifold complexities of civilized society to a point where an inductive science founded upon simple and measurable data can be begun. Its final purpose is also its conclusion: an objective social science can only be made by developing an impersonal technique for reducing to order the only social data we have which are comparable to those from which the natural sciences developed. These are the data of the interaction of human beings, to be found in what they do to one another.

One

The Countryside

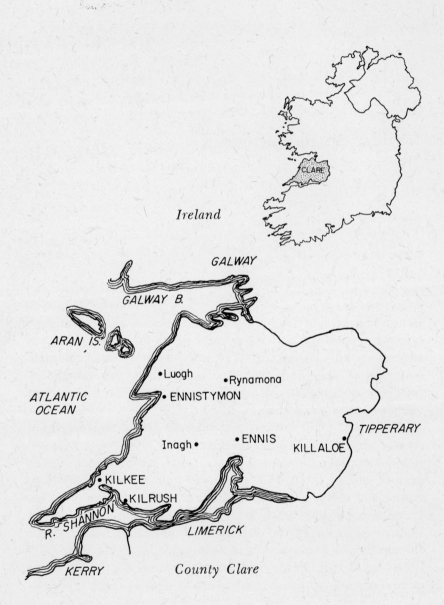

Ireland

GALWAY

GALWAY B.

ARAN IS.

ATLANTIC
OCEAN

•Luogh   •Rynamona

•ENNISTYMON

Inagh•   •ENNIS

TIPPERARY

KILLALOE

•KILKEE

•KILRUSH

R. SHANNON

LIMERICK

KERRY   County Clare

CLARE

1

The Small Farmers

Censuses have laid bare the existence of two widely different types of agricultural activity in the Irish countryside. There are two widely different groups of persons whom we can tentatively designate as large and small farmers. Indeed, the statistics, if used correctly, give factual base to the divisions the Irish reckon in the countryside themselves. They remind one continually that the large and small farmers are different beings and belong to ways of life which are quite opposed.

In general, the differences are such as to present two groups of persons defined by two different ways of adapting themselves to nature and carrying on the business of agricultural production. Large farmers differ from small farmers in their techniques, in their products, in the use of the soil and the land. They differ in the way in which numbers derive support from their farms. They differ significantly in the organization of labor upon those farms and presumably in consequence in their relations with other ele-

3

ments of the community. Family labor characterizes the small man, hired labor the big fellow.

No one, of course, expects this to be an exact correspondence in which one gets perfect correlations in each instance between the size of the acreage and other factors. A typical small farm economy might well exist on a farm very large in area, and often does so in mountainous areas, where much of the land is useless. Again, a farm small in area might be exclusively devoted to the sort of economy which is usually found on very large farms. In any single case, statistical generalities do not hold, of course. But in the large kind of correlation which a count of varying factors affords, bulk correspondences turn up with complete regularity.

The course by which this conclusion is reached takes one through the devious labyrinth of Free State Government statistical abstracts. In 1926, the last census year before the authors' field work was undertaken, the numbers living in country districts, "outside villages and towns with 200 or more population," made up 63 per cent of the Free State's population of almost 3,000,000. They were 1,815,496. Of the 1,307,662 classed as "occupied persons 12 years of age and over" for the whole Free State, 672,129, or 51 per cent, were engaged in agriculture. Any attempt, then, to understand the human setting of Irish farming involves an inquiry into the forces motivating the lives of well over half the country's people.

In 1926 this agricultural population produced a total output valued at £64,757,000. Industry in Ireland produced goods to the value of only a little over half that figure (£34,000,000 net output).

In the agricultural output of that year, the proportions of the various products indicate the character of the agriculture. Foodstuffs, with livestock products among them, made up the bulk of the output. Milk products accounted for £13,600,000; cattle, exported alive or slaughtered within the country, accounted for another £13,800,000. Pigs and eggs made up £9,800,000 and

4

£6,690,000 respectively. Other livestock such as poultry, sheep, and horses accounted for the rest, in that order of importance. Wool and sundry items such as honey brought in a mere £700,000. All of these, the total output of livestock, reached a value of £50,555,000. The figures illustrate the preponderant importance of livestock and particularly cattle and pigs in Irish economy.

The remaining £14,000,000 was made up of crops and turf, the latter alone accounting for £5,938,000. Among the crops, potatoes came first, with a value for the year of £3,786,000. Oats, cabbage, and barley accounted for about £900,000 each; and there were a few other items of smaller values, the largest of which was fruit at £466,000.

These figures of the agricultural products rather under-estimate the amount of tillage products raised. In the words of the Census Report, they "do not include any part of the prod-uce which was used for further agricultural production in the Saorstat whether that part was used on the farm on which pro-duced or sold by one farmer to another — e.g. milk fed to calves, potatoes fed to pigs, hay, turnips, mangels fed to cattle, corn used for seed, horses used for farm work." [1]

Within this generality of the monetary value of the goods pro-duced, one can begin to take account of the wide difference of the sizes of the holdings engaged in this agricultural produc-tion. A glance at the figure illustrating this kind of economy by relative size of acreage (Fig. 1) will bring the matter out.

The agricultural community carried on this production upon farms of very widely different character. Holdings range in size from one acre or less to 500 or more. Those under 30 acres com-prise 23 per cent of the total acreage of agricultural land in the Saorstat, those of 30–50, 17 per cent; those of 50–100, 24 per cent; and those of 100–200, 19 per cent. Farms larger than 200 acres cover only 16 per cent of agricultural land.

[1] *Agricultural Output of Saorstat Eireann, 1926–27* (Department of In-dustry and Commerce, Statistics Branch, Dublin Stationery Office, 1930), p. 5.

Figure 1

Production on Large and Small Holdings, All Ireland, 1926 Census

Use of Land

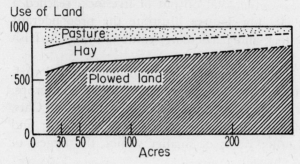

Cattle

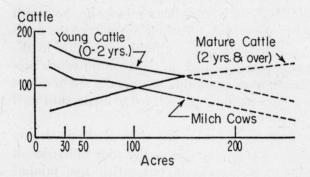

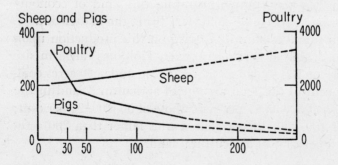

In general, the smaller ones practice the more generalized economy, their production being markedly different from that of the large farms. The latter, especially in the midland counties, where they are most numerous, raise little more than beef cattle. Their owners are the graziers or "ranchers" of current political controversy in Ireland. The different economies express themselves in the census as follows:

The numbers of acres ploughed and the numbers under hay per 1000 acres of agricultural land decrease continuously as the size of the holdings increases; the numbers of milch cows, of young cattle, of pigs, and of poultry also decrease but the number of dry older cattle and of sheep per 1000 acres increase as the size of the holdings increases. The contrast between the smallest and the largest holdings is exceedingly great and is very great even between the second smallest and second largest. Contrasting the holdings 30–50 acres with holdings 100–200 acres the table shows that on equal areas of agricultural land, the smaller holdings have 32% more ploughed land, 29% more hay, 54% more milch cows, 53% more cattle under one year, 16% more cattle one to two years old, and 9% more cattle of all kinds, 80% more pigs, and 139% more poultry than the holdings 100–200 acres, but the latter have 24% more sheep, 52% more dry cattle, 2 to 3 years old, and 209% more dry cattle 3 years old or over than do holdings 30–50 acres.[2]

In County Clare, the area of our investigation, agriculture presents much the same character and the same difference between small and large farmers as does the whole of Ireland. Clare occupies a middle place among the counties; neither the large nor the small farm predominates. Almost always the small farmer has a garden in potatoes and cabbage with a few oats and turnips and perhaps some rye. The rest of his land will be under several meadows in hay, grazed during the winter months, and in fields (pasture land) grazed during both summer and winter, if sheltered. In rough mountain areas sheep are common, par-

[2] *Agricultural Statistics, 1847–1926, Report and Tables* (Department of Industry and Commerce, Statistics Branch, Dublin Stationery Office, 1930), p. xxi.

ticularly in the Broadford and Tubber districts. In addition to cattle, the smaller holder generally has a large flock of ducks, geese, and hens, and he keeps several pigs. These are also fed upon the oats, potatoes, cabbage, and milk left over after the other livestock have been fed. Specialization in poultry raising is still rare, though poultry stations are being established here and there under the supervision of agents of the Department of Agriculture. Certain areas, of course, show minor specializations, such as Miltown Malbay, a seacoast region known for its cabbage, and Newquay, known for its oats; but an entire farm is seldom, if ever, devoted to one crop.

With few exceptions, then, the chief occupation of the small farmers is the production of cattle. Milk is sold direct to the creameries in areas where they have been established. It comes to occupy the largest part of farm production in such counties as Limerick, but in Clare the creameries are still being introduced. Where there is no creamery, the milk is used for food in the form of butter, or sold as fresh and salted butter in nearby centers, or it is fed to livestock. For the small farmer may keep several dry cattle and calves in addition to his milch cows.

The ideal is to have as much grass as possible, even with those small farmers who do most tillage. A farm is described among them as "the place of [so many] cows." For this reason, hay is the principal crop of the year; in all cases, it is an important fodder. Often it is the only winter fodder. The dependence upon hay is well exemplified for all Ireland in the fluctuation of the annual milk yield. It is at its highest through May, June, and July during the period of fresh grasses, and sinks to a low in January. The range is from 3 per cent of annual production in January to 13 per cent in June.

The large farmer, typically the so-called "rancher," a grazier of over 200 acres, presents a quite different picture, though he, too, is a great cattle producer. Ordinarily, he cultivates nothing but a "kitchen garden" for household use. He utilizes his land to its full capacity for grazing cattle. Ranching of this sort is typical

8

of the midland counties such as Meath and the other counties of
Leinster, but it is found also in certain areas of Clare. The first
of these is the low-lying alluvial plain around the mouth of the
river Fergus, very rich in grass-bearing soil. A concentration of
large holdings is found there. The actual acreage of the holdings
gives little information because of the difficulty of comparing
them with holdings in other parts of the country when in the
latter much mountain land is included. The valuations, however, are exceedingly high, the full valuation of the Ennis district (which includes the Fergus plain) being £67,000 for 112,000
acres compared with the neighboring Killadysert district at
£25,000 for 62,000 acres.

The second of the "ranching districts" or areas of large holdings practicing this type of agriculture is the region in the northern part of the county called "the hills of Burren" (the Ballyvaughan area). This is a limestone country which provides rich
winterage for cattle. Consequently land there is very valuable to
the rancher who has to winter his store cattle. Grass grows there
fairly richly throughout the winter among the limestone crags,
and the cattle are allowed to forage for themselves. In several
cases, farmers own large holdings of 200 acres and over in each
of the two areas. They drive their cattle down from the winter-
ages in April and back again in November.

Certain other farms of large size, and especially in rich alluvial areas such as Clarecastle and Newmarket-on-Fergus, make
extensive use of tillage, primarily of oats. In other areas such as
Tubber, Broadford, and Feakle, mountain land is given over to
sheep.

County Clare, in fact, shows a fourfold division into sections
differentiated partly geographically, partly by the different
utilization of the soil. "West Clare" includes all the peninsula
west and south of the ridge culminating in Mount Callan and
cutting off the Fergus drainage from the Atlantic. Here the holdings are predominantly small, and the more generalized economy is common. "North Clare" covers the country of the "hills

of Burren." "East Clare" contains both the rough country of Feakle and Broadford, where small mountain holdings approximate the conditions of West Clare, and the Tulla and Quin districts, which with "Mid-Clare" and "South Clare" cover the alluvial plain of the Fergus River, where there are many "ranches" and, in parts, extensive oats tillage.

Statistics are available only for the whole of Clare; they give a comprehensive view of the county's farming.[3] All but 21.6 per cent of the population of 95,064 lived in country districts. The area they worked, 787,768 acres, was divided into 15,857 holdings, of which 1,179 did not exceed one acre, 909 contained from 1 to 5, 841 from 5 to 10, 1,108 from 10 to 15, and 3,767 from 15 to 30, 3,617 from 30 to 50, and 3,135 from 50 to 100. The farms larger than 100 acres numbered 997 in the 100 to 200 acre group, and 394 exceeding 200 acres. Clare thus fell into a category among counties in which medium-sized holdings were normal, but both the small farms and the large rancher type were present.

We have no separate statistics for Clare's produce, but we know that in June 1932 the land was being utilized in the following manner. There were only 465 acres of wheat, 335 acres of barley, 207 acres of rye, 1 acre of beans and peas, 147 acres of fruit, 3 acres of sugar beet, 57 acres of experimental ensilage for cattle, and 151 acres of miscellaneous root and green crops. The figures[4] show the small part played by vegetable products other than cabbage and potatoes used for human food. Bread, the great staple, was, of course, made from imported flour or wheat. Potatoes and oats, however, made a better showing, with 13,518 and 8,199 acres respectively devoted to them. Turnips and mangels accounted for 3,897 and 306 acres respectively; like potatoes and oats, they are used for both human and animal consumption. This was the extent of ploughed land.

[3] Figures taken from Annual Report, County Clare Council Agricultural Committee, June 1932.

[4] Report of the County Clare Agricultural Committee, 1932.

10

The great bulk of the area was, of course, in hay and pasture. There were 2,791 acres of first-year hay, 131,429 acres of other hay, and 394,791 acres of pasture.

These figures coupled with those giving the number of livestock in the county at that date illustrate the greatly preponderant interest in animal products, particularly cattle, pigs, and eggs. The figures for cattle show that Clare is not primarily a ranching county, but that there is, nevertheless, a respectable number of dry, store cattle. In June 1932 there were 786 bulls, 60,149 milch cows, and 1,696 heifers in calf; and besides such breeding stock there were 5,780 dry three-year-olds or over, 23,266 two-year-olds, and 47,918 yearlings. There were also 58,708 under a year old.

Returning again to the conditions for all Ireland, it will be seen in how many respects Clare duplicates the various types of agriculture for all Ireland. The Report of Agricultural Statistics, 1847–1926, describes statistically the difference in farming between large and small holders over the whole country. It finds that for the whole country

milch cows were densest (in 1926) in the Southwestern Counties [Clare is one], a region of medium sized holdings, next densest in the Northwest with its numerous small holdings and least dense in the Central Eastern Counties . . . The 13 latter counties included 11 of the counties of the largest percentage of land under holdings of 200 acres or over, 11 of the 13 densest in dry cattle 3 years or over, 10 of the 13 densest in dry cattle 2 to 3 years old and 10 of the 13 densest in sheep . . . The counties densest in the older dry cattle coincide closely with the densest in large holdings.[5]

Of tillage the Report states that

small farmers adopt a crop rotation very different to that of the large farmers, putting much more of their ploughed land under roots and green crops and much less under corn . . . Farmers with 1 to 30 acres devote to potatoes nearly three times as large a proportion of their

[5] *Agricultural Statistics, 1847–1926,* p. xxiii.

11

ploughed land as farmers with over 200 acres, and the latter put twice as much . . . under barley and under turnips as the small farmer and a much larger proportion under oats and mangels.

As regards the smaller crops "the small farmers show a distinct preference for cabbage and rye." [6]

"Poultry are influenced more than any other class of livestock by size of the farm . . . They are nine times as dense on holdings of 1 to 30 acres as on holdings over 200 acres . . . Counties densest in poultry coincide with the counties densest in small holdings." [7]

Pigs, however, "seem to be influenced more by densities of tillage and of milch cows than by size of holdings . . . The Southwestern Counties [Clare is one of them] have dense pig herds and the largest bacon factories." [8]

The difference reflects itself likewise in the distribution of agricultural implements and machinery over the two types of farm. The figures, dating from 1917,[9] are two decades old, but, in spite of the subsequent increase in mechanization, Irish farming is little given to abundant use of machines, and proportions hold much as at that time. In the words of the Report in discussing the tables it presents, giving numbers of farm implements and machines, enumerating ploughs, harrows, turnip and mangel sowers, corn binders, mowers and reapers, horse-drawn hayforks, and potato diggers per thousand acres of ploughed land or specific crop, on various sized holdings:

The figures rise regularly to a maximum (in the column representing holdings of 50 to 100 acres) and then fall away regularly. Small figures for the small holdings presumably mean that the less efficient implements are used (the spade in place of the plough, the scythe in-

[6] *Agricultural Statistics, 1847–1926*, pp. xxvi, xxvii.
[7] *Agricultural Statistics, 1847–1926*, p. xxvi.
[8] *Agricultural Statistics, 1847–1926*, p. xxvi.
[9] *Agricultural Statistics, 1847–1926*, p. lv.

12

stead of the mower), not that cooperation . . . exists to any appreciable extent.[10]

That large holders do not proportionately increase their use of such implements and machines after the 50 to 100 acre maximum is reached lies in the fact that "the small figures for the largest size holdings show that the machines on the smaller farms were more than sufficient for the type of agriculture carried on."[11] For instance, on farms of 30–50 acres there were 137 ploughs to every 1,000 acres of ploughed land. But much less than half that number were sufficient for the same acreage of ploughed land on holdings over 500 acres. The difference reflects itself statistically not only in the goods produced but in the tools and techniques used.

More important, however, for an understanding of the social behavior involved, is a further great difference to be seen in the numbers of persons living upon the various sized farms. The numbers of persons supporting themselves upon the small holdings are much greater than those upon large farms. Figure 2 shows this graphically. County Mayo there represents one extreme of "congestion" and County Meath another. County Clare is of such mixed character that its position looks anomalous. The figure deals only with farmers and does not, as we shall see, represent the real situation, for it leaves out of account those who work the farm along with its farmer owner.

In 1926 there were 268,930 farmers in the Irish Free State, the largest block of which supported themselves upon farms of from 15 to 30 acres, that is, upon small farms. Their number was 75,225. Farmers numbering 51,196 worked farms of from 30 to 50 acres, and 41,052 farms of from 50 to 100. On smaller farms than the 15–30 acre norm there were 11,608 farmers on 1–5 acre

[10] *Agricultural Statistics, 1847–1926,* p. lvi. We shall see that this statement is not entirely accurate, though there is no large-scale village cooperation as in Balkan and Slavic lands.

[11] *Agricultural Statistics, 1847–1926,* p. lvi.

Figure 2

Proportion of Farmers on Each Size Holding (1926)

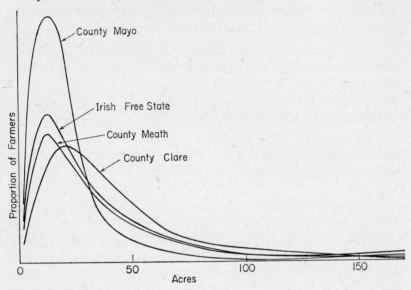

farms and 29,180 on 5–10 acre ones. On larger farms than 100 acres there were, however, only 22,660 farmers.

The counties, of course, differed widely in this respect, but in general the counties where large holdings were numerous supported a much smaller farm population than those where smaller holdings prevailed. Thus Meath, a ranching county of 577,000 acres, supported only 4,403 farmers, while Clare, with an area only about one and one-half times as large, supported 10,320 farmers in a much less rich and more mountainous soil. Indeed, it is one of the anomalies most regretted by the present De Valera government (among others) that Ireland's population is concentrated in the poorer and more mountainous parts of the island. Clare, of course, does not present such an extreme case as the so-called "congested" counties of Mayo, Kerry, and Galway.

14

In County Clare small farmers are, of course, definitely in the majority. The number of true "ranchers" is few. In 1926 the proportions were 3,020 male farmers on farms 15–30 acres (the largest group), 2,280 on farms 30–50, 2,033 on farms 50–100. In the groups smaller than 15 acres there were 828 farmers on farms 10–15 acres and 486 on farms 5–10. Farmers living on farms under 5 acres are few (180). Those on farms up to 200 number 597 and above 200, 218.

When the total population engaged in agriculture is considered rather than merely the farmers (owners), the greater numbers living upon small holdings become even more apparent. A full report based upon the 1926 census had not yet appeared, but a report was published upon the 1912 figures at the time the 1926 figures were released.[12] From that report it is at once apparent that the difference between large and small farms extends to the population engaged upon them and the type of labor employed. This new difference demonstrates a marked contrast, still apparent today, in the way in which large and small farmers carry on their economies.

In 1926 the number of farmers and relatives assisting them in the Saorstat was 533,025 and those otherwise engaged in agriculture numbered only 139,104. The figures of the Report, based upon the 1912 census, show higher numbers, but the proportion of hired to family labor had not materially changed. From the tables of the Report, it is established that "only 26% were wage earners," that is, were not farmers and their relatives, working without periodic monetary recompense on an employee basis. Relating this to size of farms, it was discovered that not only were "5 times as many persons working on farms of 15 to 30 acres and 3½ times as many on farms of 30–50 acres as on farms of over 200 acres,"[13] but that also "family labor accounted for 89% of the total on farms 1–15 acres but only 24% for farms of over 200 acres . . . Taking all holdings into account, 74% of the per-

[12] *Agricultural Statistics, 1847–1926,* p. liv.
[13] *Agricultural Statistics, 1847–1926,* p. li.

sons working on farms consisted of farmers, their wives, sons, daughters, and other relatives," and only "15% were permanent wage earners and 11% were temporary employees." [14] In other words, the small farm is generally worked by the family of the owner, while the large farm, particularly the ranch, is worked by agricultural laborers employed by the owner.

In Figure 3 the tables are reduced to a graphic representation which shows well how much truth there is in the Irish assertion that "the smaller the farm, the larger the number of people it supports." One has only to look at it to understand much of Irish political currents.

In Clare the same situation is present. Most, if not nearly all, of the work of the small farmers is done by the family relatives. And for the whole county in 1926, 83.5 per cent of all males engaged in agricultural pursuits were farmers or farmers' relatives (and 99 per cent of the rather small number of females). Only in the two districts which we have already mentioned as regions of large holdings and ranches, Ballyvaughan and Ennis, did the percentage fall appreciably below that figure (to 73 per cent and 75 per cent).

Figure 4 presents this difference in organization of labor for all Ireland in 1912.

Small farmers and large farmers make a different disposal of their products. At the same time there is an exchange of products between the two groups.

These facts are to be got from the many statistics reflecting the internal trade carried on within Ireland. There we can follow the movement of the goods of production through the population.[15] The writers deal with the statistics reflecting conditions before the advent of the De Valera government (1932) because they are the more complete and because changes introduced since then by the Fianna Fáil domestic and foreign policies had

[14] *Agricultural Statistics, 1847–1926*, p. lii.
[15] *Agricultural Output of Saorstát Éireann, 1926–27*, pp. 6, 10.

Figure 3

Number of Persons Actively Engaged in Agriculture in 1912

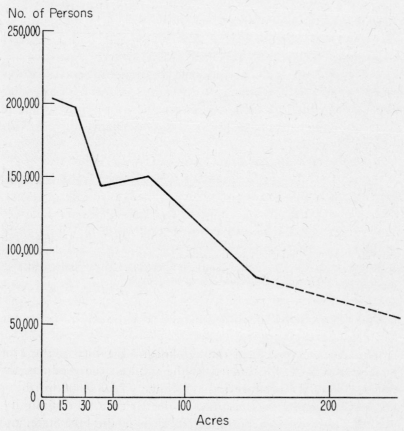

These are the actual numbers arranged proportionately, in true descending scale, with the size of the holding. Figures for all Ireland. The figures are quite comparable with those of County Clare for 1932, where in records published in the local newspaper by the County Council Committee on Agriculture it was stated that on farms of 15–30 acres, the median-sized holding, on which the plurality of the farm population live, there were 10 acres to each person. But on farms of 200 acres and over, more than 35 acres were required for each person the farms supported.

Figure 4

Organization of Labor, 1912

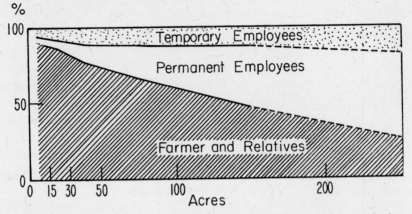

The chart again shows a constant progression. The larger the farm, the less the dependence upon other members of the family and the more often hired hands are present. The chart begins on the left with a figure of 89 per cent of farmers of 1–15 acres depending upon family help and ends at the right with 24 per cent of farmers of over 200 acres depending upon such help.

not yet (1935) had time to become the settled habit of the people at the time of the study.

In 1930 the majority of the agricultural produce of the Free State was exported. Estimated by the value of the products, the destination of the produce was as follows: £23,000,000 worth, or about 35 per cent, was consumed by the agricultural community; about 17 per cent was consumed by others in the Free State; and about 43 per cent was exported. The greater consumption of agricultural products in the country does not, of course, imply a better diet necessarily, since we are disregarding for the moment the large imports of foodstuffs made by both town and country districts, and since much of the country consumption went into further animal production.

Export, of course, was designed for the English market. In terms of specific products, 81 per cent of the cattle and sheep production was exported, 59 per cent of the pigs, 37 per cent of the output of butter and cream.[16]

In other words, only a small part of the output of more expensive cattle and sheep was consumed at home, but, at the other extreme, the cheaper stuffs stayed on the farm. The great bulk of the potatoes and turf produced, and just about one-half of the output of such dairy produce as whole milk, butter, eggs, and poultry, were consumed by the producers. Tillage crops tell the same story; they remained at home. The chief and overwhelmingly important exports were live animals and live animal products, such as butter.

Of these exports, of course, cattle were the most valuable item and represented the great export staple. They were likewise the crop to which most other produce could be devoted when not used as human food. That this kind of conversion of other stuffs into cattle could take place is to be seen in the figures for milk. Though the Free State produced in the year in question a total of 589,000,000 gallons of milk, including both whole milk and butter, comparing favorably with such an output as Switzerland's yearly 528,000,000 in 1923, only 43 per cent of it was exported, while in Switzerland the export was 67 per cent of the Swiss total.

The figures for exports introduce a new factor of difference between the holdings of large and small size and their populations. Small holdings do not share equally with large holdings either in the consumption of agricultural produce or in its export. In both consumption and export commerce in the Free State, small holders and large holders play distinct roles.

Taking the first of these considerations, the figures for consumption reveal the difference. The estimated human consumption of whole milk (as milk) was some 90,000,000 gallons, according to the statistical record of the year 1928,[17] of which 70,000,000 gallons were consumed by agriculturalists and

[16] *Agricultural Output . . . , 1926–27*, p. 10.
[17] *Agricultural Output . . . , 1926–27*, p. 18.

19

Figure 5

Consumption per Capita per Year, 1926

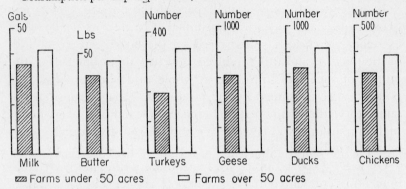

Milk Butter Turkeys Geese Ducks Chickens

▨ Farms under 50 acres　　□ Farms over 50 acres

Notice that in each instance the smaller farms produce more, consume less. The great "money crop," cattle, which neither party consumes to any great degree, tells another story.

20,000,000 by the remainder of the population. It was estimated that on the farms 38 gallons were consumed yearly per person. But that is the figure for all farms. There is a considerable difference here between types of farms.

Thus, in this case, on farms less than 50 acres only 36 gallons per person per annum were consumed, it was estimated, while on farms of over 50 acres, the consumption was 42 gallons. In Munster, the chief milk-producing province, the difference is even more marked, the indices being 35 gallons and 44 gallons.

Similar differences hold as well for the consumption of milk as butter, a commodity of which the Irish consume more than any other civlized country. The difference between farms under and farms over 50 acres can be expressed in the spread between 40 and 48 pounds annual consumption per person. For poultry and for eggs, great farm diet staples, similar differences hold. On farms less than 50 acres, 197 turkeys, 601 geese, 672 ducks, and 3,177 ordinary fowls, we are told, were consumed in the year in question, for every 1,000 persons living on such farms;

while on farms over 50 acres, 325, 884, 873, and 3,823 are the respective figures. "As might be expected, the difference between average consumption on large and small farms of valuable fowl like turkeys is very marked." [18]

In the case of eggs, of those consumed per 100 persons on farms in January 1929,[19] the figures are for small farms 530, for large farms 582. All of these figures reflect a difference of diet the more marked because the small farmer population is so much the larger.

In Figure 5 this difference of consumption is represented in the form of blocks depicting the contrast between small and large farms. One could conclude quite rightly from this kind of picture that in each instance the smaller farms produce more per person at work and eat less. In terms of production, then, the small farm is the more productive. In terms of monetary return, it is a different story. Cattle, of course, are the Irish "money crop," much like cotton and wheat in parts of the United States.

Observation makes it clear that this difference of diet is more marked than even these figures reveal. But figures for other items of diet appearing in agricultural production are not available in correlation with farm size. The home consumption of meats from the farm animals, except pigs, is negligible among both kinds of farmers. Nevertheless, we can gain a substantial insight into the difference in meat-eating between large and small farmers when we realize that, out of the comparatively small total of 123,000 cattle and 504,000 sheep and lambs slaughtered for consumption in the Free State in 1926, a per capita count of average consumption by dressed weight gives such a predominantly large-holding county as Westmeath a weight of 34 pounds per consuming person, counties with large urban population rising higher, while the same count gives such a predominantly small-holding county as Mayo a weight of only 13 pounds. Clare,

[18] *Agricultural Output . . . , 1926–27,* p. 37.
[19] *Agricultural Output . . . , 1926–27,* p. 39.

21

where small and medium farmers are predominant in the population, shows a similar small consumption of meat, a similar count giving only 19 pounds per person.[20]

In fact, the large farm population shares a meat diet with the cities and larger towns that is unknown on the small farms. The fact is evident when it is observed that Dublin, Cork, and Waterford counties (each dominated numerically by the city of the name) count an average meat consumption taken on the same scale of 69, 40, and 37 pounds per capita respectively.

The difference between the two kinds of farm shows itself again strongly in the export trade from Ireland and in the roles of each in the transfer of farm produce to its ultimate market. The two kinds of farm make a totally different disposal of their produce, particularly their cattle. In this fact we see for the first time that in some regard they have a complementary role. Between them Irish cattle trade is carried on.

The huge internal Irish cattle trade is thus significant. It reveals itself in the figures as a movement from small farm to large, an interchange between the two kinds of farmers which shows once again their distinctness. The trade is both geographical and social, in the sense that it flows between two sections of Ireland and between her two great agricultural classes.

To get at the facts which show the case demands looking at the statistics of cattle in the Free State. These illustrate clearly how far the internal cattle trade shows up the great difference between the two types of farm. It is necessary to take into consideration the age groups of cattle in the various areas and in the possession of holders of various acreages in those areas. This roundabout course of determining the outlines of internal cattle trade is necessary because there are no barriers or *octrois* at which count might be made as the cattle move from dealer to dealer across the country.

The seven southwestern counties are the areas predominant

[20] *Agricultural Output . . . , 1926–27,* pp. 48, 49.

in milch cattle production; they are the areas of the calf-producing cow. Clare is one of these. A chart of birth dates of cattle in various parts of Ireland demonstrates that the majority of the calves in the seven southwestern counties are born in March. A large majority of the calves in the eastern part of the country, the thirteen central eastern counties, are born in April, and a majority of the calves born in the northern tier of counties in the area of the Free State, a region we shall call the six northwestern counties, are born in May. This sort of progression of the birth dates of cattle through the spring months is, of course, related to climatic conditions.

Because such a progression exists, an annual count of cattle taken on the basis of age, undertaken each June first, the beginning of the butter export season, when cows are in full milk, would lead to the strong presumption that cattle recorded as under one year of age at that date would, in fact, nearly all be under three months of age; yearlings so recorded would, in fact, be under fifteen months, and so on. When an actual count was taken in 1926 of the cattle in Ireland, this presumption was borne out. On it is based the following picture of internal cattle trade to be derived from the Report on Agricultural Statistics already quoted.

Following the reasoning of the Report we learn that since "exceedingly few calves are either exported from or slaughtered in the Saorstat and . . . on June 1st, 1926, there were 78 cattle under one year per 100 milch cows, it follows that any district or group of holdings . . . with much less than 78 must have exported them." [21] Then, transferring this device to the annual count of cattle by age, it becomes readily apparent that all of the central eastern counties who count many over 78 cattle under one year of age per 100 milch cows on June 1, 1926, must have been importing, while the northern counties, Donegal and Leitrim, and the southern counties, Cork, Kerry, and Limerick,

[21] *Agricultural Statistics, 1847–1926,* p. xvi.

with figures much less than 78, must have been exporting. The last three counties named are the principal members of the group of seven southwestern dairying counties.

A great cattle trade thus takes place between the southwestern dairying area and the "ranching" counties of the central eastern area. When yearlings are taken into account by the same statistics, a fuller picture of this trade emerges. All but one of the central eastern counties has considerably more than 100 yearlings for every 100 calves under a year old, showing that the area is continuing to import the cattle as they grow older. The other sections of the country have considerably fewer than 100 yearlings for every 100 younger cattle, and have been continuing their exports. The principal dairying counties again have the fewest yearlings and are again the leaders in export.

Likewise in counting two-year-olds, the same proportions hold, and in counting cattle over three years old they hold again. In the last two cases, however, northern counties show a greater export than do the dairying counties of the southwest, the latter presumably having got rid of a larger proportion of all cattle not designed for milk production at an earlier age.

The importing central eastern counties are devoted largely to raising and fattening dry store cattle for the British market. And since this is the case, it can be seen that the statistics given above reflect a continuous movement of cattle, calves, yearlings, and two-year-olds to the rich grazing lands of the central plain. Yet to regard this trade as exclusively geographical would be misleading and obscuring, for the profound differences between small and large holders which we have been examining are involved here as well.

Further statistical inquiry demonstrates that the trade takes place as much between the different sized farms as between the regions of different soil and climate. If we correlate proportions of cattle of various ages with the size of the holdings in the various county groups we have already named, rather than with the counties as a whole, this great internal cattle trade takes on the new aspect we mention. For example, figures for calves under one year reach 78 and over per 100 milch cows on holdings of all sizes in the thirteen central eastern counties, holdings of all sizes above 30 acres (the average size) in the northern counties, but only on holdings above 100 acres in the calf-producing dairying southwestern counties. That means that, though holdings of all sizes are importing calves in the "ranching" areas, in the other areas only large farms are importing them.

Taking yearlings next, figures on the table showing more than 100 yearlings per 100 calves under one year old appear on all holdings in the thirteen county midland areas except on the very smallest farms, but in the northern and southwestern areas such figures appear only on the very largest holdings. The midlands import yearlings, particularly in the large farms, and in the rest of the country large farms do likewise, but small farmers get rid of them. Thus in the southwestern counties, holders of 200 acres and over, with a count of 118 yearlings per 100 calves, are importers of cattle produced on other farms, as are holders of 100 acres and over in the northern counties, where the counts of yearlings are 132 for the 100–200 acre group and 154 for the 200 and over group. But small farmers in all counties, regardless of the section of the country in which they live, are exporters, not only in dairying Kerry but even in the flatlands of Meath.

Taking a similar count of dry two-year-old cattle, we find that all small holdings in all areas are still exporting, though the size of holding at which exporting ceases is lower in the central eastern area (the 50–100 acre group), and all large holdings in all areas are still importing, though, conversely, the size of holding at which importing begins is higher in the dairying county region.

For a graphic representation of this argument and its conclusions, let the reader turn to Figures 6 and 7. Figure 6 gives the numbers for various kinds of cattle by various size holdings

25

Figure 6

Proportions of Store Cattle to Milch Cattle on Various Size Holdings in the
Areas of Distinctive Economy in the Irish Free State
(All cattle except milch cows on June 1, 1926, per 100 milch cows on that date)

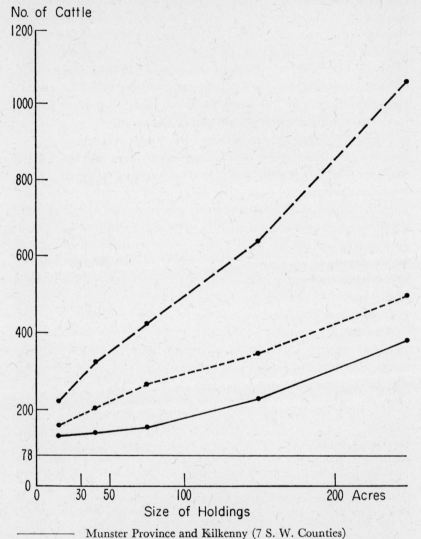

No. of Cattle

Size of Holdings

———————— Munster Province and Kilkenny (7 S. W. Counties)
— — — — 3 Ulster Counties, Mayo, Sligo, and Leitrim (6 N. W. Counties)
—— —— Galway, Roscommon, and all Leinster Province except Kilkenny
(13 C. E. Counties).

separated out for the three groups of counties.[22] It shows the characteristic increase of the numbers of store or dry cattle, for export upon holdings as one goes from small to large and from the northern and southern areas of intensive small farm production of different kinds, based upon different soil and climate, to the rich grazing country of the central plain. It shows that one is really dealing with two kinds of increase of holding of dry cattle; the first, the difference of area, and the second, the difference of size of holding. The last seems to be the more important since it has a characteristic influence in each of the areas.

Figure 7 completes the picture. In *A* one sees the characteristic relative absence of milch cows upon large holdings. In *B* one sees that calf production is fairly uniform everywhere. In *C*, however, one begins to see the movement of cattle from small farm to large as the calves grow older. Small holdings have dropped out as possessors of older dry cattle, and through *D* and *E* continue to do so. As the dry cattle mature they become more and more concentrated upon the large holdings. The figure demonstrates at a glance that it is not a geographical trade that is involved so much as it is a trade between the two kinds of economy, between the two rural classes in the Free State.

Numerical statement of the movement of cattle thus shows us that the internal cattle trade in Ireland is in reality a trade between two types of farmers. It reflects again the great difference

---

[Note to Figure 6 continued.]

The three areas are those of distinctive climatic and soil conditions. The northern and southern areas are alike in being suppliers of young cattle, the central area in retaining herds of dry cattle. Yet one can see at a glance that the difference among the broad areas reflects real differences in cattle-holding on small and large acreages. Points on the graph express for each size holding the number of non-milk-producing cattle per 100 cattle. The number of non-milk-producing cattle then ranges from a proportion of 78 to 100, to over 1,000 to 100.

[22] The figures are based on tables given in *Agricultural Statistics, 1847–1926*, pp. xvii, xix.

Figure 7

Cattle Trade between Classes of Irish Farmers, 1926

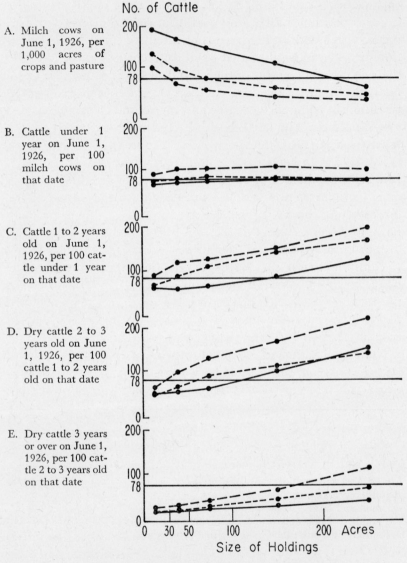

No. of Cattle

A. Milch cows on June 1, 1926, per 1,000 acres of crops and pasture

B. Cattle under 1 year on June 1, 1926, per 100 milch cows on that date

C. Cattle 1 to 2 years old on June 1, 1926, per 100 cattle under 1 year on that date

D. Dry cattle 2 to 3 years old on June 1, 1926, per 100 cattle 1 to 2 years old on that date

E. Dry cattle 3 years or over on June 1, 1926, per 100 cattle 2 to 3 years old on that date

Size of Holdings

——————— Munster Province and Kilkenny (7 S. W. Counties)
— — — — 3 Ulster Counties, Mayo, Sligo, and Leitrim (6 N. W. Counties)
—— —— Galway, Roscommon, and all Leinster Province except Kilkenny
(13 C. E. Counties)

in the economies of large farmer and small, and shows that this difference extends to their participation in the business, commerce, and export trade of the country. The large farmers are directly concerned with preparation of cattle for direct shipment to the English market; the small farmers are concerned only remotely, for the large farmer himself is their immediate market. They deal in much younger cattle and prepare them for sale to the middlemen and the big farmers.

Consequently, the small farmers are much less immediately affected by disturbances in the cattle trade with Great Britain. The fact has been evident throughout the years of the De Valera regime. It has blasted the prognostications of those who argued that a restriction and interruption of the trade with England, such as grew up in the "economic war" which followed De Valera's retention of the land annuity payments and the English retaliation in the form of import duties on cattle, would alienate the farmers' support of De Valera's government. It certainly alienated the large farmers, who were immediately affected, but the "farmer" of the politician is not always the whole population of that name. It left the small farmer relatively undisturbed. He was at one or two points removed from the actual trade with England and saw it only as a sale to big farmers. With the small farmers, the economic argument of De Valera's opponents failed.

However this may be, the conclusions as to the great division among farmers that statistics and the cattle trade have yielded us are borne out equally well within the separate counties. County Clare, for instance, shares fully in the internal cattle trade. And in Clare, the trade flows from small farmers to large. There are no statistics on the matter, but the generalities hold. Clare occupies a middle place within the system of exchanges. It is one of the seven southwestern dairying counties we have dealt with. But it does not always follow them statistically. As we have seen, Clare is a county of mixed holdings. Both the midland type of big farmer and the small farmer of the west and south are present. The cattle trade within Clare is a miniature of that of

29

Ireland. Clare buys in as many cattle in certain sections as it exports in others. Those who do the bulk of the buying are big farmers from the flatlands along the Fergus estuary or the hills of Burren. The small farmers of the remaining sections do the selling.

All this tedious statistical inquiry has not been without its purpose. It has established for us through the medium of economic inquiry the existence of two distinct kinds of orientation and adaptation to the soil and two kinds of agricultural activity. In doing so, in marking the first distinctions and differences to be observed among the dwellers of the countryside and showing us something of the relations between them, it has introduced us to the first great group with which we must deal: the small farmers.

2

Small Farm Economy

The small farmers' family groups inhabit the holdings or plots of land from which they make the livelihood we have described numerically. Except in a few and special cases, there is no physical separation of house plot from fields; the individual family's plot is usually a continuous one, and the other forms of settlement present in Ireland are rapidly being reshaped with that condition as the ideal. Consequently, the farmhouse is most often, though not always, a comparatively isolated house standing upon its own ground and forming an integral part of the holding. In it the farm family group spends its entire life, sleeping, eating, giving birth and dying there, and sallying forth every day for work upon the fields.

The farm family lives and performs almost all of its work within this spatial unit of land and house. And the unit is identified with the family in the eyes of its community in name and ownership. Outside this range, the farmer has little participation in affairs in comparison with others of the population. His

31

wife and children have even less. Within this range most of the activity marking the relations of the human beings who make up the group takes place.

The "land," as we have seen, is usually divided into "field," "meadow," "garden," "bog," and "mountain," according to its character and agricultural use. These divisions make up the holding and represent the productive activities in small farm economy. The plots so designated are devoted, respectively, to cattle-grazing, hay, tillage crops for human and animal consumption, and turf for fuel, and rough summer grazing. Nearer the house is the farmyard or "haggard," in which the hayrick and turfrick are and other supplies, such as potatoes stored in straw bins, stand ready for household and farm use.

The house opens directly into the haggard. There are the cabins, in which the cattle are housed, and the various sheds and stalls, often built out of the dry masonry of the house itself, in which the farm machines, traps, sidecars, carts, and other vehicles are kept. Hens and other poultry roam at will through the haggard and are fed and housed there, and in one of the sheds the pig or pigs find their quarters. As for the house itself, which gives orientation to the haggard and is responsible for the spatial arrangements in it, we shall have occasion to discuss it somewhat later.

Figure 8 gives a schematic view of the kind of farm called "all-purpose land" by the Irish Land Commission. This view is a composite and represents no single farm, but it is taken from direct observation of many in Clare. It depicts a mountain farm in which bog land is included. Otherwise it would do for any area.

Figure 9 gives a schematic view of a house and haggard also in Clare. This is modeled after a house in which one of the authors spent considerable time as a guest, and is carefully and faithfully depicted. But it serves, too, as a general plan for all such houses of small farmers.

The daily activity of the farm family and the daily work which

Figure 8

LUOGH
Diagrammatic Scheme of Small Farm (20 acres)

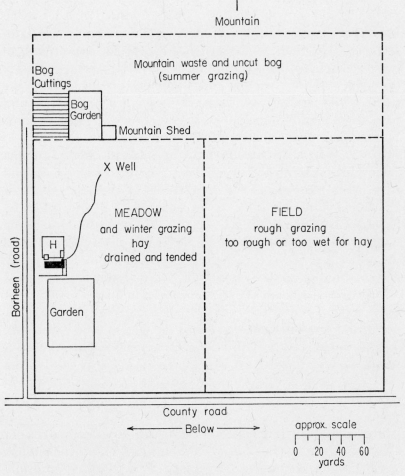

Schematic representation (not to scale) of composite Clare farm of about five to fifty acres.

Figure 9

Schematic plan of a typical small farmer's house and farmyard, illustrating his familist economy and functional division of his household.

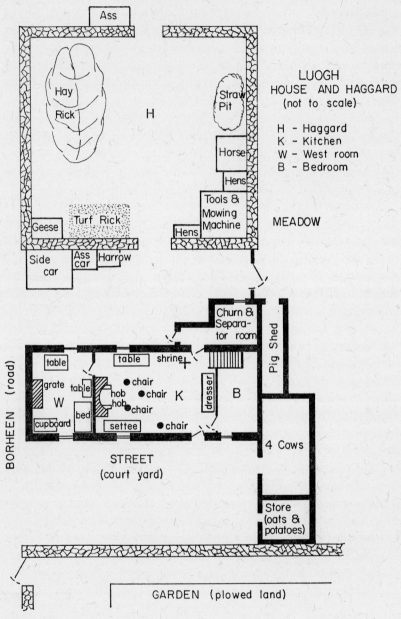

LUOGH
HOUSE AND HAGGARD
(not to scale)

H – Haggard
K – Kitchen
W – West room
B – Bedroom

its members carry on center round the house and haggard. Even for the men, whose primary work lies in the fields, gardens, and meadows, work centers in and round the house for a good part of the year. A short sketch of the daily activity which may be observed in any peasant farmhouse will throw into relief the work done by the various members and the organization of effort involved. It is to be expected, of course, that there is a great deal of variation at different seasons of the year, a fact which makes it impossible to describe farm activities without reference to seasonal change and the requirements of various crops. Nevertheless, the work round the house is constant and less variant than that outside on the "land," and for that reason it is significant to begin with it.

A typical winter day begins for the farm family about seventhirty in the morning. At other seasons the family rises earlier, but the long wet days have reduced outside work to a bare minimum and confine the work of the family members within doors. To the woman falls the first duty of the day. She must rake together such live ashes as remain in the slaked turf fire in the hearth, put down new sods for the fire, and rekindle the blaze. This done, she hangs the kettle on the hook, making ready for the first tea of the day. For the rest of the day she must keep the hanging kettle ready, for at any moment of the day she may be called upon to serve a cup of tea to her husband, children, and all visitors. With the first tea comes breakfast, usually of bread, eggs, and milk. By the time breakfast is finished, the household is ready for its workaday existence. The farmer father and husband is dressed and ready for his daily tasks, in which he relies upon the aid of whatever grown sons may still be at home, and who now take their breakfasts beside him. Similarly, the farm wife and mother who serves her men, husband and sons, and stands by unwilling to take her place at the deal table before the window at one side of the kitchen hearth until they have eaten their fill, is ready to begin her daily round with the help of the daughters and young children of both sexes who wait their turns with her.

In the household the responsibility of day-to-day housekeeping belongs to the woman. Hers, too, is the care of the children. If they are of school age, she must dress them, feed them, and get them off to school. She does all the cooking and washing up after meals and keeps the teapot always ready. Each morning she sweeps the house, makes the beds, and so on. The clothes of the household are her care as well, and the indispensable and constant mending of them which rough wear makes necessary all falls to her lot.

This household work is familiar to us; the point of itemizing it is merely to make clear the confined sphere in which the woman's recurrent and indispensable duties fall.

But her work stretches beyond the house door. In the morning after breakfast she takes the milk buckets and milks the cows in the sheds in the haggard. This is merely one of the many trips she makes in and out of the kitchen doors for fuel, or water, to feed and tend the animals and the fowl. Her milking finished, she must bring the milk in and separate it. In recent years, more prosperous farms have been able to make use of the separator. If there is none, she must set the milk in large pans and allow the cream to rise. The whole process of the conversion of milk to butter is her charge.

After the morning milking and the feeding of her human charges, she must turn her attention to the feeding of the farm animals, especially the young ones. The cows and horses are not her province, but all the care of the calves, pigs, and fowl falls to her lot. She prepares a mixture of warm milk and grain for the calves, feeding them from a bucket. They must not be allowed to suck, as the milk is meant for human consumption. Then she boils a large kettle of potatoes over the fire for the chickens and the pigs, or takes them the leavings of the previous day.

Before noon she hangs another kettle over the fire filled with potatoes for the use of the family. In season she adds white cabbage and nearly always includes a portion or two of bacon, some of it home cured in brine to resemble salt pork. By the time this is ready, the men are in from the fields impatient for their dinner.

In the meantime the men have been engaged upon work of their own. The farmer rises when he hears his wife busy herself in rekindling the turf on the hearth. If there are sons, he wakes them. After that he goes to the cow barns in the haggard to inspect the cattle housed there overnight and tend to their wants in water and hay. After breakfast, if the day is fine, neither too bitterly cold nor too soakingly wet, he sallies forth into the fields to whatever work the time of the year demands. If he finds himself confined to the house, he still has plenty to do in house and haggard.

If he and his sons go to the fields, he probably returns about eleven-thirty for the noon meal, the heavy meal of the day. Long habit calls forth his hunger and identifies it with the house. Several countrymen have remarked that they never feel hungry away from the house but are ready to eat when they get inside. The dinner unites most of the family for the first time during the day since breakfast. Only the small children of school age are absent. Their share of the meal is often saved for them until they return about four o'clock.

As at breakfast, the men sit down together immediately, falling to the steaming plates of cabbage, bacon, and potatoes the woman sets before them. As they eat, she stands ready to refill their plates, talking with them about the morning's work and the news of the neighborhood. It is the chief time of family conversation. During the meal the woman has boiled tea and, when the men finish with their plates, she clears away and lays bread and tea before them. Sometimes there is a longer interval between tea and dinner, devoted to smoking and talk.

As before, the women and children do not eat until the men have finished. They take their places together when the men have left or have moved off to smoke an after-dinner pipe, an indispensable part of the meal for them. The children may sometimes not come to the table but eat sitting upon the settle or the hearth seats. They are very silent children. They take little part in the family discussion between older members unless questioned directly.

After dinner the men return to their work. The women begin their household and farmyard tasks anew. The fowl have grown so hungry, meanwhile, that they are invading the kitchen and the woman must "hunt" them out of the house. From what remains of the pot of potatoes (which may often hold as much as forty pounds) she feeds them and feeds, too, the household pets. They eat what the family eats, though meat comes their way only upon special occasions.

This done, the woman's chores for the afternoon are much the same as those of the morning. Another large pot of potatoes, mangels, and turnips must be prepared for the pigs, more milk and grain mixed and fed to the calves, turf brought in for the fire, water fetched from the well, and rooms cleaned and swept, in an endless cycle of activity. Should the routine duties come to a pause, there is still always plenty to do in washing, mending, and knitting the clothes of the household. The woman's hands are never idle.

There is another important daily activity within the house. The great staple, bread, is baked daily into round cakes or loaves upon the "griddle," an iron tripod, on the hearth. The woman may bake at any time during the day and, if necessary, more than once. Even late in the evening, when the whole family is gathered round the fire, her last task may be to bake bread for late evening tea.

After four in the "evening" (as the countryman divides the day), the children arrive from school and must be fed. The woman sits down with them, talking over the happenings of the day, for children are important purveyors of news. An hour or so later the man brings the cattle in from the fields, if they have been grazing during the day. He is ready for evening tea.

At that hour the work of the men is over for the day, but that of the woman goes on. She must prepare, serve, and clean up after the tea, and then go milk the cows brought in from the fields. Her work ends only with the separating that takes place when she brings her milk into the house. Even then, while the men may sit round the fire talking over the day's work or the affairs of the community, she is not idle. If the children need help in lessons, it is she who gives it to them. She puts them to bed, and, if she returns then to join the men at the fire, she continues with knitting and baking. When the whole family has finally gone off to bed, it is she who must close up the house at night and slake the fire in the hearth.

Work round and inside the house is continuous and varies very little from day to day and season to season. It involves a continuous activity by which the household group orders its life and fulfills its needs of nourishment and shelter in the midst of a carefully patterned regularity of habitual behaviors. What variation there is in the accepted pattern is itself confined to narrow range. Certain chores indispensable in the day-to-day habits of the people are divided among days of the week. One woman informant, a small farmer's wife in Inagh, gave as her weekly round a much more rigid daily division of tasks than is actually to be observed. On Monday she did the washing, on Tuesday the ironing, on Thursday she made butter, on Friday she went to market, on Saturday she got ready for Sunday, and on Sunday she went to mass and did as little as she could. Really, however, it is only on Sunday that there comes any serious alteration in the daily round.

Work in the land beyond the haggard and the house is less restricted and more varied. It has a greater range of activity over the farm and over the round of the year. Coupled with such greater variety, there is also a greater freedom of choice among necessary tasks. The necessities imposed by soil and climate permit a wider range of action and a less narrowly repetitious routine than do the ordered regularities of a household.

Yet within the greater range of activity there is still a constant and nearly invariant pattern of work. The progression of the seasons brings a recurrent demand upon the farmer in the care of beasts, crops, and the land itself. Each season brings a task which must be performed, begun, or ended if the farmer is to raise his produce successfully. Similarly, the custom and rivalry of the community exert a further restriction upon his activity. He works within the influence of a long-established tradition of ancestral experience which has established for him the best dates for planting, for reaping, for breeding cattle, and for most of the tasks of his yearly round. The community holds that tradition in common, and the farmer is caught in the midst of a mesh of rivalries, competitions, and gossip in praise and condemnation, which binds him the more strongly to the accepted patterning of his yearly activity.

The seasonal rhythm of farm work reaches its lowest pitch in winter. Activity is confined to house and haggard. On bitter wet days little can be done beyond the haggard wall, but within it there is always a variety of necessary tasks involving care of farm machinery, implements, and buildings, and the housing and feeding of the cattle who cannot be driven to graze in the open field. In the house there is much that can be done. Harness can be patched, boots fitted with new soles, plates, and spikes, furniture repaired and occasionally new pieces made.

These tasks fall to the males of the household, the farmer father and his grown or adolescent sons. Any discussion of the annual round of farm work necessarily describes their labors, for all the tasks not strictly connected with the household fall in their province. We shall have occasion later to examine fully the sexual dichotomy of labor such a division of tasks represents.

For the countryman the Christmas season, from the beginning of Advent to Epiphany or "Little Christmas" (January 6), is the dead of winter. It is a period in which all farm work is at a standstill. The farmer has completed the last of his harvest and brought in the last of his potatoes from the field. The cattle are securely housed against the winter cold. The farmer feels himself free to sit round the house during the cold wet days and devote his season to holiday. The working day is at its shortest. Outside, the weather is usually unsettled, a cold rain falling on the sodden fields. It is for him as though the course of the year had stopped and were waiting, gathering its forces for the new year.

It is a period of great social activity in the local community. The very important religious ceremonies of the season call forth an intensified activity in the parish. There are constant visits back and forth; each house is ready to offer its hospitality to its neighbors; and the community gives itself over to dances, cards, talk, and calls. Not until the religious season closes with Epiphany does the countryman feel that the year begins anew.

With the beginning of the year, the cold uncertain weather with its succession of bitter wet days, leaving the fields too wet to work, does not end, but the Christmas season has marked the transition. The farmer must now make his plans for the spring planting, lay in his seed, repair machinery, and make ready for the season about to begin. On drier days he can busy himself in the field in cleaning ditches and drainages. In the evenings much of the conversation on visits and at home revolves round the coming planting, and both new and traditional experience with types, varieties, growth cycles, yields, and care of seeds and cattle passes round by word of mouth.

The first of February, St. Brigid's Day, marks the beginning of spring. For the countryman the return of the "hard" days of wind and clear weather herald the season of the land's drying off. Through February and March the gardens must be prepared, potatoes planted, and the fields made ready for the return of the cattle to them. Each hard day is a welcome opportunity, for only then can work in the fields go on. With favorable weather, the work of preparation is over in the beginning of March, and the actual planting begins. By St. Patrick's Day, with its promise of continuous hard weather, the gardens are ready for a second planting.

41

The potatoes demand the greatest attention. A fortnight after they are planted, they must be manured well with manure brought from the pile near the cattle cabins, and the ground must be leveled so that the plant will not go to stalk and thus fail to produce tubers. A fortnight more and the ground must be "softened" and the earth round the plant, which now shows its first leaves, must be "stirred." By the time May is reached, the potatoes must be "landed." Earth must be taken from between the long ridges in which the potatoes are planted and heaped up over them from each side. Thereafter nothing remains until the harvest but a summer spraying against blight.

Throughout the spring the cattle have demanded attention. March and April see the birth of calves and the beginning of the milk season and intensified butter-making. The great spring cattle fairs take place. The farmer must devote himself to the all-important business of buying and selling his milch and store cattle and his calves. At home the cattle demand constant care against hunger, disease, and cold as he mixes their diet of fast diminishing hay with the slowly returning pasture grass.

The farmer's work in the gardens does not end with the "landing of the potatoes." Mangels and turnips and whatever grains he may grow must be planted, the soil prepared for them, and the growing crop weeded and tended. With the planting of the turnips, the last crop to be "put down," often as late as early June, his planting season is over.

With the return of warm weather and the drying off of the land, Irish summer begins. May is the first summer month. And by early May the bogs are dry enough to allow turf cutting to begin. The farmer must ordinarily find time between plantings to cut his year's supply of fuel and stack it into "reeks" to dry under the summer warmth. The turf cutting, though not connected with growing plants or animals, is an indispensable farm activity and takes its place among the never varying tasks of the agricultural round.

Once the turf is cut and stacked, the fruits of the farmer's labor begin to appear. His first crop is cabbage which was planted in a small garden near the house at odd free times during the early spring. Cabbage is practically the only green vegetable of the small farm diet, and the old people remember "Hungry July" or July *an chabáiste* when a delayed potato crop might condemn them to a month or more of semistarvation in which cabbage was the only food. Today new varieties of potatoes have been introduced which mature as early as late June.

The mature potatoes mark no harvest. They are left in the ground to be turned out of the ridges with spade or plough as occasion for them demands. Not until late November will the last of them be dug up.

The first true harvest and the most important one of the year is the haymaking. The cutting of hay begins in late July or early August. It is not only the most important activity of the year, insuring a year-long supply of fodder for the farm animals and the income-producing cattle, but it is also one that calls forth the united efforts of the whole family. It is a race, too, against time and rainy weather, and every effort must be bent to mow, rake, and let dry, and stack the meadow grasses, first in small haycocks, then in a great hayrick in the haggard, before rain brings rot to the lush crop. The farmers well speak of the harvest as "saving the hay."

No sooner is the hay saved than the corn crops demand attention. Rye and oats are ready for the scythe or the mowing machine (only the larger farmers have reapers) by late August. The farmer and his sons must bind it, stack it, and leave it for several days drying. Later they will return to the fields and cart it back to the haggard for threshing. Not long ago the flail was still the most frequent means of threshing among the small farmers. In recent years steam-powered threshing machines make the rounds, and threshing, which under the older system seems to have taken place as need arose for the grain, takes place now more regularly in late September and early October.

With the bringing in of the corn, the agricultural year draws to a close. Through October and November turnips and mangels are ready to be "pulled" and stored in the fields, near at hand to the haggard, in straw- and earth-covered pits. The potatoes which remain in the ridges must be turned up with spade and plough and similarly stored for the winter. All the root crops are indispensable supplies for men and animals during the months to come when there is no grass. The winter's supply of turf must be brought to the haggard from the reeks alongside of the bogs, where it has been drying for the summer. The carting is an intermittent labor, performed by the men at odd times when they are free of other duties. As winter comes with November cold and rain, the cattle must be housed and made ready for the long, dark days of no grass to come; and the farmer is busy with them acquiring and disposing of his stock, as he was in the spring, for the autumn fairs bring him an important market.

If he has been fortunate and industrious, nothing remains for him to do but to prepare his fields for the next year. The soil he has used for root crops must be turned, and the gardens which he intends for grain are ploughed. As he follows the furrows, he can look back upon a year ended, and forward to another to begin. By the time his ploughing is finished, the dead of winter and the holiday season of Christmas is upon him and the yearly round is over.

Yet it is over only to repeat itself. For within the range of the seasonal variation and the demands of growing and maturing crops and animals the pattern of farm work in haggard, garden, meadow, and field is a constant one. Much the same progression of labor flows along year after year, and follows the farmer from boyhood till death. Yet there is much less restriction in choice of operation to be performed, in movement over space, in the possibility of day-to-day variation than in the case of the work of the household.

3

Family Labor

At crucial points in the annual round we have sketched out, the whole family lends its labor. Particularly at the turf making, the hay saving, and the potato planting, all members work together in bog, garden, or meadow. Though tasks vary according to age, sex, and relative status, the group works in a unison of effort in which a definite rhythm can be observed. Under the direction of the father, the husband and farm-owner, the variously divided tasks are correlated to the end in view. The periods of common effort in which all the family members, even to the children, are working in unison are also those in which the greatest speed is needed. At such times the pattern of daily household activity suffers; the regularities belonging to it are transferred to the field. Tea and bread, and perhaps sometimes heavier fare, make their appearance at the regular times, no longer within the house but on the edge of bog or meadow.

Within this concerted effort, a division of labor between the sexes and upon the basis of age appears. The division, however, is not confined entirely to farm work. It covers the whole field of the behavior of the individual. It divides obligations, duties, sentiments, and values of the group, and is enforced by the group. It pertains both among the members of the family groups and in the community at large. It controls individual action and attitudes and gives a standard of comparison between one's own farm work and that of one's fellows. The interests and the desires of the individual concur in large measure with the norm, and he finds reward and pleasure in it. He can rely upon similar obligations and duties toward himself on the part of others.

The greatest scope and variation in activity which we have seen to fall to the lot of the male takes its form in part from his relationship to the others of the household. On the normal farm there is an adult male farmer who is husband, father, and owner of the farm. Within the group he has the controlling role, subject to conventional restrictions of his authority. In farm work, as we have seen, he directs the activity of the family as it works in concert. In his special province he looks after and cares for the cattle, has full control over them, and takes complete charge of buying and selling them. He disposes of the income they bring in. But all this he is obliged to do in the interests of his wife and children. Should he fail to get a good price or prove a bad judge of cattle or handle them badly, his wife and children are entitled to a just anger against him.

As we have seen, all the work requiring heavy effort in garden and field falls to his lot. He makes and tends the drains, fences, barns, and shelters, which protect both cattle and garden produce. He works the fields and gardens with plough, mower, harrow, and spade. All the agricultural implements and the heavy work involved in their use and in the use of the horse are his province.

The produce which such work assures is his to be disposed of, as is all income derived from it. He may order it as he sees fit; yet his first charge is to the family he heads. The division of income between household needs and the demands of farm and

46

livestock springs from his decisions; yet it is a matter of nice adjustment between himself and his wife in favor of the group as a whole. Custom and his own desire demand that he provide for his household to the best of his ability. Though he can make what disposal he will of the funds earned by the labor of the group, his wife and children can expect as of right that he shall make it for the family as a whole in which each member receives his share. For the work of his wife is complementary to his, and in its own sphere of as great importance to the livelihood and the organization of the family unit. While he may demand and expect of his wife that she fulfill her household duties, so may she demand and expect that he fulfill his in the management and working of the farm and in providing for herself and the children.

As regards income, all money derived from the sale of eggs and butter, the chief concern of the women beyond the house itself, belongs to her to dispose of as she sees fit. Yet the fruits of her labors are also subject to the needs of the family unit, husband and children.

The division of labor between the sexes arises within a field of larger interests and obligations. It is part of the behavior expected reciprocally of husband and wife. It is a functional element of their relationship within the family.

The training each sex receives from childhood in farm work reflects this fact. Each learns his or her part in farm economy, not as a vocational preparation but as a making ready for marriage. The boy acquires his man's skills and techniques for the farm and farm family he may head himself some day; the girl learns the woman's role as an integral part of her future state of wife and mother. Each learns to expect of the other not only the loving consideration of husband or wife but the proper skills in farm economy.

Among the small farmers this dichotomy of tasks assigned to the sexes in the economy of the farm family is more even than the reciprocal duties of husband and wife, father and mother. It

47

is also an integral part of the personalities of all men and women of the peasant's own kind. One can get many expressions of attitude of this sort. They show that the division of labor between males and females is regarded as corresponding to the natural propensities of the two sexes. That a man should concern himself with a woman's work, such as the sale of eggs or the making of butter, is the subject of derisive laughter, while a woman's smaller hands make it "natural" for her to be a better hand at milking the cows.

Even when the communal labor of the family is demanded and women take their place in bog, garden, and meadow, a definite role is assigned them. Usually it is the lighter tasks which are known as women's work. There is no formal taboo confining a woman to women's work. Heavy work is merely felt to be a hardship upon her. At the potato planting the women do the arduous work of planting the sprouts which they have prepared, bending over to put them into the ridges prepared by the men. They do their share, if necessary, of cultivating, but they are not generally accustomed to the spade, which like the plough, the harrow, the mower, scythe, and turf "slan" is regarded as a masculine implement. At the potato lifting they go along behind the man who turns the potatoes out of the ridge with spade and plough, and pick them up. At the haymaking, the pitching, raking, and some of the building of the haycocks are left to them. But the mowing, especially where it involves the horse-drawn mowing machine, and the building of the rick in the haggard, are masculine skills. In all cases of field work of this sort the role of the woman is usually auxiliary. The same holds in turf cutting. The men do the actual cutting in the bog trenches, while the women knead the peat into briquets and pile it for drying.

The many attitudes and beliefs which surround this type of division of labor illustrate again the socially determined character of the distinctions and their genesis in the intersexual relationship. Just as the man's work is the harder, the more various, and the wider in scope, so the attitudes express a greater

48

valuation of the men's work within the limits of the restriction. Thus on several occasions the authors have heard men admonish a woman for interruption with such phrases as: "Woman, be silent while we [men] are talking about ploughing." Ridicule and laughter greet suggestions that either sex busy itself with the work of the other, though in the case of a woman doing a man's work some of the praise bestowed upon surprising successes meets her if she does it well. There is also an entire body of popular belief and superstition surrounding the dichotomy in farm labor.

These beliefs and attitudes serve to uphold the conventional division and to evaluate the necessary behavioral specialization which is basic to the interrelationships within the farm family. The connection between family status and labor performed brings about an identification between them. Ridicule and graver charges of unmanliness and unwomanliness can be brought to reaffirm the conventions against the offender in either sphere. Just as in the noneconomic life of the family, behavior is enjoined upon members on the basis of sex, so, when the group acts in economic enterprise, different but complementary roles become conventional for each sex. The interesting point is the identification. For the farm family, farm work is as much a family matter as is sharing the same table.

Within the framework of the division of labor on the basis of sex, there is another just as great division on the basis of age differences. Though all the males of the farm family share the work which is regarded as the masculine province, there can be immediately observed great differences in the practice of the masculine technique by the male family members; the same can be observed in the feminine province.

These further divisions of tasks likewise reflect family status. They are part of the behavior expected of the farmer as a family member, and take their form in the complex of his relationship to his fellows within the group. The controls exercised among members in work and in the life of the family in general show themselves a constant pattern to be observed from farm to farm wherever one elects to examine the daily and annual rounds of activity.

Thus in any of the tasks which the group must perform in its economy, the division of labor between the adult farmer-father and his sons may be observed. The father is owner and director of the enterprise; in him the farm and its income are vested; in the community it is known as his and the sons are spoken of as his "boys." Thus in the draining of a field or the sale of cattle in a fair, the sons, even though fully adult, work under their father's eye and refer necessary decisions to him.

Perhaps the best method of illustrating this relationship is to present it from the point of view of the growing individual who takes his place in the farm family. He forms part of the productive unit which is his own family. The techniques of farming are passed on to him, and he learns them under the direction of his father, uncles, and brothers. At their hands he acquires the conditioning which will fit him to form a farm family of his own, thus to continue the traditional pattern. Naturally, his conditioning is more than merely technological; he gets on the farm the full training which makes him a member of his class and time.

The growing child ordinarily sees his father as owner and principal worker of the farm. When the whole family group of father, mother, children, and whatever other relatives may be living with them, works in concert, as at the potato planting, the turf cutting, and the haymaking, it is the father who directs the group's activities, himself doing the heavy tasks. The father looks after and takes care of the cattle, delegating minor tasks connected with them to his sons. Even though the cattle may be generally discussed by the household, he has full control of them, disposes of them, drives them to the fair, handles and uses the money got for them. If he fails to get a good price, handles the beasts badly, or proves himself a bad judge of them, the criticism of his wife and neighbors soon establishes the value of careful husbandry in the son's mind.

The father does all the constant heavy work necessary to keep the land in condition in so rainy and treeless a country. He makes drains, ditches, fences, walls, shelters, and barns, as we have seen. As the son grows older, he learns to help at these tasks, finally taking them over. The father prepares the garden, ploughs, plants, and harrows, does all the spade work of cultivation and everything involving the use of horses and agricultural implements. The son soon learns that these are men's tasks, and he gradually assumes his share of them. The adult men of the neighborhood rival one another at these tasks; they chaff and boast back and forth over their prowess. The son cannot fail to hear and value the techniques which he acquires.

He learns those techniques in a narrow school. Where tradition is still so strong and the incursions of trained agriculturalists still relatively infrequent, as among the small farmers, there is little variation from the tried and true way. Each operation and each tool demand a technique of their own. The father makes sure that the son learns it well. Command, rivalry, ridicule, and many an adage and bit of folklore all conspire to the same result.

The father must make sure that the son has learned the right and traditional technique. For he must be ready to stand his ground with anyone in the community in farm skills. Every operation becomes the intimate concern of his neighbors; a man must hold his head high. More important, many skills are plied in cooperative activities, in turf cutting, haymaking, and much of the work of the garden. In such cases, a definite rhythm is necessary for greater effectiveness among the cooperating workers, and any deviation from the accepted technique destroys such unison. This, too, the son learns at his father's hands.

At home the son learns that building and repairing the houses, sheds, and other structures of the farm is men's work and that

51

the duty of performing it devolves on the father. He watches his father buy and use all the feeding stuffs needed for farm animals and learns something of the nice adjustment which must be made between the expenditures of this kind and those demanded by the women of the household for food, clothing, and household needs. He finds himself included in the family deliberations which impress upon him the economic interdependence of the family and the division of labor between men and women.

The process is a gradual one. It is an integral part of daily experience protracted over many years. In his earliest childhood, of course, the mother looms larger in the child's consciousness than the father. The child's first duties, as soon as he can speak and walk, are to run on petty errands to neighbors and nearby "friends." Soon he is taking his father's meals to him in the fields or going on errands to the nearest shop. Until he is seven and has gone through First Communion, his place is in the house with the women, and his labor is of very little importance. After First Communion, at six or seven, he begins to be thrown more with his elder brothers, and comes to do small chores which bring him more and more into contact with his father and with the other men of the neighborhood. By the time he is ten or eleven he will be brought home from school, if needed, to take his part in the important agricultural work of the year, particularly at spring sowing and hay harvest. But not till he passes Confirmation and leaves school (generally at the same time) does he take on full men's work. Even then, as he becomes adult and takes on more and more of the heavy tasks of the farm work, he never escapes his father's direction until his father dies or makes over the farm to him at his marriage.

If economic apprenticeship is also a process of conditioning within the family, so likewise the direction of economic enterprise coincides with the dominant and controlling role of the parent within the family. The son is subordinated in both spheres to his parents, particularly the father. Rather, the spheres are one.

For the child grows up within the full complex of life within the family. The petty errands which constitute his first steps in farm work are a mere incident in the conditioning he receives and the relationships he builds up with his fellows. He develops the sentiments of affection and dependence upon his mother and the other family members in those years in the care and attention he receives at their hands. He learns the code of conduct which constitutes the folkways of his group and the reciprocal relations within his family in a gradual process of training over years. This conduct ranges from the errands he runs for family members superordinate to him, to the learning of his prayers and the development of the sentiments which make of sexual behavior of any kind an offense and of that within the family, incest.

Thus the same landmark in his life which marks his beginning to do the minor chores of farm work after six or seven marks a change of his life within the household, for thereafter he sleeps with his brothers and the separation which begins to take him from his sisters in work and play now separates them within the household.

Later his sharing of chores with his brothers in farm work is again merely incidental to his long years of life with them. By the same token the commanding position which the father (and the mother) exercise over him in farm work is but one aspect of their control. We shall have occasion to see in a later section how this dominance expresses itself in household arrangement and in the grouping of individuals in other spheres than farm work.

This parental dominance continues as long as the father lives. Even though the major work of the farm devolves upon the sons, they have no control of the direction of farm activities nor of the disposal of farm income. They go to market and fair from the time they are twelve years old, but they buy or sell little, if anything, for themselves. Thus the small farmer and his sons are often seen at the fairs and markets together, but it is the farmer-father who does the bargaining. Once when one of the authors asked a countryman about this at a potato market, he explained that he could not leave his post for long because his full-grown son "isn't well known yet and isn't a good hand at selling." If the son wants a half crown to go to a hurley match or to take a drink on market day with friends, he must get it from his father. The authors have seen many sons, fully adult, come into shops to buy some farm requirement, such as a bag of meal, and say that the "old fellow" will pay for it. And a few days later the old fellow arrives to pay for the goods "my young fellow got." The son may, of course, earn money in employment off the farm, as many do at work on the roads in occasional employment with governmental bodies or large farmers. But in this case he is expected to contribute the larger part of the money to the general household expenses as long as he remains on the farm.

The procedure of the Land Commission, a government body, in providing additions to small holdings from the break-up of large estates illustrates well this retention of parental authority. It is the policy of the Commission to employ local men as much as possible in the reclamation and fencing work necessary at the division of an estate; the owners of the holdings to be enlarged are entitled to the work. Consequently, when the work is given, the farmer owners are assigned it. But it is the sons who do the work, and at the pay-off the "old fellows" walk sometimes many miles to be paid the wages their sons have earned. In one case of land division which the authors witnessed, a Land Commission official walked about the estate pointing out the plots which the selected farmers were to get. The farmers followed in a body at a respectful distance, each ready to step forward when his name was called. Behind them came all the young men of the neighborhood, the farmers' sons. When it was necessary to send someone back to a farmhouse or to cut up stakes to mark boundaries, the orders were transmitted from the official to the farmer and from the farmer to his sons, though these were in the majority of cases adult men. Likewise in country post offices, even after the farm has been made over to the son and the "old people" have the old-age pension, it is the son who comes to collect it for them.

Even at forty-five and fifty, if the old couple have not yet made over the farm, the countryman remains a "boy" in respect to farm work and in the rural vocabulary. A deputy to the *Dáil* (the Irish parliament) raised a considerable laugh in 1933, which echoed into the daily newspapers, when he inadvertently dropped into the country idiom and pleaded for special treatment in land division for "boys of forty-five and older" who have nothing in prospect but to wait for their fathers' farms. Likewise, a countryman, complaining to one of the authors about his position, said: "You can be a boy here forever as long as the old fellow is still alive."

It goes without saying that the father exercises his control over the whole activity of the "boy." It is by no means confined to their work together. Indeed, the father is the court of last resort, which dispenses punishment for deviations from the norm of conduct in all spheres. Within the bounds of custom and law he has full power to exercise discipline. Corporal punishment is not a thing of the past in Ireland, and, especially in the intermediate stages of the child's development, from seven to puberty, it gets full play.

It is during those years that the characteristic relationship between father and son is developed in rural communities. The son has suffered a remove from the previous almost exclusive control of his mother, in which an affective content of sympathy and indulgence was predominant, and is brought into contact for the first time with the father and older men. But the transfer is not completed. There is a hiatus in his development through the years of school when his participation in men's work and his relationship with his father has little chance of developing into an effective partnership. A real union of interests does not take place until after Confirmation and school-leaving, when for the first time his exclusive contacts and his entire day-to-day activity, particularly in farm work, will be with his father and the older men.

This fact colors greatly the relationship of father and son, as far as affective content goes. There is none of the close companionship and intimate sympathy which characterizes, at least ideally, the relationship in other groups. Where such exists, it is a matter for surprised comment to the small farmers. In its place there is developed, necessarily perhaps, a marked respect, expressing itself in the tabooing of many actions, such as smoking, drinking, and physical contact of any sort, which can be readily observed in any small farm family. Coupled with this is the lifelong subordination the retention of the name "boy" implies, which is never relaxed even in the one sphere in which farmer father and son can develop an intense community of interest — farm work. Nothing prevents the development of great mutual pride, the boy in his experienced and skillful mentor, tutor, and captain in work, and the man in a worthy and skillful successor and fellow workman, but on the other hand everything within the behavior developed in the relationship militates against the growth of close mutual sympathy. As a result, the antagonisms inherent in such a situation often break through very strongly when conflicts arise.

The division of labor in the masculine sphere between father and sons, then, is more than an arrangement in farm management. It is very directly part of the systems of controls, duties, and sentiments which make up the whole family life. The apprenticeship and the long subordination of the sons in farm work are reflections of the entirety of their relationship to parents; it is impossible to treat the two spheres of behavior separately.

Similarly, the relationships in farm work between the other members of the household cannot be treated separately.

On the other hand, the relationship of mother and son has a very different content. Like that between father and son, it is the

56

product of years of development. It is marked, too, by a similar retention of subordinate status on the part of the son. In farm work the boy is subject to commands of his mother even when, fully adult, he has passed over exclusively to men's work. It is for this reason that many Irish farm widows with grown sons can successfully manage a farm for many years before they ultimately make it over upon a son's marriage, and from their restricted scope within the household and haggard effectively direct operations in the masculine sphere. In such cases, the woman retains control. Even in such an important matter as her son's eventual marriage she has a very dominant voice.

But within the scope of such a subordination there is a quite different affective history. The relationship is the first and earliest into which a child enters. It is very close, intimate, and all-embracing for the first years of life; only gradually does the experience of the child expand to include brothers, sisters, and, last, the older male members of the household.

Until seven, the child of either sex is the constant companion of its mother. If the family is numerous an elder child, usually a sister, may take over much of the mother's role, but the mother is always nearby. As the woman works in the house or fields, the child is kept by her side. In the house it usually sits in a crib by the fire or plays about on the floor, but always within sight and sound. It learns its speech from its mother, amid a flood of constant endearments, admonitions, and encouragements. The woman's work never separates her from the child. Custom imposes no restraints or interruptions in her solicitude. She looks after its comforts, gives it food, dresses it, etc. She constantly exercises restraints and controls over it, teaching it day by day in a thousand situations the elements of prudery, modesty, and good conduct.

The controls she exercises are of a different kind from those of the father. She is both guide and companion. Her authority most often makes itself felt through praise, persuasion, and endearment. Only when a grave breach of discipline demands a

57

restraining power greater than hers, or when an appeal to ultimate authority is needed, does the father begin to play his role. Especially in the years before puberty, the farm father enters the child's cognizance as a disciplinary force. The barriers of authority, respect, extrahousehold interests, and the imperatives of duty rather than of encouragement make it difficult for any intimacy to develop.

Even after Confirmation the child's relationship to his mother is not materially weakened. He becomes confirmed, it is true, in a masculine scorn for feminine interests and pursuits, but he can and must still look for protection to his mother against a too-arbitrary exercise of his father's power. In family disputes the mother takes a diplomatic, conciliatory role. From her intermediary position she can call upon the strongest ties between herself and her sons to restore rifts in parental authority and filial submission.

Throughout the years of the son's full activity in the farm economy under the father's headship, the mother still remains the source of comfort and the preparer of food and is still infinitely solicitous of his welfare. It is only at marriage that the bond is broken and undergoes material transformation. If the child must leave the farm for other walks of life, the closest possible relationship is still maintained. When one goes home, it is to see one's mother. There is always an attempt to carry on a correspondence. In exile, the bond lingers as a profound sentimental nostalgia.

4

The Relations of Kindred

The relations of the members of the farm family are best described in terms of the patterns which uniformity of habit and association build up. They are built up within the life of the farm household and its daily and yearly work. The relations of the fathers to sons and mothers to sons fall repeatedly into regular and expectable patterns of this kind that differ very little from farm to farm.

If we are to understand them, then, we must trace them out of this setting and see in what manner they offer us explanation of Irish rural behavior. In terms of a formal sociology, such as Simmel might give us, the position of the parents is one of extreme superordination, that of the children of extreme subordination. The retention of the names "boy" and "girl" reflects the latter position. Sociological adulthood has little to do with physiological adulthood. Age brings little change of modes of address and ways of treating and regarding one another in the relationships within the farm family. The relative positions of the parties must be stated in terms of the events taking place between them. These events run over the years and redefine relationships in their course. This kind of development characterizes and gives form to the family relations we have already detailed. We shall see now that it gives form to all of them and to the farm family itself.

The long years of intimate association in the acts and events of a common life build up very complete adaptations and very close emotional bonds among all those who share the life together. The bonds must be compatible; adjustment is made all round, again through gradual habituation. Otherwise conflict is ready to set off young against old, men against women, persons against one another. There is reciprocity of obligation and expectancy.

But the point of interest here is that it is the bonds that must be dealt with for understanding, not anything within them or the activities associated with them. Here there is an absolute coincidence of "social" and "economic" factors within single relationships. In the case of a small farmer and his son, there is only one relationship; to separate their social from their economic activities is meaningless. They are one in fact, and, as far as the peasants are concerned, they are one in name.

Thus any of the words designating status in the relationship, such as father, son, owner, employee, heir, etc., might well be used, but in actual practice the first two of them are sufficient to cover all the activities of the relationship. Only the statuses of father and son are distinguished by the country people. These words are the only designations of status that are to be heard among them. All others are unnecessary. They are not part of the experience of the small farmers except as they become so when the outside world breaks in. Consequently, terms designating status are not to be understood or interpreted on a basis of *a priori* or philological meaning, but as references to the events in connection with which they were used.

Thus when it comes to understanding the force of such terms

for the small farmers who use them, we are able to see why it is that the terms are emotional symbols of very great power. They are part of the peasant's own experience in the very relations we have been discussing, and they make definite and reinforce the relations for him. They cannot be divorced from the patterns of relationships which they symbolize, and their role cannot be understood except in the fact.

If then we turn back to the common life of the families of the small farmers, it is these very terms which give us the clue to the relationships which that life builds up.

In the Irish family, the sons and the daughters are equally subordinate; there is no formal distinction made between them. The kinship terms of both the English and the Irish languages reflect this equivalence of siblings. In either case, one term, son or *mac*, reflects the unity of the position of all male children, the procreated generation, from the point of view of the elder or procreant pair, the mother and father. Similarly, a single term in both languages, brother and *dearbhráthair*, expresses for the siblings their common occupancy of that position. Rural Ireland knows neither primogeniture nor junior right. Except as age differences separate them informally, the brothers occupy the same status both within and outside the family group. Thus neighbors and other outsiders refer to them all alike as "the boys" of the farmer's family.

Accordingly, their equality reflects itself in farm activity. All are on an equal footing there. The brothers are all alike under the father's direction and control as long as they remain on the farm. They work together, and the years of common effort and common dependence create a strong solidarity between them. Though only one of them may ordinarily expect to inherit land and cattle, the others renounce their rights as it were in the interests of the identification of the family group with the land they work. The bloody faction fights which used to disfigure Irish country life have practically passed away, but the forces which brought them into existence still continue. Many a country fight

61

involving a dispute over rights of way and water courses brings in the adherents of all the brothers of either house, and, though the cases nowadays find their way into the courts, a very common defense is that the feud is very long-standing and that "the two grandfathers" began it. The tales written in the last century by William Carleton, who wrote of a life he himself knew intimately, describe faction fights in which whole parishes became involved, but the center of disturbance was invariably a family dispute in which the brothers of a family ranged with their friends against those of another. So fierce is the solidarity which the identification of brothers and their land calls forth that even today in Clare the name "defending Tim Flanagan's title" is jocularly given to forcible resistance to eviction, after a famous stalwart of the last century whose ten sons fought valiantly for their father's farm.

In fact, this emotional attachment is strong enough sometimes to preclude the breaking up of the family. Two instances of this sort came under the authors' special notice out of the many which occur. It is difficult to get the exact figures, since census materials deal only with the marital status of farm owners, but many of the bachelor-owned farms of Clare may be of this type. In the first case, two brothers and four sisters occupied a small holding of twenty-three acres and a four-room house for over fifty years. Several of them at various times had tried to break away; in fact, two brothers did, but the ones who stayed gave as their reason first that they hadn't wanted to leave the old people and afterwards that none of them had wanted "to be the first to leave." The second case was very similar. Two brothers and a sister had stayed on to work a small farm for their old parents, but, when the old couple died, none of them wanted to leave and each felt too old for marriage.

Whatever differences make a rift in this fraternal front are matters more of preparation for leaving the farm family than of internal differentiation in status and behavior. On most small farms only one son can be kept at home as successor to land and chattels. The family property, house, stock, and land, descend to him intact. The other sons must be provided for elsewhere.

In choosing the son to remain upon the farm, the father has full power of decision. His interest lies in choosing among his sons the one he thinks will carry on most successfully. There is no rule or norm in the matter; and the brothers are united in expecting an adequate return for their years of service. But none of them may claim more than the other, and they are all dependent upon the father's sense of their fair deserts. In many cases there may be an early difference among them in the inclinations they show in adolescence. But the special position a brother occupies in this regard is a matter of agreement among them all and easy enough of adjustment.

Turning now to the other relationships neither fraternal nor parental within the family, it is obvious that those among the females and between females and males build up in the same way as the ones we have already discussed.

The family makes a formal distinction between the female members and their male fellow members in terminology, just as it builds a dichotomy of behavior upon the sexual difference. Thus in the procreated generation daughter and sister, *inghean* and *deirbhshiúr,* correspond to son and brother; for the daughters occupy equivalent positions in a common subordination to the parents.

These terms express merely a classification of the female individuals and their positions in the complex of reciprocal relationships between family members. What has been said of the conditioning of the boy can be repeated of the girl, with, of course, a difference in the techniques acquired. And no less than in the boy's case, farm work is merely a part of the total adaptation the girl makes toward her fellows and toward the environment in which they live.

The work of the women is as important in farm economy as the men's. The coincidence between family status and economic role holds for them as well. Women's work on the small

63

farm is complementary to that of the men, as we have seen, though, of course, it is quite distinct. The young girl growing up on the small farm learns this, just as the young man acquires the masculine techniques. The girl is thrown constantly with the mother and the older women of the household. After she is seven, her pursuits differ completely from those of her brother and, except as she is in very close constant association within the household, she has no working contact with her father.

Many minor tasks fall to the girl as she grows up, particularly driving and milking the cows. Her conditioning prepares her to fill the role her mother occupies in the household. All the interior of the house, the immediate vicinity of courts and haggard where the fuel is stacked, the well, the poultry yard and sheds, are her concern. She learns to milk cows, feed the pig, tend the chickens, and look after all the young animals through helping the older women. She learns the lore of disposing of eggs, butter, and occasionally of some of the vegetable produce of the garden, potatoes and cabbage, and occasionally goes to market with her mother.

In the chief business of the women, the house itself, the preparation and serving of food and the repair and upkeep of clothing, she serves a never-ending daily apprenticeship. A young girl may often be delegated to look after the hearth, make and keep the fires going, etc. Only the mother makes small purchases of food and household goods. Only the mother bakes the great variety of breads. But by the time she leaves school, the girl may be proficient in these tasks too. So also with the butter making. Income derived from this and from poultry belongs to the older woman; the girl has no share until she herself has married.

In the past century (and in isolated regions still) most of the clothing of the small farmers was made at home by the women. Now, however, it is nearly all shop-bought. Certain vestiges of the former practice remain, however, in knitting sweaters, gloves, socks, and scarfs; and in the country districts, at least of West and North Clare, there is a custom which demands that some woman of the house be always at work. If there is no other task on hand, they must occupy themselves with knitting. In former days, the daughters of the community might gather in a *meitheal,* or cooperative work group, under the supervision of older women for carding and spinning flax and wool. In any event, the younger woman, the girl, is at the older woman's command.

Much the same content of emotion and sentiment exists in this relationship, subordinate as the daughter must remain, as in the case of the boy. But in the case of the daughter there is never a readjustment, and there is never a period of community of interest with the father. Nor need the mother fear a competition with an impatient oncoming successor as must the farm father who knows he cannot put off forever his relinquishing his farm to his son. For, eagerly as the daughter may look forward to her own marriage, she knows that marriage will bring in a rivalry over household control with a totally new person in an entirely new scene. It is her husband's mother, not her own, to whom new adjustments must be made. The implication of this fact, and the struggle it entails, will bear examination in the discussion of marriage.

Still another relationship exists within the household under normal circumstances. The relationship of brother to sister has its reflection in farm work. But it is a relationship with a different history from the relationship between siblings of similar sex. Sexual differences in behavior have made a different habit, beginning very early in the child's experience. And, for each of them, the sexual differences are colored a great deal by the norms which mark the relationship of their parents. Thus there is a good deal of the boy's regard for his mother in his attitude toward his sister. Likewise for the sister, especially in the years when both are fully adult, the brother comes to have much of the position of the father, especially if he is older. He shares the masculine ultimate control of farm and household. If she remains on the farm after her brother's marriage, she must look to him for her dowry.

The country people have a good deal to say about the strength of this bond. Deep-rooted in the years of common subordination and common association, it survives the removal of the sister to another house and farm. It means much visiting and a close relationship with the coming children. The country people marvel that a young child may often like its mother's brother better than its "own uncles." They mean thereby that the bond survives in equal strength with that where the common patrilineal interests of a common family name are in question, as in the case of two brothers and their children.

That the complete family is the complete unit of life both social and economic to the small farmer is admirably illustrated by the incomplete families of the countryside. By the term "incomplete" the authors indicate those many small farms which are worked by spinsters, bachelors, widowers, and widows.

In such farms, control is exercised by the person owning the farm. A widow is usually helped out by a male relative, brother, nephew, or son. Here again the male devotes himself to the tasks which in ordinary circumstances would fall to the father in a full family unit. The control over expenditure and the disposal of farm goods rests, however, with the woman. But even then the bargaining in such typically masculine enterprises as the cattle fair would be delegated by her to her helping relative. In one instance which came to the authors' notice a young widow called her unmarried brother to live with her and directed his efforts in draining a large field. The two of them ran the farm very successfully, though the brother grumbled. In another, a "landless" young man pleaded successfully to a Land Commission official for an addition to his aunt's holding, presented his case, and carried out the negotiations, but the final reference had to be made, of course, to the aunt for whom he worked, for in such a case the feeling that the man must repre-

sent the family and farm unit in the community at large is sufficiently strong to push a subordinate "boy" into the position
usually filled by the farm husband and father.

Similarly with several old bachelors. A nephew moves in and
works the farm, but the old fellow keeps strict control even to
regulating the nephew's expenditures for amusements. In one
case, where a widower had a small son, the son was taken in by a
childless sister and raised by her, and when he grew up and married he inherited the sister's farm. His father remarried and
raised a second brood. In another, two spinsters spent their lives
on a farm worked by their two cousins.

The attitudes of the country people to these arrangements
show that incomplete farm families are felt to be departures from
the normal; they are subjects for commiseration. Such phrases as
"It's a hard life she has with only the brother and no husband to
help her" and "He's all by himself with only his son there on the
land, poor fellow" are commonly applied to them.

The policy of the Land Commission in increasing farm holdings is very significant in this regard. The officials recognize the
social value of the full family explicitly. According to the official
in charge of land division in Clare, who has had successful experience in other regions as well:

An old-age pensioner without family could not be considered for an
addition of land, nor could a couple of spinsters . . . Where the
question arises, a household consisting of father and mother and
sons, rather than daughters alone, would have a prior claim. But, regarding the position of the wife, it is a fact that, if the husband goes,
the wife keeps the farm up. She is the person who saves the money
and governs everything.

Again:

Twenty to twenty-five acres of all-purpose land where the mother
is normal and the father energetic is sufficient to keep a farmer and
his family. It is the province of the mother to look after the fowl, the
milk, the butter, the pigs, the calves, and the milking of the cows. A

67

woman on a small farm can milk five cows in thirty minutes. She also takes care of the children, though she sometimes has a girl in to help her for a time. She also makes and repairs the clothes. She does the buying for the house and the husband only for feed, seed and fertilizer. She has the responsibility regarding medical attention, and where she has any showing of culture the family pushes on ahead. In fact, on the mother depends the organization of the family in all ways.

Such evidence points to a situation in which the immediate family of husband, wife, and children, the group basic to Irish society and especially to Irish rural life, carries on a corporate economy. The roles of the component individuals are assigned them by virtue of their position in the family. The character of the economic effort, its control, direction, and purposes, are part and parcel of the life of the social group.

Beyond the family economy of the small farm, there exists also a certain amount of cooperation in the Irish countryside among the small farmers. Agricultural labor upon the individual farms is not performed in isolated competition, but is permeated with a give-and-take of reciprocal aids. That cooperation takes the following forms:

1. Lending tools, or doing the work with one's own, for friends and neighbors who have not the requisite tools, especially in mowing, spring sowing, harrowing, ploughing.
2. Lending a boy at turf making, spring sowing, hay harvest, oats harvest, or driving cattle to a fair; that is, at any time that the farm needs an extra hand to get its work done quickly.
3. Of women: making up a tub of butter, or firkin of salted butter, thus pooling resources, the proceeds to be divided proportionately.
4. Of women: lending a girl on any occasion that an extra hand is needed in the household.
5. Helping at times of distress, or when one household is short or a crop delayed, with gifts of cattle, food, or labor.
6. Working together communally to get a harvest done, particularly the oats reaping and threshing. Here again the actual work is

done by the "boys," who are lent by their fathers, though, of course, the latter may also take a hand, if necessary.

7. Obligations surrounding *rites de passage* and ceremonies.

In former days this cooperation was more widespread, according to the testimony of the older people. But even today the oats harvest, which used to be celebrated locally by a large dinner and dance at the expense of the farmer whose crop was being reaped by "friends"[1] and neighbors, still calls forth some cooperation of the next to last type.

In recent years the farmers have been wealthy enough to acquire their own horses, carts (called "cars," only two-wheeled vehicles being used, at least in Clare), and mowing machines. In the last century, however, these were less numerous and, as an older countryman put it: "Once if you had a horse and car, you'd have forty or fifty people helping you with the turf."

Similarly, before the mowing machine became general, ten or a dozen "friends" and neighbors would work each other's meadows in turn with the scythe. Nowadays, the owner of a machine need only go about to his "friends" and cut their hay for them, getting their aid in return in building his own stacks and hayricks.

The commonest form of cooperation is that which involves lending a boy to a "friend" whenever he is needed. In order to illustrate this form of cooperation and to give the setting in which it takes place, it will be well to describe the hay harvest in a country district. We choose the district of Luogh. Luogh is a mountain region of small holdings, none of them larger than twenty-five acres, divided among twenty-four households. There was only one large farmer in the immediate vicinity; he worked his lands through a herdsman and, as he had his own hired hands, did not figure in the haymaking. All the rest of the holders had what is called "general purpose land" by the Land

[1] Used here in the sense explained in Chapter 5.

Commissioners; they had some bog, some meadow, several fields being grazed over, and a garden of potatoes, rye, cabbage, and oats, always less than an acre in extent. The number of cattle each had ranged from six cows, two calves, and two bullocks held by one holder with sixteen acres of mountain land and an addition about three miles off in fertile bottomland (he had got this, eight acres, several years before from the Land Commission) to none. The person having no cattle was an old bachelor, an old-age pensioner, who lived by himself on a farm of four acres stocked only with a few hens.

The hay was early, the weather favorable, and the harvest began in mid-July. All the holders except two were Luogh people related by complicated ties of blood and ancestral association to the land and to each other. There were three lone bachelors, a widow helped by her brother, and three widowers helped respectively by one son, three sons and a daughter, and two sons. The other holders were married couples with each a son or two and perhaps a daughter present, if they were old, and many growing children if they were not. The region was one of large-scale emigration, so that a smaller number of young people were present than is perhaps usual.

As the hay ripened and the weather turned fine, the families began to save the hay, mowing it, letting it dry, and stacking it as soon as possible, first into small grass cocks, then into the usual six to eight foot haycocks. After several weeks it would be moved into a single great hayrick in the haggard. There was a great deal of interest and much comment back and forth over the progress of the various families, the probable weather, and the yield of the various meadows. The men seemed to feel a general rivalry to do their work well and quickly. About half the families had horse-drawn mowing machines. Those who had them mowed their own meadows as quickly as possible, working from earliest morning as long as light held. They worked with the aid of their sons and with that of boys from the families who had no machines of their own. At each subsequent stage of the harvesting, a boy or young man not a member of the family whose meadow was being worked could be seen giving his labor in aid; he took his place at meals during the day.

The mowing done, the farmer then took his machine to the farmer whose son had helped him and mowed the meadows belonging to his friend. In one instance a youngish farmer mowed the meadows of three others; in another, of two. Certain meadows were full-handed enough not to require extra hands, and in five cases no help was given, though the mowing and stacking took a very long time with them in comparison to the others, and they were obviously short-handed. Two of these were bachelors who lived alone, and two more were the "strangers." Two other families had insufficient meadow of their own and were forced to buy hay on the so-called "conacre" system (buying the hay as it stands and reaping it oneself within a stipulated time).

Here then was an example of an important agricultural operation undertaken by the local community in which provision was made (except in five or six cases) for effective cooperation over and above the usual family economy. This is not an isolated instance; in Luogh it has been the practice from time immemorial. Old people here remembered the day when, there being no mowing machines, scythes alone were used. Then the cooperating groups would have been larger and a more pronounced rotation of the working groups from meadow to meadow could have been observed. The same custom occurs in other places; in fact, during late July and August the entire small farm population of Clare can be seen at work. Given the different techniques, the same cooperation had taken place in Luogh and elsewhere at the turf cutting, the oats harvest, and the potato planting.

Yet there was no monetary wage or payment involved. In the community of Luogh and surrounding townlands, the only hired labor was to be seen in the meadows of the large farmer (a cattleman with over three hundred acres), who had not cooperated with the small farmers and whose entire way of life, as well as the agriculture he practiced, was different from theirs. Except in so far as the agricultural operation the small farmers were undertaking was economic in itself, it was evident that an interpretation of the incentives for this cooperation must include other factors.

Driven to social rather than economic explanation, the authors were able to ascertain that in each case of this cooperation there was an extended family relationship involved. Thus Carey, who had mowed the meadows of Dennis and Seamus Molony and Brian McMahon, was second cousin to them. Peter Barrett was first cousin and uncle respectively of the two farmers whose meadows he had mowed. The young men or boys who had worked Carey's and Barrett's meadows with the latter's wives and children were also relatives; they were sons of the relatives for whom Carey and Barrett had mowed.

So it went over the townland. In no instance, of course, had a man mowed for all his relatives; it was not necessary to do so. In one instance a man had mowed for a neighbor who, while not a relative, was a great boon companion. Furthermore, the bachelors whom no one had helped had, of course, been able to help no one. And the two strangers who had moved into the townland, in one case fifty years before, in the other thirty, had no relatives "on this side." One of these was a man who had never got along with his neighbors, accused the whole townland of plotting against him, and was cordially disliked in return. The other had the help of a boy sent by a cousin in a near-by townland.

The generic term "cooring" is given to all non-monetary cooperation of this sort in many parts of Clare. The word is a direct borrowing from the Irish *comhair,* which is similarly used, originally meaning cotillage, now having the added meanings of alliance or partnership. But more interesting was the fact that the small farmers explained their cooring in terms of the "friendliness" of the place. So, we shall see, the term "friendly" is applied to the extended (and also immediate) relatives or "friends."

When asked especially why they were cooperating, the farmers' answer was that they "had right to help." In general terms they would phrase it that "you have right to help friends," or again that "country people do be very friendly; they always help one another."

Now the phrase "have right" is an expression in the brogue or English dialect spoken in Ireland (and in Clare) which, like "friendly," is a translation of a Gaelic idiom. It expresses an obligation, duty, or the traditional fitness of an act. The Gaelic word for which it is a substitute is *cóir,* and a bilingual countryman translates the Gaelic phrase *is cóir dom* (the obligation is on me) into "I have right to." The countrymen of Clare, at least, do not ordinarily use or understand the phrase "I am right" to mean "what I have said is true." The countryman is explaining his economic acts in their traditional family setting as part of the reciprocities of act, sentiment, and obligation which make up family relationships.

That he is doing so becomes evident when we find that the habitual, obligatorily performed acts toward extended relatives are similarly described, where the context is definitely not economic nor connected with agricultural labor. Thus in the townland where we examined agricultural cooperation there takes place the same lending of a boy or girl and the giving of a hand in aid at such festivals of social and family life as weddings, christenings, wakes, and funerals.

This aid is felt to be in the same category. Thus one farmer speaking of another, his second cousin, could say:

He is the best friend we ever had; we can make bold on him. When the children were little and our cow died on us, Johnny sent down a cow and calf worth twelve pounds to us and didn't want anything for it.

And in more general terms, another farmer could explain:

Everybody's friends in the country here are very good to you. They lend you a horse with the hay or a boy going to the fair, or they send down to know if they can help when somebody dies with you.

Thus it is part of the "friendliness" for the relatives to make up and serve the food at wakes and weddings, to dig the grave for the dead, and to keen (wail) over the dead. The obligatory character and something of the reciprocities involved in such behavior are well expressed by one countryman who gave as his reason for going to a funeral (at a time when he was needed at home for farm work): "I have right to go [to the funeral of a second cousin]; they always come over to this side."

Likewise, when in Luogh a man's wife died and his sister took over the child, she was praised for doing the "friendly" thing which she "had right" to do. In the very same terms a man called upon his brother-in-law to lend him his son to help drive his cattle to the fair. In a case similar to the last, a violent quarrel arose because an uncle, who "had right" to lend a son badly needed in doing some fence work, refused to do so. And in the same scale of value a family which did not attend the funeral of a relative was subjected to great criticism for being "unfriendly."

In fact, failure to fulfill the pattern of conduct demanded by extended family obligations leads often to punitive action on the part of the aggrieved party. Near R——— a small farmer, who neglected his garden and forced his father-in-law to send up loads of potatoes for his wife's support, was finally beaten up one night in his own house by the irate in-laws. Ordinarily, of course, failure to fulfill such obligations either in directly social situations or in agricultural cooperation does not lead to such violent conflict, but rather to an estrangement. The niggardly "friend," especially the one who refuses or fails to return an obligation, is held up to general condemnation, not only by his kindred but by the whole community. The position of a small farmer near but not in Luogh was the result of such failure. He was regarded by all his nieghbors and kindred as a "miser" and a "Jew" and on several occasions was accused of petty thefts by

74

them, which perpetuated the breach. As a result he lived as a recluse, refusing even to visit others; in return he was not greeted by his "friends."

The obligation of this sort[2] extend to visiting and to the hospitality which the Irish countryman deems so great a virtue. "A sup of tea" and such food as eggs and bread is "put down before" the countryman who is traveling to town or to the fair or who is merely making the evening *cuaird,* or visit, at which the older men of the local community gather round the hearth to chat and retell the old stories of legend and folklore and discuss the news. Niggardly treatment in this regard leads to disputes, as does abuse of the privilege by the visitor. A standing joke in Luogh was the treatment given to her too-voracious relatives there by a woman who exercised considerable ingenuity in starving them out without offending them.

Similarly, the obligations extend to such occasions of good fellowship and holiday as the fair day and market. "Friends" treat one another at the local public houses on meeting in town. Thus one countryman complained to the authors that he dreaded the fair day, for he must drink up all his profits with his "friends." Others are able to strike a happier balance; and a religious pledge of teetotalism likewise surmounts the difficulty.

The sum of the evidence presents the small farm economy as a family situation in which economic effort, individual and cooperative, is controlled by the social forces operative within the family. Labor connected with agriculture is merely one feature of a total constellation of behavior, enforced through obligations reciprocal in nature and maintained by sentiments and sanctions in a traditional setting.

[2] The word *cóir* (a fit and traditional right or duty) corresponds almost exactly with the full range of the small farmer's obligations, as we have seen. It well reflects the farmer's habit in two other uses. The phrase *cóir mhaith* means good food. When the speaker says, *tá cóir mhaith agam ansud* (there's a good feed for me there), he refers not so much to the food itself as to the social situation in which he finds himself well provided for. And the term of address, *duine cóir* (worthy fellow), indicates that "worthiness" springs from a fit observance of one's obligations.

5

The Kinship System

The mothers and fathers who order farm life are themselves
sons and daughters. They have or have had (before their creation of a family of their own upon the farm) much the same relationships with their parents as their children have with them.
Indeed in many cases households comprise three generations.
Grandfathers and grandmothers of the children live in the house.
Family structure is not confined to the immediate present family group, but descends with each generation as the boys and girls
reach social maturity at marriage and the creation of their own
families.

This descent forms the basis of any kinship system; it provides
also the basis upon which the "friends" to whom one has obligations in rural Ireland are reckoned. The individuals comprised
within the system are so because of their sharing of that descent
in common. These are one's "people" or "friends," in the countryman's vocabulary.

76

The terms express the generic category into which the kindred fall. Both terms are, in a sense, translations of Gaelic idiom. The first, people, corresponds exactly with the Irish *muinntear*. The second in ordinary rural usage refers not to a comrade, as in English, but to one's relatives. Even in the towns, one's father, mother, brothers and sisters, sons and daughters, are referred to as "immediate friends." In the countryside one speaks of one's kinsmen as one's "friends," particularly if they occupy one's own generation; one's father's relatives, even his brothers, become "my father's friends." A "distant friend" refers not to distance in space but to that in cousinship.

Before we detail the individuals included within this category, let us make two points clear. The first of these is directly associated with the dominance of the father within the family. He comes, as it were, to stand for the group which he heads; the farm is known by his name, and wife and children bear his name likewise. For the Irish family is patrilocal and patronymic, to use the technical terms. Farm, house, and most of the household goods descend from father to son with the patronym; we shall follow their general movement in a later section.

This patrilineal descent gives a certain accent upon the kinship system; it chooses one line of descent out of the many possible and gives those who make it up a common name. There is a reflection of this fact in the groupings of Irish rural life. To outsiders a person may be known as "a boy of the Shannons" or a "man of the Flaherties," but in a sense these groupings are merely linguistic conveniences. For in many cases two families of Shannons may live side by side, yet not be considered "friends." None of the obligations of kinship bind them. For in the phrase of the countryman: "They are not the same Shannons or, if they are, they are too far out."

Our examination of the various ways of reckoning kinship will make the statement clear. Patriliny is merely one device, an extension of the father-son relationship, by which individuals are included in one's group of "friends."

A second observation upon the kinship system springs from the fact that the family relationships regulate sexual conduct. Indeed, our examination of farm agriculture leads us to see that the technological training of the individual goes hand in hand with the sexual. Marriage prohibitions, like the sanctions of the exercise of sexual rights in marriage, are part of and take their form in the family group. Consequently, in the wider and larger alignments of individuals springing from the family which make up the kinship system, similar prohibitions occur.

For the kindred are the group within which marriage is prohibited. In a sense the formulation of the individuals in it as a group is an abstraction. Kinship bonds come ready formed to the newborn human being. The child is soon brought to know and adopt requisite behavior and sentiments toward the individuals with whom the other persons of his family are reciprocally bound.

Thus the Irish child very early meets his mother's and father's brothers and sisters; he runs errands and receives small gifts from them; as soon as he is able he carries presents. In later years of boyhood he does odd jobs for them; his labor is lent at cooring; he takes his place with them at the family table or round the hearth on visiting. At various times of crisis in his career, such as First Communion, Confirmation, and marriage, he receives gifts from them which signalize the intimacy between him and them. They share his parent's superordination to him, for they belong to the same older generation as his parents.

He is very likely, too, to be thrown constantly with their children, especially if they are substantially of the same age, where his uncles and aunts remain within visiting distance. In country regions, such as Luogh, nearly all of the families are united by complicated, reduplicated bonds of marriage and descent. There the boys and girls grow up together in constant association, both as "friends" and companions. It is with them that the natural course of development creates bonds of sentiment and mutual aid, quite like those within the family, which take the form of

78

that "friendliness" at once obligatory and pleasurable seen in the account of farm work.

Likewise, if such development of relations is carried a step higher, the brothers and sisters of the grandfather and grandmother, with their families down to the generation of the growing child himself, can retain an interest which springs out of the original brotherhood or sisterhood between them. The "friendliness," the give-and-take, the "welcome put down before" the individual, come quite naturally to the child at the hands of these relatives. His parents visit their own uncles and aunts, take occasional presents, lend them labor, and so on. The child finds himself included; and he finds himself expected to adopt a similar intimacy of behavior with the children of these houses which he visits.

In the generation of the father, his father's brothers and mother's brothers are known as uncles; their sisters are known as aunts, both terms being the usual English classificatory ones. In both Irish and English among country people, however, descriptive terms seem to be preferred, though the English terms have been taken into the Irish as *aintín* and *uncail*. In the countryside these classificatory terms are still felt to be slightly foreign, and, as is always the case even within the immediate family relationship, kinship terms are seldom used in address. There is no distinction made between parents' siblings upon seniority. The terms niece and nephew exist, but are used by farmers only in legal contexts. Descriptive terms, such as brother's son, take their place.

In the direct line of ascent, parents' parents are "grandfather" and "grandmother" in English, according to sex, without reference to the sex of the immediate parent of the speaker. In Irish, terms correspond exactly: *seanathair* or *athair criona, seanmháthair* or *máthair criona*. In the direct line of descent, however, only the English terms for children's children, grandson and grand-daughter, are classificatory and neglect the intervening child. The Irish terms are completely descriptive, specifying

79

the sex of the child whose children are the grandchildren in question. They are *mac mhic, mac inghine, inghean mhic, inghean inghine,* respectively (i.e., son's son, daughter's son, son's daughter, and daughter's daughter).

Father's and mother's siblings' children are called, as in English, cousins, or more specifically first cousins, a classificatory term without distinction in sex. The term, however, is never used as a term of address. In fact, "returned Yanks" who bring back the American usage of prefixing the word to the name of their "friends" in address are ridiculed. The word seems to be slightly foreign to the brogue. "Friend" is the usual designation, or a descriptive circumlocution is used both in Irish and English, such as "our fathers were brothers," or *clann na beirte dearbhráthar,* in which relationship is established by reference to an immediate family connection in the ascendant generation.

Irish terms for these relatives are various. The commonest is *col ceathair.* This term is interesting because it introduces the type of reckoning upon which the kinship system is built. *Col* is the term used to refer to blood relationship within which marriage is prohibited. By extension it refers to consanguinity and to an ecclesiastical impediment to marriage. Thus the phrase *cia an col atá agat leis* is used to ask, "What is the blood relationship you have with him?" and to go to the priest for a dispensation removing an impediment to marriage is known as *ceannach col* (buying *col*). Among the English-speaking countrymen of Clare the word "call," pronounced quite similarly, is likewise used to signify relationship. Thus one "friend" is said to "have a call on" another. Whether or not the words are one and the same we do not know; in any case the English word seems to refer both to the obligations and the blood relationship.

First cousins then are known in Irish as *col ceathair* or fourth *col* whenever the specific designation of these relatives is required. The choice of the numerical adjective is presumably determined by counting the number of individuals or, better, personalities separated by reciprocal relations within which *col* or prohibitions arise. They are, for instance, myself, my father, my father's brother, and my father's brother's son. Here the accent upon the kinship system makes use of the two consanguine reciprocals within the immediate family: parent-child and sibling-sibling. Through the working of the principle of equivalence of siblings only two generations, my father's and my own, are considered. Thus the same reference to an immediate family relationship as we saw in such circumlocutions as "our fathers were brothers" is contained in the term.

Another set of terms exists in Irish for reckoning these relatives. The authors have not heard it in use in Clare, however. In it, first cousins are said to be *a dó a's a dó i ngaol*. The phrase means literally "two and two in blood relationship." Here accent is placed upon the lineal father-son (parent-child) descent, for brother and sister are called *a h-aon a's a h-aon i ngaol* — that is, "one and one." The reasoning here traces back to a common parent; in the latter case there is but one step, in the former, two.

The Church uses the system embodied in this last terminology in determining consanguinity. The following slightly abridged quotation indicates that it also recognizes a different system in Roman civil law.

The civil (Roman) law founded its degrees in the number of generations. Thus between brothers there are two degrees, between first cousins there are four. [Compare *col ceathair*.] Canon law still follows this system in determining inheritance, but the Church for marriages computes, in the collateral line of consanguinity, one series only of generations, and if the series are unequal only the longer one. Hence, the principle of canon law is there are in the transverse or collateral line as many degrees of consanguinity as there are persons in the longer line counting the common stock or root.[1]

Thus brother and sister are in the first degree, uncle and niece in the second, because niece is "two degrees from grandfather." First cousins are likewise reckoned in the second degree for the

[1] *Catholic Encyclopedia,* article, "Consanguinity."

same reason. Here, as in the counting *a dó a's a dó i ngaol,* the accent is upon the parent-child reciprocal. The Church calls this the *linea recta* of descent. It bases its prohibition of marriage (incest) in the *linea recta* upon divinely ordained natural law. No dispensations for this type of marriage are ever granted.[2]

Another system is perhaps commonest — at least in Clare, where the authors have met it on several occasions — among the methods used to determine kinship in order to maintain the bounds within which alliance is forbidden. It appears both in Irish and in English speech. The system reckons descent by "generations." The Irish phrase is to *réidhteach gaol* by counting *glúin.*[3] *Gaol,* we remember, is the word for blood relationship in general; *glúin* refers first to a knee joint, then by extension to a step in family descent, a generation. In this reckoning, first cousins, that is, parents' siblings' children, are said to be in the *triumhadh glúin,* or, in English, "the third generation."

Here the accent is again upon two elements in the constellation of reciprocals within the immediate family: the parent-child reciprocal and the equivalence of siblings. By counting back to the common grandfather or grandmother the *gaol* or "blood" is determined through three generations, i.e., ego's, his father's, and his grandfather's. Each person in the line of descent seems to represent a generation. All so descended in ego's generation are "friends."

Still another system of reckoning cousinship may be contained in certain idiomatic terms for the cousins. The authors here rely only on the Irish language dictionaries, for they have not heard these terms used. First cousins are designated in the phrase *tá siad i n-ó amháin,* which can only be translated in some such terms as "they are in the one grandson(ship)," for the word *ó* or *ua* was in ancient and medieval Irish the term for grandson and today seems to survive chiefly in the *O'* of surnames. This

2 *Catholic Encyclopedia,* "Consanguinity."

3 Cf. Canon O'Leary's *Mo Sgeul Féin,* where he has a chapter (*Mo Shinnsear*) in which he reckons his ancestry in these terms.

last idiomatic usage is merely a restatement of the reckoning by generations, and corresponds with English and Irish usage in explaining cousins by saying that they had the same grandfather.

All these systems of reckoning first cousins we have seen to be extensions outward of immediate family reciprocals to include the parents' siblings' children on the basis of their common descent with ego.

The process, however, does not stop there. For the descent is carried a step further back to a common great-grandparent. Marriage taboos and extended family obligations go backward and upward with the reckoning. Thus second cousins are recognized as being within the kindred and within the prohibited degrees. In fact, in the authors' experience the obligations of cooring and "friendliness" were equally strong with them.

To include these, all the various terminological reckonings of cousinship undergo an expansion. By the various terminologies, the group of kindred who are common descendants with ego of the same great-grandparent become *col seisear* (sixth *col*); relatives in the third degree (as reckoned by the Church); *a trí a's a trí i ngaol* (three and three); members of the *ceathradh glúin* or "fourth generation"; and lastly, in the idiomatic terms for cousinship, *ar a dá ó* (thus: in the second grandsonship).

The first of these terms, "sixth *col*," illustrates again the reckoning through counting the persons separated by reciprocal relations within which prohibitions arise. They are, for instance, patrilineally: ego (1), father (2), father's father (3), father's father's brother (4), father's father's brother's son (5), and the last's son (6) who is again normally within ego's generation. By counting the common root, for instance, again patrilineally, father's father's father, four generations are counted together. These four explain the *ceathradh glúin*.

Now both the Church and Irish rural society reckon descent bilaterally; all possible roots, male and female, are counted. In that case, the count gives thirty-two kinship personalities in ego's own generation who come within this group of first and second cousins. These can all be counted as cousins or "friends." They are within the range of *col* or marriage taboo. They make up the extended family whose behavior we have examined above. Of the thirty-two, only two (father's brother's son and father's father's brother's son's son) in ego's own generation bear the same patronym as he; but the total number of personalities within the system bearing ego's patronym is nine, if the immediate progenitors back to common great-grandfather are counted.

Consanguinity is carried one step further by the Church. As a barrier to marriage, or diriment impediment, it extends to the "fourth degree." This includes the group taken from a common descent yet a generation higher. It brings in those relatives known in English as third cousins.

These include all those descendant from a common great-grand-grandparent, described in the various terminologies as "third cousins," *col ochtar* (eighth *col*), members of the *cúigeadh glúin* or fifth generation, or people *ar a trí ó*. As before, the emphasis in each of these terms is to link together all those kindred of one generation who have common descent. When all possible roots are taken into account, the personalities so linked ideally number 128. The total within the whole system, including those of all generations ascendant, bearing the same patronym as ego, is thirteen, and five contemporaneous generations are comprised.

This last group is formed then by extension outward of the same principles found within the immediate family which determined the formation of the smaller ones of first and second cousins. Ego's descent from his parents is extended upward through the ascending generations and downward through his children to the descending generations. But ego and his siblings are equivalent in their relation to their parents. So, as the parent-child reciprocal is extended vertically, a lateral extension of the equivalence of the first siblings occurs concomitantly. In this way, an ever-widening circle of individuals are brought into reciprocal relationship with ego, expressed through their bearing a name in common, as his line of descent is traced further back. The marriage taboos within the immediate family follow the extensions both vertical and lateral.

Recapitulating, then, the relationships of ego with his kindred depend upon his place in the successive generations of descent through either male or female progenitors. The emphasis in the system is twofold. In the first instance, it places the individual within a given series of parent-child relationships, and in the second it establishes a commonalty between him and the other individuals who occupy the same place within that series. The structure of the restricted family functions identically; that of the extended family uses the same mechanisms to effect an integration of individuals upon a larger scale. The great proliferation of methods of describing this kinship system arises from a cause inherent in the system. All the terms we discussed are attempts to categorize the widening circles, lateral and vertical, of kindred; the desire to establish reciprocal terms to designate the members of the widening circles;[4] there is no need to particularize except in the horizontal and vertical lines.

When these two emphases upon the kinship system are recognized, it becomes evident why there is a lack of terms describing those individuals appearing above and below ego's generation but not in the direct line. In the direct line we do have such terms as grandfather, grandson, etc., but the others do not figure. They are not named except descriptively, and even then usually only in reference to the generation which they occupy. Thus father's father's brother is called "my grandfather's brother." The term granduncle exists, but it has not found its way into the countryman's vocabulary.

Similarly, though uncle, aunt, nephew, and niece have be-

[4] The extension of sibling equivalence to embrace widely one's generation is further exemplified in the Irish terminology. *Bráthair,* the word etymologically cognate with *frater,* brother, is used to describe all kinsmen of one's generation; a different word, *dearbhráthair,* or "true-brother," is reserved for one's father's son.

come fully acclimated to Ireland, there is still a marked pref-erence for descriptive terms. The son of a cousin is described in such terms, and the immediate progenitors of the cousin are thought of in terms of their place in the precedent generation. They are thus "my father's friends," though they are, of course, within ego's kinship group. In this way, two distantly removed cousins can often establish a relationship and adopt the requisite behavior to one another through establishing a more immediate connection in a parental generation.

The bounds of the consanguine group are naturally not rigid in this type of extensional structure. There is a gradation of intensity in the taboo as it extends toward the peripheral rela-tives. First and second cousins, to use the more convenient Eng-lish terms, are tabooed, the first more strongly than the second. Third cousins, felt to be "very far out" and sometimes "not counted" by the Irish, are nevertheless formally tabooed by the Church. Yet dispensations can be obtained with relative ease for kindred of this degree. They are granted for all alliances within the system for "cause" inward even as far as first cousins and uncles and nieces, but never within the restricted family.[5] When the dispensation of the Church is obtained, there is no feeling of horror at such marriages. They are, however, always felt to be anomalous and are a matter of comment. In the country areas where there is a necessity among the farmers of keeping farms and dowries within the extended family group, or where the introduction of an outsider is difficult because of class and re-gional antagonisms, marriages between first or second cousins are not uncommon. Nevertheless the general feeling of the com-munity condemns this type of union. Too close intermarriage of this type is a common charge used by townsmen in condemning the country folk. The authors unfortunately had little chance of observing such alliances in their rural setting.

At marriage the individual acquires a new group of kindred. This group is also within the marriage prohibition and the *col;*

[5] *Catholic Encyclopedia,* "Consanguinity."

they are "friends." In the formal or ideal arrangement all those related to one's wife become related to oneself in the same degree. This is the view taken by the Catholic Church. A marriage, the doctrine goes, unites husband and wife as "one flesh." "Affinity from a true marriage is a diriment impediment to the fourth degree of consanguinity of the deceased spouse." [6] A widower "may not marry any of his deceased wife's blood relatives as far as the fourth degree of consanguinity." [7]

In other words, the union of man and woman brings a union of the two extended families from the point of view of the marrying individuals. In the eyes of the Church, the husband stands in the same relation to a wife's relatives as does the wife herself, and vice versa. So strong is this provision in the eyes of the Church that sexual intercourse with any of the wife's kin creates a barrier to the exercise of conjugal rights over the wife. A dispensation as well as absolution from the sin of adultery must be obtained before normal relations of husband and wife can be resumed. This is the effect of the infringement of the marriage taboo upon wife's relatives.

In a patrilineal, patrilocal structure, such as the Irish one, the wife is brought into the husband's family, given a place therein, and takes his patronym. Yet the inclusion is not complete, and, though a woman takes the husband's name, especially among the upper classes and at law, becomes the mistress of the husband's house, and in a thousand ways is oriented to her husband's group, her origin is never lost sight of. Her kindred are referred to as "my wife's friends," yet through the integration of the two families at marriage they become likewise "friends" of the husband. Kinship obligations extend to them.

From an internal point of view, however, marriage is a destruction of two former restricted families, insofar as two individuals leave them in order to form a new restricted family in which the individuals are husband and wife. Perhaps be-

[6] *Catholic Encyclopedia,* "Consanguinity."
[7] *Catholic Encyclopedia,* "Consanguinity."

cause of this disruptive effect on the paternal families, there is no provision made for a closer integration between them. No terms express the new relationship; the emphasis of relationship by affinity is restricted to the point of view of the marrying couple. Where the primary accent is upon vertical descent through blood kindred, there is little scope for a lateral rapport between the parental families of the marrying pair.

From the point of view of the marrying pair, however, an extension of kinship bonds is made. They are now one. Thus the immediate family of ego's wife are included in ego's kinship group. In the English terminology these relatives are called father-, mother-, brother-, sister-, son- "in-law." It must be noted that the terms brother-in-law and sister-in-law do not include wife or husband's siblings' spouses. The British and American usage extends the term to them, but neither the Church nor the Irish farmers include them within the kinship system. Marriage taboo, which the Church calls diriment impediment, does not extend to them. For this reason two brothers may marry two sisters under canon law, and a man his stepson's widow. There is no "blood" connection. For the same reason, the spouses of mother's and father's siblings, who are called uncles and aunts in American and British terminology, are not included in ego's group; *col* does not extend to them; they do not "belong" to ego.

The explanation of this exclusion of all relatives by affinity except those brought in by ego's own individual marriage lies in the concept of marriage uniting only the marrying individuals. For in the Irish system blood descent alone determines kinship: from the point of view of ego only those within a common system of blood descent are recognized as kin. Accordingly, on marrying, only those within a common system of descent with ego's wife become kin. Such a rigid adherence to the principle of descent does not prevent the development of very amicable and prescribed relations with such individuals as one's father's brother's wife. It merely excludes them from one's own kinship group.

The Irish terminology expresses the same reckoning of affinity. The word *cleamhnas* covers both marriage and relationship by affinity. It also indicates a "match." The word *céile* is used both as an adverb with the sense of the English word "together" and as a noun meaning "mate." *Céile* is the root of various expressions, such as *céilidheacht,* referring to marriage. In Irish, father-in-law is called either *athair cleamhna* or *athair chéile,* mother-in-law *máthair chéile,* as in the proverb:

Bean mhic is máthair chéile,
Mar chat agus luch ar aghaidh a céile

(mother-in-law and daughter-in-law like cat and mouse together).

Similar terms are used for brother- and sister-in-law. But in both languages the tendency is again to use purely descriptive phrases analogous to those we found in designating blood kindred. Thus "my wife's brother" and "my wife's mother," etc., are much more often heard among the farmers, both in English and in Irish.

The Irish language, however, has a separate term for son-in-law. It is *cliamhan,* which is related to the word *cleanhnas*. It is the only nondescriptive term in general use, for daughter-in-law is rendered as "son's wife" (*bean mhic*) in Irish. It may be that the singling out of this relative among those united to one by affinity reflects the greater importance put upon males in a patrilineal system.

The relatives by affinity just described include all those of the spouses immediate family. The principle at work has been to coalesce ego's immediate or restricted kindred with his wife's. Beyond this group to whom the extension of the kinship behaviors is primary lies the total group of the wife's extended kindred. They are referred to as "my wife's friends"; there is a general tendency to extend kinship behavior to them; and they lie within the prohibited group. They are what might be expressed as potential kindred in the same sense that ego's third, fourth, and fifth cousins, their progenitors and descendants, are potential kindred. Should the need arise, the common descent may be remembered. At times of family crises, particularly at funerals, this sort of bond comes into active force.

In this fact lies the peculiar character of a kinship system based upon extension rather than rigidity of form. The demarcations between the kindred groups of one individual and the next are not rigidly drawn. The individual can expand and contract the group outward from the restricted family to which he belongs. If he is important in the community, he can command the respect and the services of a great number of kindred; it becomes an advantage to the peripheral relatives to establish the reciprocals of behavior which the system allows. On the other hand, if the individual is without personal importance, the scope of his actual integration through behavior to his kindred may be narrowed down to include only members of his immediate family.

It is the potentiality of extension and contraction within the kinship group which is both praised and condemned in such phrases as "A neighbor is nearer than a friend" and "The higher the man, the more people he has." If the individual attempts to rise above his fellows or to forget them in his way upward, the cry immediately rises that he is "forgetting his friends." In fact, disloyalty to one's kinship group is felt to be a deadly crime against the group.

The Irish extended family, combining in different degrees of intensity of solidarity all descendants of a common ancestor through five contemporaneous generations, is not a rigidly defined structure set off from the other groups of society. On the contrary, the extended families present a picture of a series of interlocking pyramids in which each individual is assigned a definite place, but in which no two individuals (unless siblings) occupy quite the same place. It is a group of kindred reckoning common bilateral descent, and linking as equals all individuals occupying the same step within that descent to the number of five such steps, and including the corresponding group of the spouse's kindred. It is in no sense a clan or gens, as its bounds are not constant, but descend and ascend through the total group of possible kindred. That is, an existing group resolves itself into a number of new ones, as descent proceeds from father to son. It is because of this that farmers having the same patronym and living side by side yet may not be "friends."

Through the workings in and out of the interlocking series of pyramids mentioned above, an isolated area of small population can soon become inextricably intertangled. Hence in the poorest and most isolated regions we find the greatest amount of intermarriage. Evidence is not definite on this score, but the indications point in that direction. As these have been generally the last regions to lose the Irish language, it is there that we find the greatest proliferation of terminologies whose purpose is to preserve the structure and to determine the precise limits set for marriages. Marriages under such conditions force a nice adjustment of reduplicated kinship bonds. Dispensations are obtained under the conditions we have mentioned, and accordingly the parish priest is made a party to every marriage, a great extension of his authority.

Through such intermingling, it very often happens that a comparatively large area will be peopled entirely by individuals standing within near degrees of kinship one to another. In such a case the local group attains the added solidarities of common kinship. To an outsider, such a group, closely integrated through kinship bonds, occupying the same general level of social stratification and the same general place in the economic system, and dominating a large or small area (sometimes as large as a parish), presents a united front. It exhibits a very effective solidarity against outsiders. It is this solidarity which gives rise to the assumption among outside observers that the clan still exists in rural Ireland. It is this solidarity, too, which expresses itself in the political cohesion of large sections of the countryside.

In the appended figure (Fig. 10) one can get a view of this reckoning of descent within this kinship system as a whole. The

Figure 10

Kinship and Descent

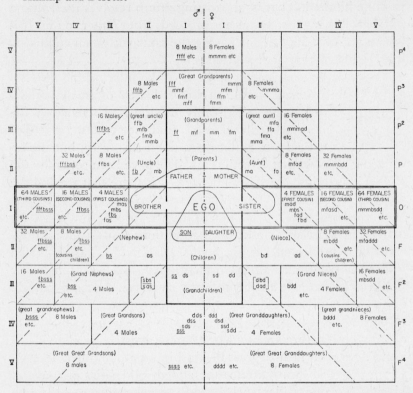

figure is arranged in block form and divided between left and right by male and female sex. The generations are numbered after the fashion of a checkerboard, and each block or square represents a kinship personality. Each square is contingent to that of its parent of the same sex and to that of its child of the same sex. Thus the lines of descent strike one's eye at a glance. The English terms adorn each square, and small letters in each square give the abbreviation for the designation of the personalities whose place the square represents and who are grouped together under a common term. A number is included which lists

92

the number of personalities in all possible descent lines represented by the square.

Anyone interested in explaining to himself the Irish reckonings, such as for instance "fourth *col*," need only count off the
squares from ego.

The groups usually designated are shown within blocks united
under heavier margins. Thus those grouped in double black
margin across the whole diagram, taking in all the generation
marked horizontally as I and O, are ego's "friends." They are
members of his generation, united by common descent reckoned
back five generations to common great-great-grandparent.

It goes without saying, of course, that, except for minor variations, this system is essentially that of all northern and western
Europe. It is that of the United States. It is technically a descriptive, bilateral, patrilineal system. Like all kinship systems without exception throughout the whole world, it provides for reckoning in a comon scheme nine generations, five of which must
already occupy the past. Like all others, it represents a self-con-
sistent system built up of the relationships within the immediate
family.

6

Demography and Familism

Of the demographic phenomena the small farmers present, the decline of population is most easily isolated. The facts are as follows: There has been a continuous and characteristic decline since the great famine of 1845. Numbers have fallen from 6,548,000 in 1841 to 2,963,000 in 1926. With the exception of Dublin, the whole of the country has suffered in this decline. On the whole, however, the country districts have suffered at a greater rate than have the towns. In 1841, 80 per cent of the population was rural; today only 63 per cent. In other words, since 1841 there has been an almost continuous increase in the town population at the expense of the rural, though the two have shared a common decline. Put in terms of percentages: since 1841, the country districts have lost 64 per cent of their population, towns from 200 to 500 49 per cent, towns from 5,000 to 10,000 25 per cent, and towns other than Dublin over 10,000 13 per cent. Dublin, on the other hand, has gained 47 per cent. That the enormous emigration associated with this de-

94

cline is a matter of the contemporary generation is evident when it is recognized that 30 per cent of the native-born Irish were living in other countries in 1926.

The closest approach among European countries is the case of Norway, where 15 per cent live outside. Italy, which has provided so many citizens for the United States and the Argentine, has only 4 per cent of its natives residing in foreign countries. Since 1911 there has, however, been a check in the decrease; only 5 per cent of the population was lost between 1911 and 1926. The region of our investigation, County Clare, shares in this general loss, falling in population from 250,000 in 1841 to 95,000 in 1926. Since 1911 it has lost only 8 per cent.

As the statistics show, this loss of population is in the main a problem of the country districts. The towns have gained proportionately to the countryside; though in a lesser degree, they have, of course, shared the common loss. Many causes for this decline have been operative and, as the excellent work by Dr. William Forbes Adams, *Ireland and Irish Emigration to the New World,*[1] shows, emigration is no new factor in Irish life. The great impetus for an enormous exodus of population was the famine of 1845, but since then emigration has flowed on continuously, coming to an end only in 1932 when for the first time for at least a century more Irishmen returned than left the country.

But far from the famine's having started the emigration from the present Free State, "the growth of emigration between 1815 and 1845," concludes Dr. Adams, "not only made possible the flight after the famine, it caused that flight. The thirty years before 1845 spread the emigrating spirit through all but the highest class until it became the favorite remedy for hard times. The tremendous rush of the next fifteen years could not have taken place without aid from the earlier emigrants." Since then, the land agitation, dissatisfaction with British rule, and periodic hard times have taken their toll, coupled with what Adams calls the greatest single cause of human migration, the work of pow-

[1] New Haven: Yale University Press, 1932.

erful interests developed first in the early days of Irish emigration, "organizing and developing (immigrant) traffic for their own profit." The movement began long before the great burst of the fifties and has been continuous ever since.

Many attempts have been made to find causes for this emigration. Perhaps the most successful have been those dealing with economic factors. Among the most frequently suggested is the change in agriculture since the famine. The assumption advanced is that the change from tillage to livestock production has cut down the rural employment, which in turn has driven the rural population to emigrate. Undoubtedly, there has been a correlation, particularly in the earliest years and at the time of the land clearances after the famine. In fact, from 1847 to 1852 (the famine years) there was a huge decrease in the area under small holdings of 1–30 acres, a decrease of 1,395,000 acres, but since then, in the years from 1852 to 1909 (after which holdings began generally to be increased), the corresponding decrease was only 155,000 acres.

The Report on Agricultural Statistics, 1847–1926, published by the Free State Department of Agriculture and Commerce, from which the figures are derived, comments that "this comparatively small transference of land from small holdings with high densities to larger holdings with low densities had but little effect upon reducing tillage or increasing livestock,"[2] the agricultural changes which are supposed to have affected emigration. The Report demonstrates that between 1854 and 1912 the smaller the holding, the larger the increases in densities of all livestock, except dry cattle two years old and over, and the larger the decrease in density of ploughed land.

In other words, the change in agriculture, whatever may have been its effect upon employment prospects for the small farmer outside his own farm, proceeded more rapidly on the small farms. The tables of the Report show that large farmers decreased their tillage at a more rapid rate than small farmers only

[2] *Agricultural Statistics, 1847–1926,* p. xliii.

in the periods of 1917 to 1926 and 1854 to 1874, while continuously over the whole period 1874 to 1926 small farmers "got out of tillage more rapidly than large farmers." Too close appeal accordingly cannot be made to changes in agriculture for an understanding of Irish emigration.

In fact local densities of population do not now and never have shown a great deal of correspondence with densities of tillage. The highest percentage of agricultural land ploughed (29 per cent) was reached in 1851. Since then it has fallen steadily, to 13 per cent in 1926. Sweden comes nearest to this low percentage of tillage, with 52 per cent of her arable land tilled. Consequently, the Irish population was at no time solely dependent upon tillage crops.

Before 1881 a correlation could be drawn with some accuracy between the decrease in tillage and the decrease in rural population. Thus in poor law unions (administrative areas) in which ploughed land decreased population also decreased as shown in Table 1.[3]

Table 1

Relation between Decrease in Ploughed Land and Decrease in Population

Decrease in Ploughed Land (per cent)	Decrease in Population (per cent)
0–20	13
20–30	26
30–40	28
50 and over	34

But since 1881 similar tables show that there is no correspondence between the decreases, and that even those poor law unions in which tillage has increased show an ordinary loss of population. Consequently, decline in tillage had little effect upon emigration after 1881. This becomes even more evident when it is understood that in both 1854 and 1912 the thirteen

[3] *Agricultural Statistics, 1847–1926,* p. lxi.

counties densest in rural population included only six of the counties densest in ploughed land. "Dense tillage was in the east, dense rural population in the west," [4] as it still is.

In the same search for economic causes, a better case has been made for the change from milch cattle to beef cattle production. As we have seen, milch cows are characteristically associated with the small farmers. During the period of emigration, the number of dry cattle has risen in proportion to the number of milch cattle almost steadily; the range is from 2,372 total cattle to the 1,000 milch cows in 1854, to 3,334 to the 1,000 in 1926; fluctuations have been very slight. It is true that the number of milch cattle has also risen steadily, if slowly. Such a change in actual numbers of cattle and in proportions of dry to milch cattle, the latter capable of yielding the greater amounts of food for farm consumption, may have had some effect upon the displacement of human beings by cattle, but certainly not a great enough one to determine the emigration. The lack of correspondence between these changes is evident when it is remembered that the change has taken place principally in the former tillage areas, and also that in 1926 the areas of greatest milch cow density were substantially the same as in 1854. The very little direct correspondence there can be is well exemplified in the contrast between County Clare, which fell from a population of 336 to the 1,000 acres of crop and pasture to 129, while milch cows remained practically the same in number (100 to 110 to the 1,000 acres), and County Mayo (a poorer region), where population fell only from 375 to 245 and milch cows also remained practically the same (90 to 100).

From these figures it is evident that the decline in rural population is not directly correlated with decline in tillage or change in cattle production. The failure of employment coincident upon that change cannot be assigned as the sole cause of emigration.

As the decline in population has been more characteristic of

[4] *Agricultural Statistics, 1847–1926,* p. lvi.

the small farmers, it may be possible to associate it with social conditions pertaining among that class. They have participated in the very agricultural changes which are thought to have caused their dispersal. They enjoyed the high prosperity of the closing decades of the last century, and won the progressive reforms of agrarian tenure. Yet they continued to send forth thousands of emigrants. Fluctuating economic conditions have undoubtedly had their effect, but factors whose greatest demonstrable result is merely to stay or hurry the stream of emigration cannot be evoked as efficient causes. In taking the problem directly to the small farmer, it will become possible to sketch the social setting in which emigration takes its form.

Clearly connected with the decline in population are other demographic statistics, particularly those of marriage. They present features which are unique among civilized peoples. Inasmuch as they are again indications of an underlying uniform social pattern whose occurrences they record, it is necessary to analyze them in terms of the behavior patterns of rural Ireland. Like emigration, they are more characteristic of the country people. Springing from marriage, they are thus directly indicative of social forces within the small farmers' family economy.

Briefly stated, they present the following characteristics: In Saorstat Eireann in 1926, according to the census then conducted, there was a larger proportion of unmarried persons of all ages than in any other country for which records are kept. Marriage, furthermore, did not take place until a comparatively late age. Thus 80 per cent of males between twenty-five and thirty years of age were unmarried in 1926, 62 per cent of males thirty to thirty-five, 50 per cent of males thirty-five to forty, and 26 per cent of males fifty-five to sixty-five. The significance of these figures springs from their comparison with other countries. In the United States only 39 per cent of males twenty-five to thirty are unmarried, 24 per cent between thirty and thirty-five, and only 10 per cent between fifty-five and sixty-five. Denmark,

99

A
301.35

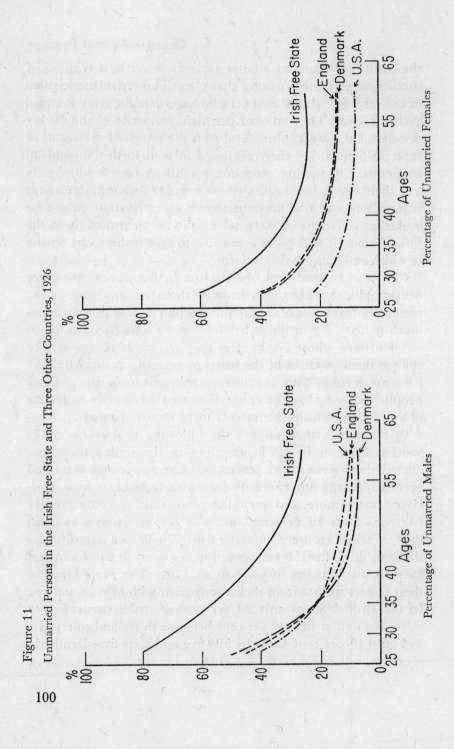

Figure 11

Unmarried Persons in the Irish Free State and Three Other Countries, 1926

an agricultural country similar in many ways to Ireland, had only 49 per cent, 25 per cent, 15 per cent, and 8 per cent of these age groups not yet benedict, respectively. In England the percentages were 45 per cent, 25 per cent, 16 per cent, and 10 per cent, a great contrast to the sister island. Indeed, in the Free State the percentages of unmarried among the males of each age group are usually double those of other countries.

Unmarried females are also very numerous, though not so excessively so as in the case with the males. In the age groups twenty-five to thirty, thirty to thirty-five, thirty-five to forty, and fifty-five to sixty-five the percentages are respectively 62 per cent, 42 per cent, 32 per cent, and 24 per cent. In Denmark the same groups showed only 39 per cent, 25 per cent, 19 per cent, and 14 per cent; in England, 41 per cent, 26 per cent, 20 per cent, and 15 per cent. Figure 11 gives a graphic comparison between the Irish Free State and three other modern countries.

Later marriage and high incidence of bachelorhood is, like population decline, more pronounced among the country people. And among them, it is highest in those areas where small holdings prevail. In County Clare 88 per cent of the males between twenty-five and thirty in rural districts were unmarried. This percentage is not abnormally high for Ireland, as Sligo, Galway, Mayo, and Leitrim, areas of small holdings, have 90 per cent and Roscommon 91 per cent. In Clare 90 per cent of women between twenty and twenty-five were unmarried, yet six western counties have higher percentages than Clare's.

In fact the thickly populated and poorer western counties show a higher percentage in all age groups of unmarried than the eastern counties. In spite of this, however, there is a higher percentage of all females in eastern than in western counties. This fact is directly correlated with the difference in the sex ratio between eastern and western counties. In Dublin and the other large cities the female population exceeds the male, while in country districts and smaller towns there is a male excess. The proportion of females per thousand males is lower than that of any of the other twenty-one European countries. It is greater, however, than that of such new countries as the United States. There are 973 females to every 1,000 males in the Free State.

If marriage is so long delayed and there are so few women relatively in the country districts, the condition in the towns is not quite so marked. Females outnumber the males there. Likewise marriage takes place much earlier. In County Clare the aggregate rural areas show 88 per cent of males twenty-five to thirty and 73 per cent thirty to thirty-five unmarried, but the aggregate town areas show only 70 per cent and 50 per cent. There is a general tendency: the larger the town, the earlier marriage takes place. Ennis, the largest town and county seat of Clare (6,000), has a somewhat lower percentage than is usual for towns of its size in Ireland. In fact, Clare's figures, 60 per cent and 30 per cent in those age grades, are better even than those for such a metropolis as Cork City, with 68 per cent and 40 per cent.

Correlations of occupation and marital status[5] support the assumption that the longest delay in marriage is found among the small farmers. Both agricultural laborers and town laborers marry younger and in greater numbers proportionately. No other occupational class, not even the professional class, delays marriage so long or has so many celibate members.

These facts obviously relate themselves to the population decline. They are, as it were, two different symptoms of the same condition. But strangely enough in a declining population, fecundity is very high. Although there are fewer married women of childbearing age per 1,000 inhabitants than in other countries (74 in Ireland, 142 in the United States, 125 in Germany, 112 in Denmark, 121 in England, and 119 in Italy), the fertility of these women is remarkably high. For every 100 married women under 45, there are 131 children under five years of age, com-

[5] *Census of Population, 1926,* vol. V, part II: Ages and Conjugal Conditions.

pared with only 77 in the United States, 71 in England, 93 in Denmark, and 75 in Germany. The number of children is higher again in western counties of Ireland than in eastern. The women of Clare under 45 produced 140 children for every 100 married women, those of Donegal 152, but in County Dublin and County Wicklow, the two eastern counties, only 122 and 124. In spite of this great fecundity there is, however, in Ireland only a normal proportion of children under 15, if Ireland is compared to other countries. The balance between high fertility and few and late marriages keeps their number down.

The kernel of the problem lies, of course, in the behavior of the country people. Marriage brings both dispersal of the farm family and change of status for boys and girls. The marriage of one of the sons brings re-formation of the whole family group upon the farm. The crux of the matter lies in this reorganization of the farm family and the mechanism of the change and continuity it provides.

The nearly universal form of marriage in the Irish countryside unites transfer of economic control, land ownership, reformation of family ties, advance in family and community status, and entrance into adult procreative sex life. It is a central focus of rural life, a universal turning point in individual histories. This form of marriage is known as matchmaking. It is the usual, in fact until recently the only respectable, method of marriage and usually too of inheritance.

In Figure 12 the reader will find a graphic representation of the description of the movement of the family and the re-formation of relations which the match involves and which is the burden of this chapter. It explains itself, and it gives a very good illustration of the generalities. Organicists should take heart at its resemblance to an amoeba expanding and budding. But the resemblance is accidental. The examples we cite come nearly all from County Clare, but literary references and interviewing in other places have been made to show that matchmaking prevails

103

Figure 12
The Match (Farm Marriage)

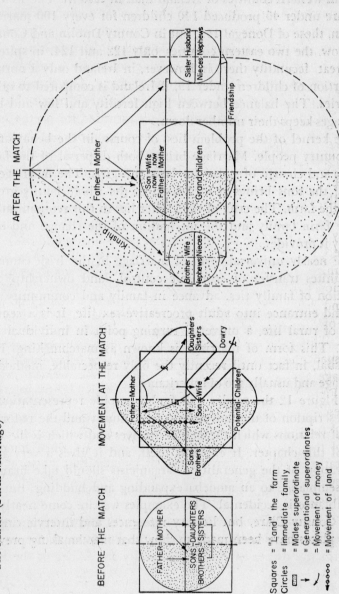

Diagrammatic representation of the re-formation of farm families at the marriage of the heir. The diagram demonstrates the rearrangement of all the constituent relations between persons and the reestablishment of the equilibrium of the familistic system.

almost universally among small farmers with very little local modification. It is furthermore imbedded in the Irish (Gaelic) tongue and very old in Irish history.

A match (Gaelic, *cleamhnas,* marriage, and *spré,* a dowry) is a contractual marriage made by the parents or families of the marrying parties and involving the disposal of properties. Generally it begins with a farmer's casting round for a suitable girl for one of his sons who is to inherit his farm. The choice of the heir from among the sons rests in the father's hands. Historically, all the sons and daughters were provided for on the land, and, where possible, this is still the ideal situation, but the closer identification of family with one particular plot of land and the difficulty of land division fostered through three generations of agrarian agitation and land reform have prevented this. One son, then, is ordinarily to be "settled on the land." Typically today only one son remains, and he gets the farm.

In the words of one countryman, the procedure would be:

If I wanted to give my farm over to my son and I would be worth, say, two hundred pounds, I would know a fellow up the hill, for instance, that would be worth three hundred pounds. I would send up a neighbor fellow to him and ask him if he would like to join my family in marriage. If the fellow would send back word he would and the girl would say she was willing [and the usual courtesies were exchanged], then on a day they agreed on I and the fellow would meet in Ennistymon [the local market town] and talk over the whole thing as to terms, maybe sitting on it the whole day. Then, before, if it was land I didn't know or the fellow came from afar off, I would walk his land and look at it and the cattle there were on it to make sure of the farm. Then we would go to a solicitor that day and make up the writings in Ennistymon. The money, say three hundred pounds, would be paid over in cash or in promissory notes, and it is usual here to divide it into two parts or sometimes more. One half is paid at the wedding, and the other is paid a year after.

This statement contains in essence nearly the whole of matchmaking. As the old fellow indicates, the initiative in the matter lies with the owner of the farm, usually the father of the boy.

When the time comes for him to relinquish the farm, he lets it be known in the district to those who have daughters ready to be dowered. On the other hand, the father of the girl may often take the initiative, letting it be known that his daughter has a dowry at such and such a figure. In either case, when a suitable boy or girl has been found, the farmer sends an emissary to his or her parent. The relative value of the farms and the "fortune" that a farmer will give for his daughter are generally pretty well known in the district, but where the two families are comparative strangers, or belong to different localities, the role of the emissary in laying the proposals of one set of parents before the other is more important. The emissary is not a relative of either party ordinarily. Certain individuals become well known locally as successful negotiators. In former days there was once a fully developed "matchmaker" or marriage broker. The office is said to exist still in Connemara, but it has died out in Clare.

Quite often a well-known shopkeeper or local politician comes to play the role. One in particular in Ennistymon (a market town of 1,200) came under the author's notice. The back room of his public house reserved for special customers became one of the centers of local matchmaking. It was there that the fathers of both boy and girl would meet and "sit on the match." Their deliberation, to the accompaniment of many bottles of stout, threshes out the whole matter of the disposal of the properties involved, the relative status of the families, and any possible barriers to the union, such as consanguinity, insanity, or notorious crime in past ancestry.

The bargaining is a matter of nice adjustment between the "fortune" and the farm. The custom known as "walking the land," referred to above, insures that the farm is roughly equivalent to the fortune, though each party strives for a higher valuation of its own claims. Thus, where a fortune of five hundred pounds has finally been agreed upon, the girl's father will have offered only four hundred and the boy's will have held out for six hundred, instancing all the prospects and advantages of his

106

farm in support of his figure. Finally, through the offices of the intermediary and after concessions on each side, the two will "split the difference" and thus reach an agreement. The decision rests with the fathers, but they will have had the quite vocal assistance of friends and older members of the kindred.

Perhaps the words of a countryman best describe the matching of values and prospects the bargaining entails. Farm and spouse are inextricably interwoven in his mind:

When a young man is once on the lookout for a lady, it is put through his friends for to get a suitable woman for his wife. It all goes by friendship and friends and meeting at public houses. The young man sends a speaker to the young lady and the speaker will sound a note to know what fortune she has, will she suit, and will she marry this Shrove? She and her friends will inquire what kind of a man is he, is he nice and steady? If he suits, they tell the speaker to go ahead and draw it down. So then he goes back to the young man's house and arranges for them to meet in such a place on such a night and we will see about it. The speaker goes with the young man and his father that night, and they meet the father of the girl and his friends or maybe his son and son-in-law. The first drink is called by the young man, the second by the young lady's father. The young lady's father asks the speaker what fortune do he want. He asks him the place of how many cows, sheep, and horses it is. He asks what makings of a garden are in it; is there plenty of water or spring wells? Is it far from the road or on it? What kind of house is in it, slate or thatch? Are cabins good, are they slate or thatch? If it is too far in from the road, he won't take it. Backward places don't grow big fortunes. And he asks too is it near a chapel and the school or near town? If it is a nice place, near the road, and the place of eight cows, they are sure to ask three hundred and fifty pounds fortune. Then the young lady's father offers two hundred and fifty pounds. Then maybe the boy's father throws off fifty pounds. If the young lady's father still has two hundred and fifty pounds on it, the speaker divides the fifty pounds between them, so now it's two hundred and seventy-five. Then the young male says he is not willing to marry without three hundred pounds — but if she's a nice girl and a good housekeeper, he'll think of it. So there's another drink by the young man, and then another by the young lady's father, and so on with every second drink till they're near drunk. The speaker gets plenty and has a good day. After this, they appoint a place for the young people to see one another and be introduced. The young lady takes along her friends, and maybe another girl, and her brother and father and mother. The young man takes along his friends and the speaker. If they suit one another, they will then appoint a day to come and see the land. If they don't, no one will reflect on anybody, but they will say he or she doesn't suit. They do not say plainly what is wrong. The day before the girl's people come to see the land, geese are killed, the house is whitewashed, whiskey and porter bought. The cows get a feed early so as to look good; and maybe they get an extra cow in, if they want one. Then next day comes the walking of the land. The young man stays outside in the street, but he sends his best friend in to show the girl's father round, but sure the friend won't show him the bad points. If the girl's father likes the land, he returns, and there will be eating and drinking until night comes on them. Then they go to an attorney until the next day and get the writings between the two parties and get the father [boy's] to sign over the land. Then there comes another day to fit her for a ring. The girl and boy meet in town some day. He buys her some present. They walk the town that day and all admire the pair and gander after them.

Several instances have come to notice where agreement was not reached and where a farmer has broken off negotiations on finding a girl with fifty pounds more. There are also many subterfuges which, though they are regarded by others as humorous occurrences, are often sore spots between the contracting parties. Thus a farmer near Ennistymon drove his neighbor's cows into his farm on the day of the girl's father's walking the land so that the other would think him richer than he was. After the marriage the deception was discovered, but too late.

In another case, a sure penalty overtook a farmer who abused the bargaining system. I give the description of a neighbor:

He's nothing but an old blatherer, he was always sitting on matches and saying he would give a fellow his daughter when he hadn't any fortune on her at all. He'd break it off by saying the girl wasn't willing and all the time it was only boasting and drinking the porter he was.

Today the boaster is a local joke, and his daughter has fled to America.

A famous local character round Ennis, a laborer now dead, once bested a countryman through a judicious whetting of the farmer's cupidity at matchmaking. The story goes that the laborer broke the countryman's bargaining resistance by distracting his attention from the cow he was selling at the fair to the prospects of a match between the farmer and a purely fictitious sister, who was dowered with an equally fictitious three hundred pounds. Later when the farmer and his friends came to town again to discuss the matter further, the wit told them elaborately that, after making full inquiries, he had decided they belonged to too respectable a family to allow themselves to make a match with his sister, since the sister had already "a little one" out of wedlock.

Another case of subterfuge practiced illustrates a variation in the match. A fellow near Ennistymon got a farmer with a daughter to back his note at the local bank to the extent of six hundred pounds. The borrowing was kept secret, and the endorser does not seem to have known that the security offered was his own farm. Accordingly, when the borrower later offered to bring in the six hundred pounds in marrying the daughter, the farmer accepted, thinking he was to receive the fortune clear of debt. He discovered only too late that he had a son-in-law whose fortune he must make good himself. The deception led to bad blood between the two, but nothing could be done.

This last example illustrates a reversal of the usual procedure. Ordinarily since the Irish farm family is both patrilineal and patrilocal, the fortune is brought in by the girl and goes to the father of the boy. When, however, there is no male heir, the incoming son-in-law must give a fortune to the farm holder. Generally the man's fortune is much larger than that of the girl. It may be that the necessity for its being larger arises from the fact that he has no land of his own. Frequently the farm into which he marries is known for at least a generation longer by the name of the girl's family, which reflects the identification of the patrilineal line with a particular plot of land, so strong in rural Ireland. It may be that the additional payment is deemed necessary to overcome the anomaly felt at the reversal of the usual roles of sons and daughters. The Irish term for an in-marrying son-in-law is a graphic one; it is *cliamhan isteach* (literally, son-in-law going in).

A quite similar case illustrates not only the position of the man marrying-in but the different aspirations which may be involved. A local politician, a farmer himself, and an automobile driver, a farmer's son, arranged a match for a girl who had lately inherited a farm and a thriving shop in a tiny country town. The prospective groom was a "returned South African" who had brought back two thousand pounds. At the last minute negotiations fell through because the young woman objected to the South African's obesity. The driver was to have got a hundred pounds out of it. We learned that several weeks later a second match arranged for the South African turned out more successfully.

The "fortune" is a prerequisite of country marriages, even divorced from its usual family setting. Many instances can be cited where returned immigrants have come back with dowries made abroad, to marry into local farms. In three cases that the authors had under particular observation, the small farmers' daughters had spent five, eight, and ten years respectively in the United States as domestic servants. Each returned to Ireland with dowry enough to permit her to marry into a local farm, in two of the cases on a somewhat better scale than the farms which they had left. The case of the South African shows how the man also may return with his fortune to establish himself in his native district after several years or even a decade or two of exile.

The dowry or marriage portion is, of course, a phenomenon universal in European peasant life. What gives it special interest here is its intimate connection with the farm family and with the land. That connection is evidenced particularly in the "writings."

After the "walking of the land" and the making of the bargain, the two parties to marry go to a solicitor. There the agreements reached are cast into proper legal form. The "writings" is a legal instrument conveying the ownership of the holding to the son. It is usually both marriage settlement and will. On the event of the stipulated marriage, the father conveys the farm and all appurtenances to his son in return for the portion brought in by the girl. The father makes also definite provisions for his own maintenance and that of his wife. Generally, these include the right to the "grass of a cow," to food and the use of the hearth, perhaps the yield of one patch of potatoes, and the use of a room in the house. The room is nearly always, at least in West and North Clare, the one known as the "west room" for reasons we shall examine later. To take care of possible disputes arising out of the failure of these provisions to work smoothly, certain very hard-headed stipulations are often included, allowing for the conversion of these rights into cash support or a lump sum.

In return for the farm, the father receives the fortune brought in by the girl and paid to him by her father. Furthermore, the provisions which must be made for other children are often transferred with the land. The father is now expected to give (if he has not given them already) portions to those of his children who are not to be settled at home on the land. Where the will and marriage settlement are one and the same document, these obligations are passed on to the inheriting son.

The following description of several "writings" (which we examined) given by an Ennis solicitor specializing in this lucrative practice illustrates the type and the possibilities of variation. The solicitor is describing certain marriage settlements, the originals of which he held in his hand:

In this settlement John F——— of C——— had one son and two daughters at home. He left the farm, you see, all that goes with it, to

111

his son on condition of his marrying the girl named here in the deed. He also made the transfer subject to the son's providing for the two daughters by giving them rights of residence and keep in the house as long as they remain unmarried, and by making them special money gifts when they should marry. He then reserved a right for his wife, leaving her a small sum, and the right to the potato patch and her bedroom free of all charge as long as she lived. In the event of her not liking the new arrangements, she was to get a monthly stipend in lieu of her keep and room until she died.

We shall go on to give this interview in some detail to illustrate the full character of the arrangements made. The solicitor continues:

If there are two sons . . . one of them gets the farm, and when the old people find a girl with a suitable fortune, and the son marries her, they give the money over to the next son, or they provide with it for the other children who haven't yet gone off. It's a pernicious system. [An upper-class person is speaking, not a farmer.] You'll go out to a small holding and see several able-bodied men and women waiting around doing nothing. They are waiting for the eldest son to get married and for their share of the fortune the wife brings in.

What may happen when such an arrangement fails to work smoothly for one reason or another may be seen from the following examples. The first is the description (recorded in the course of a general conversation, not elicited in any way) of the circumstances leading to a murder which was something of a *cause célèbre* in Ireland in 1932. The speaker is a superintendent of civic guards (the police) in charge of the area. It is instructive that the general marriage system is the same as that of Clare, though Roscommon was the county in which the murder (the Frank McDermott case) took place. The speaker began:

The lawyer for the defense at the trial had tried to establish absence of motive. I went into the case thoroughly when the question of reprieve came up. I discovered that the father of the two brothers [accused and murdered man] left the farm to the elder brother with the understanding that he should pay off the younger brother the sum of two hundred pounds to set himself up elsewhere as the farm wasn't big enough for both. The sister was also to be married off with a dowry provided for in the will. But the brother was delicate; he had an asthmatic complaint, and he needed the services of his younger brother on the farm. The farm was paying badly, and there was no two hundred pounds to pay off the other with. In this way the younger brother had no place to turn and he was kept in virtual slavery. He tried to get married in the district, but he had no prospects. The elder brother was also trying to get married to bring in a dowry to pay off his brother and sister, but no girl would have him on account of his asthmatic complaint. In the end the younger fellow decided to take matters into his own hands. He borrowed a gun from his cousin, and went out to a field where he seems to have taken a practice shot, for he apparently had never used a revolver before. No one would have discovered the thing if the cousin hadn't become alarmed when his gun was found and it was thought that he was implicated. The younger brother lay in wait for the elder brother beside a gate leading into their farm. He shot him twice . . . at any rate he left the body where it fell with the revolver beside it, evidence of panicky behavior.

By citing this fratricide, the authors do not mean to indicate that failure of matchmaking leads to such violent conclusions; they mean merely to point out the provenance of the crime in a social situation arising from the family system herein described. A case in County Clare in K——— parish[6] shows the same provenance of conflict in a disturbance of the traditional pattern. The following extract from the diary of one of the authors gives the setting of the dispute:

January 19th. K——— District Court. Nothing much in court today but the following case: Two lads about nineteen were up for having tarred the house of Tim Nihill, the publican, night before the last fair. This wasn't an isolated occurrence; attempts have been made to intimidate Nihill over a period of years. The guards agree he is himself a peaceable citizen. Both Mr. ——— , the justice, and Mr. ——— , the local superintendent of civic guards, agreed that the lads were only "tools of some one behind the scenes who is inciting them."

[6] Fictitious names for persons and smaller places have been substituted in this and following incidents.

The justice bound them over, gave them a stiff fine. Later he explained to me that a certain Mr. Mulvaney has been calling Nihill a land-grabber in the districts and setting the lads on him. Last year the house was fired into in the night. It all arises out of a farm which Nihill owns and which Mulvaney says ought to be his. Mulvaney is landless now, only a farm laborer. His mother, who had the farm, was to have left it to him, but he made a runaway match with a servant girl and his mother wouldn't let them into the house. So she sold the farm to Nihill for cash and some debts outstanding and Mulvaney has been blackguarding Nihill ever since.

This story introduces the whole position of "runaway matches," as elopements are called. There are a few instances of coercion into matches. The autobiographic sketch of one Hannah M———, an old woman, the widow of a petty shopkeeper, illustrates the form which it can take. To paraphrase her:

She is eighty-four, and guess how long she has been a widow, forty years. She's been behind the counter all the time. She has a sister in America with nine children. The sister sent her over her passage, but the family tore it up and married her here in Ennis. She wanted to be a teacher; the work was easy, the holidays (ample) and it was a good job. There were three candidates her year and she got first. At that time her sister sent over the passage money, and she was about to go when they stopped her and married her into this shop. Her sister was coming over before the marriage but her fiancé wouldn't let her go for fear someone would snatch her up too.

Ordinarily, as so many of the examples we have already given show, marriage in the matchmaking system is a matter of free agreement within the traditional setting. Love enters the situation, however, only to complicate it. A runaway match upsets the whole pattern, the interplay of dowries, land, and portions of it for children, the transition between adulthood and old age for the parental couple. There are other considerations, too, which account for the disturbance a runaway match creates, such as those of class involved in "marrying beneath" one, but they are outside our present subject.

The following story illustrates the case. A countryman is describing a happening in his district:

Tom L—— was making a match for his daughter with a fine farm of land, and they got as far as picking the gander [the name of a feast given by the bride's people slightly before the wedding]. They were all up there eating and drinking and dancing all night. Now a fellow from Ennistymon [town] came to it, but he was such an ordinary fellow he was not even invited into the front of the house but stayed in the kitchen. He was so poor and lazy, he brought a little turf to market sometimes, but that was all. Next day, the girl came down to the chapel to be married, and before they knew it, didn't she run off with this fellow. Tom cut her off and disowned her, and she's living in Limerick with her fellow now, but it might be in Australia for all Tom will do for her.

Even when matters have not gone so far, the runaway match causes a grave disturbance and destroys the cohesion of the family. The following account given by a publican in Ennis of country acquaintances shows that reconciliation occurs after a time, but that the disruptive effect upon the family is severe. We give the statement in detail in order to show the general situation as he saw it. He is a townsman, and somewhat detached.

The daughter on the farm has to wait till all the sons are got ready for their going off and maybe have been given their passage to America or money to set up in business or to settle on the land. But there are runaway matches all the time, they fall in love, they run off together, and they come in here and take work away from the laborers here. It takes a lot of love and courage because the son is usually cut off and the daughter leaves a very good place for nothing but a cabin and they get none of the money. Maybe after several years the girl will get her fortune, but not always. I remember Jerry N—— whose father was very well off as farmers go, but he wouldn't marry the girl they picked for him and took up with a servant girl instead. He's driving a hackney now and lives in a cabin with a flock of children. Jimmy L—— ran off but he gradually became reconciled with his people. The father had a good farm of sixty acres, and so had the girl, but the young fellow got nothing out of it. His father helps a little now, sending down a bag of potatoes.

Another case which the authors had under observation from time to time illustrates not only the matchmaking system but the general family setting in which marriage takes place and farm life moves. Sanctions for conduct aggrieving the families are applied by the families themselves. The case is long but worth quoting in the words of the teller for its comprehensive character:

There was a girl of the O'Rourkes from D——— , they have a farm out there and she married a fellow named Murphy up in C——— . She was a schoolteacher out in England for several years and she became great with this fellow the farmer, and she used to send him money over from England for when they would get married. She sent about two hundred pounds in all. She has an aunt up in C——— married up there and it was all the fault of the aunt. She came home and she hadn't yet told her people anything about it. She was just about ready to get married to the fellow and she told them that she was going to get married. They agreed. Then she said she was going to get married to Murphy and they tried to argue her out of it, but she said it was too far gone now and she was committed to marry him, so they hastily gave her their blessing. He lived in a big house up by C——— and had sixty acres.

Well, he was a sort of uncouth kind of chap, rough, and she was what you might say anglified, or citified. She wanted to brighten up the house and make it nice and hang up curtains and that sort of thing. He thought the reins of the horse would do for the curtains and so on, and it came to a fight between them, a clash of wills, and in the end, as it must, the stronger one won out; that is, the man's. She got hysterical and he cast round for ways of getting rid of her, and he sent up to Ennistymon for the doctor to come down and examine her to commit her to the asylum. He didn't send her up to C——— though that was nearer and in his district, but he sent up for Dr. MacNulty to Ennistymon, leaving Dr. Starr in C——— so as to get someone who wouldn't know the case.

The married sister of the wife was staying in the house at the time and he was driving her home. He told her the doctor was coming, and she said, "You are doing wrong," and made him turn round and go back to the house where Dr. MacNulty was examining the hysterical woman. Then the married sister got her brother and father to take her back to D——— .They came up with Father Brendan of Ennis

116

here and took her away down to D———— . After a time they got up a party and invited him down for a reconciliation.

After a while she went back to live with him. He started it again and got her hysterical and called in another doctor, who said that there was nothing wrong with the woman.

One night the three brothers of the girl and her father came up to the house and one went round to the back door and the others went in the front and they caught the fellow. They were going to force him to sign receipts for the money the daughter gave him. Country people demand receipts for money they give and they are right, but the girl hadn't liked to ask and hadn't got any, so her people were going to step in and get them themselves. Murphy had rifled her belongings and torn off his name from all the receipts he had sent her to England. They came in and said that he was lucky he was going to escape with his life. No one in their family had ever been in the asylum and no one belonging to them had ever been insane or robbers and that he was trying to black them with the disgrace of it. The girl ran in but they threw her out into the hall where her father caught her and held her. They said that all the people belonging to him were thieves, and that two of them, two uncles of his, his mother's brothers, were convicted for robbery and that all his people before him had been insane, and that he was trying to black the name of a good family. In the end they caught him and beat him till he consented to sign the receipts. They gave him a good hiding.

The teller drew his own conclusions from the case:

If the girl had listened to her parents, they would have told her all this and saved her. But she went on and married right ahead on her own advice. She probably thought she was doing well in marrying into sixty acres.

It is interesting that the application of sanctions does not confine itself to a single dereliction. In this case, according to the storyteller:

Murphy was a terrible lazy farmer and wouldn't even till a patch of ground for a garden for himself or his stock, and the woman's people had to send up a load of potatoes for them. They told him when they beat him if he didn't turn into a farmer and do a man's work, till his garden, and provide, they would be up again and make him do it.

7

Family Transition at Marriage

With the transfer of land at the marriage of the son who remains
to work the farm, the relations of the members of the farm family to each other and to the farm they work undergo a drastic
change. In the first place, the headship of the old couple under
whom the family group worked undergoes change. The old couple relinquish the farm, they enter the age grade of the dying,
and direction of the enterprise of the group passes from their
hands to those of the young people. Something of the change has
already been indicated in the "writings." From the point of view
of the father, it means the abandonment of the ownership he
has long enjoyed; from the point of view of the old woman it
means she is no longer the "woman of the house." Her place is
taken by the incoming daughter-in-law. Naturally, this change is
accomplished in effect only with difficulty and with considerable
reluctance upon the part of the old couple. Where the transition goes smoothly, father and son continue to work the farm

118

together, but more often as the father grows older he retires to his seat by the hearth. For example, the authors know one family, consisting of a young man and his wife, their two children, and the old couple, which was regarded as a model of family harmony in the neighborhood. The young man did all the heavy work of the farm, but his father worked by his side. Yet the initiative in agricultural matters was clearly the young man's. The man, almost eighty, did not want to remain idle. "Time enough to sit by the fire in the winter," he would say. The greatest compliment the neighbors had for them was: "Look at the C———s. Old Johnny gives his boy a hand with everything. You wouldn't know which one has the farm."

The coming-in of the daughter-in-law is sometimes not so harmonious. Disputes arise, as the provisions made in the "writings" indicate. The following quotation from an official with years of experience in dealing with country people illustrates:

As years go on, either the parents die or, if they live sufficiently long, they receive the old-age pension. Before they are qualified for this, the farms have to be made over to a son or daughter. This is done on the occasion of the son's marriage. The father reserves to himself and his wife the use of a room and the freedom of the kitchen, and they are entitled to all their food. The points were carefully discussed at length in the process of matchmaking, and the family of the future wife had no hesitation in agreeing, realizing that such points formed the final phase of a cycle of life on the farm. If the daughter-in-law has been well and properly advised by her mother, she immediately on her arrival in the new house submits tactfully to all proposals of her mother-in-law and lets the old lady feel that she is still the master mariner. If she didn't, it would cause a lot of trouble, as sometimes happens.

In such cases, the mediations of the parish priest and public opinion generally patch up a compromise, but, as far as the authors have observed, the transition is a gradual and successful one. The young woman usually serves a sort of apprenticeship at the hands of the mother-in-law in the new household, and at least during the young woman's childbearing years the older one maintains her control.

An open breach between the two couples is universally condemned, of course; "turning the old people out on the side of the road" has occurred, although the authors found no instance of it. If, however, the new family finds the old too great a burden, the old may go to the County Home, where the poor and derelict old people are maintained. A grave stigma of inability to support one's duties still attaches to this.

It is interesting that the old-age pension, originally designed in Great Britain to support the aged members of an industrial population and extended some years later to Ireland, has been incorporated into Irish farm life without upsetting, but rather reinforcing, the matchmaking pattern. The tendency is now to turn the farm over to the son as soon as the father passes his seventieth year. Receipt of the pension facilitates the maintenance of the old people and hastens the transfer of land to the son, as the farmers must divest themselves of their small farms in the majority of cases in order to become eligible for the pension.

Even from the point of view of the household expense, the pension is very welcome. In the words of one farmer:

To have old people in the house is a great blessing in these times because if you have one, it means ten bob a week and, if you have two, it means a pound a week coming into the house. You take a man like O'D——— and every Friday he will go to Corrofin [town] to collect his ten bob and he may buy a couple of bottles of porter, but spend the rest on things for the house and then come home with a few shillings which will go into the common fund.

Not only that but it adds at least ten years to a man's life because the anticipation that each Friday he is to get ten shillings will cheer him up and keep him keen. Any house which has one old person is well off in the last few years, and, if there are two, it is a great blessing.

But the blessing the pension represents is more than an economic aid in bad times. It plays a great role in the transition the match brings about in family relationships. As one country-woman phrased it:

There is no chance that the old people would give up the land but for the pension, and there is no hurrying them. Before the old-age pension the father would keep the fat of the land and there would be argument between them, the young woman and the old woman slashing each other with tongs, the doors broke, and it would be two dwellings in the house, like, but since the old-age pension, there are no rows and, if there are, then they make it up with the old people for the ten bob a week.

If the transition is smooth, there need be no such violence of dispute as the last quotation describes. Each of the members of the household must adopt a new role in relation to the others. The old man abdicates his controlling position with his transference of the farm to his son. Usually such a change goes smoothly enough. If the son can still seem to defer to superior experience and judgment and refer decisions to the old man, all goes well. The happiest compromise is that suggested in the statement of one countryman:

Every morning, even after I was married, I would go to the old man and ask him what he thought I should do for the day, and the old man would say that it is now time to do this or that or that the cows should have something done for them or the garden should be prepared. I would go then and spend twenty to thirty minutes doing what the old man said, and then go about my own business.

It is in the feminine province of farm work and household control that the transition is most difficult. Under the patrilocal type of marriage here described, the bride is a stranger and of necessity cannot rely upon the experience of an association of years in order to meet the new conditions, as can father and son. In the graphic phrase of the people, she is the "new woman."

For her the transition brings a violent uprooting from prior attachments. Unlike her urban sister, she has little of the ideal of romantic love to help her over the crisis. Consequently her introduction into the new household is gradual, and her assumption of her new duties takes place over a moderately lengthy period. Two considerations, of course, are her primary inspiration in moments of stress: first, that she is now a fully adult woman with a household of her own although she must still share its control with her mother-in-law; and second, that the customary usage of the countryside provides her with an occasional escape back to her own people still on the farm at home. The following quotation expresses one woman's remembrance of her emotional difficulty. It is interesting that it is given expression most effectively in terms of Christmas, the family festival *par excellence* in Ireland:

When I first came here, I didn't like it; I thought I couldn't stand living here, and I was always wanting to go home. I could go home, then, every fortnight. Now it doesn't matter so much and I go home about twice a year. I especially miss home at Christmas time because it is then that you miss those you always used to see, and Christmas doesn't seem right if they are not in it.

But for the bride, as for the old people, the transition brings forth a new behavior, and a new habit in her relationship with them. She must learn a nice balance between her new freedom and new full status and the continued control and the vested interest of her mother-in-law. It is a matter between the two women of the household; the father and son prefer to remain neutral witnesses to the process. The statement of one countryman illustrates well the possibilities and the type of new attitude and behavior the young woman must learn to make a satisfactory adjustment:

When a marriage is made, an agreement is drawn up so that the man hands over to his son the land, but makes certain reservations. A new woman is brought into the house. The wife may have modern ideas and be "hoity-toity" about the way to do things, and the old woman and the new woman wouldn't get along. The old man without interfering would light his pipe and go out until the squabble was over.

It might get so bad that the old woman would get up and leave and go live with her daughter. She would do this if the mother of her daughter's husband were dead, even though the father might still be living in the house. But squabbles are bad things and, if the new woman would ask the old persons their opinion and how to do this and that, there would never be any trouble and the new wife could go ahead and do just as she pleased and the old people would think that she was doing it the way that she said. The daughter-in-law, if she did what she ought, would do this and treat the old folks nice.

The theme of strife between mother and daughter-in-law is one dear to the hearts of the countrymen. It appears very frequently in conversation and in jokes. If the family is to continue its existence, the introduction of the new woman must be effected smoothly. The whole moral force of the community as well as the interest of family harmony bear upon the two women. The fear of gossip in the neighborhood operates strongly to keep the young woman with her husband, and every family makes a strong attempt to hide its personal troubles as much as possible from the general knowledge of the community.

Nevertheless, stranger as the new woman may be, the norms of the community in ordinary cases demand that the young husband take the part of his wife. The bond between them is stronger than that between son and parent. As the quotation above shows, it is usually the mother who must leave. The country people deplore such an event, but they know that the son "has right" in so doing. Many statements of this attitude are to be heard among the small farmers and any examinations of cases of dispute which end in rupture show the attitude to be enforced in reality.

That this should be the case reflects the function of the marriage and matchmaking of the farm family. It provides for continuance.

The new position of the old couple and their desires in the altered situation which has seen their displacement express this need for continuance. They are part of the pattern themselves. The statements of the blessings they bring to the farm family with their pension money are very elliptical assessments of their new place within the group.

In their new role, if the transition has been smooth, they retain, if not a dominance of control and direction of the group economic enterprise, at least a dominance of respect and prestige. They occupy a venerable and dignified place in the community and within the household. The sentiments of which they have been the object during the years of their son's youth and manhood undergo no change, even though their strict control relaxes and may disappear.

Likewise when, with the birth of the bride's children, the newly married couple begin to create a full farm family of their own, the old couple remain a part of the united group. They very soon become the objects of the children's love and respect, and enter into the complex of family relationship and family behavior which fashions the status of the children.

This new completion of the family pattern the countrymen express, as they do the reciprocities of kinship, in terms of help and aid to the economic unit of the farm. One countryman generalized as follows:

When there are children in the house, the old people are a great help to the mother because the old woman would nurse the youngsters and see that they did not fall into the fire or something of that nature, and thus the woman can go about her business. The old woman would help while the old man would keep on at his work just as long as he was able, because it was in the nature of things that he had always done so. As they grew older, they might do some of the lighter work, but they would always help.

He went on to discuss the new relationships between family members and the modification of the immediate family behav-

124

iors which the presence of the old couple brings about. His shifting the topic from help to alignments within the family is entirely unconscious; it could not better illustrate the connection between work roles and reciprocal interaction in the family.

If there was a squabble between the mother and daughter, the old woman would more than likely stand up for the daughter. She would teach her how to do things and would have more patience than the father.

Quite as before in the case of the farm economy, the strength of the pattern reveals itself in the aberrant cases. Where there is no old couple to take up new status and position in the family group, others within the family of the older generation or even of the same may be forced into such a position.

Two cases came under the particular notice of the authors. In one an elder sister became to all intents and purposes the "old woman" in the house. A widow, she owned the farm, was in the "west room," and had the place at the hob. Her younger sister and her husband, who had married into the farm, managed the farm and knew that their children would inherit it. The elder sister helped a bit with the household, but spent much of her time before the fire. Both the man and woman of the house referred to her as "the old woman," a term of respect, and one of the authors, who lived in the house for a time, learned only after much intimacy the half-forgotten fact that she was not mother but sister to the younger woman. In the other case it was a father's sister who took up the role, the product of long substitution for a lost mother, and at the match the "writings" made provision for her.

Intimately connected with the transition at marriage are all the phenomena of age grading so marked in Irish country life. The old couple advance one step in their course through life; they enter a new age grade.

Marriage transfers the boy into the adult farm-owning man, the farm father into the old man; it brings the same changes for

125

the women. Such changes are, of course, not abrupt; the groups which are substantially of the same age do not undergo disruption with the movement of one of their number from status of boy to that of man. But, on the other hand, there are general patterns of behavior which mark off these groupings in an informal manner, and which betray their origin in a social valuation of age differences.

The behavior of the different age groups is of the most intimate everyday kind, and consequently reflects those differentiations of status which are given formal and explicit recognition at marriage. Felt to be too natural a part of daily life to require explanation on the part of the farmers themselves, their behavior, nevertheless, is very easily remarked by the observer. In the ordinary countryman's house, for example, the man of the house and whatever older men may be present occupy chairs drawn up before the hearth. The hob by the fire belongs to the old couple by right. The younger people, the sons and daughters, sit behind them round the room on other chairs or on the window seats of the rectangular kitchen, which makes up the principal room of the usual small farmer's house. This arrangement shows itself best in the *cuaird* or visit, where the old men of the district drop in on neighbors and "friends" to sit around the hearth together passing the evenings of winter in conversation, singing, discussing the news, and telling the old stories of legend and folklore. At the *cuaird* younger men and women, if they attend, sit behind, usually leaving the center of the stage to the old men, and the children stand up behind in silent admiration. The younger men have their own pursuits, of course, though at present the divergence may be more marked than formerly. Lately, in Clare at least, they have taken to card playing on a gambling basis for stakes of small livestock in the country districts.

When the whole population of a country district is on the move on Sunday, the groupings are especially noteworthy. There

126

are occasional family groups driving in the jaunty car, but generally the older men walk in a group of their own, the older women in another. The young men walk together by themselves and the young women by themselves. On Sunday afternoons the young men can be seen at the nearest crossroad standing together in groups of ten to thirty, while the older men keep more to their houses or visit one another. Before mass, when the weather permits, the men congregate outside the church and do not move in until all the women have entered and the priest has arrived. As the groups stand outside waiting for the mass to begin and gossiping back and forth, the older men stand off together and the younger men keep to themselves. In wakes, weddings, christenings, the same age groupings are observed.

There is, of course, no formal prescription of such behavior nor formal taboo against its infringement; the conduct rather springs from the divisions of the family and the solidarity of the individuals occupying similar status as these forces operate in everyday life. It is evident how close a connection exists between age grading and marital status.

If behavior of this type reflects the age grading within the family and the transitions between age grades which are part of the transformation of the family at marriage, so does the arrangement of the house interior. For a graphic representation of this characteristic arrangement, let the reader return to Figure 9. The houses of the small farmers show a remarkable uniformity over great areas; it becomes at once apparent that the variations in house types and forms are more associable with differences of class than of locality. But as we are dealing only with the small farmer or peasant class, we need concern ourselves only with the implications of the striking uniformity in house form among the country people. Throughout West and North Clare the house is rectangular and consists ordinarily of a kitchen, occupying the greater part of the rectangle, and a second room, behind the hearth and chimney which occupy most of one end of the

127

kitchen. There are sometimes one or two bedrooms at the opposite end of the kitchen, in addition. In East Clare this type of house is common, but there is also a squarer type which may have a second story.

The tiny peasant cabins dating from the last century are of the West Clare type; they were and are single-gabled, rectangular blocks of one or two rooms, with steep, thatched roofs and a single half-door on each side. The half-doors open directly out of the kitchen, the one to the windward kept closed. The modern stone cottages erected by the governmental agencies and patterned after those built first by the Congested Districts Board (1893–1923) are slated and weatherproofed. Except for additional four rooms, they represent the same pattern. It is impossible to give a statistical statement of the occurrence of this type of house or to correlate its numbers with those of the small farm families, but housing records show that 36 per cent of Clare's population live in three-room dwellings, 24 per cent in four-room dwellings, and 12 per cent in two-room dwellings, which seem to point to a fairly close correspondence between the proportion of small farm population to total population.

In the small farmer's house of this type, the kitchen is the seat of family life. In it are the hearth, at which cooking is done, the table around which the family — first the adult males, then the women and children — eat, the kitchen utensils, and the religious shrine of the "Blessed Lamp" and the Sacred Heart picture before which the family prays the "Family Rosary" at night. Here also is the "dresser" found in nearly every small farmer's house, a sideboard filled with fancy china and porcelain used only for family festivals and to give to marrying relatives. The family will part with this china only under dire necessity. In many districts the year's supply of home-cured bacon still hangs from the rafters.

From the kitchen to the haggard, the farmyards, and cow sheds is but a step through one of the half-doors. There are found the sheds and outhouses where all the livestock, agricultural implements, carts, are kept and the fuel supply and the hayrick stand.

Sleeping arrangements reflect the age grading and the sexual arrangements within the family. Children generally occupy the "loft," a boarded attic covering from a quarter to a half of the space under the peak of the roof. If space is restricted, they may also occupy the "settlebed" in the kitchen, or they may be divided up between the two on the basis of sex. Older children and the married couple will occupy the bedrooms.

The room, however, which we described as occupying the part of the rectangle behind the hearth in the kitchen is of especial interest. It may or may not be used as a bedroom. It is generally so used only when space is limited. But in this room all the objects of sentimental value (except the shrine and the dresser in the kitchen) are always kept: the religious pictures, the ceremonial objects brought in by the bride at marriage, and the bric-a-brac associated with the past members of the household. Where there is only one couple in the house, this room is reserved as a sort of parlor into which none but distinguished visitors are admitted. The family heirlooms are there, and, lining the walls along with religious pictures, there appear the photographs of the members of the family, especially the familiar daguerreo-types of the last century. Whatever "fine" pieces of furniture there may be, such as highboys, cabinets, brass candlesticks, are kept there, as are all the religious objects used when mass is celebrated in the house. All these objects are inalienable in the sense that the family parts with them only when it must. They descend from father to son with the house and the farm on which it stands.

It is into this room that the old couple move upon the son's marriage. They move in among the symbols of family unity, among the religious symbols of the house, into surroundings of a certain religious or sacred character. If we can discover certain other indications of the nature of this room, we shall feel war-

129

ranted in drawing conclusions as to the nature of the change which takes place in the status of the old couple and the attitudes which surround them.

This room we have described is the "west room" mentioned in the "writings." It is so literally. With remarkable uniformity the small farmers' houses in West and North Clare face east and west, the room behind the hearth being generally at the west end of the house. Now the west room and the western end of the house are associated in folklore with the "fairies" which still flourish in the countrymen's minds, especially among the older generation.

The Irish "fairies" include the spirits of the dead. In fact, the identity between the two is explicitly recognized. It was so at Luogh, where older men could name the "good people" with whom they had had encounters.

It is the west room and the western end of the house that the fairies frequent. Where a fairy path is believed to pass the house, it passes invariably along the western end of the house. The country people of Luogh and other parts of West Clare give this as the reason why no extensions, outhouses, sheds, or other structures are built on that side; bad luck would result. In Luogh none of the twenty-five houses of the townland had any structure of any sort built there. And it is often in this room that the fairies spend the night when they visit a house on their nocturnal travels. If we remember that the old people, relinquishing their adult status and preparing for death, move into this room amid heirlooms, religious pictures, and photographs of dead members of the household, we are forced to postulate the sacred and semireligious nature of the attitudes surrounding the old couple and identifying them with the forces of the dead and the symbolic unity of the family, past and present.

The match is a mechanism, from one point of view, for preservation of family unity through the sequence of the generations. The dominant interest of the old couple in the "new woman" brings this point out most forcefully. They are vitally

130

concerned in providing heirs for the line. Consequently their evaluation of the "new woman" is made upon the score of her fertility. Their desire is as strong as hers. She must have children.

The chief reflection of this fact is not to be found in economic expressions, frequent as they are. Children mean more hands for the working corporation. The farmers express their desire for them once again in terms of "help." But help might be obtained in other ways, for it can be hired. Rather it is the continuity of the human nexus which is the true goal. The fact that much of the relationship between the old couple and the "new woman" is built around her childbearing illustrates where the motivating interest lies.

The old couple appraise their daughter-in-law accordingly. The first year of the girl's new position is a time of apprenticeship. Work is light. Pregnancy is her major duty. All during her childbearing years the old woman aids her and helps her, praising her in terms of her increase and showing as great an interest in the arriving children as the mother. One countryman puts it as follows:

This [a smooth relationship between the old couple and the new woman] carries on for seven or eight months, but, if then the old people do not see evidence of increase of young, then the boy's father's people get angry and abuse her, but if they do, they do not let her do any work and are so proud.

Family and community alike support them in their attitude. A woman could say bitterly, for she was childless:

No matter how much money you have and how good-looking you are, if you don't have children, you're no good. But if you're ugly as the worst and have children you are all right.

The husband has every right to express his displeasure at his wife's barrenness. To have no children is a source of shame to

131

him and a terrible disappointment in his desire to continue his line upon the farm. One woman put it:

> The man wants children because he is afraid others will tell him he is no good if he hasn't any. Children are the curse of the country, especially if you haven't any.

In the country districts they say that he may beat her and in their graphic phrase "bounce a boot off her now and then for it." Country belief still regards the woman as the offending partner in a childless marriage. Near Inagh one farmer, a returned Yankee, was regarded as an anomaly because, though childless, he treated his wife just as well as though she had many and did not get angry when he was twitted on his lack of an heir. They explained it by saying that he "knew it was his own fault."

The day of the "country divorce," as the farmers call it, is rapidly passing. In the old days, they say, a man might send a barren wife back to her parents, though Catholic law forbade him to marry again. There are cases which illustrate that the custom survives in altered form. They are particularly revealing in our analysis of the desire to preserve the family unity and its identification with farm and household through the generations. Here the brothers act, sociologically, as a single individual in order to insure the desired continuity. For instance, in one case, a middling farmer of Corrofin, childless after several years, got a country divorce. He gave the land thereafter to his brother in return for a thousand pounds, which the brother had inherited in lieu of the farm on the stipulation that his brother should marry. The brother thus got wife, dowry, and farm; and the identity of land and family was preserved for a new generation.

Time and time again that continuity of identification lies at the root of the behavior which follows upon the transference of control within a family.

Particularly in the case of the incomplete farm families, a wide variety of arrangements appear to effect the same transition without going beyond the group. As the following generality explains, it is only the "crabbit" farmer who breaks through the circle of reciprocal obligation:

If there is no heir to hold the land, they [the childless couple] might give it to a friend, the nearest to the husband, or the wife might give it to the nearest to her. The husband might take a boy from his brother or, if he's crabbit, he will sell it and go to town and drink the money.

But the second contingency that the wife might give the land to one of her kindred may be a source of trouble. The great emphasis upon patriliny militates against it. As the countrymen say, they "want to keep the name on the house; they are dying to have the same name on the house."

At any rate some of the matches between cousins arise, consciously or not, because of this desire. And they occur here and there in country districts, even though the full weight of the Church's authority is against them. Countrymen on occasion have explained that they are love-matches. By impregnating the girl, the boy forces the priest to allow the marriage "for cause." Soberer opinion, nevertheless, condemns such action. It is no light thing to "destroy a girl's character."

There are many more subtle ways of effecting the same end. Nieces and nephews, even grandchildren, may be brought into the house, and matches made for them. In this regard a conflict arises between legal right and social custom. The country districts recognize only vaguely the right of a woman to hold property. The patrilineal identification of family and land is incompatible with it. Whatever farm a woman works or controls is regarded as a trust for a son or brother of her husband or father.

The conflict is naturally never so phrased, nor is it ever debated. Yet there are many instances which show behavior, accepted fully as right and just by the local community, which reveal the patrilineal identification. A widow, for instance, remains upon the farm only if the children are beginning to grow up. If

133

they are very young, she returns to her parents and a husband's brother may take the farm. Even if she marries, she and her new husband merely hold the land in trust. The new husband is, graphically a "stranger to the land."

As a "stranger" he has no right to it. In a village in mid-Clare, to give an example, a "Yank" returned after many years in the United States to his father's farm, from which he and all his brothers had emigrated. His mother, now dead, had married again, and her two children by her second husband still worked the farm. D———, the "Yank," threw the husband out into the road, told him to go home, and took up the land. Later when he gave fortunes to both of the children, the village felt he had made ample amends for the stepfather's years of toil.

Whether or not there is a legally executed will, it is much the same. In Luogh, a son, inheriting a farm upon the death of his mother, allowed her old second husband to stay on with him. He was said to be "very kind to the old man." In Inagh again, though a small farmer, dying, willed the family's farm to his wife and children, a brother on a neighboring farm got most of the land. "He paid her nothing for it. He took bits of it here and there until it was all gone." Whatever protest there is must come from the growing nephews. Inagh makes none.

In matchmaking, too, legal form may be subordinated to country-bred aspirations. To insist upon the full letter of the contract, even if its purpose is not fulfilled, is meanness. It is a breach of social convention, even though quite within legal right. For the "writings" is a formal legal instrument nowadays. Not all the farmers have gone so far in safeguarding himself as one F——— in Inagh did. "He put it in the writings that he would pay the last half when his daughter was safe delivered," so we were told. For the provisions of the match reflect again the identifying continuity and the importance to all parties of the girl's bearing children for the family into which she marries. Most often the second installment of the fortune is not paid until the first child is born, or, with more legal formality, till a year

134

after the marriage contract is completed. One informant summed the matter up:

> If the woman dies after a year and the first part of the fortune is paid, the man doesn't usually claim the rest, although he may be mean enough to claim it. For the young man can marry again. If the man dies, the girl is given the money if there is no heir and is sent home. If there is, then she gets the place.

Let us re-examine the dowry in the light of this complexity of interrelated factors. As has been explained, the fortune goes to the farm owner, in ordinary cases the father of the boy. At the match, land, house, cattle, and household effects move from father to son just as kinship relationships move and as adult status moves. One family, that of the old couple in which the son was merely one of the children, is partially destroyed in order to make way for a new one, in which the son and the incoming wife are now the adult married couple. The movement of goods corresponds to social forces. And the fortune brought in by the new wife moves from her father to the boy's as if to recompense the father for his loss of the farm. It is significant that the fortune is paid always in money. Try as we might, we never found it paid in any other way. Land, cattle, and household effects are not used but are inalienably associated with the family. This is a new development. In Carleton's day, before the famine, a daughter was often dowered with goods as well. Today this is not the case, for the goods like the land are part of an indivisible and corporate whole.

In this way, when we remember that the farm is identified in popular thinking with the patrilineal and patronymic family line of the landowner and that the girl is an outsider brought into that group, the money appears as a payment for the girl's inclusion. There is significantly no corresponding recompense or payment to the girl's father. He loses both daughter and dowry. The identification of his family, both immediate and ancestral, with the family farm is undisturbed. Of course the father of

135

the girl makes sure that his prestige does not suffer. He demands that the farm she enters shall at least equal the dowry. The size of the dowry he gives his daughter is a very strong index of that prestige. It is both a duty and a great source of pride to provide well for her.

A further indication of the nature of the movement of the dowry is to be found in the terminological (formal) structure of the family which we have already described. It will be remembered that there was no integration between the boy's father and the girl's, and that relationship by affinity proceeded only from the point of view of the young couple. The two fathers-in-law or mothers-in-law are not felt to be related. No kinship terms express the new connection between them. Clearly, then, we have two patrilineal groups still unmerged, still distinct. That this is the case can be seen in Carleton's[1] descriptions of faction fights in which two families are often pitched against one another in spite of their alliance by marriage. The authors have seen some of them, not on the scale of faction fights, it is true, but ones in which brothers-in-law flared up to strike one another even though after a week or so the two connections became reconciled.

Up to this point we have failed to distinguish between wills and marriage settlements in the statement of matchmaking and transfer of farms. The confusion is justified because in so many cases they are one and the same. Nevertheless, the subject of wills made apart from the son's marriage needs discussion. If our conclusions as to the nature of farm marriage are valid, something of the same play of changes, obligations, and goods must be present.

Money in the dowry functions to recompense the farmer for his relinquishment of the farm and the break-up of the family which he headed. Similarly, in the cases where inheritance pro-

[1] William Carleton, peasant novelist (1794–1869), principally *Tales and Sketches* (Dublin: J. Duffy, 1845) and *Traits and Stories of the Irish Peasantry* (10th complete ed.; London: W. Tegg, 1864).

ceeds without marriage, money plays the same role. There are many instances in which the old farmer has demanded payment for the property his heir is to receive. Let an Ennis solicitor describe his experience with one of them:

I remember an old fellow, Jimmy B——— of K——— who was taken off dying to the County Home. He called for me to go out there and make a will for him. Seven wills I made for that old codger before he was through. He hadn't any idea of dying. He had only ten or fifteen acres of a farm, but he said he would give it to his son [only] if the son paid him ten pounds a year for it. They often do that, make the son pay from ten pounds to fifty pounds a year for the land. Then [when the solicitor pointed out that the son would inherit the money anyway as the old fellow had no other heirs], old Jimmy made me make another will leaving the money itself to the son.

Another case the authors knew involved no son. The old fellow left a small farm to his cousin and even though he was on the verge of dying, he forced the cousin to pay for it.

In still another instance, an old fellow had some land and about two hundred and fifty pounds to give away. He gave the money in a will, but insisted the son pay for the land. After that, there was a cow and a calf left over, which he reserved for himself. When he called in a solicitor to make another will disposing of the cow and calf, this time, as he lay dying in the County Home, the nun in charge said he had been awake all night mumbling to himself about the cow and calf. The solicitor and the nun finally got him to leave the money for masses.

These cases show the hold of the pattern of receiving money for the transfer of family property. It must be understood that under ordinary circumstances the payment the son had to make would be devoted to the other children, as is the dowry. But in these cases the pattern persisted though there were no other children.

Another case occurred in which a farmer named Patrick N——— left money, farm, and everything he had to his nephew

137

Michael in trusteeship to be given to him upon his marriage with the trustee's approval. Here no money was demanded, but another common feature of countrymen's wills was involved which throws light on the general family situation. The old man had other nephews who had given him a hand from time to time in fulfillment of the agricultural pattern. By mischance they discovered the content of the will, called their uncle an "old fraud" and a "robber," and stopped working for him. A generous move on the part of Michael prevented further bad blood.

English law of property gives the owner full right to dispose at will of farm and other real property as personal chattels. That right is, of course, embodied in Irish legal practice. But the situation underlying the Irish farm life is otherwise. In the first cases cited, we see a tendency to enforce payment for the farm, analogous to the dowry. In the last case, the basis for that tendency is the expectation of provision on the part of the family members. With the transfer of the farm and the break of the family at either the match or death, the other members of the family must be provided for.

(It may be for this reason, the conflict between legal right and social obligation, that so many countrymen's wills are drawn up in elaborate secrecy, the solicitor creeping out in the dead of night to a lightless cottage in the bogs somewhere to make a will for an old fellow who for one reason or another refuses to fulfill obligations, real or fancied, to his kindred and neighbors. The authors had frequent descriptions of this from solicitors and townsmen to whom the piquancy of the situation appealed, but obtained none, unfortunately, from the countryman's point of view. They did receive accounts from countrymen of their attempts to conceal their visits to solicitors in town.)

Even in these cases in which the usual sequence of events is upset or changed through special circumstances, the same concern for rebuilding and changing the family relationships in a certain definite manner appears. The dowry, like the rest of the behavior at the match, is understandable only in such terms.

Even, as in the case of wills of the kind just reported, where transfer of land alone is involved, the same concern is present. That is, the match is here by implication, if nothing else, and the mechanism of social change it provides is at work even *in absentia*.

8

Dispersal and Emigration

The internal reorganization of the family consequent on the marriage of one of their number produces a marked change in the situation of the as yet unprovided-for brothers and sisters. The other members of the family broken up by the marriage of one of their number on the home farm must be provided for elsewhere. They feel themselves entitled to portions, either in the form of dowries to marry into another farm or of some other means of establishing themselves. If such provisions in fact are not made, conflict arises, as we saw in the case of the McDermott murder. A classical case in the Ennis region of Clare was that of an old farmer of substance who married a nineteen-year-old girl when he was eighty. When the birth of a son precipitated a crisis, he had to be protected from his scandalized relatives, sons, and daughters by the police. When he died the following year, he gave a hundred pounds each to the constable who protected him and the priest "plucky enough to marry me." His sons refused to attend his funeral.

Normally, however, the transfer of land and the break-up of the family which worked it is made with the fullest possible provision for the other children. The dowry brought in is utilized to that end, and the savings of a lifetime on the farm have been used. The following observations made by a Land Commission official, himself a small farmer's son and a man with many years' experience in Irish rural affairs, attempt to give a statement of the generalities. They express, however, an ideal rather than an actuality.

The average household consists of six persons [and the parents]. Of necessity not more than one could be provided for on the holding and assuming, for example, that the family consisted of two girls and four boys, the position would be somewhat as follows:

The eldest son would in the course of years assume ownership of the holding. A second son might be provided with a secondary education and might possibly win a County Council scholarship . . . enabling him to pursue a course of engineering or medicine practically free. In the event, however, of his not being so fortunate, the thrift of the family may enable him to pursue a similar course at the university, the intervals between terms and the long vacation being spent on the farm.

Some years ago medicine was the profession usually pursued provided the boy had no vocation for the priesthood. At that time the cost of his board was appreciably reduced by an arrangement through which neighbors' sons lodged together and brought with them supplies of potatoes, oatmeal, home-cured pork, in fact, provided for almost all their own food. When the boy is qualified to his own particular calling, to his credit it may be said that he denies himself many little luxuries in order to pay back the cost of his training and thus assist the other members of his family.

The third son either got trained in business and in due course started one of his own, or emigrated where he could also refund the cost to his parents. The fourth son might possibly become a primary school teacher, a civic guard, a tradesman [artisan] apprenticed by his father in the near-by town, or again his family might give him enough to marry into another small holding.

One of the girls received a dowry or, as they say here, she was "fortuned off" into another small holding of similar status. The second girl possibly favored nursing, teaching, business, or domestic service,

141

or again possibly religion, or even a clerical position of some sort either here or abroad.

The above quotation states the generalities in terms of upward social mobility. The influx of the country people into the towns, into governmental, professional positions, and into the ranks of urban occupations must wait for special analysis in itself. It is not possible here to determine how great the effect of this movement from the small farms is upon the current much lamented overcrowding of the professions in Ireland. The point of interest for us is the dispersal of the farm group.

Naturally enough, this dispersal does not always occur so happily as in the above statement of the ideal. Yet the portioning off of the children and the success with which it is done is the pride as well as the duty of every farm family. A few examples will give the variations. They are more matters of success or failure to advance beyond the level of small farm life, but they show the genesis of the movement in the farm family. In a later section this subject will be dealt with in more detail. These examples, however, are typical, though the names are fictitious.

Leary of F——— , a farmer with sixty acres, has a daughter married near-by with a four hundred pound fortune, and another, a nun in Mercy Convent, Ennis. Four sons have entered the priesthood, an expensive training from his point of view. A fifth is at home working, not yet thirty. Leary is a "strong" farmer, highly prosperous.

Tom Casey, K——— , is a very poor holder with thirty acres of mountain and bog. Two sons and a daughter are still at home, and a bachelor brother works with him. Another daughter works for herself as a domestic servant in Ennis. One son Tom is apprenticed to a carpenter in Ennis. A daughter emigrated through the good graces of her aunt.

Michael Dunn of T——— has twenty acres, but has not prospered. His two sons left at eighteen and twenty respectively to drive hackney automobiles in Ennis, an uncle there giving them a start. Another son now thirty and a daughter are still at home working the farm.

In a mountain townland, Pat Looney's father prospered, won the good graces of the landlord's agent, amassed four farms, the largest fifty acres, the smallest eighteen. He married off two daughters with two hundred pound fortunes, settled three sons and a daughter with her husband in each of the farms. Pat himself, the eldest, now about eighty, got the largest farm but not the one he wanted. He has been warring with his brothers and his neighbors ever since. He held out against his father for five years, refusing to marry and take his farm. In Pat's youth, land agitation and reform had not yet prevented subdivision and acquiring of new farms by a successful tenant. Pat on his fifty-acre mountain farm has married off a daughter locally at three hundred pounds and sent two sons out to America. Another daughter works in England. Two sons, aged forty-three and thirty-six, are at home and Pat hasn't made up his mind yet which one shall get the land.

The examples, various as they are, need not be multiplied. The sons and daughters who are not to be portioned at home, in the words of the Luogh residents, "must travel." To that end both the savings of the family, created through their united efforts under the headship of father and mother, and the incoming dowry, are devoted. In Luogh there had been only four marriages in ten years; two of them were the usual farm-transferring matches, one a returned emigrant who married a boyhood sweetheart and bought a farm, and one a widower who took a second wife and a second fortune. An old woman described the situation: "There aren't any matches nowadays. Nobody has a fortune to give his daughter and the young men must travel." Yet the woman who lamented this state of affairs was carefully husbanding half crowns for her baby granddaughter's fortune.

Nevertheless this necessary dispersal of the members of the family at its reorganization does not ordinarily destroy the family ties. The bonds of affection and family obligation still hold. If they have emigrated, the family members send back remittances and passage money for nephews and nieces and brothers and sisters left at home. A great many farms, especially in West and North Clare, are partially supported by Christmas gifts sent from children living abroad. It is unfortunate that the authors have not statements of the amount of these annual remit-

143

tances for local districts. The total for Ireland, however, is enormous. There is a marked tendency for emigration from a local region to perpetuate itself, sons and daughters of each generation going out to join the members of the last. One district round Cross to the west of Carrigaholt, a little settlement on the Loop Head peninsula which juts out from Clare into the Atlantic at the Shannon's mouth, is said locally to be supported by sons in the Shanghai police force. The first to go became chief of police in the International Settlement there, and many places in the force have gone to men of Cross.

The authors had the opportunity of examining some of the family setting in which emigrant remittances operate in Luogh. There the greatest number of emigrants had gone out to Boston. In one family, there was a succession of nephews and nieces following uncles and aunts from the same farmhouse for four generations. In four recent cases Luogh boys and girls had married one another in Boston. In two more they had married in Ireland and emigrated together.

Remittances from sons and daughters arrive around Christmas. In one family the farmer's wife had written to children in America saying that the family were trying to acquire an addition to their holding from the Land Commission. The children sent them the purchase price. In this case the daughter sent her regular Christmas remittance as well. When she was admonished by her parents for such generosity, she wrote: "I would think it wasn't Christmas and I hadn't any father and mother if I didn't send them something."

Her mention of the festival in the same breath with her parents is understandable when it is realized that Christmas is the family festival *par excellence* in Ireland.

The role played by emigrated relatives in providing for the children upon the home farm and the role of the dispersed children in helping the old couple and the brother or sister at home is part of the general "friendliness" by which the Irish countryman sums up the family obligations. The two roles are felt to be the same, and they are described in the same terms, as the obligations of actual charity between country families, agricultural co-operation, and ceremonial assistance at marriages, wakes, and funerals. Brother and sister send back gifts to the home farm, especially when the old couple are still alive. Gifts of money, clothing, and presents of all descriptions are sent back. Geese, farm delicacies, and such mementos as shamrocks go from the farm to those relatives that keep in touch.

At family crises, such as death, marriage, and birth, the new bonds come strongly into play and, where possible, the dispersed relatives come back to the farm at that time. The emigrant returns, if he does so at all, to the very townland of his birth, either to buy the old place or to settle near-by. In fact, there are many instances of countrymen, returned Americans, Australians, South Africans, and British soldiers, who have roamed over the world but have never seen more of Ireland than their route to and from their port of embarkation and the nearest market towns.

The sentiments of place, farm, and family become so inextricably intermingled as to be almost one. Perhaps the peculiarly Irish type of song and music owes its character as well as its popularity to that fact. The laments for a dear one, especially a mother, and the pangs of exile are the major motives. They are sung to the same tunes and call forth the same tears.

The break-up of the family at the transfer of land has changed the relation between the dispersed children and the old couple, just as it has changed that between the new farm family and their parents. Control of expenditure, in fact all vestiges of the strict parental control, is perforce destroyed. The best example of this fact is the change which comes over the attitudes of the old people toward their children's personal expenditures. The economic corporation which they directed is destroyed with their headship of the group. Consequently, they no longer can demand the services of their children as before. Thus the authors saw several old couples doing their best to learn how much a returned emigrant had earned but, because of the change in position, not daring to ask outright. If the son had remained on the farm, they would not have hesitated to demand a strict accounting. Likewise, in such important matters as marriage, over which the parents would have had great authority as long as the son or daughter remained at home, the parents lose their control. More than one old couple remarked, on hearing from a distant exiled son of his marriage, that they wished him well but that he must please himself now that he was on his own.

A word more might be said to clarify the position of the dispersed relatives. They equally share the new attenuated bonds which take the place of the old closely integrated family group. But, as might be expected in the structure of a family, which, as we have seen, is based, not upon the principle of rigidity in classification as in many primitive kinship systems, but upon the principle of extensions of relationship outward from the nucleus of the immediate family, the bonds are stronger as the original relationship is closer. The children of each generation growing up on the home farm can look far oftener to a father's or mother's emigrant brother for aid when their own time comes to emigrate than to father's and mother's emigrant cousins. The closer relatives are the ones who most often step forward, though the obligation theoretically binds them all. The following incident from Luogh illustrates the clash between the varying degrees of relationship. Let the small farmer tell the story himself:

A fellow named O'Dwyer — married to a cousin of the old woman out of Ballyheline [a neighboring townland] — was home from Australia one summer, looking a fine cut of a man with a new greatcoat and a fine hat on him. I saw him one day when we were all in Considine's shop for the old-age pension and knew who he was from the pictures of him. [After they had established recognition and struck up a friendship] he asked if he could take the boy (second son) out to Australia with him, and he would set him behind his bar. [He had a hotel there.] I said, yes, he could have him. After the fellow went back to Australia, he sent over fifty pounds for passage for Seumas. But didn't Seumas's sisters write from Boston and they swearing that if I let their brother go off from them to Australia, I'd never hear from them again. So Seumas went out to America to his sisters. And I sent back the fifty pounds, and sure wasn't it the devil's own work sending it back.

The new behavior, as this example shows, is that of the extended kindred already examined. Where emigration has not removed the brother and sister altogether, they are now "friends" and are bound by reciprocal obligations and sentimental attachment. The necessary disposal of their brothers and sisters provides for the continuance of the family unit upon the farm. The very mechanism which assures that continuance does the dispersing. Yet the dispersed do not leave the family. They stay within the bonds of kinship. They are united by the new more attenuated ties of cousinship. Their displacement, like that of the old people, is a regular social movement, providing for them, as it were, a new place and status, changing radically and necessarily their old family membership, yet still confining them within the web of interest and sentiment, though upon a new footing. Henceforward the relatives see one another, of course, less and less often and rely more and more upon the proxy of mementos and gifts.

In summary, the dispersal of the family is part of a general movement arising out of the re-formation of the family group. Forces within the relations of the members of the group bring it into being. Yet the dispersal is carried out very often in ways which depend also upon familial ties. The whole movement is carried on in the midst of an orderly and organic transformation which comes over the family regularly at marriage and death. Old and new meet at marriage in Ireland. Between them social organization is passed on though a prior group is partially destroyed.

Let us recapitulate, then, for a moment. Statistical statement of productive and consumptive behavior in rural economy revealed a marked difference between small and large farmers. Within that difference the small farmers presented a great statistical uniformity. Consequently, it was necessary to look beyond the numerical count to the actual behavior of the small farmers. In referring the question to the lives of the small farmers themselves, we were led to a new analysis of their behavior and to the discovery of a new uniformity.

The new uniformity, however, is of a different nature. It is itself a coherent and consistent pattern, widely extensive, and responsible to laws of inner development of its own. We are entitled, or rather compelled, to call it a system and to give it the character of other systems, where that word is used with precise meaning and is not warped into a catchall of common speech.

For, it is evident, the intricate web of human movement and interrelationship involving objects, household and land, which the study of "matchmaking" reveals, is no random movement. It arises in response to definite needs of the family group. It performs a definite function of reorganization and recrystallization in the group. The manifold changes the match brings upon the lives of the family members, the new positions which they take up, and the new behaviors which are theirs are dependent upon its success in this function. We do not need to insist that they are fully dependent upon it. It is sufficient that they cannot be adequately understood without some assessment of its influence. If we keep this fact in mind, we are ready for an analytic interpretation of our data. The uniform social behaviors of the small farmers begin to form an interrelated whole.

Marriage, property transfer, and the dispersal of the family members derive their character from family relationships. The immediate family of father, mother, and children form a corporate group engaged in agriculture upon a small farm. The roles of the father and mother make them superordinate to the children. Theirs is the direction of the group enterprise. Within the group, technological roles correspond with family status. Economic endeavor, both upon the individual farms and in the form of cooperation between farms, is controlled through the opera-

148

tion of social forces springing from the family. In the testimony of the farmers themselves, that effort is but part of a larger constellation of behavior patterns, obligations, and sentiments governing the individual in other fields by virtue again of his place in the family group. In total, Irish small farm agriculture presents a picture, not of isolated individuals or units pursuing a course of the greatest economic gain, amassing material objects in response wholly to individual desires and selling labor as a commodity, but of a way of life, only a small part of which we have examined, in which the relations between individuals, the soil, productive work, and the material goods of the household constitute a web of social ties, bearing their own incentive and reward and determining the part of the individual in the labor and the goods of the group.

At marriage and at death, as we have seen, this web of relationships is disturbed. New individuals are introduced, old ones lost. The match brings a re-formation of the family involving a dispersal of former members and an introduction of a new set of component individuals into the relationships between land, goods, labor, and human beings.

In the light of this system and of the internal changes which are brought about within it, the Irish population statistics now may become interpretable. Late marriage and the high incidence of bachelorhood are associable with the reluctance of the old couple to renounce their leadership, the necessity of acquiring sufficient means to portion children, and the delay in dispersing the closed corporation of the family group until it is possible to establish the new one. The practical self-sufficiency of the family group makes it difficult to destroy. The identification of a single immediate family with the individual farm prevents the setting up of more than one new such group upon the land.

As we pointed out, subdivision of holdings practically ceased after 1852. Since then the struggle for land and legal reforms in land tenure have prohibited any great further division. The matchmaking system is very old in Ireland. The works of such Gaelic writers as Canon O'Leary describe it explicitly for the pre-famine period. With the cessation of subdivision of holdings came the necessity of providing for children elsewhere than on the land. From that same cessation of subdivision dates the high incidence of bachelorhood. In 1841, at the time of greatest population, age of marriage was normal. Then only 43 per cent of males between twenty-five and thirty-five were unmarried, not 72 per cent, as at present. Then only 15 per cent of males between thirty-five and forty-five were celibate, not 29 per cent as today. Figure 13 represents the percentages of unmarried males and females at each age in each subsequent census from 1841 to 1926.

Viewed in the light of this family structure, the decline of population becomes interpretable not as a flight from intolerable conditions, though economic distress had a powerful effect, not as a political gesture, though political disturbance took its toll, but rather as a movement arising from the effect of all these causes upon a family system whose very nature predisposed it to disperse population and which could, therefore, accommodate itself to that dispersal when it occurred. Emigration, no new thing in 1845, appears as the logical corollary of this dispersal. It derives much of its character, such as assisted passages and remittances, from the social forces at work in the family. It can become a traditional movement like the movement from country to town without destroying the family structure or the rural culture whose members it takes away.

The authors do not mean to imply that anything within the social forces of the family as it exists in Ireland has had direct causal effect upon the peculiar statistics of Irish population. The authors would rather point out that the forces operative within that structure are of such a nature as to allow the society of which they are a part to continue to function in essentially similar fashion through the welter of economic, political, and other events which have impinged upon the human beings who have succes-

Figure 13

Percentage of Unmarried Persons, Irish Free State

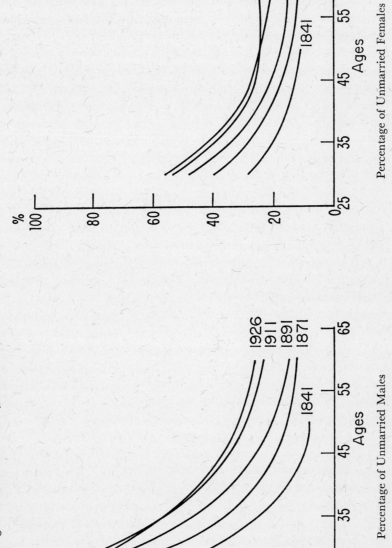

Ages

Percentage of Unmarried Males

Ages

Percentage of Unmarried Females

The figures are taken from the censuses from 1841 to 1926.

sively filled the structure. Likewise, the structure is capable of continued and virile existence in the present, governing the lives of its component individuals and modifying itself to take in new influences.

9

The Problem of the Aged

The small farmers of the Irish countryside have a characteristic way of treating differences among themselves that is based upon relationships fundamental in the organization of their communities. Naturally these folkways are connected with the norms of family life. Perhaps the most important of them is their treatment of differences in age.

Ireland is in some ways an old person's country. The percentages of the old in the population are very high. Naturally the fact is closely allied to an emigration which until recently has drained the country of its young adult manhood and womanhood. And, as in the case of emigration and late marriage, it is the rural districts, or better, the small farmers who inhabit them, that set the norm for the whole country.

A comparison of the distribution of age groups over the population between aggregate rural areas and aggregate town areas, as made in the 1926 census,[1] shows the case clearly. For

[1] *Census of Population, 1926,* Vol. V, pt. I: Ages, Orphanhood and Conjugal Conditions.

the whole Free State at that time there are 671 males per 10,000 males aged sixty-five to seventy-four in the aggregate rural areas, while in the aggregate town areas there are only 402 per thousand of that age. The proportions of females of this age to total females are higher in both cases, but they show much the same relationship. In both sexes the number of old people is greater in the country districts. Conversely, of course, the country districts show a smaller number of people of adult years. Among males the country areas in the aggregate for the whole of the Free State count only 1,115 per 10,000 aged thirty-five to forty-four, while the towns count 1,234 per 10,000 in the same adult age group.

When the various county rural areas are subjected to internal comparisons, similar proportions of old and young appear. To give only one example, County Clare counts 752 per 10,000 males aged sixty-five to seventy-four in the aggregate rural areas of the county, but only 528 per 10,000 of the same age in the aggregate of the county's towns. Likewise, Meath, a county of the midland "ranching" area, shows a proportion between rural and urban districts of 620 to 392; and Galway, in part a "congested area," a proportion of 723 to 547. Thus within counties from all parts of Ireland the same greater concentration of the old is found in the country districts.

One can remark immediately from the examples given above that there is a progression in the degree with which, for the counties mentioned, the numbers of old people of the age group selected range above or below the average number of their age per 10,000 males for the whole population of the Free State. This fact introduces us to a new consideration, corollary to the last. It is in general the poorer western counties, where small holders predominate, which have the larger number of aged individuals. Numbers per 10,000 males of the age we have selected before sixty-five to seventy-four rise regularly among the rural populations of the Irish counties from the 614 and 620 of Kilkenny and Meath to the 841 and 835 of Leitrim and Mona-

154

ghan. In such a scale, the southwestern counties, such as Clare, are again in the middle, though Clare itself with a count of 752 leans heavily toward the Leitrim side.

It becomes obvious that census records by age will all support the assumption. It is in the rural areas, and among the small farmers, that, relatively, the largest number of old people are to be found. Tables 2A and 2B [2] illustrate this conclusion graphically.

Table 2a

Old People in Ireland: Rural and Urban Areas in Selected Counties

Census Area	Males per 10,000 aged 65–74
Free State (all counties)	
Aggregate rural areas	671
Aggregate urban areas	402
Clare	
Aggregate rural areas	752
Aggregate urban areas	528
Meath	
Aggregate rural areas	620
Aggregate urban areas	393
Galway	
Aggregate rural areas	723
Aggregate urban areas	547

Table 2b

Old People in Ireland: Selected Counties Showing Minimum and Maximum in Aggregate Rural Areas

Census Area	Males per 10,000 aged 65–74
Kilkenny	614
Meath	620
Clare	752
Monaghan	835
Leitrim	841

That the large proportion of old people is a matter of the agricultural community is very evident again when the fig-

[2] Based on tables from *Census of Population, 1926,* vol. V, pt. I.

ures indicating the age of those following the various occupations are examined. This is important in gauging the provision Irish society makes for its old members, for numerically they are a large group. Not only are there larger numbers of old people relatively to other adults in the countryside than in the towns and in agricultural pursuits than in other occupations, but also there are more of them absolutely. Thus out of 550,772 males engaged in agriculture, there was one in 14 of them, or 41,130, over seventy years of age. Among all other "producers, makers and repairs," who numbered 154,016, there were only 3,655 septuagenarian males, or one man in 50. Even among the more sedentary occupations of the towns, the occurrence of old men in commercial, financial, or insurance pursuits was only one in 56 and in professions only one in 75. The occupational figures show that the old are still active and numerous in agriculture. In other fields old people are far less numerous and the numbers of retired persons are greater.

It is only among one sort of agriculturalist, the farm holders and their helping relatives, that this fact is true. Naturally the numbers of the old are high in Ireland, where they represent the survivors of a numerically larger generation thinned much by emigration and where their relative number in the total population is increased by the absence of many men and women who could, without emigration, swell the ranks of the young adult age groups. Nevertheless, within the framework of these proportions, it is the farm-holding agricultural group which sets the norm. Expressing the same proportions in percentages, agriculture counts among its male followers 9 per cent — holders and relatives assisting them — who are over seventy years of age. No other group exhibits such a percentage. The only other occupations to show any similar longevity or length of service are "makers of apparel and made-up textile goods" with 6 per cent of their number still engaged after the age of seventy. All others range much lower in percentage of aged individuals still occupied.

156

The relatively great preponderance of the old in agriculture does not extend to the agricultural laborers. They number only 2 per cent of males over seventy. It is only among the farmers and farmers' relatives assisting them that so many old people are alive and active.

It becomes even more evident that it is the farm population which sets the norm for Ireland in this regard when we compare figures of this sort with those of the total population. In all Ireland 6.7 per cent of males are over seventy years of age. Those in the adult years twenty-five to twenty-nine and thirty to thirty-four number only 9.2 per cent and 8.0 per cent of the total males. The farm population with percentages of 8.4 and 8.0 in those ages is the only occupational group to show figures below those of the total population. All others rise above the average percentages for the whole country. Naturally it is the absolutely greater numbers of the farm population which weight the averages. Yet, understanding this, we must also understand that it is among the farm population that the norm is determined.

Statistics for females present rather different ratios. They need not detain us, as they are complicated by the inclusion of a larger category entitled "those engaged in home duties." The category embraces the greater number of urban women and makes comparison with farm women by occupation somewhat precarious. On the other hand, it has the merit of grouping them about household duties and provides in itself a good distinction between urban and rural household workers. Comparing them, then, we find 12 per cent of female farmers and relatives helping farmers over seventy, and of this 5 per cent and 8 per cent aged thirty to thirty-four and thirty-five to forty-four. (We choose here ages in which most of the women who marry are already married.) But among the women "engaged in home duties" (the category which embraces most townswomen, as well as unspecified numbers of countrywomen), only 4.4 per cent are over seventy, and conversely the more numerous 11 per cent and 23 per cent are thirty to thirty-four and thirty-five to forty-four. The total female population shows percentages of 8.3 per cent over seventy and 8 per cent and 15 per cent in the younger age grades. It can be seen how these comparisons bear out the conclusions presented by those of the males. It is among the farm population that the largest number of old people are to be found. In this regard the farmers again set the norm for Ireland.

The largest proportions of the aged among the farmers prevail, furthermore, among the small farmers. One can expect this fact, related as it is to the greater emigration of this class. The statistics correlating the size of the farms and age group proportions bear out the expectation.

Table 3, based again upon census records,[3] expresses the relative percentages of males over seventy years of age and of males thirty to forty-four (the age groups in which emigration comes to an end) in the total of males ranked by age among farmers and farmers' assisting relatives upon the various sizes of farms, for the whole of the Free State:

Table 3

Old Age and Size of Farms

Farm Size in Acres	Percentage of Farmers and Assisting Relatives over 70 Years of Age	Percentage of Farmers and Assisting Relatives aged 30–44
1–5	15	10
5–10	12	15
10–15	10	11
15–30	9	12
30–50	8	12
50–100	7½	10
100–200	7	16
200–over	1	24

The table reveals a constant diminution of the percentage of the old as the size of farms increases. In other words, the smaller the farm the greater the likelihood that it supports old people. Since we are dealing with census records of occupations actually

[3] *Census of Population, 1926,* vol. V, pt. II, Table 7.

engaged in at the time of numeration, the figures again point to the fact that larger proportions of old people are still active upon the small farms than elsewhere. On the small farms then, the old do not retire. That there should be no constant increase in the percentages of the adult age groups does not detract from the validity of the conclusion. The inconsistency of the percentages can be referred to the differential emigration rates of the inhabitants of farms of various sizes. If emigration takes place at different ages and in greater or less proportions from different-sized farm holdings, as other figures not germane in this connection point out, that fact will make it impossible to select any one age group to illustrate the corresponding increase of the proportion of adult males to aged males in the farm size categories.

The table confirms the point. It is among the small holders that the greatest number of old people survive. The peasant population is again responsible for a striking peculiarity of Irish demography.

That the peculiarity is a peasant manifestation can be demonstrated upon a narrower stage. In the various counties of the Free State, the same statistical differences appear between rural areas and small holdings on one hand and urban areas and large holdings on the other. Old people are relatively numerous in the former, relatively few in the latter. In Clare, to take one example, we have seen already that the aggregate rural areas count a larger proportion of the old than do the aggregate urban areas (towns of 1,500 or more inhabitants). The Clare rural districts in which larger holdings are more numerous, Meelick and Ballyvaughan, count 2.4 per cent and 3.1 per cent respectively of their people over seventy-five, both male and female. Those in which larger holdings are relatively fewer, e.g., Tulla and Ennistymon, count larger percentages (4.6 and 4.0 respectively). Here again, within the bounds of the county, the demographic peculiarity by which the old are so numerous is a characteristic of the small-farm population. The presence of large farmers in any district is enough to weigh proportions away from the peasant norm.

159

Comparisons of occupations by age within the county yield the same result. We need not detail them here.[4]

The demographic peculiarity which gives Ireland so large a proportion of the aged in her population becomes more marked when other nations are compared. The Irish death rate is rather low. Most strikingly, only one civilized country keeping census records of age distribution surpasses Ireland in the large proportion of aged individuals. That country is France, which in 1926 counted 9.4 per cent of its citizens over sixty-five years of age, barely topping the Irish figure of 9.2 per cent. Other countries ranged far below France and the Free State, Scandinavian and Baltic countries coming comparatively near, with such figures as that of 8.8 per cent for Sweden and 7.6 per cent for Norway. Industrial Germany and England (with Wales) occupied a middle place with figures of 5.7 per cent and 6.6 per cent respectively, and such "new" countries as Australia and the United States, where the percentages are 4.4 per cent and 4.7 per cent, brought up the rear. These figures (see Table 4) were taken from national censuses of various dates in the various countries in the period 1920–1926 and compiled for the Irish census primarily from the "International Health Year Book 1928 (League of Nations)" and *Aperçu de la démographie des divers pays du monde, 1925* (International Institute of Statistics).

Table 4

Persons over Sixty-Five in Ireland and Other Countries

Country	Population Percentage
France	9.4
Ireland	9.2
Sweden	8.8
Norway	7.6
England (with Wales)	6.6
Germany	5.7
Australia	4.4
United States	4.7

[4] *Census of Population, 1926,* vol. V, pt. II, Table 12A, County Clare.

Ireland and France share eminence as abodes of the old. But they reach that eminence through different courses. A comparison of the expectancy of life in the two countries, made upon the basis of actuarial computations at the time of the taking of the census in the Free State, reveals this difference. In addition, it reveals a new factor in the question of age distribution in Ireland. At all ages from birth to eighty, the expectation of life is considerably higher in the Free State than in France. At five (a better age than that of birth to take for purposes of computation because of infant mortality) the Irishman may look forward to fifty-nine years of life, the Frenchman only to fifty-five. At forty he may expect to live thirty-eight years more to the Frenchman's thirty-five. And at eighty, if they both survive so long, the Irishman may hope to outlive the Frenchman by more than a year, their expectancies being at that age 5.8 and 4.3 respectively. As Ireland shows a very high expectation of life at all ages in comparison with other countries, especially for males (the female expectancies being considerably lower), the combination of this fact with her large proportion of old people leads to a new conclusion. Not only are the old in Irish country districts relatively more numerous, but they are absolutely more numerous since they live longer than in other countries. Consequently, whatever conditions produce the large percentage of old people among the total population in France, they are not those of Ireland. There low life expectancies go hand in hand with a large proportion of the aged. In Ireland high expectancies, especially at older ages, where they are among the highest in the world for both sexes, go hand in hand with the same phenomenon.

For this reason one cannot appeal too directly to emigration as the determinant of the demographic condition. The Irish countryside is relatively full of old people, not only because so many of the young adults have left, but also because the old people tend to live long lives.

Within this complexity of factors, emigration, a high percentage of the old, and late marriage, the small farmers set the norms for the whole country. Now we can recognize that high expectancies of life also belong to them. A comparison of life expectancies among the three provinces of the Free State will suffice to bear out the fact. Males of Connacht can expect more years of life at all ages than males of Munster; the males of Munster can expect more than those of Leinster; and those of Leinster can expect least of all three. Thus the provinces show higher expectancies the smaller their farms.

Many causes have been advanced to account for Irish longevity. The country people live long and die often very old indeed. Diet, climate, natural selection through infant mortality, racial heredity, have all been suggested by various writers. Probably all of these factors are involved, in one way or another, but the problem is one that has faced students of peasantries often.

The authors have no single efficient cause to offer. The question that poses itself for them is one of effect rather than of cause. The existence of such a large proportion of the old among small farmers presents a problem in the organization of behavior among human beings. Nevertheless, might not the longevity of peasants be after all a simple matter? In the Irish case we shall see that they live long because they have much to live for. In their own sphere of life, they are honored. They have power.

The problem is one which must be referred to the small farmers themselves. As before, it is a question of their sentiments and their conducts and any analysis of their action in the matter must follow upon the presentation of observed generalities in their social life.

Some of these generalities present themselves to the eye immediately. As we saw in the discussion of the house and family, there is a great deal of everyday conduct which expresses the differences of social valuation of age and which one age group follows in its intercourse with many others. This conduct, the sentiments which accompany it, and the attitudes and verbalizations with which it is associated, can be seen every day in the lives of the people. It is part of the mores of the community. The child learns it as he grows up upon the small farms. It prepares him to meet all others in the local community who are of substantially the same status, habits of life, and speech as the members of his own family. It provides a scale of valuation in which each individual can place any other within the bounds of variation existing in the local community, and upon which both can build sure expectancies of conduct. On another facet it gives each and every individual a place among individuals occupying similar places. In making status in this way, it governs behavior in high degree, imposing bounds upon it and exacting conformity. We have already seen something of this conduct. In the discussion of the house interior and the grouping and seating of individuals by rough similarity of age, we have seen what might be termed one focal point within the system of relations which is characterized by this conduct. The old people in the farm family occupied that point. Place of honor and privilege within the household is theirs. In their families they are objects of respect and a mild sort of veneration on the part of all younger members.

They occupy this place and receive this respect from other persons than their relatives. This respect is as much folk custom as the norms of family life. The community can on occasion enforce it upon the family members through gossip, verbal censure, and, more rarely, direct intervention in the person of the priest.

The vocabulary of the countryman and a great many of the judgments and comments he makes upon his surroundings express the valuations of the community upon age. In the discussion of the house interior it was remarked that the conducts of the different age groups were too "natural" to the farmers to evoke verbal recognition among them. The statement is true only in a sense. The farmers make no explicit recognition of the organization of behavior upon the basis of age. But they are never silent upon the implications of such organization as it affects individual conduct in daily life.

More cogent, perhaps, for our understanding are the many expressions which arise from day to day based upon the speaker's place within an age grade. A great part of the constant talk which flows back and forth among the friends and neighbors who pass their lives within a rural community takes its form so. Particularly is this true of discussion of the past, a favorite topic and one which came very frequently indeed to the authors' ears. Gossip and personalities are as frequent a theme, and a speaker rarely fails to qualify the object of his remarks with an appropriate definition of his relative age. Even to intimates a man is referred to as "old John" or "young Michael."

Perhaps it is the discussion of the past which illustrates best partiality for the things of one's own age. The older men and women describe the "old days" with enthusiasm and regret. The "old times" are a ready topic among the country people, or rather among the older ones. Many an evening an old person can be got to tell of the "old times." He or she takes little warming to the task. They were hard times, even "bad times" of famine and death, but the speakers throw a glow of courage and glamour round them. Even the mention of the lack of tools, draft animals, shoes, and many other amenities of present existence evokes comments such as "Weren't they the poor old times?" and "Wasn't it hard the work they had to do in the old days?" Phrases of murmured commiseration and headshaking regret or pity are not without a tinge of pride for listener and teller alike. Remembered necessities in the eyes of the old people who tell the tale are now feats of endurance and strength to which the new generation could never aspire. That is the point for those who tell and those who listen. Where could you get a young man today to walk from Corrofin to Ballinasloe in his bare feet forty miles and back over the stony roads? Where is the woman today who could shoulder a creel turf and carry it a hundred yards out through the bog mud to the famine road before the Board put in the road to the bog above Dunnagore?

Even the meager diet of the old times is remembered with a certain nostalgic pride. An old man, called upon one winter evening, began his remarks upon the theme characteristically:

In the old days people used to have a maize gruel "stirabout" for breakfast, but you couldn't get any of the young people to eat it now. There was a potato bread, *stampaí,* and it was very good too. The people in the old times had great teeth and, when they died, they would have every one left in their heads. Their teeth would be stronger than a horse's. When the people ate potatoes and bread three times a day, they were healthier and lived to a ripe old age. Now with all the better food, they are not as well.

Such a belief rises very frequently to the lips of the old people who remember the days of the past either in their own or their parents' experience. The implication is clear. The young people, the new generation, are not so strong nor so hardy nor even so good-natured as those who went before.

Discussions of the present fall into the same vein. Just as, for the older members of the community, the past reflects their glories and is a convenient vehicle for the expression of their superiority, so the present can be measured against the past in the same terms, usually only to be found lacking.

Often the expressions take a different turn. They become that universal complaint, the younger generation.

Young people today are not what they used to be [said one old farmer in the course of a general discussion of the golden age that was his youth]. They spend money for fags, they have to be gambling every night, or else go to a dance, and, if they happen to win a turkey, they will nearly shake the house down when they come in. There is no good in the country when things go on like this. In the old days a man used always to be out repairing his stone walls, cleaning his land, or doing something. They expect everything to be done for them.

He paused for an illustration, selected one from among his own cronies, and swept volubly on:

Wasn't Keane out every night with his cattle putting them in small fields and late in the night? He would have his supper waiting for him when he came in, but he would take off his shoes so not to waken his father, and then to bed. Wasn't he up early in the morning and out working? They cleared a nice piece of land in the common. He kept it all until he had cattle up by Ballyvaughan. You wouldn't get any of the young people to do that now. There's no control of them.

But even among his listeners, all of them "old" like himself, the young people had some defense:

But there has to be some fun for the young people. If they don't enjoy themselves, there is no heart in them. You can't expect them to be always at home.

But these statements express more than a mere rivalry between young and old. They spring from a feeling of mutuality between young and old which transcends rivalry. The old days were better, among other reasons, because the dependence of the young upon the old was greater. The present is less attractive because the young no longer help the old as they should. Both facets of such mutuality may be expressed, even though the speaker, if he is old, casts it in the form of mistrust and dislike for the young. The whole of experience can be brought within this scheme of attitudes. To give an example, let an old fellow, an opponent of the present regime of Gaelicization in Ireland, recite his misgivings about the school system:

I am patriotic and it may be a bad thing to say but I think the school system they have now is bad and the teaching of Irish is bad. In my day and before, a man might go to school when he could — maybe for only three months out of the twelve — but he would know more than they get now when they go to school all the time. The old people learned more then. When the child finished school, he could be expected to read a newspaper to the old people and to write a letter for them, or to do sums — and he would do it well.

His complaint is much longer, but enough has been given to show his mistrust of a schooling which to his mind makes no provision for the mutuality mentioned. This mutuality was and is strongest in the realm of farm work. The farm family demands the cooperation of all its members. No less, the community makes its valuation of young and old upon that cooperation. General discussions among the country people bring out this fact again and again. To illustrate again, two "old fellows," adult farmers with families, could agree upon a formula running somewhat as follows:

The men were stronger in the past, they worked harder, while you try to get any young person to do as much work as the old men now and they would laugh at you. The young people today seem to see how little they can do rather than how much, while the old men would strip down and compete with one another to see who can do the most work.

Yet they were later forced to admit:

The people in the old times were not as knacky as they are now. Isn't it true that they used to have the horse in a stall feeding him while the man would be out with a spade turning over the garden?

Most of these allusions are to the realm of farm work. Just as the rivalry between father and son in the farm family is most intimate and most constant in the economy which they pursue together, so the expression of the conflict between the generations in the community at large takes the same form and finds its expression within the frame of the work that the community must do to live.

Naturally enough, the young people do not express these attitudes. They do not agree with their elders on the score of their own shortcomings. But they have a good deal to say, among themselves, from their own point of vantage. They express the reverse of the medal. The past is not so golden to them, and there are many among their elders whose idiosyncrasies can be sweepingly condemned with some such criticism as "old fool" and "old blatherer." Like the son already quoted who gave his

167

father his head in farm work and listened patiently for orders, only to follow his own devices, they have their own valuations of themselves in which youth and strength outweigh age and wisdom.

But within a system of values in which the old represent the nexus of kinship and bear honor within the community, the young people do not see the issue so clearly. There is as much respect as there is antagonism in their verbal assessment of the older men and women. The young people recognize themselves as forming a distinct group with interests and sentiments of its own, opposed in the scheme of rural life to the elders. They use the word "we" and oppose it to "them" for the old. They recognize places, pursuits, and forms of activity as their own and find much more interest in them than in those of the other group. The young men greet the suggestion that they should take their place in the gathering of old men in something of the tone of derision which they reserve for women. But the rivalry in their sentiments between respect and egocentric feeling, like the controls imposed by their parents to keep them respectfully silent in the presence of their elders, imposes a silence upon them. Consequently, one cannot find among them the voluble expression of attitudes based upon one's belonging to a certain relative age. One must look for it rather in particular expressions of annoyance, boredom, and chafing against restraint.

Expressions of sentiment about age are the products of a system of values upon it in which the individual makes the valuation from the place he occupies. They express not only a grouping of individuals of similar age but a mutuality between groups so composed. And, too, they form a scaffolding of categorization in which each person takes his relative place.

Let us examine one instance at least of this categorization. The community in rural Ireland bestows many names and titles. They are ephemeral. They have no currency outside the immediate circle of life in the townland or village. At best, they spread through a parish. They are nicknames and express no more

168

than the individual's particular place in the hearts of his fellows. Yet some of them are generic epithets. Like "old" and "young," they may prefix a name and designate the more closely the personality of the person named. Like "boy" and "old fellow," they may express broad categories of a man's age and its associated behavior, and may designate not so much a biologic or physiognomic reality as a sociological status. The words "saint" and *cailleach* are of the last kind of epithet, in rural usage. In the brogue they refer only to the old. In strict philology both are metaphorical, for the brogue knows and makes use of the words in their "proper" meanings. *Cailleach,* the Gaelic word, means properly "hag" or "witch." "Saint," of course, is the canonized saint of the church.

The small farmer who refers to this or that contemporary and neighbor as a "saint" or a *cailleach* is making a social and moral categorization. He is not concerned with purity of diction. The old man or woman who follows a behavior proper to his or her status and is an ornament to the community is a "saint." The old man or woman who does not is the object of distrust and dislike. His or her departures from accepted conduct cause disturbance and strife in the community. Accordingly, he or she is a *cailleach.* Thus, in one North Clare community a "stranger" whom the community disliked was a *cailleach,* despite the feminine gender of the word. Likewise, the old man who lived in harmony with his son upon a farm already transferred, a leader in the village whose oldest hale inhabitant he was, could be described by a neighbor as follows:

The old man is a typical Irishman. He is a saint and there isn't a thought against anyone in him. He is always in a good humor and, if he went to town to have a drink, he could stand in the one place till he dropped. He is as gentle and harmless as a child, and it will be a great loss to the village when he is gone. He and Roche [a neighbor] are two level-headed farmers and they have met every sort of trouble. If you are in doubt about any farm advice, you can go them and they will give you as good advice as you can get, because both of them have been successful farmers. It would pay a young man to listen to them.

169

"Saintliness" of this kind is a matter of one's filling one's role. But it is one's role for the village that counts. There is nothing individual in the canon of conduct. The young person who follows ardently the conventions laid down for him is not a "saint" even if he is exceedingly chaste and religious. It is the word "holy," not "saint," which comes to the countryman's lips in describing him. Nor is a young person a *cailleach,* for, like "saint," the term applies only to the old. Both terms refer to sociological age rather than chronological age, for those old people who occupy the role of "old" only because they have been forced into that position within the farm family can also be "saints." Thus the elder sister described in the discussion of farm marriage, who occupied the west room and the hob by the fire, was known in the neighborhood as a "saint."

Relative age makes a difference in status in the local community. It fits one into a definite place in a scheme of values. And lastly, as in the description of "saint," it equips one with a definite role in communal life which one can fill well or ill.

The conduct that reflects this state of affairs thrusts itself into the observer's view again and again in rural Ireland wherever he meets countrymen of different ages together. The relations between young and old in the community, like those between parent and child within the family, are understandable in the light of the roles of such broad age groups in terms of status.

First, there is the matter of privilege and precedence. To an outsider there may seem little enough in the countryman's way of life to allow for such distinctions. But from within, that little looms much greater. The old fellows, the men of full status who head farms and farm-working corporations of sons — those who have turned or are about to turn over their control to a younger generation — are accorded a very real precedence. In their own houses we have seen it to be very great. In the community at large it is little less so. A farmer visiting another takes his place at the hearth seat. His sons lag behind and occupy the back of the room. When the community gathers in the wake house to honor the dead, the places by the fire go to the older men and women. The boys and girls must group themselves behind. They come forward only when called upon. At country "stations" [5] the elder men and women file in for confession and come forward for Communion first. On the road to the shop, to church, or to the fair, the young man must keep pace and the elder may call him to his side.

The relation shows itself best perhaps in the constant discussions that are the breath of life for the countryman. No work is too pressing to prevent the countryman from "stopping on the road to pass the time of day." In the rural community such personal communion is an indispensable bridge across the social and physical space separating farm from farm. In all such discussion it is the elder men who may regulate length and subject of conversation. When groups form in pubs, in one another's houses on evening visits, before and after mass in the churchyard, the enthralling game of presenting argument, choosing sides, directing the flow of talk, belongs to the older men. The young men must listen in. At such times the important news of the countryside disseminates itself. Political judgments are formed, and the ephemeral decisions of daily life are made. In all this the boys are silent listeners. It is a bold young man who enters an opinion of his own.

Second, there is the matter of the contacts of the community with the outside world. The elder men, these same father-owners, represent the interests of the community before priest, schoolmaster, merchant, cattleman, and government official. The younger men hang back, ready to be brought in when the elders want them, listening in and keeping their own counsel. Much of this we have already indicated, but it is necessary to cite it here again in order to round out the picture.

[5] In country districts remote from the parish church masses are said in the private houses of parishioners once or twice a year in order to allow the performance of Easter or Christmas duty by those confined to their homes through age or sickness or other cause. These are "country stations," important religious events in every townland.

The relation extends to very small matters indeed. The better cup of tea, the bigger piece of bread, the glass of whiskey, the two eggs instead of one, the pipeful of tobacco, go to the elder men. This last, tobacco, is no small matter where even now tobacco is still expensive enough to require careful husbanding. It is a custom in the country districts to pass the pipe around among one's intimates and guests for testing, for praise, and to the accompaniment of formulae still often magical in nature. But the pipe does not go to the young man. He must content himself with an occasional "fag." When there is little, the young man can go without.

For illustration there is the anecdote that one Clare farmer tells:

During the time when tobacco was scarce [the war], an old man came into Sullivan's [shop] and asked for a half-quarter [cut of tobacco]. The Missus told him to go [get it] where he always bought it. He was very cast down. After he was out the door, I said to her she should give him some tobacco because a man who is used to it all his life would miss it greatly if he can't get it. "Let the young bucks go," said I; "they don't want it. But an old fellow wants it badly." She looked at me and says, "Frank, are you serious?" "I am, faith," says I; "call the old man back." He was just a few paces down the road. She did and his face lighted up and he couldn't thank her enough.

Informal as these differences are, they are nevertheless powerful agents in the regulation of conduct among the small farmers. Without them, the flavor of country life is lost. Without them, too, one can gain no understanding of the never-varying annual round of social activity in the country districts nor any inkling of the importance of those informal activities of social intercourse which fill the nonworking lives of the countrymen. It is here that social patterns of behavior upon age difference assume importance as controls of human activity. It is here that the roles the age grades play in the organization of the community reveal themselves most clearly.

When the authors first made their way into the small farm

communities which they came to know best, they were plunged
into a mass of observation which, without knowledge of the
valuations of the community upon age, had no interpretation.
Night after night, the day's work done, their new acquaintances,
at least the males among them, walked out upon the roads to this
house and that in search of recreation and companionship.
Mention of dances, "gambles," "hooleys," sings, *ceilidhthe,*
filled our ears, belying the impression of a gray monotony of
rural life too easily gathered by town-bred minds. Some of
these sportive events were age-old survivals of ancient custom,
like the bonfires of St. John's Eve. Others were nearly as ancient
celebrations of crucial events in individual and family life, such
as wakes, christenings, weddings. But many others were less occasional and less specialized gatherings, and others wore a very
modern dress: a turkey raffle and a dance round a gramophone.

But our interest was soon caught by distinctions of participation, rather than those of kind. The people of the village participated variously. Different groups met more or less regularly at
specific houses.

For instance, the "old fellows" went out on *cuaird,* as they
called their visiting to join one another. They followed a deep-
set regular habit. As they phrased it, "a man would feel lonely if
he didn't go out on *cuaird."* In most communities, they usually
convened at a particular house. Often their gatherings bore
particular names. In one North Clare community, Rynamona by
name, the old men's meeting was known as the *Dáil.* Before the
Free State, it had been the "parliament." The name is a jocular
one, of course, but it is expressive of the participants' evaluation
of themselves nonetheless.

The young men know the *Dáil* as the "old men's house."
They stay away. One of the cronies of Rynamona put the matter
most clearly when he described the old men's gathering from
its members' point of view:

It wouldn't suit [for the young men to come]. They gather in at
Jack Roche's and they laugh and joke and play cards. They talk about

the next gamble and the next dance, and that is all they know. It is a lot of codology [nonsense, buncombe]. It is only the old men, the men with families and a responsibility on them, they are the ones that come. And in our own way we learn a great deal. If you advance any argument, you must be prepared to defend it from all attack, and John Roche, "the public prosecutor," will ask you questions till he is sure it is right or wrong. Then some evening we have real discussions in which we settle problems. Other times we discuss farming. It wouldn't suit for the young men to come in, but, when we get old and they get married, then they will gather and talk about this and that. That is the way it always has been and that is the way it always will be. There is never any bad blood between any of the village, and one reason is because we talk things over.

This statement on the old men's gathering imparts a deeper reality to what appears to be merely a companionable pastime of the old men. The evening *cuaird* of the old men takes on an institutional flavor. It is a clique, of course, a tightly knit group of males of similar interests and similar status, giving rise to nicknames within itself which, as in the case here mentioned of the public prosecutor, express the members' position in the internal arrangement of the group. It has a definite meeting place and meeting time. It excludes those of dissimilar traits; in this instance, the young men. But it is a clique which operates within a traditional setting: "That is the way it always has been and is the way it always will be."

It is a clique, too, which performs a function for a larger group than those who make it up. In this case it is claimed for it, at least, that it prevents bad blood in the local community.

174

10

The Old in the Community[1]

Let us examine the life of a local community in the rural "West of Ireland" and put to the test of observation the claim that the clique of evening visitors among the old men of the community plays a decisive role in its social life. Perhaps Rynamona already mentioned affords the best example. Yet any other community the authors knew well would afford as good a one. In all of them the old men met in much the same way and, in spite of different names and persons, acted in much the same way to form a similar old men's clique. By taking the example of Rynamona, we can throw the generalities of this conduct into relief.

Rynamona is a medium-sized townland in the limestone country of North Clare. It is like many another in the "good land" of rough limestone outcrops stretching back from the sea into the glaciated lakes strewn north in County Clare. To reach Ryna-

[1] Much of the material in this chapter is taken from *The Irish Countryman* (London: The Macmillan Company, 1936), by Conrad M. Arensberg. It is used here by permission of the publishers.

mona is no easy task, even for horse and car. The main road
north out of Corrofin to Kilfenora passes through Kilnaboy,
where twelve houses, a school, a chapel, and a post office are all
that remains of an antiquity preserved to the eye only in the
ninth-century church and graveyard.

There, beside the graveyard, a side road leads off toward
Glanquin Mountain and the hills of Burren beyond. Along it
one passes through ragged upland for a mile and a half. This is
Kilnaboy Commons, and its many small fields bear witness to
its having been a refuge of the evicted, laboriously cleared of
stones. The upland is not high. It merely gives rise enough to
start a half mile of gentle slope downward into a basin filled with
a little lake. Rynamona lies round the lake.

The fields here are cleared, too, and cut up between with limestone ridges. But the grass grows richly among the crags and
ridges. The farmers are a fairly prosperous lot.

Eight of their houses stand in an irregular cluster on the lake
shore. This is Rynamona village. Five others are scattered
through the fields and across the lake. These households and a
few more a little further off make up the community. These are
small farms of the kind we met in Luogh. No one has more than
nine cows; and only one has fewer than two. Except for the eight
houses huddled in the village, fields and meadows stretch away
from the haggard gate. In the case of the villagers' holdings, the
arrangement is not much different. Their fields are scattered
about and behind their haggards in irregular patterns. In addition to these fields, most of them have several acres, carved
out for them by the Land Commission on an estate about two
miles off.

Rynamona is a closely knit community. Reduplicated bonds of
kinship unite all the households. "We are all related one way or
another," they describe it. Cooring is the usual form of cooperation, and the village as a whole holds itself responsible amid
grumbles for the maintenance of the borheen (road) which
leads out to the outside world of the towns. Nowadays the

County Council pays the sons who break stones and lay them in the winter months, but the village still assigns a bit of the road to each householder. Small matter if the borheen is bad, for a well-trod maze of paths crisscrosses the fields in all directions from house to house and across the countryside beyond.

Old man O'Donoghue's house, the third in the village, is the "old men's house." Mrs. Ruin, a neighbor, will tell you what the old man means to the men of the village:

The old man is getting weaker and when he is gone out of it the village won't be the same. He will be the greatest loss. It is round his fireplace the men gather. Where will they go when he dies?

But the question has not yet arisen for the men who meet there nearly every night, particularly in winter, when the evening is long and the work day its shortest. Soon after the evening meal they begin to gather. Occasionally this or that habitué may not come, but it is always the same group of men who stride across the threshold with a "God bless all here," and take their accustomed places.

O'Donoghue has the place of honor in the chair to the right of the fire. He is an old man now and no longer active beyond the house door. He lives here with his nephew, a man of fifty, and his nephew's wife. The couple have no children and must depend upon their own efforts in the working of the farm. It is a good farm and the nephew works it well, deferring to the old man in occasional matters.

O'Donoghue is the "judge" in this gathering. In the nightly discussions which take place around his fireplace, he has a judicial role. He is regarded as a wise man to whose opinions all must defer. Usually they know he contents himself with a word of affirmation, or now and again a slow and measured judgment upon a current topic. He initiates nothing and only occasionally adds a nonjudicial bit to the conversation. Then he shows himself to have a fund of funny and apt anecdotes as good as any

177

other man's. He rarely generalizes. When he does, his remarks deal with the "old times."

Silent as this shrewd old man is, his is the central position in the group. Comments and questions are phrased through him. He takes the preferred verbal bit and passes it on among the others. And when agreement is finally reached, it is his quiet "So it is" that settles the point for good.

O'Halloran sits on the hob across the hearth from him. He is the "drawer-down" in the scheme of jocular titles which includes most of the group. O'Halloran is a man of fifty but mature. He owns a farm a little better perhaps than most, just beyond the village. He works it with his wife and six children, the eldest of whom is nearing twenty. As he has no parents left alive, he is the "old man" and the man of the house. But individually he is more. "He has a great head on him," they say. He has had a somewhat wider experience, once having traveled as a salesman over the roads of southern Ireland. Yet, in spite of the fact that he is occasionally a little skeptical and his politics are somewhat suspect to the villagers, who are today De Valera men to a man, he is emphatically one of them.

His title of "drawer-down" is an apt one. O'Halloran seeks information. He most frequently of them all brings up points of interest and questions of the day. These he addresses to O'Donoghue, who passes them on for general discussion. Like all the rest of them his illustrations are apt and his anecdotes definite and precise, but his chief role is to "draw the talk down" to common levels of interest which allow all to take part.

O'Loughlin usually occupies the other hob. He has no real place here. He is a bachelor, aged fifty or so, and, though he comes here, he has little to say. He is seemingly silent all the time, and he breaks his silence only to add to unanimity. For O'Loughlin is very poor and lives alone. Having no family, he can neither coor nor work his land to best advantage. And occasionally he works on the road, breaking stones with the boys of the village. Just as he has no voice here, he has no title either.

178

Roche, "the public prosecutor," sits by the fire, opposite the old man O'Donoghue. He is a man of sixty or so, with a wife of the same age and an unmarried son and daughter, both in their thirties, still at home. His is a good farm and he is still active upon it. He, too, has a reputation for shrewdness, but his role here is a different one. Roche demands "why?" He makes one bring out one's best arguments, and pursues a point to its final conclusion. There his interest stops and he makes way for O'Donoghue, who sums up the agreement of the group. Roche earns his title well. He tests out the other's mettle. No one is offended at his "prosecution," for it clears the issue and brings out the right and the wrong upon which all can agree and O'Donoghue phrase judgment.

Behind them, a little further into the middle of the room away from the hearth, sits Cullinan, the "senator." Cullinan lives across the lake, where he works a middling farm with a wife and five children. Several of the sons are nearing twenty-five and Cullinan himself is well past fifty.

The "senator" is a weighty man. His part in the *cuaird* is in character. Cullinan is the one of them most fertile in cogent and fitting anecdotal illustrations. In a scheme of references, such as this, to past events and traditional precedents, Cullinan's many memories of persons and happenings, slowly and accurately phrased, give weight to the evening discussions.

Still further behind them, and often perched upon settle or table in the kitchen, are two other habitués. The elder of them is Noonan, a man of sixty, who lives in the village with a wife a little younger than himself and two boys and a girl, out of a once numerous progeny, still at home. The children are in their twenties and help him in his still active conduct of the farm.

Privately at least, the others think Noonan a bit of a fool. He is as good a farmer as any of them, it is true, and knows how to drive a shrewd bargain. But his role at *cuaird* is not a weighty one. Noonan is a very voluble man. He can be counted upon at all times to enliven the gathering with many opinions on all subjects. His volubility makes him more vulnerable than the rest to the public prosecutor's relentless logic, but it helps too to keep the conversation alive and active. Consequently, though he has no important title, he is a member of long standing.

The younger of the two sitting in back is John Quin. His position is a little anomalous, though he is a Rynamona man by birth and blood. Quin lives on a good farm just outside the village. He married-in there, taking over the place of a dead husband. But, true to the country custom, it was not the widow he married. She brought in a sister, who, in turn, married Quin. But both women are still living in the house. The elder sister has become the "old woman" and is treated more like a parent than a contemporary. It is Quin and his wife, the younger sister, who work the farm and who regard it as their own. Their claim is a perfect one, were it not for one misfortune: they are childless at fifty.

Quin is thus neither fully a young man nor fully an old one, as the countryside reckons age status. His place in the evening gathering reflects this intermediate state. In the two years in which the authors had the old men's house at Rynamona under observation, Quin was going through a transition. It was one which he could not describe himself, but which showed itself well in his behavior.

When we first came, Quin divided his evenings between the old men's house and card playing in several of the young men's gathering places. At one of these, to be described shortly, he was an important figure. His pronouncements were listened to with respect. He had "weight," and he conducted himself importantly and showed a serious demeanor and a little disdain for frivolous pursuits. In the old men's house he looked a different person. He was often silent or contented himself with answering questions. When he did speak, it was to "act the playboy," in the country phrase. It seemed to be a periodic fluctuation with him. One evening he would be silent and the next he would be more than ready to joke, to render a song, to dance, and to break into playful banter. Sometimes his lively efforts were successful. Sometimes they were not. But the playboy role did not last long. A year later he was a constant visitor, and he had given up all other visits. He had moved in. O'Donoghue, the "judge," passed judgment one evening which affirmed his new place. "He's a bit of a playboy," he said, "but there's a good head on him."

These seven men make up the old men's *cuaird*. As the evidence of their behavior shows, they are a closely knit clique with a code of conduct and valuation of their own, one strong enough to enforce a specific personality on each of the members in accord with his role in the group.

To appraise the *raison d'être* of such a group in Rynamona, we must examine it in relation to the rest of the community. These seven are not the only old men in the community. Roche, the prosecutor, had an elder brother with a good farm across the lake on the line between Rynamona and the next townland, Carhunamadra. But the elder Roche is seventy-five and no longer stirs out the door. He is too feeble to come to the *cuaird* house, and his faculties are failing. His sons, still young men, work the farm.

But there is another as well, a more active old man. Moroney is perhaps the strongest farmer in Rynamona. His house in the village is the best also, and he has the best-stocked farm. Moroney and his wife, at sixty, have a son and daughter nearing thirty still at home. The four work energetically and the household is prosperous. Each year Moroney stands for them in the "station," and the family's dues to the church are greater than any other's in Rynamona. Such prosperity draws him a bit apart from the villagers, and occasionally in political discussions he will identify himself with the Cosgrave party, as a man with a "stake in the country."

All this draws Moroney away from his fellows. Some say there was an incident long ago when Moroney was young, but most have forgotten it. Nevertheless, there is a breach between Moroney and the rest of the older men of the village. He never at-

181

tends at the old men's house and, when he goes on *cuaird*, it is usually to the house of Oscair, whom we shall describe presently.

Furthermore, just as not all the old men of Rynamona came to O'Donoghue's, so are their households unrepresented there. Unlike the cases of the elder Roche and Moroney, it is because in these other cases the men of the house are not eligible in age.

Two houses in the village send no man to the *cuaird* house. One of these is very poor and is a case of the "incomplete farm family" already discussed in a prior section. The only man there is a lad of twenty-five or so, who lives alone with his mother. Another of these is the case of O'Brien, a man of forty, married and with a family of children, the eldest of whom, a boy, is fifteen. O'Brien is a man of uncertain temper, given to gusts of anger. He is a moody man who doesn't do much or go out much. When he does, it is to the young men's gambles. Like John Quin, already described, he is in a transitional state, but he does nothing to hasten his advance.

Among the households beyond the village, one, that of Mackey, is likewise in transition. But with Mackey the process is hardly begun. His parents are dead, but he has only recently married and sent off a brother to the towns. He still visits with the young men.

The same holds for another family of Roches. The man of the house is only a few years married. His brother is as yet unprovided for and still lives with him. Both frequent young men's meetings.

The old men's house includes all the adult farm fathers of complete families whose children have just succeeded or are nearly ready to succeed them, with two exceptions. It brings in, too, two others, O'Loughlin, the silent old bachelor, and John Quin, whose status among the old age group is still provisional. The interviews already quoted have given an insight into the function this meeting performs for the community. The behavior of the group points again to the same function. This is the seat of judgment in the community. It is the clearing house of information and the court of opinion in which the decisions of the community are reached and the traditional knowledge of the peasantry applied and disseminated. From these meetings the men return home to their wives and sons, and the formulations they have reached spread thus through the community of individuals who share life in Rynamona.

Let us examine the type of topic that comes up in the old men's meetings. If we want to assure ourselves that the meeting has the influence its members ascribe to it, a glance at the conversation that takes place there should bear them out.

The old men's meeting is an informal gathering. It arises in response to the community's interests and its immemorial custom. Naturally, different personalities and personal idiosyncrasies make the gathering slightly different in each rural community. Occasionally it may be absent altogether for various causes, such as the dying-off of a central member of the group. Often there is a sort of interregnum between one generation of old men and the next. This was the case in one Clare community studied by the authors. There the old men had lost the central figure of their group and, diminished in number, spent most of their time in enfeebled loneliness at home. Two new cliques of slightly younger "old men" were competing for central position in the community.

But despite such variation from community to community, the old men's *cuairds* act very similarly. The topics brought up and debated upon are much the same from year to year and place to place. First in importance, however, are those concerning agriculture. Times of sowing, reaping, harvesting are debated; the merits of various seeds are disputed; shop and fair prices are compared; and the community's trade often affected thus. The "old men" are conservative farmers, as are most peasants, and an innovation must be thoroughly tested before it wins, here in the evening *cuaird,* the approval of the community. Traditional methods of farming receive their strongest support

183

here in the web of legend, proverb, and reference to the past that the speakers weave around them.

Much of the community's relation to the outer world is debated here and determined by the old men's agreement. In late years, this has come to be called "politics." It is here that petitions for roads, for relief work in winter, for extension of agricultural prize schemes, and all the "political" business of the county council and its committees originates on the side of the local community. It is here too that the community reaches its unanimity in party voting. In Rynamona, for example, it was felt that it was in the interest of all that there should be no dissension on the score of politics. The old men's *cuaird* debated the matter and agreed upon support of Fianna Fail, the De Valera party, an allegiance it held for the years 1927 to the time of the authors' visits. Even O'Halloran, whose private views leaned in another direction, begged the authors that no word of his political heterodoxy be allowed to reach the ears of his neighbors. "I wouldn't want them to think I wasn't with them," he said.

Here it is too that the community makes its appraisal of its own members and those with whom it is in contact. And that appraisal tells quite heavily in the behavior the community will adopt toward the person or condition appraised. Even the priest finds each of his acts and even his sermons discussed and debated in the evening *cuaird,* and he "gets a name" according to the decision reached. In Rynamona an incident occurred which shows the type of slow appraisal the community makes and the speed with which, once its judgment is formed, it puts its decision into action. Not far away in the same general region, a gentlewoman moved back after years of absence to a small manor house which the family had had for many years. She was unknown to the farmers and, despite her friendly interest in them, seemed to be unable to establish contact with them. This distressed her, the more that her kindness seemed ineffectual in putting an end to the inevitable petty pilfering which she knew she must expect. One day, about a year later, her horse bolted on the country road. An expert horsewoman, she soon brought him into control. Thereafter her luck with the country people changed. Her exploit had made the rounds of the local community and had won approval for her. The old men agreed she was a grand lady and had a great hand with horses. And the petty pilfering sank to manageable proportions.

The community regulates its internal affairs through the *cuaird* as well. It is here public opinion is formulated. There is nothing formal about the decisions made upon the incidents arising from day to day. The local community has no implement with which to enforce its will. But it has the power of gossip and in action the power which in the critical days of the land agitation won itself an international name: the boycott.

In a later section the sanctions the local community exercises will be discussed. It is sufficient here to point out this role of the *cuaird*. An example from another community than Rynamona will throw the type of action it can take into relief.

An "incomplete family" affords the example. It was made up of an old woman and her thirty-year-old son. Theirs was a poor farm, and ordinarily they would have been an object of commiseration. But they were not. In fact, they were a constant annoyance. The son was generally regarded as bad and lazy. He neglected his farm and exhibited an obstinate disregard of village opinion in which his mother abetted him. The result was, naturally, that their house was shunned and he went nowhere to *cuaird*.

But no crisis arose till the episode of the pig. One autumn the son brought home a large Irish white sow. The sow was more nimble than most of her kind, and neither the mother nor the son took any pains to keep her at home. She wandered through the village at will and soon devastated many a cabbage patch. The village took alarm, and the more so that the sow might well prove dangerous to young children. There were angry words among the women, and the men for once backed them up. In the *cuaird* it was hinted that the sow might be found dead one

185

morning. But before such an event could take place, the son took warning and sold the pig. "Public pressure," if you will, forced his decision and resolved the conflict, but it left him as low as ever in the village's esteem.

And lastly, the *cuaird* is the seat of traditional lore and entertainment. Its members are the repositories of folklore and legend. And the official belief of the countryside finds its expression and its reaffirmation in the discussion of events and the recounting of histories and incidents. In communities still at least partly Irish-speaking, such as Luogh, most of its members are *seanachaidhthe,* storytellers in the traditional vein. And it is among them that traditional repertories of a saga, folk tale, song, and legend still get an audience. The point of importance here is that it is among the old people that folk myth and folk belief are preserved and expressed for the community.

If we are to examine in full rural behavior based upon age and its connection with the old adult clique whose function in the community we are assessing, we must offer some contrast with the behavior of other age groups.

We have already mentioned that the old men's house in Rynamona was not the only seat of visiting after the day's work, and that the entertainment provided there was merely one instance of many gatherings taking place almost nightly, at least through the winter, in rural communities. In the statements given by older men about the meeting of the young men we have seen something of the manner in which other pursuits than those of the men's house are regarded.

Indeed in all the communities which came under the authors' notice the young men were as ardent evening visitors as were the older men. In Rynamona they were no less so.

There they gathered in most often at the house of Roche, the "prosecutor." They did this from long habit, as did their elders. But they had no larger justification for their doing so. They went because "you never feel the time passing when you're in with the boys." But there were marked differences in their meeting. There was no central clique so closely integrated as that in O'Donoghue's house. There were pairs of lads, brothers, friends, and groups of three and four and five who habitually played cards or walked the roads together.

A greater difference lay in their complete lack of concern with the affairs of the community. One could get them to talk only about their own plans or the trials of their own kind and age. There was no debate, no reaching of decisions, no appeal to tradition. The skills upon which those taking part in the meetings prided themselves and for which they received their nicknames were of other sorts. Not even farming occupied a large share of their conversation, keen as their rivalry in the matter often was while work was going on.

Taking these matters in order, the young men who met at Roche's house met habitually there for card playing. Roche's unmarried son, a man about thirty, was perhaps the central figure. His cousin, another Roche, was the brother of a young man just married, who took part in no *cuaird*. This cousin helped work his brother's farm. He was another central figure. The group that formed itself round them included most of the young men of Rynamona between the ages of twenty and thirty. They played the usual games of the Irish countryside, "forty-five" and "nap," often far into the night.

Roche's house was the more informal center. It took in the younger men. But there was present in the community a custom somewhat more organized, namely, the "gamble." As often as once a week a gamble is held in or near Rynamona. Each household, as its turn comes, throws open its doors to the card players. Admission, usually a shilling, is charged and goes toward defraying the expense of the supper of bread and tea for all and toward the prize. What is left after those charges are met belongs to the householder. Often this amount reaches a profitable figure, and, where the custom is firmly entrenched, a certain commercialism shows its head.

But the gamble is a sporting event. Teams, often formed of

187

habitual associates in card playing, are pitted against one another in one form of the gamble. In another, individual high scorers win. The prize is usually a turkey or two geese, even a bonham (young pig), a side of bacon, or a calf. Elaborate rules and canons of honesty govern the play, the conduct of the players, and the obligation of the person offering the prize. Play is serious and intense, and the winner of the prize can count himself a proud man, for to be known in the countryside as a "great gambler" is a coveted mark of shrewdness and skill.

The older men seldom attend the gambles. They are the province of the young. For the latter, they are a crystallization of the more informal card playing, such as that at Roche's house, already described, and they give the successful young men a prestige in the community ordinarily denied them. For in late years tournaments have sprung up covering whole sections of the county and it is a proud team which can bring back a five- or ten-pound district prize to its home community.

From the standpoint of an enumeration of those taking part in the gambles, too, the gambles show themselves to be such a crystallization. They bring into association on more definite occasions the groups, such as that at Roche's house, which meet habitually. They unite most of the young men, especially the more active among them, with a few of the older. But it is from the young men's world of habit that their union is created.

In Rynamona the young men who gathered nightly at Roche's house were the mainstays of the gambles. They could be counted upon to attend all of them. They played well and long, as they had learned the games among themselves. But they were not the only ones to come. Most of the slightly older men of what we shall call the intermediate *cuaird,* to be described later, such as John Quin, the newcomer to the old men's house already named, came from time to time, and there was always a sprinkling of young men, kinsfolk, and "friends" from near-by communities. It was only the members of the old men's house who stayed away. They alone had given up the habits of young men. To them the gamble was "codology."

Thus the first point of difference between the visiting habits of the old men and the young men, their lack of central clique, is not without wider interest. The young men are more numerous, and they group themselves together as much as do the old. But it is upon a different basis. It is a synthesis in a looser, more widely inclusive gathering which unites smaller cliques of brothers, friends, and boon companions. The gamble is only one of many entertainments they provide themselves. Equally frequently they hold a dance. The country dance is undergoing change in rural Ireland today, but it is still much as it was in the last century, although it may not enliven the country districts as often as it did. Irish square dances, jigs, and flings, most of them variations of sixteenth-century European dance forms, are most common, although some Gaelic-speaking districts preserve an older tradition.

The country dance belongs to the young people. It differs from the gamble, from the standpoint of participants, in that it unites both sexes. In most communities it is an affair in which the whole community takes part, the old people as onlookers, the young and the still spry among the older ones as performers. In late years the more formal "all night" dance, an organized dance for which admission is charged and from which the older people are usually absent, has made its appearance. Like the gamble it draws from a wider area.

But there is a good deal of the spontaneous dancing which springs up wherever the young people of the community gather even today. The young men and women learn the skills required and value them. There are elaborate codes of etiquette round them and a wealth of proverbs and jocular superstitions. But here again, unlike the behavior followed in the old men's house, these conducts have little larger purpose than uniting the scattered cliques of young people. They are recreations. They are ends in themselves. They are good times that pass the time.

189

The gamble and the dance do not, of course, exhaust the list. The young people have other activities, games, sports, contests, and playful roles of solemn occasions, such as acting as strawboys (mummers) at weddings. But all these activities, in which the old members of the community do not directly participate, are alike in their playing no great part in organizing other elements in the community than the young people themselves. They serve other functions.

All these activities bind the young men, the young people, together in common interests. They provide them with a scope of action in which they are comparatively free, yet which keeps them divorced from the seats of a power over community life which is denied them. In this sphere they may develop complex norms, valuations, and conducts.

But such developments do not serve primarily to knit the community as a whole the more firmly. They are associated with the lesser prestige of the young people. Consequently, the old men's house comes to have in contrast a double function. It unites the old men in much the same way as the gamble and the dance unite the young men, in fact even more strongly. But it does so in terms of the old men's common position as recipients of the respect of the community and in terms of their individual positions as integrators of their families. The difference is structural. The activities of young men unite them across family and clique lines even from one community to the next. But those of the old men do more; they unite young and old as well. The integration of the young men is a looser and less inclusive one, even though the numbers ephemerally joined in gamble and dance may be greater.

In such a system of integrations, that of the old men has the greater prestige. A great gambler or a great dancer wins wide respect. But the distinction is short-lived. It is a nine days' or a nine years' wonder. It bestows great prestige among one's fellows, but it removes one very little, if at all, from one's subordinate, less valued place as "boy" in the community.

190

Where such is the case, the individual's progression through rural life under normal circumstances is not toward a greater and greater prominence in the activities of the young men's group. Rather, there comes a time when one must break away altogether. One faces perforce a new orientation of sentiment and a new kind of behavior. Growing old brings many more changes than the physiological.

The case of the newcomer, John Quin, already described, shows the necessary changes. In Rynamona it is brought out very clearly in the clique to which he first belonged and to which we have referred at various times, calling it once the "intermediate."

The clique we name so met at the house of one Joseph McMahon, more commonly known as Oscair (the Hercules of Irish saga) for his physical strength. Oscair was a rural carpenter with only a very small plot of garden and his house. But he was a good singer, a jokester, and a repository of folk tale, though he was not much past forty. He lived just at the edge of the slope leading from Kilnaboy Commons down to Rynamona. The townland was what would be called in urban sociology an "interstitial area." It was higher, rougher, and more craggy than Rynamona and Kilnaboy, lying between them. Its inhabitants were descendants of people evicted from round about who had squatted there. Most of them were "died out and left," and the place was always poor. It acted as a sort of outlying fringe of Rynamona.

The men who collected round Oscair's fire were aged thirty-five to sixty. Just as their ages were intermediate between fully old and fully young, so was their habit here. They very seldom played cards. Talk was the order of the day, enlivened by Oscair's humor and ballads. A few of them spoke of the affairs of the village with some weight. The rest did not. Those who came were as follows:

a. Young Mackey, from the village, the man recently married, still too young for the old men's house.

    b. Moroney, the sixty-year-old, "strongest" (richest) farmer of the village. One of the few who spoke with weight.

    c. Young Roche, son of the very old man, still unmarried but entirely in charge of the farm he would soon inherit.

    d. O'Sullivan, a herdsman, from near-by, who was a stranger in the community but had won himself a place, despite his being a landless man of sixty-five, by acting as the local veterinarian. He spoke, too, with weight.

    e. John Quin, already described, who spoke here with weight.

    f. Two forty-year-old Pilkington brothers, unmarried, from the Commons, very small farmers, most often silent.

    g. Oscair himself, whose role was to entertain.

Of these men it can be seen that only Mackey, Moroney, and John Quin could make the transition to full farm-owning, farm-father status of old men. Mackey had years to pass before he could so do. His eldest child was very young and he himself not long in possession of his farm. John Quin, in a somewhat anomalous position, could and did move onward. In doing so, as we described, he felt it necessary to break away completely from this group. This he did, with the result that the group, itself never stable, fell to pieces. Moroney, as we remember, had a disagreement with the villagers and would not attend the old men's gatherings.

What was it then that brought these men together? The authors could get no answer from the men themselves, other than their amusement with Oscair and, in Moroney's case, a guardedly phrased dislike of the villagers. Yet, through observation and interview in the community, it became clear that they were all passing through a similar transition. Oscair's visitors were not a stable clique, nor too faithful in attendance. Both young Roche and young Mackey were still going occasionally to the young men's meeting at the other Roche's house, but both felt too great responsibilities for gambling and cards. John Quin gambled heartily enough but was more and more impatient with the "playboys" of young fellows. Old Moroney was gruff and lonely. The others were neighbors of Oscair's and, being poor or landless men, felt awkward going elsewhere. O'Sullivan could visit as he pleased, for, as the local "vet," his word carried weight, but, always a stranger in sentiment, he felt most at home here.

The intermediate clique was a product of similarity of interests, in contrast to the interests of other better organized groups. Its members were in some way or another a little different from the ordinary old or young of Rynamona. Some of them were remote topographically, but not all. Some were without full community status, but not all, and some of a transitional age.

Oscair's house was thus a sort of catchall for those whose position in Rynamona was not clearly defined. It was intermediate between the clearly defined groups, and for the small farmers, such as Mackey, Roche, and Quin, was a halfway stage in their advance from the status of young men to that of old.

The progression of which this is the halfway stage is an upward one, metaphorically speaking. It leads no longer to a greater role as "playboy" but toward full family and community status. It leads to a new behavior and new personal desires, more highly valued. One's discarded status and one's discarded behavior fall away into lesser esteem. In terms of this progression we can understand the attitude of the old men on the behavior of the young ones. It is a transitory, impermanent, unimportant thing. It is a "codology." "When they grow older," one old man said, "and become married, they will meet just as we do."

What shows itself in Oscair's clique is a transitional state. For a moment were gathered here those who could move upward, like John Quin. Gradually, they could attain full status. Oscair's hearth for them was a roadside resting place.

With these intermediates were gathered the representatives of another anomalous social place. Both Oscair and O'Sullivan, the "vet," were important figures in the community. Their occupations and their skills won them respect and admiration over the countryside. O'Sullivan, the older man, was free to come and go wherever he might wish. But both were "landless" men.

They could never attain full peasant status. In the identifications of Irish familism, they were condemned to celibacy. Neither could feel comfortable in the old men's *cuaird*. There was no place for them except, as Oscair's behavior showed, as playboys and entertainers. So they too must occupy an interstice in the structural alignments of rural social life.

11

Familism and Sex

The small farmers' treatment of sex and the relations of men and women is no less characteristic of their communities than is their treatment of age differences. The country people are the ones among whom marriage is latest in Ireland, bachelorhood and spinsterhood most common, fecundity greatest. They are the ones among whom there is an excess of males over females, a fact which gives all Ireland a sex ratio (973 females to every 1,000 males) unexampled among the long-settled Old World countries and comparable only to those of the new countries. Yet the best evidence gives them a comparatively low illegitimacy rate, too, and the country people yield to no one in the strictness of their sexual morality.

In the small farm households of the countryside, the roles, privileges, and duties of male and female are complementary. The division of labor between the sexes is only part of separation of human activity into male and female spheres. By oriental standards, perhaps, physical segregation of the sexes may be lacking. Yet in the countryside the community sets very rigid norms of conduct regulating the relations between men and women.

Indeed, the bounds of propriety among the small farmers are quite well marked. An outsider can come to see something of them almost at once. Men and women are much more often to be seen in the company of members of their own sex than otherwise, except in the house itself. Except upon ceremonial occasions in family life or in the considerable affluence of owning a gig or a trap or a motorcar, in Clare at least they go to mass, to town, or to sportive gatherings with companions of their own sex. Till recently and even now in remote districts, a conventional peasant woman always kept several paces behind her man, even if they were walking somewhere together.

The women do not go out on *cuaird* like the men. Their sphere of interest and influence is better confined within the family circle. Women do not take part directly in the deliberations of such cliques as that described in the old men's house at Rynamona. On the other hand, they are not in the least excluded or treated lightly or in a derogatory fashion. At the old men's *cuaird* the woman of the house is nearly always present. Her being of the company does not seem to stem the flow of talk in the slightest. She remains silent or is ignored so long as their talk deals with the world of the men's interest. But when the talk swings around to her sphere, she is consulted and is ready to take an active part.

The girls, of course, the unmarried younger women and adolescents, keep to themselves and form cliques and smaller groups of neighbors and kinswomen among themselves. Occasionally a dance breaks the ordinary succession of work and evening talk in the kitchen. And then, in their more restricted place, they are ready to go about under the tutelage of parent or brother to meet the young men and boys of the community.

All this is nothing new and has been described before. Yet one must review it, because in it one can see the existence of

196

statuses of the kind we have demonstrated before. Old woman, married young woman, and girl, each term is a status in the countryside, in the same manner as in the cases of the boys and men we have already presented. The terms are summaries of status in farm economy, family life, and the cliques of the community.

Consequently the comment and attitude of the small farmers toward sexual behavior cannot be divorced from their appreciation of status in family and community. For them sexual behavior is merely one aspect, not of individual personality, but of sociological role. If one turns to any record of the sort of commentary and discussion the small farmers carry on among themselves, both in the semipublic discussion of the *cuaird* and in the more private talk of conversation among friends of a common age and status, one encounters a characteristic set of remarks and evaluations. These are for the most part discussions of specific persons in specific events. The attitudes expressed are directed now toward persons, now toward general conditions, now toward moral or ethical imperatives, now toward cosmological principle. Yet always, if sex is the subject, the status of the actors and the interests of the familist farm economy are the themes.

Women are valued and praised for their fecundity. All this is part of generally accepted convention among the small farmers, and such conversations as the following are not in the least unusual, despite the very great modesty and reticence of the farmers. A small farmer is praising an old woman, the head of the household, to one of the authors and contrasting her to her son's wife, both being listeners:

Here is a woman that has no more milk of her own. They shouldn't allow a woman like that to breed because a man should always keep his wife in the milk. The old woman, God bless her, raised every child with the didi [breast].

The country-bred boy and girl grow up in an atmosphere of constant reference to sex and breeding. There seems to be little of the ignorance about such matters which the townsman delights so in attributing to country people. In Ireland, no less than elsewhere in the world, the antagonism between town and country often expresses itself in such joking ascription of ignorance and stupidity. In Ireland, however, there is another side of the expression of town and country distrust. The countryside points to prostitution and immorality in the towns and finds something to back up its condemnations. The town returns its dislike with double measure and accuses the countryside of primitive lack of all sensitivity of feeling or restraint of impulse. But these antagonistic attitudes and ways of regarding other groups than one's own are not our concern here. They are of interest here because such ascriptions of ignorance are part of a common misapprehension of the complexity of the peasant attitudes.

For instance, to an outsider the countrymen will seem often to give a mere lip service to the attitudes of the townsman, for one is always apt to mistake the function of hearty laughter. The country people have strict moral and ethical attitudes around the question of sex, as rigid as those of any other class if not more so. Yet they have conventional licenses and conventional niceties which do not coincide with those of the other classes and are thus open to misunderstanding. And, like all classes and peoples, they have two sets of attitudes, not one, and these are "ambivalent," to adopt the Freudian term.

But these attitudes and their "ambivalent" nature, the kind of alternation they seem to present, must be understood in terms of the social relationships of the countryside. The greatest single cause of misapprehension lies here. In different contexts, toward different persons, in connection with different events, one and the same person regards the same subjects quite differently.

For example, in discussions of the peccadillos of young people and the censurable events of the district the farmers and their wives were full of animus against the "crabbit" great

"bucks" of lads who led girls astray and from whom the innocent were not safe. Yet even then, in discussing the fault of such
amorous lads and the necessity of circumspection and immediate and frequent confession for girls as their best defense, one
sees that the pure young maidens are also not without blame.
They bear the taint of Eve. "Sure the boys have no chance,"
said one woman in this respect, "for the girls always lay
the blame on them." Yet these attitudes coexist together with
other very hearty, casual, and sometimes ribald attitudes which
make their appearance in banter, joke, and repartee even between speakers of different sex. These even take the form of
taunts about prowess and mild ridicule for the possession of a
greater relish than is meet, or fanciful recitation of past magnif-
icent misdeeds. This is particularly true in the recitations of
stories and adventures of persons in the ken of the community,
where details of amorous desire and accomplishment are given
with considerable gusto, and greeted and reiterated again and
again amid hearty laughter.

Certain observers profess to find the puritanical outlook on
sexual matters on the increase in the countryside. The country
people themselves purport to see a change in their own outlook. And it may be that the last generation has brought a considerable spread of Catholic moral standards with the spread of
education and the opening of the countryside to urban influence.

In any event the laughter and hearty guffaws with which references of nearly any kind to sexual intercourse, sexual attraction, and childbearing are greeted, and the evident interest they
evoke, are very much part of the everyday behavior of the small
farmers. They do not imply in any sense an approval or acceptance of the deeds described. They are rather expressions of a
very definite judgment. They are in the nature of a condemnation in which laughter is itself a sanction upon the forbidden.[1]

[1] The authors accept readily the view of laughter as a response to a situation where socially conditioned values are threatened with upset and yet not
so deeply or irrevocably broken as to bring out a full reproval. The view is

The "earthiness" and the ribaldry of the country people is not an antithesis to their strict moral code. Rather it reinforces it. It gives its pietistic and too-respectable, churchly and town-bourgeois aspects an authentic, indigenous touch. Even more important, it makes for a modification of the conventional attitudes which fit them for the country people's social life.

In this ambivalence of attitude one can see the identifications between status in human relations and norms about sexual behavior more clearly. The one view, that "holiness" denies sex, can be reserved to suit the nonprocreant statuses of family life. The other, the hearty and open view embodying animal analogy, frank interest, overt desire, can be reserved for the persons whose roles in social life allow free rein to the amatory and procreative urges.

For the small farmers marriages are for the pupose of producing children and assuring continuity of descent and ownership. They are "forever." They are indissoluble. Sexual relations are part of marriage, its pleasure and its duty. They lead to children if one is fortunate and strong and potent. It is the will of God. One may regret that one's childbearing came so early.

---

well developed by Pilkington and agrees with that of Max Eastman. The tabloid reader is not weakening his horror of murder or his distaste for adulterous behavior, however familiar his tabloid-viewing may make them. Similarly the Englishman reading his detective stories and the Frenchman listening to his *chanteuses* are merely indulging vicarious "thrills." All of them are going through a playful rehearsal of the conditioned reflexes of social sanction, indignation, rage, and punitive action in the same way a dog growls and bares his fangs at his play fighting. The idea may seem a bit ludicrous in itself, and it will offend the moralists. But let them remember that in most persons moral and ethical activity is absolutely unreasoned, spontaneous, and without any kind of intellectual support at all. It is pure reflex. Like any other reflex, it must be kept alive by a constant restimulation. Only overzealous priests, reformers, teachers, "nice people," and prudes miss this point. They fail to understand that vulgarity often hides far stricter morality than hypocritic cant. This laughter represents a constant and not unpleasurable reiteration of the accepted canons of morality upon so important a matter.

There might have been more time for free enjoyment. But it is a regret to which one resigns oneself easily.

Thus marital and sexual success have but one criterion. One proves one's worth sexually in the marriage bed, which is in turn the childbirth bed. The proof of happy adjustment, of masculine virility, and of feminine worth is "the good long family." "Lots of women have no children," you are told, "but the men have no value in them if they don't." Both man and woman are at fault and in misfortune in childlessness. In one case of repeated miscarriages, the man might be at fault, it was said, because "he usedn't to make them [the children] right."

It is only with the married men and women who are still engaged in producing offspring that any kind of sexual interest, officially at least, is permitted or even deemed to exist. Among others in the rural communities the interest either does not exist at all, in the eyes of small farmers, or it exists only as an evil, but powerful force. As such it must be subjected to constant control. This is the case among the young. Among the old, if it exists at all, it is only as a survival of embers that should far better be long dead. For adults, in adult family life, sex is divested of any awesome, evil character. "God help us," said one woman in this regard, "what is natural can't be wonderful."

Thus one can see why it is that nearly everything the young people do seems to their elders to shape them for the goal of marriage and family headship. Much of local custom comes to have that explanation. The goal is taken for granted. It is the ambition of all the young members. Their activity either marks time until they shall be able to take their places as married family heads or it prepares them for that directly. Even the pastimes and jollities of country life in the communities the authors came to know had that keynote.

The pastimes of the young people in which the usual segregation of the sexes is bridged point toward matchmaking and country marriage.

201

Even where matches are made between strangers, some kind of sexual attraction is not to be neglected, and local custom provides for a brief introduction and a setting for courtship. Several cases came to the authors' notice in which advantageous matches were broken off when either boy or girl expressed distaste for his or her prospective partner, usually when confonted with him or her at the preliminary festivities of the country marriage. Other cases again came to their notice in which a shy suitor could be galvanized into a final decision to take matters into his own hands and press a suit, when his family began to cast around for a match for him elsewhere. Matchmaking was, in fact, far from presenting a scene of "loveless" marriages. The match is a convention like any other. For those who are trained in it, it provides occasion for arousing sexual interest and marital aspirations in young couples quite in the manner of "falling in love" in communities where courtship is more immediately a matter of personal initiative.

And, like any other convention, the match could also come to cloak another situation. The match made by the contracting families is the ideal kind of marriage, for the reasons we have discussed. But it does not necessarily imply any one kind of courtship. In many instances a couple who made their own decision had a match made for them. Even in the case of "runaways," as elopements are called, the boy and girl could often be brought back and a match made for them. And lastly, as a way of establishing respectability and providing for the movement of the re-formation of the family, even those cases of marriage necessitated by premarital pregnancy could be fitted into the dominant convention.

Thus the forms of courtship and the development of pairings among the population of boys and girls of the country communities must all be understood, even in their most unusual forms, in terms of the dominant pattern of the familistic system and the kind of marriage it entails in rural Ireland. The country people feel this. Their attitudes identify the convention with the whole code of morality and folkways of their own class and kind.

They equate any departure from the accepted norm as a sin, a lack of religion. They bring the whole weight of all their sanctions and values to bear upon it. They make the ultimate identification between their own norms and the only right conduct, particularly in this matter so central to the rural familistic system. This final attitude was often addressed to the observers, particularly, but there is reason to believe that it is as often expressed among the country people themselves. In discussions of immorality, illegitimacy, premarital intercourse, the question would arise: Would you believe such a thing could happen in Ireland? In such countries as England and America well it might, for there, the country people hear, the boys and girls just take a liking for one another and go off and marry and "never mind the money." And we remember that in this case the "money" means the re-formation of the entire two families as well.

Even those cases which meet condemnation are likewise often thought to have to do with the dominant pattern. Whether or not the suspicions of the country people are correct, the authors do not know. But they were struck with the fact that so very often in discussions of cases of immorality and unethical sexual conduct the country people made no recourse to concepts of search for pleasure or even of the overpowering force of emotion as explanations of the condemned conduct. Both explanations were to be heard in other classes. Rather, the country people insisted upon looking for a motive in terms of the system of organizing human relations which they understood. The culprits, young "bucks," tried deliberately in such cases to impregnate the girls and force marriages. They were motivated by greed for land and dowries. Sex without familism seemed beyond the country people's imagination.

But the last statement must be qualified in a definite direction. It is only for themselves that they seemed to be unable or, better, unwilling to imagine a sexuality without familism. Other patterns of sexual behavior they see and have heard of, but these are immoral and unworthy ways of doing things and acting, departures from the right and normal, sometimes disgusting, sometimes ludicrous, and sometimes mysterious. In any event they are marks of standards of a lower class and lesser dignity and respectability than that of the farmers. They are to be repudiated not only for their lack of common sense but for supernatural reasons as well.

Thus the authors heard several instances in which bad luck attended the departure from the usual familistic norm. There was a feeling, sometimes overtly expressed, that at any one time there should be only one sexually active procreant couple in a household. Young and old could well be part of the household in any numbers, but there should be only one adult married couple under one roof. Any other arrangement brought its own punishment and ill luck.

But more often there was identification between the expression of sexual impulse outside the familistic pattern and the debased conduct of the lower ranks of the landless and disreputable of the countryside, the laborers of the towns, the runaways, remnants of broken households. Or else the small farmers put the onus of guilt on other regions "more backward" than their own. At the most, wrong conduct might be the result of some occult compelling force strong enough to break through all sense and caution. The authors were struck with the countryside's version of love charms. In accounts of love charms and love magic, proof of their existence and efficacy was always to be found in the otherwise unaccountable cases in which a man or woman abandoned farm and fortune and the favor of friends for a sexual attraction. How else to explain, for instance, an old man's senile infatuation, a young boy's indiscourageable devotion to an older woman who could bring him nothing?

A word must be said here of the other ways of bringing about

204

marriage than the formal process of family matchmaking. In the last century, to judge from the accounts of the old people, and to follow the testimony of novelists on Irish life, a stage-managed elopement was often resorted to. It was a semirespectable kind of marriage. The swain and his friends kidnapped the bride out through the window in the night. They took her away from her father's house to the house of an uncle or other relative of the young man's. There dancing and general jollity reigned, and the young couple were feted. Very often all parties seem to have connived at the result. On other occasions, the elopement was obviously designed to bring about a match to which parents objected or to force parents to a decision. Staged elopements of this kind seem now to have died out in Clare, or at least to be rather infrequent. But the difference between this and a true runaway is slight. In the latter case the young couple take matters into their own hands entirely. Throughout the years many couples have eloped, run off to towns and to emigrate without parental blessing. Others have done likewise and returned to get their portions and a delayed parental sanction. Nevertheless one can see that all these forms are mere modifications upon the dominant convention.

They too must lead into the familistic pattern. A match must be made, or at least fortunes given and provision for family reformation made. In cases of premarital pregnancy, the match may be forced or hastened, but it is nonetheless the final and respectable resolution.

Even in cases of illegitimacy, if the mother comes to marry another man than her child's father, a match may sometimes save the day. It serves the social purposes and repairs the damage, though it removes none of the stain upon one's local reputation. In spite of the strictness of country standards, many small farmers have married "poor, unfortunate girls" of this kind, without irreparable loss of respectability. Yet even then the attitude of the community fits the familistic norm. Such cases are

205

felt to be very unusual and special departures from custom. They are matters for some surprise and congratulation.

The moral standards of the countryside involve a most strict control of the young people in sexual matters. Premarital virginity is the ideal. It is a double standard, of course. The young lads are not, or were not until recently, expected to be so pure as the girls.

The sexual urges of the older people are deemed adequately satisfied in marriage. Adultery very seldom seems to come into the reckoning of the small farmers. This is part of the equation of sexual appetite and familistic aspirations. The country people know something of town prostitutes and have heard of occasional marital lapses in the countryside as well. But these matters are not of great interest. The incidents, as far as one can judge, are of infrequent occurrence. Marital fidelity is not only the ideal; it seems to be the fact as well. It seems even to be taken for granted, and any other course felt inconceivable.

Thus we must look to the relations among the unmarried young couples to see the chief point of pressure in the rural system of values. That is the area in which there is nearly all the smoke and not a little fire.

Although premarital virginity and complete abstinence from any kind of sexual activity is the ideal for the young, local custom emphasizes marriage all the while. Local dances and other festivities are the chief times of meeting and play for the young men and women of the rural communities. The customs and conventions which surround them are constant reminders of marriage and its hopes and privileges.

Yet as soon as any intimacy of acquaintanceship builds up between a particular pair, they are matched together in local gossip. They are forced to take a position which is only a single step from betrothal. But, as elsewhere, lovers separate to find others. Though a once or twice fickle or jilted girl is subjected to constant gossip, her luck seems not to doom her entirely if she is attractive or a good match.

Such outings as the "patterns," [2] relics of saints' festivals, and race meetings in summer, and the dances in winter, are occasions of courtship, excitement, and philandering of sorts in the countryside. They are objects of censure on the part of those of the clergy, townsmen, and people of higher class who unite in condemning more obvious manifestations of peasant social life with little insight into a custom's function. The clergy, in particular, fulminate constantly against all-night dances. They object not so much to the jollities as to the opportunities for "walking out" among the young couples.

The following quotations from country people describe the situation. In the first a countryman is talking about "crabbit lads" who are to blame for local sexual irregularities, and comes around at last to the local dances:

They are awfully crabbit around here. If a girl has money or land and she will get it, the boys try any way at all to put her up the hill so they will marry her and get it. And the parents keep the girl away from the boys for fear it will happen. But it is no good to keep the girl in the house, because, if you do, she knows nothing. Let her knock away and she soon learns how to take care of herself. If you don't, there are ways the crabbit lads will get to her.

That was the way with the girl who married Willie Meaney[3] and he thought to get the money, but the parents said let her go. Now they are in Ennis and she never got anything. The same way with the two who married the Shaughnessy girls. They thought they would get something but they didn't get a thing. Would you believe that? America is not the only place where things like that happen. The people have crosses to bear. Every year we have a talk from the priest about the dances. He says the dances are all right but it is the going home that is bad. There is always a laugh when he says that. Then some of the parents get worried and they won't let their daughters go to a dance for a month or so, and they forget about it after that.

[2] The local name of country festivals once religious, somewhat like the *pardons* of Brittany.

[3] Names of persons and smaller places in this and subsequent quotations are, of course, fictitious and refer to no actual persons or places of such names.

207

The status of boy and girl involves a "repression" of sexual impulse, virginity, and chastity of thought and expression, but custom and the attitudes of the older people provide a constant stimulation of sexual interest in the direction of the familistic system. The status of boy and girl thus involves a definite kind of sexual organization, based directly upon social relationships.

Nowhere is this better to be seen than in the case of the young woman's "character." Here the Church fathers and the country people seem to have attained quite a unanimity. Sexual orientation is inseparable from social role. Sexual repute and status are identical. The authors do not say this identification is unique. They do not know its historical origins. But they do wish to point out its function in this setting: The young woman's "character" is her full status as a social being because the familistic system is such that sexual activity, no less than economic, is completely integrated with one's role in social life. Consequently her sexual conduct is no concern of hers alone.

In the relationships in family and community in which the young girls of the countryside find their roles, any departure from the norm of conduct on their part is cause for violent disturbance in the relations uniting others to themselves and to one another. To "destroy a girl's character" in the countryside is to upset the pattern of family and community life by overthrowing the possibility of an orderly change in farm succession. Much more than a shooting or a fight, a sexual irregularity which cannot be righted in a match is capable of destroying the intricate mutual obligations and expectancies of rural familism.

For the family whose "name" is "destroyed" and whose hopes of orderly re-formation are upset, two courses are open. One is to patch up a compromise, to accept the match forced upon them. The other is to expel the offenders bodily. Community feeling gives full support. In either case the girl concerned can no longer hope for full status. If the match is made or another husband found to father a child, time may right matters and give her full adult status as a farm wife and mother. Her failure as a girl may be forgotten, but it was a failure still. Otherwise there is little further to do but suffer expulsion. Emigration has been the refuge till recently.

The country people's attitude toward illegitimacy and pre-marital intercourse, one and the same to them, reflect well the disturbances they occasion. In discussing a local case, one woman could voice the community's opinion in the following general terms:

A young lady with a good fortune even, she couldn't get any man because her character is broken. Unless maybe he is very low. And so she usually goes to America and passes for a maiden. Everyone knows the father of the child but, if he has a good farm of land, no one would say anything, but he would be unlucky and have no family. He would get another woman [a wife, that is] with no bother. The baby might be sent to a home. And after a time they bring it home as a cousin.

But it is not always that the boys are treated so leniently, and they, too, must emigrate, driven off by public censure. For it is said by country people that "to destroy a girl's 'character' is murder." In the logic of the familistic system, the statement is true.

The following incident, described by a countrywoman in a discussion of religion, shows the fate of such cases and the verdict of the community.

There is no such place as hell. God forbid. No one would be there except a few murderers and a person who destroyed a girl's character. Sure to destroy a girl's character is murder. The C——— girl above was great with a boy who was her second cousin and she couldn't marry him here, so they made it up and he went to Canada, and she would go to the States, and they would meet there and marry. He had to go to Canada because he had bad eyes. They went away and seven weeks later she came back and in a few months had a child. Sure no one knows whether she went to the States or what happened to her. The boy was a red-haired, wild lad, and I often ask his sister above if she has heared from him. She says they haven't but we don't know whether they have or not.

209

The girl put a shame on all people. She isn't married now. Sure who would marry her now that her character is destroyed? The child died after eleven months, and she is living in the house there, and that is why she isn't married. Would you believe such things could happen in Ireland?

The last quotation contains a further consideration. Prestige and respectability are bound up with proper conduct and proper fulfillment of the role in social life one's status gives one. If the girl whose "character" is broken gets a husband at all, she must get one of lower standing in the community. She cannot expect to carry the full prestige of her own family with her, even if she does find a farm into which to take a dowry. As the woman quoted remarked, no one will take her unless he is "very low."

Failure to retain and advance in the status assigned the young of the sexes leads to the same kind of relegation to other cliques and other spheres of social participation as in the case of the followers of rural occupations other than the ownership of land.

Even among the country people improper behavior has the effect of declassing the offender. Just as the farmers attribute sexual laxity to the classes of the population they consider below themselves, such as fishermen, tinkers, and itinerant laborers, and the laborers of the town, so, by a reversal of the view, destruction of status over sexual misdemeanor condemns one to membership in such categories.

This declassing effect of sexual misconduct is, of course, strongest for young women. Apart from the moral censure misconduct brings upon a young woman and the shame it inflicts upon the people of her "name," it brings as well the destruction of her social role. It makes an end of her potentialities, for these, too, are her "character": potential motherhood of a familist line on the one hand, and potential transmission of an advantageous alliance on the other. In a familistic order they are identical. They are both based upon her sex. They make of the unmarried girl a sort of symbol of familistic aspiration. To use the symbol for any but its proper purpose of procreation and alliance is to destroy not only its efficacy but the aspirations that are attached to it. Rural Ireland, indeed, provides a sort of archetype or "pure" form of this sexual outlook, the conventional western European ideal of premarital virginity. It is important here as a living function of a closely integrated social system.

When we turn to the rural attitude toward sexuality in the old people, all those who have relinquished farm command in favor of a younger procreant couple, the norms of the small farmers present the reverse of the coin. Both rural expressions and rural standards of conduct seem to reflect the attitude that only the married have a sex life or, if others have it, they should not.

The first facet of this attitude shows itself in many kinds of situations. For instance, we have already seen that a woman whose son has married and who fails to get along well with the "new woman" may, quite without censure, move into the house of a daughter and share that house with the daughter's husband's father. Several cases came to notice in which women who had relinquished their farms moved in with the dead husband's brothers.

A famous joke between a well-loved old priest and his bishop in Clare based on a real incident plays around this last theme. On the occasion of his usual pastoral visit, the bishop congratulated the parish priest on the high moral standard of his parish. He had one reservation to make, however. He was shocked to learn that a couple who had recently moved into the priest's parish were living together openly and were not married. The parish priest caught the twinkle in his bishop's eye, but nevertheless he promised to make an inquiry and take necessary action. Next day he reported that he had learned that the couple were an old man and old woman, brother's wife and sister's husband, who had recently moved into a cottage together. They were both seventy, and had been living in the bishop's own parish for the last ten years. Since the bishop had been so shocked by

211

their taking the house together, the priest said he would send them back and let his lordship deal with the problem as he had been doing before.

In such cases, obviously, the difference of sex of the housemates as a danger to morality has disappeared. This agrees with the equation many country people seem to make between the "saintliness" of the old and their emancipation from the flesh.

By the same token, the old person who has already had his or her day of childgetting and childbearing, and yet still persists in manifesting sexual aspirations, is a stock figure of fun. He or she is the butt of endless ridicule and practical joking in the countryside. Again, of course, such laughter is best explained as playful censure. For very real censure often breaks out against such a person. It is particularly likely to break out into overt punitive action in cases where old farmers threaten the expectations of their heirs by taking young women as second wives. In fact, the one kind of man or woman of considerable age who does not command respect is this. The countryside finds endless amusement in the theme of May and November. Naturally the matchmaking system does lend itself fairly well to matings between oldish men and young women, since ownership of a farm is the basis for a match.

The most interesting point of inquiry, then, may well be the connection between the sexual status of the family members, as we have described it here, and the standing of the family. The sexual status of the members is a reflection of their capacity for carrying alliance among the other families of the countryside. Can we draw, therefore, a connection between rural familistic norms about sexual behavior and the class structure of the rural community?

We know already that marriage in rural Ireland yields us one clue to the connection. At matchmaking the negotiations between the contracting parties concern the relative standing of each. That standing is at stake. The equivalence of dowry and

212

land are arrived at through a careful enumeration of all the past history and the present material substance of the contracting families. The location of the farm, its livestock, its soil, the reputation and ancestry of the family, all these are compared. Backward places, we remember, do not grow big fortunes. Neither do many other kinds of persons and places.

We are dealing here of course only with one broad class, the country people. Yet within the boundaries of rural life there is much to be learned of the country people's treatment of relative prestige and standing among themselves. There are many behaviors in the activity of the countryside which express attitudes of social stratification. These do not only express the differences between the country people and outsiders from other classes beyond the confines of the local districts; they have much to do with the intimate details of personal relations in daily life among the small farmers as well. Intimate as they may be, however, these behaviors are nonetheless powerful. Like so much else in rural life, they find their chief expression and their most complete organization around marriage and matchmaking in country custom. In that they are directly a part of the organization of sexual conduct and attitudes among the small farmers.

From this fact springs the seeming paradox of Irish rural life, already mentioned. A social system centering so strongly round the institution of the family condemns a large proportion of its members to celibacy and long-preserved virginity. The explanation lies in the very paradox. Only through marriage does one attain full stature and one's family take its full place in the interlocking alliances of extended kindreds in the countryside. Failure to make a match is not only failure to fulfill one's own destiny of mating and procreating; it is also, as we have seen, failure to provide for the dispersal and re-formation of one's group. It is also, as we shall see, failure to maintain or establish the alliances making status among one's peers.

Thus it is the identification of sexual behavior with familistic

213

role on the one hand and attainment of status on the other that makes the problems of marriage and sex of such great social and emotional importance.

Their importance is both individual and social. Individually, the powerful dispositions and sentiments concerned give a deepseated biological and physiological basis to the institutional imperatives and the behavioral norms learned in experience of human relations. Socially, the fact that such a basis can be relied upon gives added strength to the attitudes evoked in support of the social institutions of the countryside and an added, automatic sanction to the enforcement, through public and official channels, of the accepted behaviors. In this manner, based upon and reinforced by such deep-rooted automatic reactions of individual conscience, the canons of morality, custom, personal habit, religious teaching, and social sanction form a whole piece all together. To hazard a comparison, let us select other central nexuses of custom, attitude, and emotion, among other peoples. By the process described, sexual morality becomes to Irish society, from the country people with whom we are dealing upward through other classes of society, what respect for law is to English society, what filial piety once was to Chinese society.

Let us now see how this mutual incorporation of sexual, marital, and stratificational standards works out in the experience of the countryside.

In the system of relations we have described, the fate of persons at the hands of their fellows and the repute they bear among them are closely connected. Local standing is, of course, a product of values arising in local experience. Consequently when we come upon the comedies and tragedies of life within a specific community, and hear described by the people themselves the course of events through which these little dramas took place and the impression they made upon the witnesses, we are close to observation of the experience which builds a scale of values and the place of individuals in it. The problem of local repute and

214

public opinion can be reviewed in the light of concrete events and referred to actual relationships built out of behavior.

Thus one can come to see these petty events not merely as personal histories but also as functions of the patterns of organization we have been detailing.

If then we should take up the life of a local community and its inhabitants and search it through for its family histories of recent years, we should lay bare the roots of local values. Such a study was made in one community studied. Family histories since the famine times were secured from two hundred families of a Clare parish. The histories included farms owned or rented, worked, subdivided, added or lost, in each generation since pre-famine days; names, numbers, sexes, and life-sketches of family members of each generation; occupations of each person not taking to farming; emigrations and the destination of the emigrants in each generation; marriages made in each generation, according to farms married into, occupations of husbands and fathers-in-law, and size of dowry. Much of this material was statistical in form, but along with it a considerable amount of anecdotal material was gathered, describing in detail many local incidents. This information is out of place here; and it will be reported elsewhere. But certain conclusions of relevance to the problem of understanding the social role of marital alliances in the countryside are of importance for the present discussion.

The first of these conclusions concerns the mechanism by which families without farms or with very small and "backward" ones were forced to extinction through celibacy. The second of these conclusions illustrates the means by which alliances made through the matchmaking mechanism provided a channel of upward social movement and incidentally a path of recruitment of the successful children of farmers in the "bad" or poorer lands into the ranks of those of the "good" or better lands.

The first conclusion illustrated by the material of this survey of family histories is one we have already met. Failure to make marital alliances led to failure of family re-formation and hence either to celibacy for all the children or to emigration on the part of the whole generation. In the words of the countryside, if a family could find no one with whom to marry "they died out of it."

Even so broad a question as the disappearance of the class of artisans in the countryside comes, for its explanation, under this conclusion. It cannot be understood except in terms of responses to values determined in the relations of familism. The social mechanism by which the local artisans have disappeared — whatever the historic and economic occasion of their fate in the industrial revolution and its aftermath — is something specific to the system of social organization we have described.

The few local artisans who survive today were once members of a numerous group. In the days before railroads and the growth of towns, each local community had its local artisans. Tailors, weavers, carpenters, shoemakers, and smiths followed their lifelong trades and supplied local needs. Their skills descended, like the farmer's farm, from father to son; the trade was "in their blood." Their surplus children have had to disperse to the towns and in emigration. For theirs, too, is a familistic world.

Unless the artisans in the countryside marry within their own fast-diminishing numbers, they, too, must have land and fortune. If they do not get it, they must either marry one of their own kind or stay celibate. Today one finds many survivors of this local class of craftsmen scattered here and there in the countryside. The mere memory of their trade may be all that remains to distinguish them from petty cotters. In the majority of cases they have not married. If they have, without a fortune to transmit, they can find no wives and husbands for their children. Thus the family "dies out of it." Neither alliance nor continuance can be theirs.

The mechanism by which this extinction is brought about is

clear enough. Occupational names have emotional significance far beyond their reference to skill and economic function. They are symbols evocative of social stratification, among the small farmers as no less elsewhere.

In disputes even within a family, angry reference to ties outside the family may well be a method of attack. Where, as here, such ties are a matter of one's "blood," the attack is direct and personal. One's status is part of one's person. How close a part it is can well be seen in the quotation of one farmer's account of transition in family relations at the match:

If the old people don't like the girl, then the mother and the father go to their room and fight with her every day; and if she has low blood in her, they will take her to task for it, if she has weaver, tinker, or tailor blood. If they don't like her they will not work like they used, but go out on *cuaird* and spread the bad news about her.

The familistic outlook gives all this kind of evocation and reference the character of genealogical commentary. Everything one does or is can be referred to one's "blood." Heredity is the explanation of success or failure, high position or low estate. Since one's heredity includes the occupational and other status of one's forbears and the whole gamut of relations which marked their place in the community, a continuity is preserved between the present and the past which defines one fully as a member of one's group.

Consequently, the instances of failure to find wives and husbands, the instances of courtships opposed by parental and other pressures, the instances of elopements ending in emigration, the instances of families of brothers and sisters who stuck together celibate until old age, are far oftener examples of the force of failure to find a mate of acceptable status than of any other cause. The organization of sexual behavior in the countryside is inseparable from that of the stratification of the community itself.

The second interesting point, again one in which the examina-

217

tion of family histories led to an illumination of the connection between the patterns of sexual organization and those of small farmer familism, is in a sense the reverse of the coin.

In these histories, when a countrywoman explained that she or someone she knew had married from bad land into good, or paid a larger dowry than she might have, had she stayed in her own townland, she referred to a movement that was quite readily discernible in her parish. She had experienced, and took pride in, a natural wedding of desire and ambition, which combined, for her as an individual, the instincts of a woman to be wife and mother and the demands of her group's advancement in the systems of familist alliances that made up her community. This was the individual side of the matter. Many indeed were the farmers and their wives who were careful to specify to us how successful a match had been in carrying a larger-than-might-be dowry to better land. One might grumble perhaps about one's lot, if there were anything to grumble over, but in such a case one might be proud that one had assured one's children of a better farm and a better standing than one's own.

But there was a social side of the matter which showed that this ambition was not a merely personal thing. For in the parish in which we gathered detailed information an interesting statistical movement could be seen. This movement was reflected in the geography of the district.

Marriages since 1864 in this parish have shown a tendency to move brides from the westward out of the poorer lands eastward toward richer farms. The parish happens to lie between higher, poorer soil to the westward and a more fertile area to the east. One must know the local topography and the fertility of the soil to understand the details of the movement. But its overall tendency is statistically clear. None of the marriages among small farmers and their fellows has taken place (if it took place in the County at all) beyond a six-mile range of distance between the farm married-out-of and the farm married-into. In all cases the movement is small. Yet, small as it is, it shows a distinct tendency. In general, the higher and more westerly townlands of the area made up of this parish and the contiguous parishes are the townlands from which marriages have moved brides outward. These same higher and more westerly townlands are also the ones that have lost population fastest and have been marked by the highest rates of celibacy. Since 1860, at least, families of this area have consistently paid higher dowries to establish their girls on better lands nearer urban and shopping centers. These families have married their daughters along the country roads downward and eastward, from the higher, poorer, more westwardly townlands to the better lands in lower and more eastwardly ones. Relatively speaking, there has been no movement of brides in a reverse direction. By comparison with the better lands, the poorer farms have done without brides for their young men. These poorer farms are the ones, then, who have seen their families "die out of it."

This is merely the evidence from one small parish and its neighbors. But it is instructive that it corresponds with the picture for Ireland as a whole, as the marital statistics of the censuses reveal it. Late marriage, celibacy, the marked preponderance of males in the sex ratio, are all phenomena of the western and poorer farming districts of the country.

Neither the establishment of a peasant proprietorship in the years of agrarian reform since the Land War nor the remarkable growth of prosperity among the farmers since the nadir of famine times has had any success in reversing the long-persistent trend of population decline in the countryside. They have had no effect either, it seems, upon the demographic phenomena associated with that decline. Perhaps the reason for the persistence of the trend despite all changes lies in the considerations revealed by the study of the matter in one small parish, as we have just described them. The acquisition of better lands, the growth of a greater rural prosperity, and the opening up of new opportunities at home have gone hand in hand with a persist-

219

ence of social sentiments and forms of social organization shaped entirely within the familism of the small farmers. The new opportunities have appeared first and foremost as means for personal and group advancement within the existing social and familist order.

One could hazard that the census figures represent not an "economic problem" in the sense of a flight from poverty or a fight against its restrictions but the movement of a population seizing upon new opportunities and new prosperity without relinquishing at any point the already existing organization of their social sentiments and habits. In such a view the problems of population decline in Ireland are results not of poverty but of prosperity.

However that may be, there is a close parallel between the opening of opportunities for education and for rise into the professions, the ranks of business in the Irish towns, and government, all taking place since 1870, and the demography of the small farmer class. The children of the small farmers have flocked through the doors opened to them into every walk of Irish life. They continue to do so today. The towns and their occupations continue to grow and grow, but the countryside does not. The process is one by which the long delays in marriage, the restriction of children to the few who can be well provided for, and the fierce centering of family ambition in the occupational status of its members, more usually thought of as urban, petit-bourgeois phenomena, have spread outward into the countryside and overtaken the small farmer on his farm. The mobility of a changing, democratized social order, capable of recruiting the ranks of one class from the children of another, has been combined with the fixity, the conservatism, and the rigidity of an ancient and still vital familism. It should be said that Ireland is not unique in this recombination of elements of social organization. She is unique in illustrating so well, in her special way, a social process universal in the countries of Western European civilization.

It has already been pointed out that the census figures available at the time of the fieldwork on which this book is based are those of the Irish census of 1926. Since that time some at least of the figures based on the succeeding decennial census, that of 1936, have become available. There are also a number of annual statistics which bear on the questions of Irish population. It is interesting to turn to these for the light they throw on subsequent development in the trends we have noted.

The release of the 1936 census figures in 1939 showed conclusively that the demographic trends that have marked Ireland since Famine times continue to persist. Neither the years of the establishment of the Free State up to 1932 nor the years of depression, economic war, and the experimental programs of the De Valera regime since then have affected the trends. Any of the charts prepared for the 1926 figures needs only to be extrapolated along the trend line a few points to show the situation of ten years later.

Stated briefly, these trends recapitulate and re-emphasize the points we have already made. Emigration continues to mark the life of the country, draining the countryside first into the towns and second overseas, now to Great Britain rather than across the oceans. Ireland continues to hold its record of possessing the highest percentage of unmarried men and women in the world. The population over sixty-five years of age continues to rise. The population of children continues to fall. Marriages continue to be fertile, by comparison with many other countries. But they still tend to become fewer and fewer, and the delay of marriage into middle life grows longer and longer. The ratio of females to males continues to fall, until in 1936 there were 975 males for every 935 females in Ireland, the lowest sex ratio in Europe and one of the lowest in the world.

These figures mark the continued existence of the familistic order we have discussed. They mark as well the continuance of its struggle to fit modern life. Perhaps a figure in the report of the Registrar-General for 1938 gives the best illustration of the culmination of the trends that mark this struggle. In that year slightly over half of all women who married (and only a negligible number of them were not making first marriages) were between thirty-five and forty-five years of age. The problem of delay in marriages seems to be reaching some sort of climax.

It is interesting to speculate what that climax might be and what future trend of demography it may inaugurate. It is obvious that the conditions these figures point to, rooted as they are in the social order of the countryside and of the nation, are in any case beyond the reach of ordinary measures. They have marked, as we have seen, every Irish administration since Famine days, whether native or not. They are not matters of "poverty" within the reach of immediate economic policies. If "poverty" refers to hunger and an absolute low level of living, the concept does not apply at all. If it denotes rather relative standing within a community of certain values, it has some meaning. But such meaning waits for its understanding on a realization of the form of family and community these values express.

Yet the old cry about a flight from the land has arisen in Ireland once again. Until the outbreak of war in 1939, the population question, linked now with continuing unemployment in the towns and a shortage of labor in the agricultural districts, had become a football of politics once more. The new small local factories of the regime of industrialization now have their place in the controversy. The opposition in the *Dáil* are bitter against a program they believe subsidizes industry at home out of the farmer's pocket, yet leaves him unable to employ the hands his farm requires. The government finds itself in a quandary. To accept the opposition view would be to admit itself responsible for a condition far beyond its control. To put a stop to the program of industrialization would leave the incoming farm sons and daughters with nothing to do at home. It would mean to give up all hope of absorbing them at home. Yet to build the factories is to send into the country districts the very forces of urbanism, such as wage payment, individual recompense, and a job rather than a part in group life, which wean the farm boys and girls away from a familist self-subsistence. Still the farmer of the familist tradition continues to vote the government in and continues to support the factories he must subsidize. For only by some such provision of occupations at home can he provide well for his children, as he must, by ambition and tradition.

There are farmers and farmers in Ireland. The small farmer is by all marks of social life a different person from the "big fellow." It is to be remembered that it is the little fellow who works the familist economy. Only the big fellow normally hires hands. Yet as sons and daughters leave for the towns and the town continues to make inroads on farm life, hired hands must take the vacant places. The migrant children must find new occupations with good pay and a steady hire. The process is one of continuous change at all points in the social order we are tracing out.

These population figures continue to mark, not any single cause or "factor" in social life, but the gradual, generation-slow transformation of an ancient culture, using that word in the anthropological sense. Its central core of familism is offering strong resistance to slow assault. But it changes, and along with it there changes the structure of the community that has been built upon a familistic base. The next chapters deal with these rural communities at the points of transformation: the nonfarming occupations in the countryside and the farmers' markets.

12

Occupation and Status

County Clare, like other more westerly Irish counties agricultural in outlook, presents a picture in which there is little industrial activity at all, comparatively speaking, other than that involved in agriculture, trading in market towns, and administration and communication. The fact holds pretty generally for the whole of the south of Ireland.[1] Whether the inhabitants like it or not, Ireland has long been peripheral to the huge English industrial centers. It has been little more than a market and a source of foodstuffs. A western region like Clare has been nothing more. Ireland was called not very long ago "England's bread basket." But we have already seen, where economic matters have come up, that such a view of her is a bit astigmatic. Ireland was her own bread basket first, long before she was anything else.

In rural Ireland outside the large cities, other industrial activity than that involved in agriculture is merely a matter of sup-

[1] At the time of the authors' study the De Valera government's program of industrialization had hardly begun.

ply and service, as far as the country people are concerned. The market towns, with their fairs, their shops, their banks, and their artisans and laborers, fill functions entirely distributive in nature.

This has not always been the situation. In 1810 the economist Wakefield found domestic woolen manufacture a widespread industry among the country people throughout Ireland. There seems even then to have been quite a widespread cottage industry in wool and linen, later to be destroyed everywhere except in Ulster. The peasantry displayed great ingenuity at the craft. The wool of their sheep was made into frieze at home, carded, spun, woven, dyed, and consumed there. Oils essential to the weaving process were extracted from fern roots, and dyes were got from alder, walnut, oak, and elderberry. This craft survives today as a cottage industry only in remote parts of Donegal and Kerry and in the Scottish highlands and isles. Such home-spinning was once widespread, probably universal. It survived here and there down to a very late date. In Ulster and northern England the industry was gradually brought into the factory, where it laid the foundation for the industrial revolution. But in the rest of Ireland industrial production of woolens was confined to Dublin by 1840 and, as a commercial enterprise, the wool trade was dead except in the region of Belfast. A few small factories survived in several towns, for example at Limerick, Clonmel, and Bandon, but there was no life or power of expansion in them.

Other manufactures originally native to the country repeat the story of wool. A few attempts at cotton manufacture died out. Linen suffered the same fate. At one time flax was grown extensively throughout Ireland, and a home industry of weaving linen was practiced widely in both town and countryside in many parts of the country. O'Brien[2] cites evidence that the older

[2] George O'Brien, *The Economic History of Ireland from the Union to the Famine* (London, New York: Longmans, Green & Co., 1921). See also O'Brien, *The Economic History of Ireland in the Eighteenth Century* (Dublin and London: Maunsel & Company, Ltd., 1918).

custom in linen making, strongest in Ulster, but not unknown elsewhere, by which weavers occupied plots of land and supplemented their income by farming, was gone by the famine time. Otway[3] describes the weavers of Drogheda in 1840 subsisting on conacre gardens (plots hired without right other than to the current crop) in circumstances of dire poverty.

O'Brien sums up his *Economic History* by concluding that the result of the first fifty years of the nineteenth century was that Ireland abandoned all pretense of being an industrial country and came to rely on agriculture to a greater extent than at any time formerly and even than in the eighteenth century. The accounts of Ireland at the time of the famine and after it bear him out. They show a very great lack of any kind of industrial activity other than agriculture.

The petty crafts of the countryside, which never gave any promise of reaching industrial proportions as those in the town centers might have, suffered a similar decline. But with them the decline seems to have come later and to have been part of the general change brought by the industrial revolution. All the supply crafts of the countryside have now come to be concentrated in the market towns. Nevertheless, through western regions, at least, local craftsmen, often with garden plots to help them eke out a living, seem to have long continued to be part of the local scene. In the novels of Carleton written just before and after the famine, many local shoemakers, cobblers, weavers, carpenters, smiths, coopers, nailers, and other followers of small trades appear. Upon them, the agricultural population depended for much of its tools and goods for local consumption. It is impossible to determine now how many of these were rural, since censuses of occupations before 1926 do not distinguish occupations in towns from those in country districts. But these men were part of the generally greater proportions of country

[3] Caesar Otway, *A Tour in Connaught* (Dublin: W. Curry, Jr., & Company, 1839).

dwellers before the rise of towns and the opening up of the rail-roads during the last century.

Another very great occupational change, though it does not show itself in any great numbers in census records, has been connected with the disappearance of the landlord from the western counties. A whole series of occupations clustering around the management of estates or the tastes of the local gentry and their families has gradually disappeared. Even the adoption of many of the conventions and habits, once exclusive marks of the Ascendancy, by other classes of the population has not served to stem the change.

If we fasten our attention directly upon determining what occupations are characteristically found represented in the countryside rather than in the towns in Ireland today, we get a picture of rural economy in which the followers of other occupations than farming are few indeed in the countryside. The occupations predominantly rural in Ireland are nearly exclusively those of farm ownership or farm labor. Only in recent years has there been any further development of rural pursuits to take the place of those going out with the changes brought about by modern communication and distribution of factory-made products. The chief of the new influences is not yet represented in full, even in the census of 1926. It is too recent a development. The introduction of creameries had not yet made its mark in that year. Plans for industrialization, since undertaken by the De Valera regime, had not yet even been drawn up.

To get a picture of rural life and the view of technological adaptation which it entails, we can look through the figures for a comparison of urban and rural industry in the years of the study.

Volume VI of the Irish census of population of 1926 entitled "Industrial Status" gives a view of the industries of the whole country and a preliminary view of the chief forms of industrial organization. Though the volume is largely concerned with unemployment, it also contains tables which classify those at work in the Free State according to occupation and employment. It distinguishes between employers (those employing persons for pay in their principal business) and employees (those working for others) and counts the latter by trade or industry or, if farmers' employees, by size of farm in acres. It further distinguishes those persons working on their own account and those assisting relatives. Persons employing domestics only are not classed as employers. Even in keeping these categories separate, the census ran into difficulties. The following statements indicate the troubles met in separating the smaller farmers from those who engaged in nonagricultural occupation and from hired farm labor.

Large numbers of small farmers and their sons work as agricultural laborers, road laborers, etc., as opportunity offers and many described their "principal occupation" in the census (1926) as agricultural labor or road labor. (In gathering agricultural statistics in 1927, they were recorded, however, as farmers.) This is the chief reason why the numbers of farmers, male and female, shown in censuses of population were always so much less than the numbers of occupiers of agricultural holdings as compared with the agricultural statistics.[4]

The introduction to the volume then compares occupiers and farmers from figures of 1929 and 1926 respectively, and finding the occupiers much more numerous than the farmers, particularly in Leinster, the writers conclude:

It is evident that large numbers of small farmers in all parts of the country did not describe themselves as farmers in the census and that this was more common in Leinster than in Connacht, as more employment can be obtained on the large farms and elsewhere in Leinster than in Connacht.[5]

Thus the presence or absence of big farmers in a district seems to have an effect upon the occupational status of the small farmers, in affording them the chance of employment away from

4 *Census of Population, 1926,* vol. VI: Industrial Status, p. ix.
5 *Census of Population, 1926,* vol. VI, p. x.

their holdings but within their own area. In such cases the small farmers are both employees and employers employing their own families.

In regard to such difficulties the introduction makes the following final qualifications of its own categories of industrial status:

As regards the numbers returned as employers, persons working on their own account, persons assisting relatives and employees, it should be explained that persons employing domestic servants only were not classified as employers, that persons assisted in business only by relatives who had no contract for wages were classified as persons "working on their own account," . . . persons working on their own account and persons assisting relatives were classed as employees (e.g., clergymen, nuns), and finally that many employers having small concerns (blacksmiths, dressmakers, etc.) described themselves not as employers as they should have done but as persons working on their own account.[6]

It is clear that, in segregating country occupations from those of the towns, industrial status as defined in the census is less significant than occupation itself.

For the whole country, taking in all industries, there were in 1926 as totals at work and out of work over twelve years of age some 850,000 men and some 341,082 women. Of these, those employing others numbered 62,605 men and 16,509 women, a fairly large proportion for employers. About 232,340 men and 62,949 women worked on their own account, and 196,034 men and 73,062 women were returned as assisting relatives. Employees of others numbered 402,631 men and 176,324 women. The figure for men, at least, indicates that those working for others were less in fact than those carrying on for themselves and families. The same fact is indicated for women, too, but only after the large figure of those engaged in "home duties" (a class which, according to the census, belongs in no industry at all) is

[6] *Census of Population, 1926,* vol. VI, p. xii.

included. At the time, 1926, the census recorded 6.9 per cent of men and 3.4 per cent women as unemployed, figures to be added to make industrial totals. The percentages were very low, and by the advent of the De Valera regime in 1931 had increased considerably. However numerous they are, they do not change the industrial picture very much in Ireland. Small enterprises predominate, and very little of the great developments of the machine age is present. The supply and service industries are in a definite preponderance, and in that fact reflect the country's dependence upon its agriculture and agriculturalists.

The Census of Occupations is quite different in purpose from that of industries and industrial status and proceeds by different counts. To quote the notes:

The difference between statistics of occupation and industries must be kept clearly in view . . . A person's occupation is defined by the operations he performs in earning his living: grainmiller, jamboiler, tramdriver, packer, clerk. A person follows his occupation within a certain industry or service. Some occupations are peculiar to a single industry or service . . . others are found in very many industries and services.[7]

The Census of Occupations is obviously in many ways an elaboration of that of industries. The two overlap frequently. Yet they are distinct enough to give us an alternate view of Irish industrial activity of great detail. If now we examine this view for what it will tell us of the survival of rural industry, we see again that occupations other than those of farming are very few indeed in the country districts.

Table 5 records the occupations of the whole country classed within industries. It lists followers of occupations living in rural districts in the left-hand column and followers of those living in urban districts in the right-hand column. Weighting the figures for all occupied persons properly between towns and country districts, we find that on the basis of chance expectancy

[7] *Census of Population, 1926,* vol. II, p. 5.

Table 5

Comparison of Rural and Urban Occupations, 1926
Irish Free State [a]

The table lists in the left-hand column, under the heading "Rural Occupation," those occupations 67 per cent or more of whose followers live in country districts or places under 1,500 population. It lists in the right-hand column, under the heading "Urban Occupations," those less than 67 per cent of whose followers live in country districts or places under 1,500 population. Percentage figures near 67 per cent are usually given; those greatly divergent are omitted. Industrial categories grouping occupations are listed at the head of the occupations. Figures for females of each occupation, and sometimes for males, are omitted if very small.

Rural Occupations	Urban Occupations
I. Agriculture and Fishing	
Farmers, male	Gardeners and nurserymen, 62%
Farmers, female	Gardeners' laborers, 62%
Sons assisting farmers	
Daughters assisting farmers	
Other relatives assisting, male	
Other relatives assisting, female	
Farm managers	
Agricultural laborers living in	
Agricultural laborers living away	
Woodmen	
Other agricultural labor	
Fishermen	
II. Mining and Quarrying	
Coal-mining	
Quarrying and other mining	
III. Producers, Makers, and Repairers	
a. Makers of Food	
Creamery workers, 80%	Employers, managers, 62%
	Bakers, pastry cooks, biscuit makers
	Sugar, sweet, jam makers
	Grain millers
	Other skilled food makers, including foremen
	Other unskilled food makers
b. Makers of Drink and Tobacco	
	Employers, managers, foremen
	Maltsters
	Other skilled workers
	Other makers of drink
	Makers of tobacco and snuff

[a] Based on Irish Free State Census, 1926, vol. II, Occupations. Categories are sometimes not exactly those of the census but are occasionally grouped together for convenience.

231

Table 5 *(continued)*

Rural Occupations	Urban Occupations
	c. Textile Workers
Breakers and scutchers, 89%	Employers, managers, foremen
Knitters, female, 67%	Spinners, piecers, carders, winders
	Winders, female
	Weavers, 49%
	Weavers, female, 30%
	Knitters, male
	Hand-lace workers, female, 65%
	Other skilled textile workers
	Other textile workers
	d. Makers of Apparel and Textile Goods
	Employers, managers
	Boot and shoe makers, 40%
	Cutters
	Tailors, tailors' machinists, 50%
	Dressmakers, female, 50%
	Sewers and sewing machinists, female
	Embroidering, female
	Other skilled workers
	Other workers
	e. Workers in Hides, Skins, Leather, not Boots or Shoes
	Workers in hides, skins
	Saddlers, 50%
	Other makers of leather goods
	f. Workers in Wood and Furniture
	Employers and managers
	Carpenters, 57%
	Cartwrights, wheelwrights, 28%
	Sawyers and wood machinists, 28%
	Coopers, 20%
	Basket makers
	Boat and barge builders
	Cabinetmakers
	Upholsterers, coach trimmers
	Other skilled workers
	Other workers
	g. Metal Workers
Employers, managers, 67%	Foundry workers
Smiths, 67%	Motor mechanics, 30%
	Cycle mechanics
	Mechanics
	Fitters
	Plumbers
	Tinsmiths, sheet-metal workers

Table 5 (*continued*)

Rural Occupations	Urban Occupations

Machine-tool workers
Boilermakers, shipwrights
Other skilled metal workers
Other metal workers

h. Electrical Workers

Electrical fitters and wiremen

i. Workers in Chemical Processes, Makers of Fertilizers, Soaps, Paints, and Workers in and Makers of Paper and Cardboard

Skilled workers
Other workers

j. Printers, Bookbinders, Photographers

Employers, managers, foremen
Compositors
Printers
Bookbinders
Photographers
Printing-machine setters and minders
Machine assistants
Others

k. Builders, Bricklayers, Stone and Slate Workers and Contractors

Foremen and overlookers, 75%
Masons, 75%
Platelayers, 75%
Contractors' laborers and navvies, 74%

Employers and managers
Bricklayers
Plasterers
Slaters, tilers
Other skilled workers
Builders' laborers, 25%
Other workers

l. Painters and Decorators

Employers, managers, and foremen
House, ship, general painters
Painters of vehicles
Other workers

m. Other Producers, Makers, and Repairers

Watch and clock makers and repairers
Workers in precious metals
Electroplate workers
Makers of bricks and earthenware
Makers of glass and glassware
Brushmakers
Other skilled workers
Workers in gas works

233

Table 5 (*continued*)

Rural Occupations	Urban Occupations

IV. Transport and Communication

a. Railway Workers

Station masters and railway officials, 50%
Locomotive engine drivers
Firemen
Cleaners
Guards
Signalmen, 58%
Shunters, level-crossing keepers, 40%
Ticket collectors, checkers
Railway porters
Other special railway occupations

b. Road Transport Workers

Proprietors, managers of motor car garages
Drivers of motor vehicles, 40%
Drivers of horse vehicles for passengers
Drivers of horse lorries, carts, vans, 25%
Tramdrivers
Tram and bus conductors
Grooms, 53%
Other road transport workers

c. Water Transport Workers

Ship owners
Harbor officials and stevedores
Navigating and engineering officers
Petty officers, seamen, deck hands
Firemen, donkeymen
Barge- and boatmen, 40%
Dock laborers
Other water transport workers

d. Other Transport Workers

Post office sorters
Postmen, 61%
Telegraph operators
Telephone operators
Telephone operators, female
Messengers
Porters
Other workers

V. Commercial, Insurance, Finance

Cattle, sheep, pig, horse dealers, 53%
Shopkeepers, male, 43%
Shopkeepers, female, 39%

Table 5 (*continued*)

Rural Occupations	Urban Occupations
	Shop assistants and salesmen, male, 30%
	Shop assistants and salesmen, female, 30%
	Buyers
	Agents and factors (coal, drapery, etc.)
	Commercial travelers
	Van salesmen and canvassers
	Hawkers of coal, vegetables, etc.
	Newspaper sellers
	Bank officials not clerks
	Insurance officials and agents
	Auctioneers and valuers
	Other commercial, insurance, finance occupations

VI. Public Administration and Defense, excluding Professional Men and Typists

Civil service officials and clerks
Local authority officials and clerks
Civic guards, 60%
Army, commissioned officers
Army, others
Others in defense

VII. Professional Occupations

Rural	Urban
Catholic clergymen, 65%	Other clergymen, 60%
Schoolteachers, male, 65%	Nuns and postulants, female, 34%
Schoolteachers, female, 67%	Christian brothers and monks
	Religious lay brothers
	Theological students, 54%
	Church officials, 50%
	Barristers
	Solicitors
	Medical doctors
	Dentists
	Veterinarians
	Midwives, female, 40%
	Sick nurses, female, 40%
	Music teachers
	Civil engineers and surveyors
	Chartered accountants
	Analytical chemists
	Professional students and articled clerks
	Journalists and authors
	Other professions

VIII. Personal Service

Rural	Urban
Gamekeepers, 87%	Domestic servants living in, male, 60%
	Domestic servants living in, female, 58%

235

Table 5 (*continued*)

Rural Occupations	Urban Occupations
	Domestic servants away, male, 40%
	Domestic servants away, female, 45%
	Hotel and restaurant keepers, male and female, 25%
	Publicans, male, 56%
	Publicans, female, 53%
	Bar attendants, male, 46%
	Bar attendants, female, 54%
	Waiters
	Laundry workers
	Hairdressers
	Caretakers
	Charwomen, office cleaners, female
	Others in personal service

IX. Clerks and Draughtsmen and All Typists, but not in Civil Service or Local Authority

Heads of commercial sections of business
Clerks, 14%
Typists, male
Typists, female
Clerks, female

X. Other Gainful Occupations — Entertainment

Race horse trainers and jockeys, 78%	Proprietors, managers
	Actors
	Musicians
	Other occupations, sport, entertainment

XI. Warehouses, Stores, Packing

Warehousemen and storekeepers
Packers and other warehouse assistants

XII. Other and Undefined Gainful Occupations

Stationary engine drivers
Timekeepers, gatekeepers
Watchmen
General and unclassified laborers, 25%
Other and unclassified occupations

XIII. Persons Twelve Years Old and Over not Gainfully Occupied

At school, 12–18, male, 69%	Retired from active occupation, not army or navy, 57%
At school, 12–18, female, 69%	Retired from active occupation, female, 50%
	Ex-officers of army and navy not described, 39%
	Students over 18, male, 50%
	Students over 18, female, 50%

any occupational class should have about two thirds of its members in the country districts and one third in the towns. It follows then that any occupation two thirds or more of whose followers are still recorded as country dwellers can safely be called a rural occupation. Any occupation whose followers are less than two-thirds country dwellers can be called urban.

In the table, therefore, occupations 67 per cent or more of whose followers are rural are listed in the left-hand column. They are called rural occupations for our purposes. Those occupations which have less than 67 per cent of their followers residing in the country districts are listed in the right-hand column. They are called, for our purposes, urban occupations. In some cases the percentage of the followers of an occupation who are country dwellers is given for reference, particularly where it is near the critical percentage, 67 per cent, but in most cases, where it is not close to 67 per cent, it is omitted.

In actual number the followers of nonagricultural occupations in the countryside are not a small army. They are 249,930 persons, to compare with 658,800 agriculturalists of one sort or another. Of this army the largest single total is to be found among the "other producers," that is, those not listed in the recognized census industries, such as transport, communications, trade and commerce, the professions, or "personal service." There are 194,969 "other producers" in the country districts today.

A glance at the left-hand column of the table shows that there are practically no characteristically rural occupations left other than agriculture and the small occupations of fishing, coal mining, quarrying, creamery working. Breaking and scutching and hand knitting are still country occupations, but their followers are few. The rest of the textile workers are characteristically townsmen today. Tailors and shoemakers and woodworkers, even carpenters, are townsmen today, overwhelmingly so, though among carpenters quite a few rural ones still survive. Smiths and employers in smithing and other metals businesses,

237

many of whom are presumably smiths employing a few hands, often their sons, are still country dwellers characteristically. Masons and foremen and overlookers of construction and building are still country dwellers, as are contractors' navvies and platelayers. Except for the smith, therefore, there are no characteristically rural artisans left outside the building trades.

Those in the building trades or in construction, in the west at least, are not highly skilled men at all, not even the masons. They are largely laborers and landless cotters who work for local authorities as stone breakers and suppliers of gravel and broken rock for road construction. They are often farmers' sons who get work off the farm whenever they find work is to be had. Yet the local mason who puts up stone houses in the countryside, and the petty contractor ready to get up a crew of local boys for any sort of building, are still characteristically rural dwellers and part of the rural scene.

In transport industries the only occupation which is even nearly rural in complexion is that of postman, for obvious reasons. The local post office is usually a small crossroads shop in the western counties. The post office workers are members of the rural communities they serve.

In commerce, in spite of the two currents at work, no occupation is characteristically rural. Dealers in animal produce, however, come closest to it. Yet most livestock and animal produce dealers are now townsmen, often town shopkeepers as well. The country shop at a crossroad is still important but not characteristic.

Civic guards, clergymen, and schoolteachers make up the only other occupational classes in the country who still live in the rural districts and are part of rural communities.

Three other occupational classes, according to the table, are also characteristically rural still today. These are gamekeepers, race-horse trainers, and jockeys. These are, of course, employees of the landed gentry who follow the cult of the horse. They are

238

more often to be found now in the eastern midland counties than elsewhere today.

In County Clare rural occupations other than agricultural are equally rare. There the figures necessitate a slightly different definition of rural districts, since certain towns smaller than 1,500 possessing local self-government are included in the town areas. But, by the same procedure as before, we can divide the proportions of total population into rural population in the county and then classify the occupations in Clare according to their rural or urban character.

In Clare, of course, there are no very large cities. The county counts 5,023 males and 5,522 females in town districts, and the overwhelming majority are country dwellers as one would expect in the agricultural west. The total rural districts in 1926 numbered 45,048 male inhabitants and 39,471 female. As befits a largely agricultural area such as the county, occupations and industries show a little different distribution. The population is for males 89 per cent rural and for females 88 per cent rural. Those gainfully occupied in rural districts number for males well over two-thirds of the total population, for females only one-fifth of the total, so that for men, at least, the numbers recorded as unoccupied are negligible. The low figure for occupied females is due to the inclusion of housewives among the unoccupied. The rural-urban ratio upon which we can build expectancies of proportions of followers of occupations to be found in towns or countryside is 92 per cent for males and 84 per cent for females. As for the whole country, female occupations are found only in the towns.

The table for Clare (Table 6) repeats practically exactly the same story as that for Ireland as a whole. In fact, the dropping away of rural occupations other than agricultural is even more marked. Yet the smith, carpenter, mason, building contractor, employer, and foreman, and their navvies and laborers are characteristically rural producers. Only they of all the occupations

239

Family and Community in Ireland

Table 6

Comparison of Rural and Urban Occupations, 1926, County Clare[a]

The table lists in the left-hand column, under the heading "Rural Occupations," those occupations 89 per cent or more of whose followers live in country districts or places under 1,500 population or in places having local self-government (a special case). It lists in the right-hand column, under the heading "Urban Occupations," those occupations less than 89 per cent of whose followers live in country districts or places under 1,500 population. Percentages near 89 per cent are given; those greatly divergent are omitted. Industrial categories grouping occupations are listed at the head of occupations. Occupations represented in Table 5 which are not listed here have so small a following in Country Clare that they are included among "Others." Figures in parentheses following occupations give the total numbers for County Clare.

Rural Occupations   Urban Occupations

I. Agriculture and Fishing

Agricultural occupations, male, 99%   Fishermen, 84% (199)
(23,572)
Agricultural occupations, female, 99%
(5,307)

II. Mining and Quarrying

Mining and quarrying, 92% (21)

III. Producers, Makers, and Repairers

a. Makers of Food

Employers, managers, 60% (21)
Bakers, 50% (82)
Makers of foods, female, 61% (13)
Others, 20% (80)

b. Makers of Drink and Tobacco

Makers of drink, 99% (12)
Makers of tobacco (0)

c. Textile Workers

Textile workers, male, 95% (43)
Textile workers, female, 87% (15)

d. Makers of Apparel and Textile Goods

Employers, managers, 70% (48)
Tailors, 67% (180)
Bootmakers, 65% (141)
Employers and managers, female, 70%
(14)

[a] Based on Irish Free State Census, 1926, vol. II, Occupations. The Census does not divide occupations within this category between rural and urban districts for Clare. It gives merely the total for the category of occupational classifications.

240

Table 6 *(continued)*

Rural Occupations	Urban Occupations

Dressmakers, female, 71% (304)
Milliners, female, 50% (43)
Others, female, 50% (13)

e. Workers in Hides, Skins, Leather, not Boots or Shoes

Saddlers, 67% (45)

f. Workers in Wood and Furniture

Employers, managers, foremen, 71% (38)
Carpenters, 84% (491)
Cartwrights, 40% (27)
Others, 60% (66)

g. Metal Workers

Employers, managers, 84% (56)
Smiths, 85% (199)
Fitters, 67% (31)
Plumbers, 50% (11)
Motor mechanics, 40% (91)
Other mechanics, 80% (69)
Others, 80% (112)

h. Electrical Workers

Electrical apparatus makers and fitters, 80% (87)

i. Workers in Chemical Processes, Makers of Fertilizers, Soaps, Paints, and Workers in and Makers of Paper and Cardboard

j. Printers, Bookbinders, Photographers

Compositors and printers, 100% (16)

k. Builders, Bricklayers, Stone and Slate Workers, and Contractors

Contractors' laborers and navvies, 91% (2,054)

Employers, managers, foremen, 88% (136)
Bricklayers, 40% (5)
Plasterers, 42% (28)
Masons, 87% (114)
Builders' laborers, 43% (121)
Others, 78% (88)

l. Painters and Decorators

Painters and decorators, 43% (65)

m. Other Producers, Makers, and Repairers

Others, 50% (50)

IV. Transport and Communication

a. Railway Workers

Railway officials not clerks, 84% (21)
Locomotive engine drivers, 67% (34)

241

Table 6 (*continued*)

Rural Occupations	Urban Occupations

Firemen, 33% (16)
Porters, 60% (45)
Others not clerks, 60% (41)

b. Road Transport Workers

Proprietors, managers, foremen, 50% (21)
Motor drivers, 50% (231)
Drivers, horse vehicles for passengers, 60% (13)
Drivers for goods, 50% (96)
Others, 50% (6)

c. Water Transport Workers

Dock laborers, 9% (54)
Boatmen, 88% (116)

d. Other Transport Workers

Postmen and post-office sorters, 89% (190) Messengers, 50% (39)
Porters, 13% (63)
Others, 80% (5)

V. Commerce, Insurance, Finance

Cattle, sheep, horse, pig dealers, 65% (69)
Shopkeepers, 62% (574)
Shopkeepers, female, 55% (341)
Shopkeepers' assistants and salesmen, 50% (378)
Shop assistants, female, 54% (263)
Commercial travelers, 40% (25)
Van salesmen and canvassers, 50% (15)
Insurance canvassers and agents, 50% (19)
Others not clerks and typists, 47% (83)
Others not clerks, female, 80% (10)

VI. Public Administration and Defense, excluding Professional Men and Typists

Civil service officers and clerks, 68% (102)
Local authority officers and clerks, 59% (78)
Civic guards, 82% (260)
Army officers, 5% (42)
Civil service officers and clerks, female, 86% (93)

Table 6 (*continued*)

Rural Occupations	Urban Occupations

Local authority officers and clerks, female, 30% (15)

VII. Professional Occupations

Rural Occupations	Urban Occupations
Catholic clergymen, 90% (120)	Other clergymen, 69% (13)
Theological students, 90% (32)	Christian brothers and monks, 35% (14)
Mental attendants, female, 91% (37)	Nuns and postulants, 50% (227)
Schoolteachers, male, 86% (200)	Solicitors, 40% (10)
Schoolteachers, female, 91% (322)	Medical doctors, 77% (46)
	Dentists, 13% (8)
	Civil engineers and surveyors, 79% (28)
	Other professional, 63% (90)
	Other professional, female, 75% (23)
	Mental attendants, 50% (33)
	Registered midwives, 75% (4)
	Sick nurses, female, 77% (121)

VIII. Personal Service

Domestic servants, male, 83% (63)

Domestic servants living in, female, 78% (1,312)

Domestic servants living out, female, 75% (451)

Hotel and boarding-house keepers, male, 78% (45)

Hotel keepers, female, 50% (157)

Publicans, 70% (229)

Publicans, female, 75% (145)

Bar men, 75% (76)

Barmaids, 76% (113)

Waitresses, 67% (15)

Laundry women, 60% (27)

Charwomen, 30% (24)

Others, female, 40% (11)

Hairdressers, 30% (19)

Others, 57% (57)

IX. Clerks and Draughtsmen and All Typists, but not in Civil Service or Local Authority

Clerks, all typists, male, 45% (153)

Clerks, all typists, female, 57% (82)

X. Other Gainful Occupations — Entertainment

Entertainment and sports, male, 59% (42)

XI. Warehouses, Stores, Packing

Warehousemen and assistants, 75% (23)

Table 6 (*continued*)

Rural Occupations	Urban Occupations

XII. Other and Undefined Gainful Occupations

Stationary engine drivers, 80% (45)
All others, 50% (33)
All others, female, 60% (41)
General laborers, 48% (387)

XIII. Persons Twelve Years Old and Over not Gainfully Occupied

Rural	Urban
Retired, 87% (637)	Ex-officers, ex-soldiers, etc., 69% (137)
At school, male, 87% (3,504)	Students over 18 not elsewhere recorded,
At school, female, 86% (3,482)	83% (92)
Others, male, 90% (1,620)	Not yet at work, male, 77% (281)
Engaged in home duties, female, 88%	Not yet at work, female, 75% (336)
(17,657)	Others, female, 83% (3,602)

and crafts survive in rural districts, with the exception of the very few textile workers. But the figures for the weavers of Clare are somewhat deceptive, since one of Clare's few industries was a tweed factory in Sixmilebridge, a town just too small to be excluded from the rural districts. Actually except for them the rural weaver is nearly entirely gone.

In Clare, as in the whole country, two professional occupations are still rural. Priests and schoolteachers are country dwellers. And theological students, characteristically "strong" farmers' sons destined for the priesthood, are rural too. That female mental hospital attendants should be characteristically rural in Clare is a statistical accident due entirely to the fact that the County Mental Hospital happens to be just outside an urban boundary.

The statistical record restates the fact that today in Ireland no less than elsewhere social differentiation on the basis of occupation and technique is an urban matter. The countryside has been relegated entirely to the agriculturalist. Only very few others occupy the countryside with him in the face of the extreme division of labor of modern industrial civilization. The Irish countryside is an extreme example of the relegation of the rural districts to agriculture. Nevertheless the statistical record shows us that a few of the rural artisans survive. It demonstrates too

244

that a few men of professional status still serve the rural community. Even the crossroad shopkeeper is an important rural figure still, though he does not count a sufficiently large number to
distinguish himself statistically as a rural occupation.

Occupational and technological differentiation is thus not entirely lacking in the country districts. Such division of labor of
a nonagricultural character as still persists in the country communities is very simple. Yet it is an interesting part of community life. It affords status to local artisans in the lives of the
small farmers.

The families upon the separate farms are not, of course, entirely self-dependent units. We have already had occasion to examine the kind of cooperation called cooring, often based upon
the extended family which flourishes in the country districts.
Such reciprocal aids in ordinary farm work are only one part of
the fabric of services which one meets among the country people.
Another part can be distinguished. It takes account of what ele-
mentary specialization in local techniques and handicrafts exists.
The man or woman skilled in some particular branch of work is
called the "handy man." The handy man is an important person
at the times when his or her special skill comes into use. The
local reputation of such a specialist is sufficient to keep the recognition of his skill alive between periods of use and to afford
him a definite status. In the country districts of Clare even full-
fledged artisans, appearing in census records as full-time carpenters, smiths, and the like, sons of fathers and grandfathers
who followed the same trade, are not much more than local specialists.

Many a farmer is still a jack-of-all-trades, ready if need be to
turn his hand to shoeing his horse or resoling a boot or building
himself a house. Only where the products of factory and foundry
have become deeply entrenched in farm life, embodying skills
of distant workers abroad, do local goods and services represent
techniques the small farmer cannot come close to emulating.
For example, the smelting of iron is a process completely un-

245

known, and neither the local blacksmith nor the farmer can do more than rework the iron they have at hand. But the blacksmith and the farmer both can do it, though it is the blacksmith who has the greater skill. In the countryside the techniques and the products of specialized labor are open and visible to everyone, and in some measure they are part of the lore which each man learns. Not all the men come to practice them, but they have all seen them or heard them described, and they are part of the fund of conversation, precedent, and value which is common coin among the people of the community. One's special craft does not segregate one from one's neighbors or take one outside the community here. Rather it is one's mark or sign, one's reputation and status within it.

This is the case particularly where, as here, most of the craftsmen of one sort or another have always depended upon a plot of land or a kitchen garden behind their cabins, with perhaps a pig or a cow or two, nearly as much as they depended upon their craft. By this dependence they were never segregated from the rest of the local population, either physically or occupationally. They too were agriculturalists of a sort and shared farmers' tribulations. Just as the farmers knew something of their techniques, so the local craftsmen were nearly always proficient in the ways of agriculture. Today in rural Clare the handy man may be anything from a veterinarian or bonesetter to a building contractor. He is always without benefit of law, apprenticeship, or formal training, and merely follows a technique of which everyone knows something. The farmers are ready to pass upon his skill, to debate the technical points of his work, to build up or tear down his reputation.

Down to the time of the World War, in the last generation, the close acquaintance the small farmers had with the special skills of the countryside was reinforced by the interest the farmers had in putting their sons to a trade. They could often find a place for them thus. In the towns even today formal apprenticeships, into which the farmer must pay for his son to enter, still flourish.

The statements one can get about the local specialists, at least of those of the better recognized trades, are direct and intimate. The following words illustrate something of the character of apprenticeship. A small farmer is speaking of his own knowledge of local conditions:

Before the war there used to be about twenty shoemakers in the neighborhood, but now they've mostly gone away or are in the towns. One of them went into Ennistymon. Whenever a farmer wants a strong pair of boots even yet, he will not go to a shop but he would go to the shoemaker. It wasn't always the case the son of a shoemaker would follow the trade because there was good money in it. With it they would buy a farm and so for his sons, and they would go to farming. If a farmer had a crippled son, he might send him to the shoemaker to teach him the trade. Papers were signed that bound the boy for three years to the tradesman, and then the boy would go live with the shoemaker. At first he would be taught to tap, then to stick, then to sew, and the last thing would be to cut. If a boy left before the three years were up, no one would give him a job, and no other tradesman would take him on to teach him a trade. The father had to give twenty pounds to twenty-five pounds to teach him. At the end of three years the boy was given his indenture papers which meant he could set himself up any place in the country or, if he had not enough money to do that, he would work as a journeyman for someone else and his papers would give him the right to do it.

There were a great many tailors and smiths too. The time of work was three years. A boy who was a cripple might be sent to tailoring. He was taught three years and then he could set himself up. It was the easiest of them all to get along with because it required no money to start with. In the old days the tailor used to come to the house and stay for a week or so and make clothes for all the men of the house and go to the next house after.

The smiths trained boys also. When I was small, a cousin of mine had a forge below on the road and any wet day all the boys used to gather there and watch and talk. I started out by blowing the bellows and then doing other things until finally I was as good as anyone. If I had the material I could make shoes, and I always shoe my own horses.

247

Of these local specialists only the smith survives in any strength today. He shares with the mason the admiration the country people feel for physical strength and prowess. Perhaps it is this that made the more sedentary occupations of weaver, shoemaker, and tailor of less prestige. Thus the crippled son, as the quotation says, might be put to one of them.

The tailor was often a peripatetic. He moved around from house to house and community to community where he was known, living and eating among the family. He was made welcome, not only as a maker of clothes but also as a carrier of gossip. Today the few tailors who survive in the country districts are petty cotters with only a memory of their trade. The few still active ones have retreated to the towns. Most of the farmers' clothing is now shop-bought and factory-made.

The weaver was perhaps the most sedentary of the local craftsmen. He is the one who has failed to survive even in the towns. The women of the farm families carded and spun the wool into yarn until home spinning died out, and broke and scutched the flax for linen, but the weaver made it into cloth. He spent all his days indoors, moving from one side of his loom to the other in a small room heavy-laden with fluff and lint. The farmers seem to remember most strongly the unhealthiness of the life, but they tell one also of the weavers' arrogance when their skill was in great demand. The following is the kind of description one can still get, the first part of it discoursing on weavers in general and the second relating the history of the local man:

In the old days the weaver might have enough work to keep him busy for four months and, when you went to see him, he would put you off and tell you to come back in a fortnight for your goods. It would be no good for you, none in the world, if you didn't take a bowl of butter and a few dozen eggs to him as a way of getting him to start on your yarn in a hurry. If you didn't, he would not do it until he got ready. They were independent, all right, and then when they were finished, you had to reach down into your pocket and pay for what he did. There used to be a lot of weavers here, but they are all gone now. The women have got out of weaving the wool.

248

A weaver here, Paddy Seán R——— , was a very fine fellow though he drank a lot. You cannot blame him for that because his job was a mean one and bad on the health. He worked to keep his mother out of the workhouse and till the day she died he would not let her go there. Wasn't that a decent thing for him to do? Afterwards he went to Galway and then he came back here and as an old man he died in the workhouse. But wasn't it a decent thing he would not let his poor old mother go and her going up the streets of the town every morning collecting the urine from the people who lived in the houses [to use for bleaching].

These three occupations were the meaner ones in the eyes of the country people. It was not that they degraded their followers. Rather it was that they were intrinsically of less value than the more robust crafts of outdoor life. Something of the sexual dichotomization of labor was involved in this attitude equating sedentary, house-bound pursuit with the feminine spheres of activity.

The chief exponents of the robuster, more masculine crafts within local ken were the carpenter, the mason, the house builder, and the smith. But there were many others. Between the landless or "backward" cotters and laborers, who might turn their hand to anything, and the small farmers, who were themselves occasionally forced to turn to harvesting abroad or to road-mending and stone-breaking at home, there were as many specialists as there were activities in which special renown and skill could be attained. In fact, the development of local skills seems restricted only by the limits of the *matériel* which peasant life requires.

Other local experts were the thatcher, the cattle doctor or "vet," often a herdsmen with a lifelong experience of cattle, the butcher, expert at pig killing and skinning (pigs are regularly butchered on the small farms), the expert at rigging the great hayricks which stand in the farmers' haggards, and, lately, the threshing machine experts. All these robust, outdoor specialists are male. The feminine sphere of life does not seem to have bred such specialization. Yet many women were known

249

also for their special skill at this and that branch of women's work and were consulted accordingly. Nevertheless, the only traditionally feminine crafts to develop and flourish apart were witchcraft and midwifery.

A local craft or proficiency seems to develop out of some special crucial activity in local life. A local craft or skill of the kind that meets us here builds up directly out of social life itself. It is a development of habitual association about any person who gradually builds a reputation for a particular proficiency. The proficiency may center around some traditionally established technique of peasant life, like the weaving of homespun and shawls, the clothing of the small farmers, or else it may build up about local conventions having no direct economic value. Dances, gambles, and other entertainments and ceremonies of local social life may likewise afford areas in which a special skill gains recognition, gradually to grow into an occupation.

Thus the local specialists included fiddlers, singers, poets, storytellers. In the last century, in a day of great poverty and much displacement from the land, each of these skills gave an occupation to many wanderers along the roads of Ireland. Their followers found employment in the rural communities among the small farmers. Even itinerant dancing masters once flourished in the country districts during Carleton's day.[8]

The existence of other conventions leads likewise to the habitual utilization of persons specially skilled in them. They are the ones to whom the small farmers habitually resort. Thus legal sanction might become necessary for matchmaking as soon as land reform made the farmers legal owners of the farms they transfer in the match. But a long experience of court tangles and reprimands by judges was necessary to establish the licensed solicitor as the channel for negotiation. The handy man who was a legal expert and had a fine copyist's hand in the country districts flourished quite a while longer, and flourishes occasion-

[8] Students of Gaelic culture have described these artists very amply. See Robin Flower, Daniel Corkery, et al.

ally even now. In the country districts, down to the present, these local specializations were acquired through personal association of one kind or another with former specialists. Very often skills are deemed hereditary in the eyes of the country people. But actually they are acquired as often through gradual development of habit begun out of interest and imitation as by inheritance and parental instruction. They are passed on quite often to others than sons. The following extract from field notes illustrates the development of such skills:

The local man who cuts hair here is a handy man; the man Donnolly, who goes about and kills pigs for his neighbors is a handy man. When we asked, we were told by Flanagan that Donnolly was the butcher and handy man. They butcher only sheep, goats, and pigs. Cattle would be killed by the town butcher. Flanagan said Donnolly was not a true butcher, for he did not serve his time. If they want a boy to be a butcher, they send him to town and pay a fee and he would be trained there. Then they take out papers binding him. Donnolly said he learned it when he was a young man, but now that he was getting old he was not doing it any more. It takes several men to hold the pig, put a hook through the mouth, and kill it with a heavy blow on the head. They take it home, lay it on a table, and take a knife and cut it up. Then it is hung up, salted, and cured. Afterwards the butcher is given a bottle of stout for his work, as well as some fresh meat, while the husbands who helped get nothing.

The country people distinguish between these men who are handy men and have had no formal induction into their trade and those who are legally recognized as "tradesmen." But the line of formal distinction is thin, and more recognized in the abstract than in the concrete. Thus in the story of the development of one local mason, one can see that the difference lies rather more in the kind of remuneration than anything else. One farmer's account of the "tradesmen" of his knowledge led him on as follows:

There are other men who are carpenters and masons who are handy men, but they usually work for pay because the job might take several

251

days, and no neighbor could stay away from his work with a friend for that length of time. Donovan is a mason and he taught himself. He built his own house and several others. A man cannot build a house because he would not know how to do it. Donovan is a very intelligent man. He has a terrible head on him.

That the difference of remuneration is seized upon by countrymen as the distinguishing mark came to the authors' notice again and again. The handy man is the local resident who fits into the local pattern of courtesies, barter, gifts, as in the case of the butcher, described above, who got his reward in the shape of the meat shoved under his arm. In cooring, of course, one never pays. In any act of "friendship" and alliance in a familistic setting no formal remuneration of monetary payment is ever present. We have already seen that it is only at the crucial period of family reorganization, when the whole system of relations between members undergoes change, that any considerations of money enter the schedule of rural services and rewards. The same absence of money payment is the point of distinction here. It distinguishes the relations between the men of a local community and one of themselves who is "handy" through special experience from those between formal client and tradesman. Money payment is the mark of the outsider; gift and barter that of the fellow in the local community.[9]

For example, O'Sullivan, the "vet" of Rynamona, already mentioned, was a herdsman who did his cattle doctoring in his spare time. His services were always at the call of his neighbors. He seems to have been fairly good at his practice. He was quite widely sought after. His interest led him even to an experimental turn of mind. He said he often cut up cattle to see what killed them. In every description of him given by his neighbors they insisted he never took a penny for his work.

[9] Weavers, carpenters, thatchers, and masons may, of course, receive payment for their work, and do so. But such payment is made usually either where a farmer is in no position to return favors or does not want to enter a permanent relationship of cooring. The methods are alternatives.

252

The many bonesetters, whose help is much sought after, reject payment too. They are so numerous that a local dispensary doctor in Clare could complain that he had never been trusted to set a fracture but was consulted only to make sure a fracture had occurred. Even townsmen always emphasized in justification of local custom that the bonesetter accepted no money. Legal requirement has something to do with it. Statutes protecting legitimate doctors and veterinarians from this sort of competition exist and can be invoked, but that is only part of the story. The greater part of the matter lies here: The handy man is part of the local community. He is one of the farmers who has specialized, and thus he is within the pattern of reciprocal services and mutual aid.

Such a figure as the blacksmith, who follows a recognized trade and is paid for it accordingly, distinguishes carefully between the services for which money payment is possible and those which cannot be so remunerated. In the following case we can see that he distinguishes nicely in this tact indeed, for he can be paid in other communities for services for which he cannot accept payment at home. A blacksmith in North Clare is telling of himself in paraphrase:

He is called the blacksmith by the people around; his place is called the forge. He is also the local horse doctor. He has about a hundred and twenty horses which he shoes for the surrounding farmers. His father, whose place he has now taken, is too old to work and so he does it all.

A rainy day is the time when the farmers bring their horses in to be shod, for it is then that work cannot be done on the farms. That's the time he will be busy all day, and it is very hard work. The shoe must be made to fit the horse. You work the fire with the bellows and put on the special coal for the forge. Usually the man whose horse it is will work the bellows for him.

He buys the iron in long strips and makes it up himself. The price is six shillings for a new set of shoes and three shillings for refitting an old set.

He keeps account of what the farmers owe him and usually between the first of November and the beginning of the new year they come in and pay. They pay once a year and he never sends an account or presses for the money. If they are poor people, he never charges and overlooks it until they have the money to come in. They come from about four miles around and he has the same ones year after year. He never charges them for looking at the horses. His father was a great horse doctor, better than himself. He was great for growths, sore teeth, or internal trouble. From miles around the farmers would come to have their animals treated. No charge was ever made for this of any man who had shoeing done with him, but a man from a distance would be charged. His father took a trip once through Galway and Connemara curing the ills of horses and he charged enough to pay his expenses and a little more.

Here we see the same consideration at work as in the case of the handy man carpenters and masons. When the exercise of skill is expanded to a point where it fills the workman's working existence, clearly setting him off from the farmers, the farmers recognize his role as a fit subject for money payment. When his work is only the occasional avocation of one of their own kind, they do not. For this reason the midwife always differed from the local nurse. The midwife got her reward in presents, gifts, and whiskey, but not in money. Money, however, would be profferred to the nurse.

That the factor of payment in money should be crucial is really the cloak of the set of dispositions arising from habitual relations. In the local community the handy man is not paid, since, like "friends" and neighbors, he is one of themselves. Since he is one of the countrymen, he is caught within the system of much the same habitual relations of reciprocal service and mutual aid which make up cooring in agriculture.

To see this point, we must describe the action of the local community in respect to the work to be done once again. Cooring is a form of reciprocal exchange of goods and services. One old fellow described it aptly when he said that it meant that for a day of work given you would receive a day in return. We have already seen its connection with familism and the extended family. But besides cooring, there was another form of the custom known as *meitheal* (mihil). The word *comhair* (coor) referred to the reciprocity, the word *meitheal* to the band of men and teams acting together to perform a task. On various occasions when work beyond the capacity of cooring families was to be done, a *meitheal* of men or women or horses could be made up.

As described by the old people who still remember its heyday, the *meitheal* rested on a foundation slightly different from the reciprocity of cooring. The work was done by a gang of local persons got up for the purpose through the wish and custom of the local inhabitants, but without expectancy of individual return in like measure.

Bands of men and women were got up in rural communities by *meitheal* for the following purposes, of which the authors heard record:

1. Mowing and harvesting for priest and school teacher.
2. Mowing and harvesting for an old couple without children who could not do it themselves.
3. Hauling and moving where many horses were needed, as a *meitheal* of horses, for bringing sand or seaweed manure from the coast, or moving and resettling a family.
4. Rebuilding a house and resettling an evicted family.
5. Collecting a *meitheal* of girls with their spinning wheels from all the community's houses to spin after shearing.
6. Collecting a *meitheal* of men and girls for various processes connected with the conversion of flax to linen.

There were probably many other more extraordinary kinds of cooperative action. But the above list exhausts those which are remembered by the local communities the authors knew in Clare and which are unconnected with the more directly reciprocal and familistic pattern of cooring. The difference between *meitheal* and *comhair* was not a contrast, however, by any means. The term *meitheal*, applied strictly, referred to the band of persons and their tools got together. Yet there was a certain unanimity in the country people's feeling that the word *meitheal*

255

should be reserved specifically for occasions of the local community's communal action. In *meitheal* work no individual or family expected a like return.

Community action in concert, in which bands of workers are got up for specific purposes, is nowadays very different. Most of the characteristic actions of *meitheal* remembered by the old people are no longer carried out. Just as in the case of cooring, the need of the small farmer for his fellows is no longer so great. Monetary hire is spreading into the country communities. Yet even today the schoolteacher and the priest are donated services at hay harvesting occasionally, though nowadays schoolteacher and priest rely no longer upon bits of land and garden for support but upon fixed monetary salaries from state or church. Such aid is of little importance in their economies. Likewise, old age pensions and other benefits have removed the necessity of action by *meitheal* for the support of the aged and childless. General prosperity and the spread of machinery and tools have made it unnecessary for such concerted action in other cases, and local self-sufficiency is no longer so complete.

Nevertheless, the foundation of mutual relations between members of the local community upon which *meitheal* was based still exists. It can be called into play in emergency or under special circumstance still. Not all the townsman's accusation that the spirit of self-help and self-sufficiency has gone out of the country people is true by any means. They still will buckle to a community task, if necessity forces action, quite willingly. But they have learned that they have a voice nowadays in the kind of activity to which public funds and public works shall be put. This awareness is part of the extension inward into the community of the lines of relationship with persons and institutions external to the farm community which is so characteristic of the age. Such relationships are now made use of where before there were none of them beyond appeal to a landlord.

Some description of the former kind of activity might be of

interest here, though it is in the nature of a digression. The techniques of the last century, particularly those of wool and flax, were different from those of today; yet the situation is in other respects quite like that of today as far as the organization of persons in the community is concerned. The age groups of old and young, the sex division of activity between men and women, and the reciprocities between family groups and the direction of the community in the hands of the old men were even more marked than they are today. But nothing fundamental has changed except the techniques.

The following is an account of the older custom in weaving:

A man would go to town and buy two or more pottles of flax to sow. Then on the first of May he would go to the garden and plant it. In August he would pull it up by the roots and lay it in small bundles to be made into stooks. Then they would take it and put it into a bog and leave it there fifteen or twenty days, after which they could dry it in the house by hanging it from the rafters. About the first of November you would take it down and some men would come in and help break it. They would then put it back and later take it down and scutch it with a pronged tool, drawing the flax over it and breaking it.

Some time about Christmas time you would have a *meitheal* of girls come in and they would sit in a semicircle round the fire and clove the flax. It would take several days depending on how much you had. The girls would stay with you all that time. At seven in the evening they would be through and within half an hour you could hear them in the hills leaping and shouting. About eight or eight-thirty the boys would begin to arrive and there would be a dance and be no more good out of them for that night. They might have a dance every two or three days. You fed them good.

The next thing was the hackling, and this might be done by men or women. You had a box with iron prongs sticking up and you would hit the stalk against the irons and the small particles would fall into the box below. It might take several nights. Old man Roughan was a great man at the hackling, but he was always great for nothing else to do with flax. It was fine if you got him to come and help you and he would be glad to do it. Then you might be good

257

at something else and you would go and help him with that. Some men were good at one thing and others at something else and they would help each other.

After this the next thing was the spinning, and this was done by the woman. She would sit in this corner by the fire and she might be there every night, or whenever she had the time, spinning the flax fiber into thread. She had no one to help her and it was a hard job. After it was made into thread, it would be taken out and bleached and rewound and then taken to the weaver. The weaver made it into cloth and you would use it for sheets and shirts and other things. Flax was a hard thing and there was a lot of hard work about it.

They have been out of growing it for thirty or forty years and now they would never think of growing it but must be running to town and buying what they want.

The process of conversion of wool to yarn and thence into cloth was equally difficult. It demanded the concerted efforts of most of the rural community. It gave scope for the development of specialists who could give their skills back and forth even though, as before, their skills were part of the equipment of all the young people in the community. Two other old fellows of Inagh combined in the following account:

With the wool it was sheared on May 15 and, if that fell on a Monday or Tuesday and the following was Saturday in town (market day), you would see the men there with wool to sell while others would be there to buy it with large baskets in which to put it. The first thing was to card the wool. About the first of June you would get ready to spin it. For that you go around to all the neighbors and ask for a loan of a girl to spin the wool, and if you got eight or ten you must get the loan of that many spinning wheels. Then they come to the house on a certain day and I have seen eight wheels in this room and two in the other, all the girls spinning and talking away. It might take several days before they were through and they would have a dance and the boys would come around. You want to be sure to get the girls early for there is a great demand for them. After the yarn is spun, it is placed on the wall to be taken to the weaver later on.

All this was part of the pattern of work in which the members of the community were accustomed to work in close association.

258

The behavior described here is that which we have already looked at in the discussion of the obligations of cooring. The *meitheal* referred to the working gang rather than the system in which the local habits were set. That setting was a constant play of habitual work relations between the "friends" and neighbors of the local community in which the characteristic organization of the community aligned sex and age groups and associated the skills of individual experience and prowess with one's place in such groups.

In dealing with local techniques and local specializations, it is impossible to divorce them from this social setting. The attitudes of the country people support this view. Their emotional outlook on work gives added proof of the identity between work role and the social relations it involves. Solitary work is difficult and tedious. It offers little incentive. Communal effort on the other hand has a pleasant and variegated rhythm which works up an emotional satisfaction which can counteract fatigue and monotony.

Consequently, concerted effort and hard work are not often divorced in the minds of the country people, to judge from what they say of it, from their experience of the *esprit de corps* which they feel. The old people as usual deny any value to present-day activity. The young think the doings of an older day the behavior of savages. We have already seen how the attitudes which express one's age status color one's view of life in the countryside. That is the case again here. If the old people deny the existence of community effort today, it is because they think of the zest of working in unison in youth long ago and remember the times when emotion was highest and the solidarity of communal effort greatest. And the young people forget this. Listening to the accounts of such mighty effort, they think only of the hardship and the ignorance of labor-saving short-cuts it entailed. Similarly the old people forget or fail to see that the young people go through the same experience as they once did.

Thus one can hear such a description of communal effort and

259

the joys of work in common as follows from the old people and at the same time one can still watch a harvest where cooperative action and competition in skills is just as great. And we can know that the essential patterns are the same, though the techniques may change:

And at the time of the saving of the hay and up to the War didn't it used to be that a man's place was done in turn and there would be fifteen or twenty men working at a time on the one place. There would be one man make the hayrick and there were no round ricks in it then, they were all long. There would be another who would rack it and two above on the rick putting hay into it. The other men and women would be in the fields bringing the hay in on their backs, and the children would be there too. Each would do as much as he could. Then the man whose field it was would have half a barrel of porter and the men would all drink. At noon and in the evening the neighboring women would come in and spread a great feed with jam and sweet breads and other things out of the ordinary, and in the evening there would be a tea for all of them in the fields.

Then at the cutting of the turf the man might have porter, though the hay saving was a bigger time than the turf cutting. There would be several working together at the cutting of the turf, some cutting and others laying it out, and they would be given a feed and some drink for it. There was a man who agreed to cut turf for a widow woman who had several small children. After he arrived, he was sorry he came, for there was no one to lay out the turf for him. But the widow and children were there and worked all day and never a sod did he get ahead of them. As soon as he had one cut, there was a child there to carry it away.

The people also helped each other with the ploughing and the planting of the garden, several men working to help and be called. There was one woman who would help one neighbor today and another the next and so on. It would kill you if you had to do it alone but you never feel the work when there are several of you all working.

There is none of that today. Everyone is begrudging the other if he manages to get along tolerably well and each man does his own. Then the women used to work together. They had what they called a *meitheal*. On an appointed evening all the girls would gather at the house and work on the flax, scutching it, and they might be there for several days or a week working and living in the same house until all the work was done. Then they might go to another house and stay there. We had a great fortnight long ago at the Murphys here. The young men would be waiting outside to whisk them away or to have a dance.

Then when they ground the oats, they had a quern and the men and women would come together and each take a turn at grinding so it was not tiring and they would have a big supper of spuds and milk for all of them before they would go. Then they would get together for the carding and spinning before the thread was taken to the weaver. The young women might be carding and the old women spinning and the *meitheal* of girls would work away. They would get a dance when they would be done.

All the above description of close concert and deeply imprinted habitual work relations among the members of the local communities in the framework of the organization of behaviors of age and sex depict the now dead past. The same activities today, though certain techniques are different, bring out the same picture of work relations in an emotionally charged unison among persons of similar status within the community. The present-day hay harvest is very little different, though mowing machines are used. The great hayrick is still built in the same setting, and still calls for celebration. Everyone still waits for a signal from the hayrick rigger, a personage of considerable importance on such a day.

The unison of working on oats harvest with flails is gone. But in its place is a threshing machine, and its owners come around and a local crew is got up out of the local men. The same jollities still reign. In all this our chief interest is not in changing custom. Rather it is from this kind of observation that a new conclusion arises. The factors of differentiation about skills and techniques in the rural communities give rise to statuses of the same kind as before, statuses based upon the development of a specialty by a member of the local community which is recognized and valued within the habitual activities of his

261

fellows. Here is an opportunity to see the embryonic form of division of labor and development of occupations in terms of the life of a community. It is a continuous process.

The formally recognized artisans of the country districts represent a sort of halfway stage in this process. The blacksmith is the most important of them, through historical associations and because his skill suffers so little loss of demand. Others, such as the weaver and tailor, are in process of disappearance; others perhaps in process of emergence. It is the incorporation they experience into the habitual relations of the group that determines their presence or absence and determines whether or not their skill shall develop or be lost.

Take, for instance, the few cases of persons who return to their native communities in the countryside from abroad. They find adjustment extremely difficult. The "returned Yank," if he has been long away, is declassed and to an extent deracinated. This is true of all his behavior, through all his relations with those from whom he went. The process of reabsorbing him is slow and painful. None of this shows itself better than in his inability to fit himself in again technically and occupationally. If he takes a farm, he is better off because he is independent. But otherwise he must learn a different kind of organization of work relations, a different tempo, and he must wait upon the slow development of the relations with his fellows which alone can give him full occupational status among them. This is the reason why innovations of all kinds seem to be infinitely slow in conservative rural life. Ardent agricultural reformers all too often fail to recognize this enforced tempo of habitual working relations in agriculture and suffer disillusionment accordingly. In fact, it is the rock on which most well-meaning reforms or innovations break. Change and innovation do come about, surprisingly quickly from one point of view. But they proceed through social relations; they do not overthrow them. They come about through a new habit's achieving a compatibility with old ones.

In the Irish countryside the organization of the community

262

upon an occupational basis can be understood not in terms of such considerations as income, wealth, or skill, or any such factors, but in terms of the place and function of the persons specializing among their fellows. It can be understood in terms of social relations and the organization of habit. Status based upon technical differentiation is built up out of personal relations in the work experience of the community members.

If then we take inventory of the kinds of goods and objects which make up the *matériel* of peasant life, and draw up such an inventory to illustrate for us the connection between social relations and these goods and objects, we can construct a series of charts which connect community life and the exchanges and uses of goods, services, and objects in one comprehensive view.

In such a chart those goods and services which come to the farmer from those within his own community come to him in connection with traditional social relations uniting fellow community members. They are the ones transferred under the pattern of cooring: through "friendliness" and nonmonetary reciprocal obligation.

Those goods and services which come to the farmer and his family from without the community come to him in connection with more recently developed nontraditional relations uniting him to persons outside the community. They fall into quite different patterns of activity. Likewise any person whose occupation makes him both a member of the local community and part of the outside world, by virtue of his relations extending beyond, is also in a position of oscillation between the first and the second relationships.

For there is a continual attempt to extend the pattern of cooring, as with all local familistic and communal obligation and sentiment, outward on the part of the farmers, and a continual extension inward on the part of outsiders of other patterns of relationship. Much of the enduring pattern of town and country relationship evolved in Irish society hinges on this point. Much of political life is explained here. Gifts and personal favors, fash-

263

ioned on the pattern of the extended family and local community, besiege (or used to besiege) magistrates and government officials. Before land reform they besieged such links with the outer world as the older estate system provided, like the bog warden, the land steward, and the other functionaries of landlords. Yet against this pattern's sway there runs a continual incursion of other patterns which the institutions extending their sway from town life and higher social classes downward provide. In this meeting and conflict of social patterns much is to be learned of the structure of Irish social classes and of the continuing course of Irish social life.

The matter is of interest here only as a summary of the life of the rural community itself. It occupies us only in so far as it points to a conclusion about the kinds of relationship which build up within the local community between the farmers and those of their fellows who are not farmers. There is always a primary distinction among them. There are those who have, quantitatively speaking, most of their activities taken up in relations within the local community alone, and there are those who are divided between the local community and the outside world and who make a bridge between. The former fall in one way or another into the pattern of cooring. They are a "cut below" the farmer, yet his intimates. They are the ones in relation to whom the farmer is the dominant party, since it is the farmer who commissions, hires, or otherwise sets off the other's activity, expert as it may be. The secret of the equivalence of the status of these persons with that of the landless boys lies in these facts. For the boys are in exactly the same case.

The others, however, who are in one way or another part of the outside world, are alike if only in that. Various as they are, they are never in the same case as the local handy men and the boys. For them the patterns of dominance by the farmer, of recipiency of gifts and cooring favors, of articulation with the peasant cliques in the local community, are never complete, because of their conflict with other, external ties. The crossroad

Table 7

Relations of Farmers and Non-Farmers in Three Rural Communities in County Clare

The table which follows is a chart of relationships between farmers and non-farmers in the rural communities of Clare. It lists those of different skill or habit with whom the farmers have relations. Those who fall under the pattern of reciprocities, gifts, and cooring, and the goods and services they provide the farmer, appear in one list. Those who fall under other patterns, who do not figure in the obligations of cooring, are listed in another. At the right of each item in each list is a word or phrase characterizing the initiation of the actions taking place between the farmer and the non-farmer in the course of the provision of the goods or services described.

Read another way, the lists arrange in two groups all the local specialists with whom we have been dealing. They show us that the differences are to be found in social relations, not in goods or services rendered or any other factor. All the specialists of whom the authors got information in the country districts are here. The first list describes the specialists whose relations to the farmers are "internal" to the community. The second list describes those persons who connect the farmers with the outside world and are thus "external." List I gives those who enjoy superior prestige and local standing, whose contacts with the community proceed through the heads of families, the adult men, and who are capable of initiating action among them. In that limited sense only, they are dominant over the farmers and make a higher class. List II gives those who share inferior prestige and local standing, who form cliques with the "boys," and who are not ordinarily capable of initiating action among the adult members of the community except in a course of communal action employing their special skill. These are a lower class in the country districts by such definition.

This configuration of factors reveals the lines of relationship within the community and those extending outward from it.

The reader may judge for himself how close the connection is between the familistic system of farm life and the structure of the rural community.

List 1

Extra-Familial Relations within the Local Communities, Internal

Occupation or Technical Status	Goods or Service Provided Farm Family	Character of the Relations[1]	Activity Initiating Relations Involving Provision of Goods or Services[2]
Weavers	Homespuns, shawls, cloths blankets		
Tailors	Clothing		
Carpenters	Furniture, houses, buildings		

[1] Unless otherwise indicated, in each case this consists of gifts and cooring.
[2] Unless otherwise indicated, in each case the farmer commissions the labor.

Table 7 (continued)

Occupation or Technical Status	Goods or Service Provided Farm Family	Character of the Relations	Activity Initiating Relations Involving Provision of Goods or Services
Smiths	Farm implements, horseshoes, tools, repairs	Gifts, annual payment, and cooring	
Shoemakers	Boots, shoes		
Thatchers	House thatching		
Hayrick experts	Hayrick building		
Masons	House building, sheds, walls		
Wall builders	Walls		
Whitewashers	Limewashing of houses, sheds		
Water diviners and well diggers	Finding and building of wells		
Threshing-machine operators, owners	Threshing	Payment, gifts and cooring	Farmer commissions labor and machine and pays hire
Midwives	Attendance at childbirth		
Bonesetters	Broken bones		
Local "vets"	Treatment of sick animals		
Local "doctors," wise men or women	Treatment of sick; magic		
Domestic servants	Household aid	Wages only for outsiders not kin	Farmer hires and pays hire, otherwise kinship relations hold
Agricultural laborers, employees of big farmers	Occasional aid in agriculture		Either party requests aid
Gravekeepers	Records of grave locations, tending of graves	Wages by priest, gifts and cooring from farmers	Unobserved
Slate quarrymen	Building and roofing slates	Unobserved	Unobserved
Sextons	Tending of churches	Wages by priest	Unobserved
Limekiln and lime burners	Fertilizer	Gifts and cooring from local men, payment for outsiders	Unobserved

Extra-Familial Relations with Local Persons Extending Outside the Local Communities, External

		Special Cases, Occasional Relationship	
Tinkers Dealers, hawkers, feather-mongers	Asses, pots, pans, repairs Odds and ends, small trade articles. Feather mongers buy feathers from farmers.	Occasional trade at the door Occasional trade at the door	Tinker makes rounds Dealer makes rounds
		Habitual Relationships	
Crossroad shopkeeper	Supplies liquors, foodstuffs, tobacco, sundries not bought in town. (Most trading of staples done in towns, however.) Collects eggs and butter for sale to produce dealers.	Farmer an habitual client, purchasing on long-term credit. Relationship overlaid with obligations of "friendliness," involving reciprocal gifts and occasional advances. Barter significant only in the shopkeepers' acting as depot for eggs and butter sales.	Relationship habitual over long term (see other columns)
Civic guards, (police) officials and uniformed men (*Gardaí Siochána*)	Local protection of person and property, apprehension and prosecution of misdemeanor and felony. Informally, police settle disputes, report grievances, give amateur legal advice, and gather census data for governmental departments.	By law, civic guards must be neither members of the communities in which they are stationed nor related in it by marriage. They are instructed to maintain close rapport and very friendly relations with local people, and seem to succeed. They go in for much sport with the local young men and boys. They are attached to local barracks but, if they are married, maintain homes in the local community.	Assigned to stations on departmental orders

Table 7 *(continued)*

Occupation or Technical Status	Goods or Service Provided Farm Family	Character of the Relations	Activity Initiating Relations Involving Provision of Goods or Services
Agricultural instructors, horticultural instructors, poultry instructresses, etc. Permanent officials, employees of local authority, county councils, and members of government departments	Instruction and demonstration through experimental plots, prize contests and schemes, assignment of grants, evening lectures, etc.	Agricultural instructors of all kinds make home visits and hold classes locally but have large districts and are often townsmen. Informal contact with farmers slight.	Instructor either pays a visit of inquiry or is called upon by the farmer for his advice and aid; farmers make inquiries at central offices.
Land commission officials and staff	Division and regulation of land holdings provided by land law in breaking up former large estates, often affording occasional employment for young men	Usually entirely official and administrative; very little informal contact; tempered, however, by indirect political influence originating among farmers	Land commission proceeds officially to estate division; farmers petition for increase of holdings at local offices
Commission of Public Works officials and staff	Provision of public works and relief works in connection with drainage, conservation, government projects, supplying occasional local employment for young men	Usually entirely official and administrative; very little informal contact; tempered, however, by indirect political influence originating among farmers	Public works commission proceeds officially to put a project into effect
Local government authority, County Council, officials and staff: a. Rate collectors	Collection of rates, taxes, land annuities	Make collections in person, most frequently at farmer's house, though also by post. Usually owe jobs to local influence and are most often of the farming class, but collections are large and contacts not wide	Rate collection proceeds under orders of administrative staff of County Council

b. Road engineers, foremen, overseers and staff	Maintenance of roads through direct labor or through contracts with the farmers for supply of local quarry stone or paving materials. Relief work and road building an important source of employment of young men.	Permanent officials employees of the local authorities, the County Council; foremen, overseers, and "gangers" often chosen from the farming community; much local influence exerted through county councillors	Road work proceeds under orders of administrative **staff** of County Council
c. County councillors	Local political representatives on local authority. In practice present local needs, wishes, and grievances, smooth the local administration of governmental bodies, and carry out the official duties of the County Council, not delegated to permanent staff.	Elected by voters of rural electoral districts through universal suffrage of all citizens over thirty years of age (1935) in periodic local government elections. Have very often been crossroad shopkeepers or influential local big farmers; nowadays, however, are often small farmers as well. Depend for election upon canvassing, personal contacts, and attention to constituents' business, though political party endorsement is not unimportant.	
d. County Board of Health, officials and staff, local dispensary doctors, nurses, and home assistance (relief) officers	Investigation and report of cases in need of assistance, relief, etc., and provision of same	Employees or appointees of local authority; usually townsmen, and not members of the local community. Their duties, however, demand that they maintain friendly contact and acquire considerable local information.	Farmers petition Board of Health or County Council or apply at dispensaries

Table 7 (*continued*)

Occupation or Technical Status	Goods or Service Provided Farm Family	Character of the Relations	Activity Initiating Relations Involving Provision of Goods or Services
Big farmer	Occasional employment of local young men; occasional aid to small farmers and local purchase of corn, vegetables, animals, produce	Of a higher class and wider contacts than the small farmers; most often a townsman by culture and even by residence. In the countryside, close informal contacts with others of his kind over a wide area; interest in fashionable recreation and sport. Contacts with small farmers often friendly but usually few, except where big farmer is active politically.	
Cattle and produce dealers	Purchase of produce and livestock, providing chief monetary income of small farmers	When not townsmen, whom the farmer meets only at periodic fairs and markets, these men are usually big farmers. Buy "from the land" (that is, from individual farmers not gathered at the local fairs and markets) very rarely; butter and egg dealers nearly always buy through crossroad shopkeepers.	

Parish priest and curate and other clergy

Religious leadership and moral control. Regulation of personal conduct and family behavior. Settlement of conflicts and disputes. Recommendation of "characters" before the outside world. Regulation of formal beliefs and attitudes, supervision of education in the interests of the accepted mores. Priest supplies ceremonial and cultural leadership and takes an active part in nearly all recreational and cultural activity, along with the schoolteacher, in country parishes. Only at times of high ceremony or special devotion, as at marriages, or in pilgrimages and retreats, does the small farmer make use of town churches, though he and his wife often contribute to them.

In country districts today formal religious relationship seems to be superseding older paternalistic dominance of parish priest. Little informal contact except in the case of young curates in local sport. But the priest still commands greatest respect and reverence and, in many cases, the love of his parishioners. He is still the local court of appeal and the arbiter of local custom. He is consulted a great deal by both men and women. His parishioners are jealous lest he overstep his sphere of authority, particularly in politics, yet they concur in granting him obedience in everything else. Nevertheless the older magical power he possessed once is gone. Today he is often superior to the small farmers in wealth and education, and is not one of them. His more usual associates are other clergy, big farmers, and townsmen.

271

shopkeeper, the policeman, the schoolteacher, the priest, the big farmer, even the local man who becomes a county councillor by election, are always a "cut above" the farmers. They come to form a group apart. They take over near-urban standards first. Some of them, of course, priest, schoolteacher, and policeman, are often residents for only a short term. They have come to the country district that they serve as strangers and outsiders, if only from the next parish. But a certain aloofness and a certain difference clings to these men even if they are natives by ancestral descent. Contact with the outer world brings in the outer world's ways and sets them apart and a little above.

Only the wanderers, the tinkers, the itinerant beggars, hawkers, and "dealing" men and women, many of them uprooted urban laborers, whose ties are with the towns and whose visits in country districts are short and predatory, fall outside this pattern. They are a special case. They are also many a "cut below" the farmers. They are an outcast lowest class.

13

Markets and the Community

In rural Ireland what we have called the "rural community" is no simply defined geographical area. Any one of the recognized divisions of the countryside in Ireland, a townland, a group of townlands, a parish, an old barony, a mountain upland, a portion of a valley floor or plain, except perhaps the newer administrative divisions, is in a sense a community. The lines of relationship among the small farmers are continuous from one of these to another across the land. Geographic barriers serve only to deflect the lines of this continuum, not to divide it.

We observe of a farmer of Luogh, for example, that he coors largely in Lough townland. But he has kinsmen scattered around about as far as Mount Elva, four miles to the north, and Liscannor, three miles to the south. He attends the parish church of Killilagh, a two-mile walk from his house, but sends his children to school at Ballycotton, only a mile off. He does most of his shopping in Roadford, a crossroad settlement two miles away. Yet he takes his larger produce for sale and his larger needs of

273

purchase to the market town of Ennistymon, some eight miles off, or the smaller one of Lisdoonvarna, some five miles off. He votes and pays his taxes as a member of a certain electoral district which overlaps exactly none of these regions. He associates himself in tradition with Clare and Munster as a North Clare man, rather than with Galway and Connaught, though he may have seen very little of either beyond his market towns. The small farmer of Luogh has allegiances to all these communities. He is quite ready to find his emotion stirred in any one of them. He is ready to back the men of Luogh against the men of the neighboring townland; to back those of the mountain region against those of the valley lands; those of his parish against the rest; those of the countryside against the towns of Lisdoonvarna and Ennistymon; those of North Clare against other sections of the county; those of Clare against all other counties; those of his class against all others; of his religion against all others; of his nation against all others. Each one of these allegiances has a geographical base, though in the last analysis each one of these is built up out of his personal experience of human relations.

A study of the local community among the small farmers must thus be a study of the geographic basis of their relationships. In the course of such study an inquiry into the spatial relationships involved in the distribution of produce and shop goods between the farms and the market towns is a first step.

The chief agencies of distribution in the countryside draw upon well-marked areas. Each crossroad shop, each hamlet, each market town, each fair, has its own hinterland. In recent years creameries have grown up at strategic places. Likewise, in the same years, larger towns have pushed their hinterlands farther back into the country districts, and motor lorries go even into the back roads.

The definition of such market areas and the demarcation of those into which such a rural county as Clare can be divided is a relatively simple task. It can be reached by plotting out on the map lists of customers' names and addresses obtained from each

274

of the myriad crossroad centers and clusters of shops sprinkled over the county, combining them with others obtained from records of tolls paid by farmers in larger centers. This information can be checked with the testimony of farmers themselves as to where they do their buying and selling. It can be checked again with testimony upon the part of shopkeepers in the market towns as to the area from which they draw their clientele.

Plotting out these lists gives a picture of many superimposed areas. The smallest of all of them groups only a few townlands together about a crossroad or a hamlet. These areas about hamlets cluster together in turn, along the roads, to form larger areas about a village. The area about a village groups together with that round other villages, again depending upon the terrain and the roads, to form a larger district around one of the larger towns. These town-encircling areas themselves fall together to form still larger districts embracing all the farms trading in the largest centers such as Ennis, the county seat of 6,000 population, Kilrush, the metropolis of the West Clare peninsula of 4,000 population, and the city of Limerick. For Limerick draws farmers along the main roads as far as Newmarket-on-Fergus, fifteen miles into Clare. The whole county, of course, centers ultimately in Limerick, since rail, road, and river all lead there rather than over the upland divides to Galway city to the north.

Local fairs figure in this plotting. Traditional long-established fairs are sometimes not held within the confines of a town of the present day, though all but a few of them now take place in the streets of some town or on a modern fair-green set aside at one edge of a town. Nevertheless, the areas from which farmers come to fairs yield the same picture of overlapping distributions. The smaller fairs of little attendance draw from the smaller areas, which group together in turn. Widest of all are the areas of the largest fairs, held at Ennis and Kilrush. And there is not a village to be found on the map that does not have its fairs, carefully scheduled so that within the immediate area there will be no conflict of schedules. The farmer may go this week to a small village fair two miles or so away in one direction, next week three miles or so in another, and the third week to a larger town.

The list of cattle, sheep, horse, and pig fairs within County Clare given in Table 8 is taken from *Old Moore's,* the farmer's almanac. *Old Moore's* has hung in every farmer's house for nearly a century. It is his infallible guide. A glance at the map of Clare will show how many are the fairs within even a very small compass of a few miles.

Table 8

Calendar of Fairs in County Clare, 1934

Ballina, March 28
Ballyket, March 22, July 4, August 17 (cattle) , December 1
Ballynacally, February 28, April 14, June 14, July 30, September 16, November 8
Ballyvaughan, May 29, June 24, September 16, December 18
Bauroe, *see* Feakle
Bridgetown, January 24, April 18, June 10, November 25
Broadford, April 13, June 21, September 13, November 21
Carrigaholt, June 1, July 5, August 19 (cattle, pigs, and sheep)
Clare Castle, May 30 (pigs day previous), November 11 (pigs day previous)
Clonroad (Ennis), May 8, July 31, October 13, December 2
Connolly, January 2, April 17, July 18, October 3
Corofin, February 19, May 20, July 20, September 12, November 22, December 14 (cattle, sheep, and pigs)
Doonbeg, February 8, April 1, May 2, July 1 and 26, October 8, December 16
Ennis (*see also* Clonroad), January 5 (sheep), 6, 11 (pigs only), February 2, 8 (pigs only), March 2, 3, 8 (pigs only), April 4 (horses and sheep), 5, 10 (pigs only), 16 (cattle), 18 and 19 (sheep), May 10 (pigs only), June 14 (pigs only), July 12 (pigs only), August 9 (pigs only), September 4 (cattle and sheep), 13 (pigs only), October 11 (pigs only), November 8 (pigs only), December 13 (pigs only)
Ennistymon, January 22, February 12, March 24, April 15, May 15, July 2, August 22, September 29, November 19, December 13. Pig market last Tuesday of each month
Feakle, January 24, February 17 (Bauroe), March 24, April 24, May 17 (Bauroe), June 20, July 24, August 17 (Bauroe), September 24, October 24, November 17 (Bauroe), December 20
Kilclaran, June 1
Kildysart, January 21, Febuary 20, March 15, April 24, May 22, July 15, August 27, October 24, December 18. Pig fair second Thursday of each month
Kilenena, March 11, June 13, September 12, December 12

Kilfenora, February 25, April 9, June 2, August 15, October 9, November 4 (cattle, sheep, and pigs)

Kilkee, January 8, February 24, April 15, May 13, July 10, August 13, October 5, November 26. Pig fair second Tuesday of each month

Kilkishen, January 20, March 15, May 9, August 31, December 23

Killaloe, third Monday in January, February 28, March 28, April 12, May 20, June 26, July 16, August 12, September 3, October 20, November 17, first Tuesday after Christmas, cattle and sheep

Kilmihill, January 7, February 15, March 30, May 19, July 18, August 15, September 28, November 1, December 13

Kilmurry M'Mahon, May 24

Kilrush, last Wednesday in each month, for pigs; January 16, February 22, April 13, May 10, June 12, September 1, October 12, November 16, for cattle and sheep; March 25, first Thursday in June, October 10, November 23, for horses

Labasheeda, June 10, August 10, October 10, December 10

Liscannor, January 6

Lisdoonvarna, April 1, May 1, November 1, December 1

Miltown Malbay, February 1, March 9, May 4, June 21, August 11, September 10, October 18, December 9. Pigs first Thursday of each month

Mullagh, January 1, March 17

Newmarket-on-Fergus, December 20

O'Brien's Bridge, March 18, July 25, November 17

O'Callaghan's Mills, June 27, November 14

Quin, July 7 (cattle and sheep), November 1 (horses, cattle, and sheep)

Ruane, June 17, September 26

Scarriff, January 5, February 1, March 3, April 3, May 1, June 2, July 5, August 2, September 6, October 4, November 3, December 9, pigs day previous

Sixmilebridge, December 5

Spancil-hill, June 23, 24

Tulla, last Tuesday in January and February, March 25, April 25, May 13, June 15, July 19, August 15, September 29, October 19, November 9, December 7

In these ever-larger overlapping market areas the natural physical divisions of the countryside are well represented. The great central mass of Mount Callan divides West Clare from the rest of the county. It divides as well the market districts of Ennis and Kilrush. In the valley of the Fergus River, which drains the highlands of Mid-Clare to the north and East Clare beyond the corcasses (rough marshlands) to the east, the human flow of trade and produce exchange tends downward to the towns of Ennis and Clarecastle, at the head of tidewater. The high country marking the divides over into the Inagh and Cullinagh rivers and into the lake country of North Clare, just south of the

277

gaunt hills of Burren, divides the market district of Ennis from the smaller districts upon which the villages of Ennistymon, Corrofin, and Lisdoonvarna draw. Yet these villages in their turn are within the region of Clare from which the farmers converge upon Ennis. In each case a center, whether a larger market town or one of the smaller villages, serves a natural area demarcated by the configuration of the land and the course of the roads.

In such natural regions, particularly in more remote and mountainous country, the roads determine the intercourse of the communities with one another. Today each focal point is joined with another by a motor road. As the roads wind out from the larger centers, shops come to be placed at the strategic crossroad; a public house springs up; perhaps a schoolhouse, a parochial house, a chapel of the parish, rise beside them. Nowadays creameries are put up at these or still other points along the roads, where they are most conveniently accessible to small and medium farms producing milk. Even more recently lorries have begun to come direct to the crossroad to pick up produce that once, before motor traffic, had to be carried by the farmers themselves all the way to town.

Plotting out the market areas of the towns and villages of the countryside reveals a characteristic of social and economic space even here where the deepest hinterlands are never more than a half-day's leisurely trip by horse and cart. Any list of customers plotted by residence around a minor center gives an area which extends considerably farther in the direction away from the nearest larger center than it does in the direction leading to it. The minor centers draw principally from the hinterlands behind them and their areas extend only a little way along the roads in the direction of the next larger center. Ennistymon in North Clare draws custom twelve miles to the north, but to the south its influence reaches only three miles up the valley of the Inagh River, where the region of the larger center, Ennis, begins. Ennis itself serves all Clare, and its own immediate area extends, to judge from the residences of the farmers who come to buy and sell in her markets, beyond Ennistymon to the north and as far as Killadysert to the south. In the direction of Limerick, the metropolis of southwest Ireland, however, the influence of Ennis ends at Newmarket-on-Fergus, a scant five miles off.

Today the roads both great and small provide all-weather routes for every kind of local traffic. They carry many lorries and not a few buses in competition with the only local railroad — the small and winding West Clare Railroad, which joins Kilrush and Kilkee to Ennis and Limerick in the east, and Gort and Galway in the north, tapping Ennistymon and Corrofin on the way through, all this in the roundabout leisurely fashion of the earlier days of railroading.

The main roads are much more direct. They follow divides and occasionally cut right across high bog country. Today they negotiate bogs, which once would have prohibited any sort of transportation during wet weather, by dint of side ditches and high crowns of gravel and dirt. Over high country they have better foundations and wander in comparatively straight fashion through the country.

At various points along these main roads there are branches today penetrating the countryside. These are rougher and simpler constructions of crushed stones taken from local quarries, leased by the County Council. The stone is broken by laborers and small farmers of the district through which the road runs. In the case of the smaller roads each landholder is responsible for the bit of the road that runs by his land. "Road metal," as the crushed stone is called, is spread during the late autumn, winter, or very early spring. When the weather is dry, in summer, a fine white dust rises after every vehicle. But in the rainy months of spring and winter the roads are soft and full of chuck holes, and new stones must be laid down. Then the heavy iron-tired carts of the farmers break them further and press them into the soft roadbeds.

The interlocking net of roads covering Clare high and low must have been fairly complete at an early period. In high country many of the roads were "famine roads," built to give relief during the "bad times." In lower, richer land they are older. They ran originally from one concentration of estates to another, reflecting the older social order. Even today there is still a considerable amount of new road building carried on by local authorities, opening up districts which formerly had little or no communication with the outside world. There are still many farmhouses and village clusters of farmhouses far away from any improved road in higher country. Their inhabitants rely on rough borheens and stony trails leading from the nearest road. Many such isolated houses were originally built in inaccessible parts of hills and bogs to keep their owners from the eyes of bog rangers and estate stewards and to hide them from the threat of eviction.

Today the roads are kept up by the county government and the state. The system of road labor is very old. Private contracts for stones, maintenance, and repair and gang work under county officials are still important sources of outside work for the farm communities and occasions of local relief important in county politics.

The small farmer today uses five principal methods of travel. Choice among these is determined by the nature of one's errand and the status of the traveler.

The motor car is the newest and most costly method of transport. Small farmers do not own motor cars. They hire them from the towns when occasion arises. The motor car is still in process of introduction into the Irish Free State. In the countryside it is used only in time of crisis and high ceremony. If a member of a farm family needs hospital attention, he is removed to the nearest hospital, either in a private motor car or in the free county ambulance. At a wedding or an important funeral a family may engage two or three motor cars for important guests and the principals. At election time the local political organizations of the national parties provide free transport to the polls for the old and lame. In all else the motor car is the mark of the townsman, either the produce-collector in his lorry or the man of influence on a jaunt.

Even at such times of high ceremony as weddings, funerals, and elections the country people still use the horse and trap or sidecar. This is the traditional mode of polite travel, and it retains its popularity today. The trap is used only by the whole family or by its adult farm-owning members. It is used only in connection with activities of importance which mark their own status and those to whom they travel. It is always used at funerals and marriages. It sometimes transports all the family in Sunday best to church. It is brought out to honor a visitor or announce the arrival or departure of a friend. And it is used occasionally on visits of state to the town. Sunday clothes always go with it. It would be a very big farmer who used the trap in all his trips to town.

The vehicle-of-all-work, and the one on which produce goes to market and shop-bought goods come back, is the common two-wheeled cart. The farmers call it a "car." With the addition of side boards it becomes a "creel" and can carry small livestock, turf, and many another bulky object. Occasionally it appears on Sunday, but one never sees it in times of high ceremony such as in a funeral procession. It is the vehicle of everyday working life. Even the younger members of the family may use it sometimes in going about their work. But it is most often to be seen in the hands of the man of the house.

The ass and car, on the other hand, ordinarily has no such eminence. The donkey cart is a woman's vehicle. It takes her and her farm produce to and from the crossroad center. In a town market it is no accident that one can find the ass-carts among the poultry sellers or with the pigs, but seldom in the corn or cattle markets.

Another modern vehicle has worked its way into farm life. The bicycle is used by all ages and both sexes. But in poorer districts it is principally used by adult men, especially among the smaller farmers. Children go on foot. The bicycle is an in-

281

formal and individual means of conveyance, ideal for visiting, for the pursuits and pleasures of young men and women, and for quick trips to the local crossroad center.

Finally, the country people travel a great deal on foot. At work one travels nearly always on foot. Distances are short, and the vehicles one has are needed for carrying. On Sunday most people walk to mass, even where it means a long walk over the fields. In any procession of country life the majority of persons taking part are always afoot. In running petty errands to "friends," neighbors, and the local shop one goes on foot. Habit wears many paths across the fields in many directions. It makes one very expert at avoiding hazards of mud and wet. But nearly all foot journeys find the road soon or late.

To complete the picture of rural travel, one must add perforce two more vehicles. One is very new and just beginning to make its influence felt, though only on the main roads between the large cities and towns. This is the motor bus. Today a few persons have begun to travel beyond the market towns to the cities for their more important business, and in the movement lies much of one side of the picture of the decline of the middle-sized towns in rural Ireland. The other and last means of transport is the horse. Only adults among the country people ever ride him, either for sport or for transport. The horse is first a work animal, then a sporting beast. In either case he is the special care and interest of the adult man.

The methods of transport in the countryside are related to the distances to be traveled and the errands to be run. These things are matters of the organization and relationships of family and community. It is not only the means of transport which can be related to the constituent relationships of country social life. Each kind of farm product exported and farm need purchased involves a different distance of travel, a holder of a different status in family and community, and a different relation with the outsider.

The goods the farmer produces travel to the centers at which they are exchanged over distances which are commensurate with their value, their importance in farm economy, and their association with the status of the persons in the rural communities under whose charge they are produced. Horses take most care, are most valuable, and are the very special charge of the man of the house. The horse fair accordingly draws from the largest area. Cattle are the great money crop, the export staple. Accordingly the cattle fairs are among the chief lodestones of the larger centers, drawing from the deepest hinterlands of the major market areas. They are masculine affairs. Likewise potatoes and corn crops, oats, come to market only in the major centers. Farm fathers bring them down by horse and car from the deepest hinterlands.

Pigs represent a much shorter period of work and care. They are often in woman's province. The pig fairs are smaller gatherings, held in small centers, drawing from small hinterlands. Lesser vegetables, principally cabbage, travel no such distance as potatoes, and women often sell them. Finally, butter and eggs travel the shortest distance of all. They are often bartered at the crossroad centers. Before creameries were introduced, salted firkins or tubs of butter, representing a longer accumulation, went longer distances to the village centers.

Creamery associations were not established until the middle of the time of research in County Clare. They are part of a new economics which brings distributing agencies to the farmer's door. Consequently they do not fit this picture and are among the great forces of gradual change. They have made dairying the pursuit of the farm father, as it was not before. Like motor lorries, they represent the new geographic order that is gradually overcoming the old.

The goods that reach the farmer cover distances between their ultimate distributing center and consumer in the farm families in the same proportion as they are bound in with the statuses and relationships in work and life of the familistically organized groups. The men go to the larger towns with or without their wives for the larger annual purchases of boots and cloth goods or furniture or tools and implements. The boys may go for the more ordinary purchases of flour and foodstuffs and feeds and so on, to be bought in their fathers' names, to the local centers and villages. The household needs from day to day are the women's province. Tallow, candles, oil, sugar, tea, are to be had either in the villages or in the crossroad centers. The only need the men may fill so close to home is the recurrent hunger for tobacco and drink.

If we turn this view of travel and distribution and personal relationship into generality, we see that the pattern is such that it fits those of community life we have described. In the masculine sphere of life the disposal of produce means masculine travel and masculine building of relationship with the outside world of greatest geographical range. Taking each item of masculine produce in the descending order of its importance to the farm families, the area out of which the product is brought to a center is progressively smaller. The same fact is true of the feminine produce, with the difference, of course, that the range is smaller to begin with. The area of widest contacts established by women and the areas drawn upon by women and the areas drawn upon by centers of distribution of women's produce are always much less in extent than those of men.

It is not enough to point out that the distance to be traveled and the size of the area which a center serves are in direct proportion to the monetary value of the goods concerned. This is the case. It is an old story among economists. But like all generalities it does not fail to have many exceptions. The point of interest is not the monetary but the sociological aspect of the matter.

Areas of distributive service coincide roughly with areas of personal contact and habitual travel. They coincide also with areas of effective social relationship. Thus there is a direct correlation between the area over which a peasant moves and has social relations and the value of the product he raises, as the economist would point out. But the source of this correlation is not to be found in economic considerations alone. The economic matters are themselves the outcome of the patterning of activities between persons. They show us the interdependence of the internal organization of the peasant community and the relationships making that community's articulation with the outside world.

Nothing in the world prevents any small farmer from going to Dublin markets to sell his cattle, not even the price of the ticket, for he has that. But he goes only so rarely as to make the fact negligible. On the other hand, the big farmer, the cattleman, in County Clare habitually goes farther, buying and selling far beyond the confines of the local market areas, purchasing his household and family goods in the great urban centers, patronizing even a Dublin tailor sometimes. The difference in travel is a part once again of the difference by class and economy between large farmer and small. The small farmer's community is made up of the persons related to him who are also small farmers and the persons who connect these men with the outside world. This we saw in the discussion of occupations. The market areas are the areas of effective, habitual relationship among farmers. They are definable only in terms of social relations made up of the acts of specific local persons. Such relations differ in duration and the frequency of the events making them up. Change such relations and geography is changed. For a human setting geography is merely the locus of relationship. The system of distribution that orders space in rural Ireland functions to do so within a system of social relations, which we have called familism.

It is not surprising that the relationships existing between the small farmers and their local distributing agencies go farther by far than economic acts of barter, purchase, and sale. The country crossroad shopkeepers, especially, win very special status in rural communities out of these relationships. In Ireland and in Clare shopkeeping is predominantly an urban and small-town trade. Yet shops are numerous and important in the country districts, and a word must be said of them.

In typical western rural communities the smallest and poorest of the crossroad shops, serving the minutest areas, are ordinary cottages of farmhouses. The slightest alteration has sufficed to turn one of the rooms into an emporium where makeshift till, counter, and shelves carry little more than tobacoo, matches, oil, and a few sweets and small sundries.

Such a shop is usually run by a woman, who subsists upon it and a plot of land or garden. She is often a widow, or the wife of a local tradesman. In many cases the little shop is the local post office as well, and a salary from the state contributes to the owner's upkeep. Such a shop is sometimes, too, a local gathering place for the boys, in the way the local smithy once was such a gathering place. The boys get their fags here. It is encumbent upon the woman who keeps the shop to make them presents at Christmas time, in recognition of their custom. Everyone agrees that the woman subsists only because she is a part of the local community. Though she charges a bit more, she spares one the longer walk to the village center.

Country shops are often larger than hers. Sometimes where the distance to the village center is greater, they sell nearly everything one could get in town, outside the specialized drapers' or hardware, boot, and shoe shops. They sell all the farm staples, such as groceries, sugar, flour, tea, and tobacco. Here people may come from two or three miles around. The farmers all know they pay more, but the shop is a convenience. It may get the only newspaper in the district, and men drop in to hear the news. In the evenings, a local school of cards may flourish here and the boys foregather.

The country shop reaches its zenith at the crossroad, where a church, a parochial house, a school, and a creamery may stand as well. Here the shop often dates from the days just after the famine and has had a long history of prosperity. In the past generation many such crossroads produced county councillors, and the

286

rewards of public service often meant the acquisition of several rich farms in addition to the shop. The shop serves the surrounding countryside and collects its produce, and it derives its reward from the service it performs.

The position of the country shopkeeper is to be found in his place within the system of relations which make up the community of small farmers behind his shop. His function as economic agent of distribution is only part of his role. He is in a situation which must be described as a perpetual seesaw. If he is drawn too far within the local community, he loses contact with the outside world. If he is drawn too far outward, he loses touch with his customers. He must maintain a balance in a delicate equilibrium.

He is caught within a pattern of mutual obligations to the farmers on the one hand and the social system of the town classes on the other. Let it suffice to show his place that in a recitation of such a shopkeeper's intimates and associates it is most often not the farmers but the members of the community who are in a similar position who figure. His associates are the parish priest, the schoolmaster, the local police, and the local "rancher." When marriages are made for his daughters, they are made with big farmers, and husbands are got at considerably greater distances than in the case of the small farmers. Along with his associates, he makes up the rural middle class, at once a halfway point and a channel of movement for the infiltration of gradual change, poised between the small farmers of the countryside and the middle and upper classes of the urban centers.

Other agencies of exchange and contact between rural communities and the outside world are as much overlaid with social sentiment and custom expressive of valuations upon local status as is the position of the crossroad shopkeeper. The form of exchange is ceremonial, and a ritual exists to express much more than the mere mechanism of contact and exchange.

The two chief occasions of economic exchange outside the shops at the crossroad or in the towns are the best examples of such ceremonial. Let us take the fairs first. The fairs are still the most important mechanism of exchange between the small farm producers and the middlemen who start farm produce upon its journey to the ultimate consumer. Nothing has risen to threaten them seriously even in this day of economic complexity. The farmers of the rural hinterland of towns and villages journey with cattle, pigs, corn, and wool to market, to sell them that day or else to carry them home again. Some big farmers sell from the land direct to dealers and jobbers. A few small farmers sell direct to neighbors. These are exceptions, and sales in market and fair are well-nigh universal.

The fairs are not only universal, they are also elaborately conventional. How much, if anything, survives of medieval commerce in them and how much comes down from the days of the medieval Irish *aonach* is a matter for the historian. In ancient times the fair was a gathering for purposes much more widely embracing than exchange of produce. The *aonach* was often the occasion of a royal or chieftainly court, a bardic contest, and local games. Nothing of this remains today.

Cattle, horse, sheep, and pig fairs are fixed, habitual occasions. Their dates and places of meeting are universal knowledge in the countryside. An extension of medieval English law has made most of them proprietary, making of the right to hold a fair a legal title to be bought and sold and charged for in the shape of tolls. But they are public occasions none the less.

The lore of fairs is an inexhaustible fund of information among the small farmers. Among them, indeed, the size of the local fairs is a matter of local pride. It is an index of the industry and wealth of the region. The state of prices is as much a clue to the fate of the local universe as the financial vagaries of Wall Street or the City reveal the destinies of the world.

All this is natural enough where fairs and local markets represent the chief outlets for produce and the chief source of monetary income. As cattle are the chief concern of the males of the family and source of ultimate success or failure for the family, so the cattle fair is the great testing ground for male prowess, skill, and intelligence. In the market place of the cattle fair, the male command of the family corporation and masculine representation of that corporation in the community makes public display of its stewardship. On this stage, the farmer can meet the outsider on his own terms and with his own weapons of shrewdness and experience.

The farmers criticize bitterly any departure from customary procedure. Even though they complain that the fair gives advantage to the buyer rather than to themselves, they would change nothing in it. Prowess in bargaining is recognized and valued in every person. A man who is a good hand at bargaining or a good intermediary between bargainers soon makes a name for himself. The man who can drive a hard bargain gets a hearty respect from his neighbors and wins a grudging respect even from his victims, but the man who lets himself be bested wins scant sympathy. At the same time, however, sharp or unfair practice soon wins condemnation.

All this lore the child learns as he does man's work. He is taken to fairs from the age of ten or so and stands on the fair green or in the streets the long hours from dawn until the last buyer leaves. He learns from actual experience and finds his lessons reviewed again and again in the constant discussion at home and on *cuaird* of prices, buyers, famous bargains and bargainers.

At home the approach of a fair leaves no doubt as to the importance of the event. Farmers talk of prospects for days ahead. Each man is asked what he intends to try to sell, and the merits and prospects of each beast are common coin. Every man hazards his opinion as to what prices will be, how they will compare with those of recent fairs in surrounding villages, and what beasts will find the readiest market. In the light of all this discussion the ordinary farmer makes up his mind either to try his luck or wait for a better chance.

Should he decide to try his luck in the coming fair, he has a well-established procedure to follow. He gathers his stock together, gives them any special attention they may need. If the fair is a long way off, he drives his bullocks and heifers halfway there the day before and puts them overnight in the field of a "friend" along the road. In this he has the aid of a boy or a "friend," after the pattern of kinship reciprocities.

On the day of the fair he is up as early as one or two in the morning. To dress, snatch a cup of tea, and bless himself takes only a moment. Usually he has arranged for companionship, and he and his neighbors drive their beasts along the roads together. Company makes the night less lonely and the handling of the animals easier. Driving them is a skilled task against the dangers of the road, both natural and eerie. The men hope to reach the site of the fair before daybreak. They want to arrive in time to find a "good pitch," as they call it. They want to take their stand in the drawn-up lines of men and beasts where buyers are most likely to notice them. His pitch taken, each man stands over his beasts, ready for the inspection of buyers, careful that his beasts do not wander off or get mixed up with the others.

As dawn breaks, the buyers arrive. They are nearly always cattle dealers and big farmers. Only occasionally are they local men. One can recognize them as they hurry about, businesslike, wearing trench coat, bowler, and leggings. The costume is practically a uniform with them, quite different from the drab coats and boots of the countrymen. They carry chalk or scissors and pencils and a notebook to mark the beasts of their choice and record their purchases.

In the good days of high prices, as during the World War, the buyers arrive even before dawn and buy by lantern light. All the good beasts of the fair may be gone by the time the sun comes up. On occasions of little demand, however, the buyers have time to look about carefully and make the exhaustive tests of quality that long experience has convinced them are the secret of commercial success.

The procedure of choice, bargaining, and sale is as unchanging a ritual as any church provides. The buyer — dealer or farmer — strolls unconcernedly along the lines of farmers and their beasts. Here and there he greets an acquaintance. But he is appraising the animals all the while. Rigid custom forbids his breaking in on a bargain already begun. He must find a farmer who is free for the moment. Should he catch sight of an unoccupied owner of a likely animal, he crosses over to him and begins the business of the day. His first move is to ask the price, knowing well he will get one larger than the farmer really hopes to receive. This first exchange is merely the occasion for the closer inspection of the cattle and a notice to the other that a bargain is in process.

Such a move is a signal. As questions and offers pass between buyer and farmer, a crowd of bystanders soon collects. They offer suggestions, shout out commentaries, encourage one party or the other, contributing animatedly to the debate, which will eventually culminate in a sale at a price which instantly becomes the knowledge of buyers and sellers alike.

One of the bystanders almost invariably adopts a well-recognized role. He becomes an intermediary between buyer and seller. He turns all his energy, backed by the plaudits of the crowd, to the consummation of the sale. He may be a friend of either buyer or seller, brought in for his shrewdness or experience or skill, or he may be a wandering tinker in hopes of a commission from one or the other. He may even be only an interested bystander.

The intermediary is almost always a major factor in the transaction. He is the one who forges an agreement over the distrust and shyness of the farmer and the autocratic impatience of the buyer. All the parties are vociferous, the farmer in praise of his wares and the buyer in depreciation of them. The intermediary turns grandiose claims into laughter, wears down the resistance of the farmer by wit, and raises the offers of the buyer by appeals to fair dealing. Time and time again he will drag back a buyer who rushes off in well-feigned disgust at an out-

291

rageous demand or push forward the hand of a reluctant farmer to be seized by the buyer in the handclasp that marks completion of the sale. Amid the encouragements of the bystanders, he repeats the old bargaining cries. He shouts, "Split the difference!" when taking-price and asking-price approach one another, and he wrings concessions from each party until agreement is reached. They end with a handshake between them. The sale is made.

If the buyer is ready to pay for his purchase on the spot, the older custom, all three parties step off the fair ground into any convenient near-by pub. There they celebrate the transaction at the expense of the buyer, the purchase money changes hands, and they make assurances all round. The seller turns back a "luck penny" out of the purchase price. This is a payment often as large as half a crown, depending upon the transaction, repaid to the buyer in token of good faith.

Custom is changing here. A large-scale dealer may have little time or inclination for such amenities. He may give the seller a ticket or slip of paper as his record of the transaction and arrange to see him later in the day. He stands, slip in hand, ready to receive payment in his turn. Later on, then, at the time arranged, the farmer takes his place with the others with whom the dealer has been dealing during the day. Even then the farmer usually gives back a luck penny, even though he knows the dealer may reckon it a reduction of price rather than a ceremonial gesture. For it is a traditional gesture of independence and equality on his part.

Fairs beginning at dawn are usually over by noon. By that time the farmers are clear that they must sell at a sacrifice or drive the beasts home unsold to wait for another day. If prices are good, eager buyers have snatched up everything except unsalable scrubs.

For the farmer this mart is more than a simple economic exchange. The form of exchange is as important as the exchange itself. It is an instance of traditional behavior on the part of the small farmers, supported by sanctions and sentiment. In the ritual of bargaining and exchange in the fair, many relationships are acted out: the relations between farmer and farmer; the relations between farmers and their sons and the boys of their kindred; the relations between farmers and persons from the outside world of big farms, business and trade, and the towns. Throughout the whole of the proceedings one can see all these get a periodic, ceremonial reiteration here.

The economic circumstances of the fair are only part of the picture the fair presents. The fair and market are almost the only sources of monetary income for the farmers. They are the chief occasions for realizing the labor of a year's agricultural work. Consequently they are also the traditional occasions for settling debts, for making payments on accounts with shopkeepers. They are also the occasion of stocking up with everything from boots and clothes to feed and manure.

Indeed the fairs are the chief occasions of commercial and monetary activity in the agricultural counties. They are periodic high points of local activity in which laborers and local government have as much interest as the farmers. They are great events at which the economy of the western and southern parts of Ireland gets its only general, public, and spectacular circulation of funds. Yet they have a ceremonial side equally vivid.

The lining up of the farmers and their sons before their cattle to await the inspection and commencement of bargaining we must not idly dismiss as a mere convenience in bringing cattle to the attention of the prospective buyer. Like the other conventions of conduct in the fair, it deserves a careful treatment. These conventions can be put under a common explanatory scheme with those of farm life. In the arrangements of events in the fairs there are new events among persons which follow the same course as in the daily life of the family members at home on the farm and in the rural community. But in this case there is a far different setting.

At a fair the dealers or buyers initiate transactions or ter-

293

minate the bargaining at will. They are free to choose both the cattle they shall buy and the farmers with whom they shall deal. This is the same organization of relations between farmers and outsiders as that which prevails in the local community. The efforts of the intermediary and the emotional connotations of the luck penny as well as the grumbles of the farmers fit into this pattern of social and economic relations. There is some antagonism here, of the farmers against the others, but the solidarities of the two parties carry their own check. Prices may be so low that the farmers refuse to sell. Buyers band together to force a low price on various occasions. Resentments are mutual and common enough. But the ceremonial survives. It is an enactment of the community relations of the small farmers. It will change only as those relations change. The familistic farmer stands for himself, and his community is built only on gossip, public opinion, and common values. His mechanism of economic exchange expresses his social order and the community it serves.

Beside the cattle fairs there are fairs for dealing in sheep, pigs, and horses. These take much the same form, their complexity and importance depending upon the importance of the animal sold. Sheep, for example, are not so important in farm economy as cattle. Neither do they command such high prices. Consequently, sheep fairs are less imposing affairs, often held in conjunction with cattle fairs. The conventions are the same as in the cattle fairs.

Horse fairs again are very similar. Because of the higher value of the horse and the use of the horse for sport and ceremony among the upper classes, the horse fairs are less frequent than cattle fairs, but more elaborate. In the case of cattle, the farmer must usually drive the beasts he has sold to the station himself. In the case of horses, the buyer exercises a greater care. A deal is closed not only by the usual handclasps but by the change of halters as well. Horses are put through their paces very carefully, sometimes in secrecy off in a side field or down a dark street.

The majority of horses are sold between farmers and destined for farm work, but there is always a strong atmosphere of riches and brilliant chance about the proceedings. Many are the tales of half-bred horses, picked up for a song, that have come to win all before them.

Since most of the fairs are legally proprietary, they are protected by law. In many cases the towns have bought out the rights to tolls from private families, finding them a welcome source of revenue. To safeguard these rights, action may be brought against illicit buyers and sellers. In practice, however, it is only in horse-dealing that the owners of the tolls exercise vigilance, since there the tolls are so great. All this contributes to the atmosphere of importance that surrounds the horse fairs.

Pigs are sold more frequently, especially as they represent a great deal shorter period of development. Every town has its bonham and pig market. Every Saturday may witness a few transactions complete with the same rituals of inspection, repartee, and bargaining, but there are times of greater activity as well. It is generally only in pig markets that women are to be seen at fairs.

The second chief occasions of economic exchange, which afford further examples of the ceremonial surrounding the small farmer's mechanisms of contact with the outside world, are the produce markets of the towns. In them similar enactments of family and community relations are to be seen.

Each market town has its weekly market day. The day is fixed so as not to conflict with that of any other center. Only in the central largest town of a whole area is Saturday the market day *par excellence*. In Clare, for instance, only Ennis and Kilrush have Saturday markets. Smaller centers set other days of the week aside.

In the larger towns such markets may be held in stores and yards owned by the municipality. More often custom has set aside a section of a street or a central square for each kind of produce. In Ennis a separate yard and shed serves as a butter market, another yard and shed with a weighhouse serves for corn and wool. Pigs, lambs, cabbage, and other vegetables are sold in the streets.

The principal commodities sold at the weekly markets in Clare are oats, mangels, turnips, wool, potatoes, hay, straw, cabbage, calves, lambs, kids (an Easter delicacy), pigs, bonhams, chickens, geese, other poultry. Records of these sales itemize the commerce of the whole hinterland in agricultural produce. Public institutions in the town buy through contracts awarded to various suppliers, the weighing and delivery taking place through the public market. Dealers for each product visit the markets. Even those who have come recently to use lorries that tour the country crossroads still appear at the weekly markets.

For those interested in a typical view of this kind of commerce, Table 9 presents a picture of the tolls received in the town of Ennis during the years 1927–33. The table is arranged as a calendar and gives average toll receipts for each product for each month during the period. One can see the monthly fluctuations at a glance and the annual periods of activity in sales. The chief change during the period was the dropping off of butter sales, a fact accounted for by the rise of creameries in other parts of the county and the introduction of the lorry. Otherwise sales were of much the same volume each year. As the tolls were constant during the period charted, the figures are a very good index to the local produce marketed.

In buying and selling in the town markets, bargaining ritual is very much the same as in the fairs. Every seller must negotiate for himself, but the luck penny is neglected. The sexual division of labor on the farm is amply represented. The women stand over and bargain about their eggs, butter, and poultry. Men alone are to be seen dealing in pigs, lambs, wool, and corn. Yet it is not unusual to see a woman dealing for a sack of potatoes or for bonhams.

In all these transactions the usual ritual of bargaining ap-

296

Table 9

Sales of Ennis Market, 1927–1933

Toll receipts are given in pounds or hundredths of pounds except in the case of the last two, which are given in shillings. The figures are average total receipts for the month named over the six-year period.

Item	April	May	June	July	Aug.	Sept.	Oct.	Nov.	Dec.	Jan.	Feb.	March
Cattle	£54.00	?ᵃ	0	0	0	20.00	?ᵉ	0	?ᵍ	30.00	41.00	44.00
Sheep	£19.00	?ᵇ	0	?ᶜ	0	?ᵈ	?ᶠ	0	?ʰ	3.00	4.00	5.00
Butter	£ 8.00	18.00	25.00	27.00	32.00	28.00	26.00	15.00	6.00	4.00	3.00	4.00
Potatoes	£14.00	9.00	6.00	1.00	2.00	3.00	5.00	6.00	7.00	9.00	9.00	17.00
Roots	£ 3.00	.75	.13	0	0	0	0	2.00	3.00	5.00	4.00	4.00
Corn	£ 3.00	.50	.13	0	0	12.00	30.00	29.00	17.00	8.00	5.00	9.00
Hay	£13.00	1.00	.13	.13	1.50	2.00	2.00	2.00	3.00	4.00	5.00	9.00
Wool	£ .75	2.00	13.00	7.00	3.00	4.00	7.00	2.00	.50	.20	1.00	.50
Pigs	s62	56	37	46	76	118	115	118	118	94	84	90
Bonhams	s122	155	111	84	94	99	117	115	64	42	59	112

ᵃ Figures only for 1928, 1932 (£49, £11 respectively). Presumably no fairs tolled other years.
ᵇ Figures only for 1928, 1932 (£22, £17 respectively). Presumably no fairs tolled other years.
ᶜ Figures only for 1932 (£4). Presumably no fairs tolled other years.
ᵈ Figures only for 1931, 1932 (£8, £12 respectively). Presumably no fairs tolled other years.
ᵉ Figures only for 1932 (£18). Presumably no fairs tolled other years.
ᶠ Figures only for 1931, 1932 (£35, £37 respectively). Presumably no fairs tolled other years.
ᵍ Figures only for 1932 (£11). Presumably no fairs tolled other years.
ʰ Figures only for 1931, 1932 (£9, £10 respectively). Presumably no fairs tolled other years.

pears. It is customary, though in a curtailed and abbreviated form, in the purchasing that the small farmer does in the shops. It appears wherever persons of diverse allegiance are brought together in the life of the farmers. It appears, as we have seen, in the making of a match between two families. Like monetary payment for services, it figures only in the external relations of the farmers' groups. Indeed, it is the behavior characteristically connected with monetary payment.

Occasionally a small farmer buys from another in his own community, but the practice is rare. Goods change hands rather through the mechanisms of borrowing and gifts in the patterns of kinship and cooring. The difference of behavior must be referred to the different relationships.

14

Conclusion: The Framework
of Relationship

Enough has been said already to demonstrate the conclusion to which the study of rural behavior and social organization in the communities of the small farmers leads. The sociological conditions of Irish rural life are those determined in a system of relationships among persons based upon the Irish form of the family, family subsistence, and familistic custom. The demographical indices of population cannot be understood except in such a context.

Each topic of local life and custom, and each statistical index, as we have examined it, has led us back into this nucleus of organization among the small farmers. Something in the course of events prescribed there by the habitual arrangement of human lives existing in the small farmers' homes and communities has always lain behind the form of custom and the kind of attitude we have encountered. Something in that course of events has always likewise lain behind the numerical indices demographic count has yielded the census-taker.

This something is of the nature of an interdependent variable. The Irish small farmers of the present day behave as they do in the matters in which we have investigated them because they are members of a social system of a certain kind. A system implies a state of equilibrium in which elements are in mutual dependence. If change is introduced at one point, change follows at another. If the first change is not too great — that is, if it is not so great that destruction of the system ensues[1] — then subsequent changes do not alter the situation out of recognition. Far from it, since the elements are woven into a common whole, the effect of the change is soon dissipated. The system reverts to its former state. It may be said to have thus an equilibrium which it regains after each disturbance.

The doctrine of mutual dependence within a system helps us far more in understanding the events of life among the country people of Ireland than any ascription of cause and effect. The sorts of behavior we have dealt with do not have a single cause. They must be referred to a setting which must be looked at as a whole. Likewise the historical, economic, or personal events which impinge upon the country people of our communities do not ever succeed in changing very much either the people or what is really coterminous with them, their pattern of life. The traditional custom of life persists and continues to wield its power in essentially similar fashion decade after decade and generation after generation. Change goes on, in plenty, but it is gradual change of outlines already existing. It is no new departure.

Yet that custom operates always within a framework of relations uniting the same persons by various paths in space and hav-

[1] For a discussion of the theory of the equilibrium of a social system, the reader is referred to *The Social Theory of Pareto*, by L. J. Henderson (Cambridge, Mass.: Harvard University Press, 1936).

ing various histories in time. On each farm and among most of the farms of each area one cares to describe, these relations have certain uniformities. They turn up over and over again, and the course of events which they follow repeats itself in essentially similar fashion over and over. Circumstances alter cases, but not very far. Custom is not to be separated from this framework. The followers of customary behavior are those related in uniform fashion through the recurrence of similar events.

We are now ready, therefore, to make a summary and tentative definition of the communities and families of the Irish countryside. The definition is also an interpretation of the behavior of the persons concerned. It is also, too, an explanation of the events of human life in which they take part. And lastly, it is a social psychology of the country people.

In the discussion of each topic, the outlines of such a summary have become clearer and clearer. New events and new patterns of action fell into place as we drew their connection with old ones. Recapitulating this progress, let us take a step toward putting these connections in an abstract and general form. The sociology of the Irish rural life and small-farm subsistence is largely a matter of the anatomy of two institutions of characteristic form. These are the family and the rural community. The latter, in turn, cannot be described apart from the former. It is a framework of long-term customary relationships uniting persons beyond their family ties. Together these two unite essentially all the persons of the rural areas. With a few other institutions not here described (not, however, autonomous as are family and community), such as the parish (the formal, hierarchic community of religious belief and observance), they make up the entire anatomy of the small-farm class, the largest in the land.

Taking these two alone, however, what can we say of this framework of relationships upon which custom moves? It is a master system articulating five major subsidiary systems. These five comprise:

1. *The relationships of the familistic order.* These are the pattern of family life and subsistence, and its extension in kinship reckoning, obligation, and cooperation. They undergo periodic re-formation at the match and effect the dispersal of emigrants and the continuity of the pattern of farm subsistence.

2. *The relationships of age grading, or generation.* These are uniform habitual relations of persons of locally subsistent families who are similar and dissimilar in age. For each person we can trace them to specific events of interaction patterned by custom and compatible with the behavior of familism. In the large, they make up a structure of cliques or age groups, usually of persons of similar sex. Such cliques are opposed to one another, yet integrated under the headship of one of them, that of the heads of families, the so-called "old men." They are characterized by activities of discussion, gossip, and recreation, and make for common and long-established values and opinions, and membership in them bestows certain status, limited, however, by family status.

3. *The relationships of sex organization.* These are relations among persons, similarly the growth of habitual conduct, uniting the same persons of locally subsistent families who are similar and dissimilar by sex. They make up an organization of behavior canalizing the sexual drives in the direction of family life and forming a common attitude toward sexual behavior and a common norm of conduct and standard of sexual morality. This organization is compatible with that of familism and that of age grading and may be said to reinforce both. It also is capable of providing a standard for differentiating farmers from others.

4. *The relationships of local division of labor.* These are still other relations, similarly formed among the same persons, uniting those of similar and different occupation and technical skill. These involve action dealing with goods and services of practical value to the farmers and their subsistence. They fit the persons of a locality into two categories of relationship, depend-

ing upon those persons' association with other local persons on the one hand and their connections with persons beyond local ken on the other. The customary behavior marking the relations of the first of these categories duplicates that of familism in many ways and affords status similar to that found in age organization. The behavior marking the relations of the second of these categories does not. It is in this latter case only that class difference makes its appearance in the country districts. Those of higher class than the farmer, in his own community, are those who have connections extending beyond the range of his associates.

5. *The relationships of economic exchange and distribution in fairs and markets.* Finally there are still further relations among these persons, uniting them over space among themselves and with others from outside the local area in effecting the transfer of farm produce outward and the distribution of non-local goods and services inward. These relations are habitual, customary, and in many cases ceremonial, as in the fairs. They represent a form of organization reflecting familism, age, sex, and local technical organization.

These five classes of relationships summarize the incidents, biographies, and events that are here observed and described. They are a classification of them that has explanatory force. They do not themselves explain every event. But they point out to us, as does any faithful map, where we must look. All together they make up a configuration of social patterns, set off and different from others in Ireland. All together as a system, they determine events in the countryside. No event can be understood without reference to them. No sociological or demographical index can be interpreted without them.

This master system is the framework of social life in the countryside. It is the form of the social network in which the greater part of the Irish population are points. It is the system of forces in which any doing of the small farmers, or anything done to them, is a movement, a change of direction, an impact either from within or without.

If a view of the conditions which administrators or legislators of any institution, governmental or private, might wish to attack is to be realistic and adequate, it must take this master system into account. It must be wide enough to allow for its existence. It is not enough to plan an attack as a unilateral action from above. One must know and assess the place in the system into which an action might fit. It is not enough to institute an agency of reform or take an economic measure or put into effect regulatory devices on the basis of a single limited purpose or a single simple diagnosis. The equilibrium of the system must not be forgotten. If it is forgotten, disaster will not follow, in the ordinary case. The social organism is very tough and can stand a great deal of rough handling. But failure of the measure will follow. If the measure is merely a wishful effort, a sop to constituents, a gesture of good will, or an act of ritual or propaganda, its failure is no matter. But, if it is a sincere attempt at changing conditions, for whatever purpose or desire, its failure will be all the more perplexing. Today, in all the civilized countries, conscious efforts at social change are being made. Complexity is too great and problems too pressing to continue to rely as of old upon the traditional tools of politics: intuition, compromise, and a flair for practicalities. Great centralized bureaucracies have grown up in each country, even in one so small in Ireland. If they are to be effective, they must know the societies they serve. For them an understanding of local scenes and local social organisms, so remote from bureaucratic headquarters and national capitals, becomes more and more essential.

The foregoing remarks do not apply to Ireland any more than to any other country. The extension of central authority is a universal phenomenon of the age, probably a result of the new technology of science. Yet it has its applications in the case of Ireland as well. It is not for foreigners, such as the authors, to offer suggestions to the Irish people and their government. The

Irish have demonstrated quite amply an enviable ability to rule themselves. Besides, the role of the academic man is to provide the tools of the theory, not the recipes for action.

Nevertheless, one of the central problems of Irish economic and social life today stands in great need of a theoretical formulation such as is here advanced. The matter of demographical conditions — continuous emigration, decline of population, delay of marriage, and rise of bachelorhood — is a persistent and recalcitrant phenomenon. It seems to resist every change and every attack. No one knows why.

Yet the reason for resistance is simple enough. The matter escapes every observer and evades every attack upon the problem merely because no observer has conceived it adequately. Social conditions are the products of social systems. Yet attacks on them are predicated, as in this case, on the assumption that they are simple effects of simple causes.

The argument is the familiar argument. The phenomenon is conceived only as an economic one. Human action is merely the pursuance of economic goals. In this case, the argument runs specifically, the matter is the result of poverty. Since the condition persists, it is a matter of "endemic" poverty. One has only to change the cause, do away with the poverty, and all else with right itself.

Such a view is inadequate by virtue of two counts. On the first count, it hides a fallacy that vitiates it from the start. The fallacy is this: It asserts, in its very premise, that people act according to logic in pursuance of their wants. As a statement of a theory of economic exchange, the assertion is impeccable. As an approximation to what men actually do in social life away from the market place, or as a description of what in particular those men who are the marriage-less small farmers do, it is valueless. None of the many very well designed attacks upon the problems of rural poverty and rural employment in Ireland has had the slightest effect on demographic conditions. Yet the level of prosperity, by every account, is much greater than ever before.

305

Whatever makes the country people act as they do in these matters, it is not poverty alone.

On the second count, such a view is inadequate because it offers nothing further to learn. If the problem is a matter of wealth or of goods or of material conditions alone, supply the goods or right the wrong and the job is done. But such a remedy tells us nothing about other and related problems of human life and social behavior. It offers a practical rule of thumb for a particular instance, no more. We are already well along the way to a science of the practical. The production and transportation and distribution of the necessary goods and material services should be done easily enough today. It awaits only the knowledge of the "human element." But a science of the human element, capable of predicting, manipulating, and directing the growth of social life and institutions, controlling for any purpose the forces of human emotion and habit and will, is lacking and continues so. It is lacking, for one reason, because too few people of all kinds, whether official, academic, or what not, are aware that it is needed, or willing to work to develop it.

Two

The Town

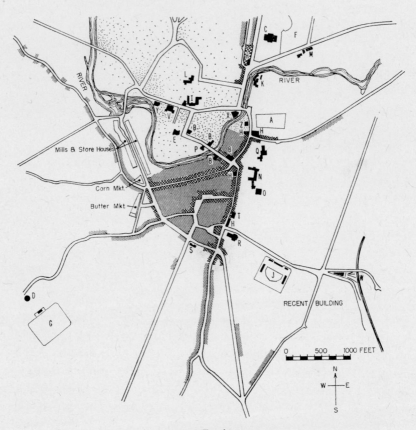

Ennis
County Clare
Pop. 5518   Census 1926

▨ Shop and Business Area
▨ Laborers' Cottages and Artisans' Houses
▨ Well-to-do Residential Quarter

A	Franciscan Abbey (in ruins)	J	State Inebriate Reformatory (converted to working men's dwellings)
B	Banks	K	Constabulary Barracks
C	Court House	L	The College (Protestant)
D	Cattle Pen	M	Monastery and School
E	Church of Ireland (Protestant)	N	Mercy Convent
F	Fair Green	O	Orphanage (girls)
G	Agricultural Show Grounds		
H	Hotels		
I	County Infirmary		
P	Post Office		
Q	Catholic Church		
R	Catholic Cathedral		
S	School		
T	Town Hall		
V	Masonic Hall		
W	G. S. and W. Railway		
X	County Club		
Y	Ennis Club		
Z	Abbey Club		

15

The Town: Setting and People

The people of the Irish town that is about to serve as the locus for our probings of their customs and groupings call their home "Ennis." It is a name full of the history of Ireland and her people. The cities and towns of Ireland were once a foreign growth, the importation first of the Danes and then of their successors, the Norman-English; but the walls which once separated and protected these invaders from the Irish have long since fallen down, and towns and cities today are as Irish as any remote countryside. Our town, Ennis, has also had such a history.

It is a market for a rich and varied countryside and draws its economic life-blood from a hinterland of farms both large and small over a considerable area round about. It is the seat of government and administration for an ancient Irish county and an episcopal see. It is not large in size, its population numbering only some six thousand. But in this it is in the middle range of Irish towns, a representative of the census group of towns most

309

numerous and most characteristic of urban settlement in southern Ireland.

Like all such market centers and administrative seats in southern Ireland, the town is impossible to visualize apart from the rural hinterland that it serves. The two have always had a close connection, even when Ennis' freemen were all English and Protestant, holding the only franchise in an Irish and Catholic population. The town has shared the ups and downs of Irish history and prospered or suffered as the county and the province grew rich or poor.

Before the reformation and the plantations, Ennis, on the banks of its river in a fertile plain, was a royal residence, and a great medieval abbey flourished there. The royal residence has long since disappeared, but the ruin of the great abbey still dominates a section of the town. In the Elizabethan wars the English set up their first court there, and spread a new and foreign jurisdiction over this corner of the Celtic land.

Town and country around Ennis suffered Cromwell equally; and plantation, not perhaps so sweeping as in some other parts of Ireland, saw the Norman-Celtic chieftainry dispersed and a soldiery established in the castles and the manors of the countryside, a soldiery that would soon become a landed aristocracy. From that day the courthouse in the town was the center of the land; and the procession of the assize judge, the high sheriff of the king, and the grand jury (made up of the owners of the land), opening each quarter's session, was a circumstance of pomp and state. And at a later and a much more recent date, when the mantle of local authority fell from the shoulders of the landlords to those of their erstwhile tenants' sons, the town and the courthouse were still the county seat.

In all the long struggle for land and independence, for religious freedom for Catholics under Protestant domination, for economic security for tenants-at-will, for political autonomy for the subject people, Ennis and her people played a part and

310

made a rallying center for the factions of the countryside. Daniel O'Connell trod the streets and spoke from the central square. Parnell followed him. The Tans patrolled the streets, and the patriots of what the town now calls the Anglo-Irish war gathered forces or cached arms in the lanes and byways of the town. When the trouble broke, men died in fratricidal civil war; and in the long healing process since, the town's central square has echoed to the speeches of all the parties of today's democratic Irish state.

In another realm of struggle, too, the town has borne its part. And as in all the west and south of Ireland, religious dissension is a thing of the past. The Protestants, unlike their fellows of Ulster and the north, have become a minor leaven in a Catholic loaf. The ancient abbey, no more than a monument now, may be still in the hands of the Protestant church, but a larger edifice, a great stone cathedral built in the seventies of the last century, now lifts its spire into the sky to guide the people in.

All this is Ireland's history, rather than that of Ennis only. But the two are inseparable. And so it is with economic life; Ennis the market center of a rural hinterland, is a miniature of the country of which it is a part.

The fertile valley plain is drained by a winding river that finds its way to the sea not many miles away. Ennis is an inland town, but, as with all the south and west, as with even the great central plain of the Midlands in Ireland, the sea of this North Atlantic island surges somewhere in the background as a reminder of the isolation of the Gaelic western world. But round about the town at the edge of the valley floor highlands rise up and shut the sea winds out. The green carpet of the rich lush pasture land, and the browner green of the river corcasses, or marshlands, give way to rougher, craggy, rolling uplands, with patches of grey rock or brown bog on the shoulders of the upper courses of tributary streams. Trees are rare, though here and there protected by a hollow of the land or a landlord's love of

311

game, a patch of them may lend a darker green. And beyond, the mountains that rim the island all around make a green and brown and purple wall that marks the valley's limit.

Down river from the town, the valley floor spreads out, the farms are larger, and old demesnes are met with here and there along the roads. In parts, the farms are quite extensive, in this country of little farms, and here and there a so-called ranch grazes large herds of two- and three-year-old cattle designed for beef. But the kind of farming that its enemies describe as requiring and supporting no more than a man, his dog, his stick and gun is here, too, and a solitary herdsman or two, with no more work to do than to watch the bullocks grow. And side by side there are large farms where tillage has held its own from the time before the American West and the Argentine turned Ireland into a land of milk and beef. Both ranching and mixed tillage farming flourish within the town's reach, and make a representation of the economy of the eastern half of the nation in the south and west. The ranchers and tillers are the "big farmers" of the current Irish economic and political scene, men of many acres. Here two or three hundred acres is a very wide domain.

But up the river and off toward the valley sides in the poorer and higher land lie the many smaller farms that make the economic backbone of the country and house and feed the greater share of all its people. Ireland is a land of the small subsistence farmer, the peasant, and the region that Ennis serves has its full quota of small farmers who flock to trade each Saturday in the shops and markets of her streets and bring their annual crop of calves to her fairs.

Ennis is no manufacturing center. Her whole economic life and nearly all the trade her shops supply depend upon the farmers, large and small, who make up her hinterland. She takes their produce from them, all of it that leaves the circle of subsistence at home upon the farm, and in return does the many things upon the performance of which the townsfolk live. She feeds the farmers through her shops, importing bread and tea and flour, and gives them fertilizers, tools, machines, to work with on the land. She clothes them and sets the fashions, got from the outer world, that they follow haltingly.

She shrives and blesses them and gives them prayer, for the cathedral, a Franciscan monastery, and another church give them a richer pageantry than a rural parish church supplies. Ennis educates the farmers, too, supplementing the rural primary schools. The Christian Brothers, a lay teaching order, and a convent of the Sisters of Mercy offer secondary education to those who live within a certain radius. The large, imposing Diocesan College at the gates of the town gives training to many a farmer's or townsman's son preparatory for the university or the professions, and sends young men to seminaries from which they return to parishes like those from which they first came.

Here in the town the professions have the offices to which the hinterlands come, or the hospitals in which they are healed or die. Entertainment comes to be centered more and more for all the countryside. Dances, sports, and cinema draw more and more widely, taking the young people away from purely rural jollities. For the town is the center of diffusing the new and changing the old no less in Ireland than everywhere else in the urban civilization of today.

And lastly, even in democracy and universal franchise, the town rules its hinterland. Law and administration center there. The representatives of even the farthest townland come to Ennis and make their bargains. The edicts of central government and the dictates of the nation, as they affect the farmers and their lives, are channeled through the town. In the hurly-burly of politics the countryside quite often imposes its will on townsmen. The administration of law and the enactment of legislation and ordinance are ultimately responsible to the predominantly rural electorate. Political parties organize in every rural parish. But decisions are made, taxes imposed, appeals brought,

313

and officers chosen in the town. For in the county, the county town is the only common ground for all sides and factions. It is a capital.

Ennis has all these functions and does these many things. Yet in addition she has a life and a being of her own. She is a microcosm where all these very things are also done among the townsmen for one another.

The physical aspect of the town reflects this double character. In the narrow winding streets, the rows of varicolored cottages, the austere angles of churches and public buildings, an artist might have much to admire. He would be struck with the fact that even in so small and drab a little country town there is a jumble of young and old and a variety that grows as one comes to know it better. Were he historically minded, he might find something vaguely medieval in the crowded huddling of shops and houses, and be fascinated by the tumbled ruins of houses and mills and warehouses he would meet here and there, all of them telling of recent history as the shell of the great abbey tells of a far older day. If he valued the picturesque above human convenience, he might even regret the touches of modernity that mark the town's liberation from its narrow bounds. Neat new rows of artisans' houses, the mark of slum clearance, and more portentous reminders of suburbia push out into the surrounding fields. Motor roads cut straight into the town's central mass. A railway station, a little older and already a little grey, turns the town outward. Government buildings, old and new, incongruous formal masses, fringe the outer boundaries. In a little residential section, a few tall brick houses from a London square mark respectability.

But an aviator would see the essential pattern of the town more clearly than any artist on the ground. He could watch the country roads winding inward to convergence in the town. He could see the long fingers of shops and cottages that line these roads and stretch out in all directions into the countryside. He could follow the same lines to the central square, "the height of the street," at which the three main spokes of thoroughfares meet and the biggest shops and the banks stand. He could see the clustering of narrow lands and older buildings round the market squares, and sense thus the kinship of marketing farmers and the town's poor. He could sense as well the segregation of the residential district on the other side of the river that cuts the town in two, the old genteel segregation of the professions from mere trade.

He could see one or two of the more spacious residences that bring the country house tradition almost to the edge of town, and he could see something of the walls outlining the cottage farms that mark the line between small cotter and urban laborer. But amid all the contrasts the essential pattern would stand out. The town is the hub of a long-spoked wheel, and its shape reflects its functions.

The first weeks the authors spent in Ennis made both these views of the physical self of the town unforgettably clear. The weeks were spent in plotting out and charting all that caught the eye. It was a plotting and charting of the outermost externals of the town, but it was a necessary prelude to the knowledge that would lead behind the house doors, the shop fronts, and the grey institutional walls. None of these things — the houses, the streets, the yards, the buildings, schools, churches, either inside or out — has any meaning apart from the human beings who make use of them. They are the chrysalis of the life within. In relation to that life, however, they tell much of the story. Examined in that relation, they tell much of the kinds of persons whose action toward one another makes up its life.

When we examine the structure which that action has and thus anatomize the community which Ennis and her hinterland make, we take upon ourselves a task imposingly large. The town itself has only six thousand people. The market area, the hinterland exclusive of those who regularly trade at some other town, may well number twenty thousand or more. The county numbers all told between eighty and a hundred thousand; the diocese, as it is not entirely coextensive with the county, somewhat more. Each of these aggregates heads up in some way to the town that we have set ourselves to understand. The town has two aspects, then: its own life and its functions. And both of them we must understand. The people have two immediately discernible roles: their lives among themselves and their places among their fellows in society. We must make a record and build a general scheme for them both. Let us turn to the people of the town.

One need not be long in Ennis to learn that there are many kinds of people there. Their lives and their aspirations, their loves and their hates are quite different. The persons one meets on the streets of the town are all Irish, most of them are Catholic, and they are a homogeneous lot. They are of one tongue, however deep their brogue. They are of one tradition, and within that tradition most are of the provincial brand that marks the county. They have a common nationalism. They have a common front toward the stranger and a common hospitality for him, too. But there are many kinds of them beneath this sameness, and to know them one must know these variations and know what they imply for life.

As one walks about the streets and makes acquaintances in the first several weeks, superficial marks make many of these kinds stand out. One comes to recognize a farmer very soon. One learns even to judge, as the townsfolk do, the number of his acres from his manner and his dress. Shopkeepers, publicans, and their assistants, as one comes to know them enough at least to exchange greetings, are a different lot from the few members of the professions one meets. One soon thinks one can distinguish the neat black or dark brown of officialdom and the clerical pursuits. One comes to know that certain cuts of cap and boots and a muffler at the throat are the badge of the laborer. The signs are subtle and the costumes unpicturesque, perhaps, but if one has an eye for that sort of thing they soon become very clear. If

316

one's eye roves farther, one soon learns that equal differences mark the women. Feminine finery may change with taste and pocketbook, but there are rough parallels to the differences among men. One comes to know what a shawl or coat of a particular cut and wear connotes. The vagaries of dame fashion are not all matters of caprice.

But should one want to make something of these outward signs of similarity and difference and learn something of the groups that make up Ennis' population, one could not rely solely on such impressions. A hundred factors would upset any prediction. If, like the authors, the observer were a foreigner, the signs that catch the eye, like the actions that pique curiosity, might well have quite another meaning from their meaning for the men of Ennis.

For an objective record of the actions of human beings upon one another, the significant signs of similarity and difference are those that the people of the town recognize among themselves. These are the signs that stand for categories that have a real existence. One can hear of them and learn that they are felt to be real things. To them emotion and value are attached, and of them each man is felt and feels himself to be a part. These, in brief, are the categories that give status and provide a role in which each man acts and each can be met by his fellows.

The people of Ennis are keenly aware of the differences that economic interest build, and like many others today, they extend occupational names to cover social classes. They count themselves as members of this or that great economic class, and with the name laborer or farmer, tradesman or merchant, professional man or government official, they think they summarize the whole pattern of their lives. As we shall see, the terms are very elliptical indeed, and, in the events of the life of the town, not one of them coincides exactly with the group of real persons it designates. But still the terms serve well, and the observer who does not know their use and meanings (those traditional in the civilization of which Ennis is but a part, and those specific for the town), or the observer who confuses them, will gain very little understanding of the place.

A count of industrial status shows us that, as in the rest of Ireland unaffected by the transformations of the factory system, most men still work either on their own or in an organization numbering only a few. The government offices, the Church, and the railroads are, with the exception of the banks, the only large hierarchies that figure importantly in the town. In agriculture, as we saw in Part One, hired hands make a smaller proportion than either working relatives or farmers working for themselves; hired labor is important only on the big farms, and even there the hands are usually not numerous. Manufacturers are few indeed in Ireland, and there were none at all in Ennis till recently. Production is a matter of local artisanry, craftsmen working on their own account to supply local needs. Construction work claims a horde of workers, the vast majority being building laborers who make up a large, only partially employed reservoir of labor in the towns. Nearly all are employees of the local authorities. Commerce and finance and the professions, especially in smaller centers like Ennis, are still in the hands of independent men who employ only a few persons outside their families. Shopkeepers and their assistants, trading from small, separate shops, make a vast army in the country. Thus, all in all, in spite of the large numbers working in domestic service in the towns or, in such a county town as Ennis, for the government, those who work for their relatives or for themselves far outnumber those employed by others. The economy of Ennis is the economy of small, independent units, whether on the farm or in the town itself. One must learn what these units are and what they do.

The traders who supply the countryside from the shops or move the farmers' produce to the outer world reflect their place in the town's life by the goods with which they deal. Most of them are little fellows, general provisioners. But they specialize

318

enough to show us the needs that they supply. The industrial
census records list the kinds of trading that they do:

Horses	Boots and shoes
Grain and forage	General drapery
Eggs and poultry	Metals, tools, jewelry, watches,
Coal	clocks
Bread and cakes	Paper, stationery
Fresh meats	Department stores
Fish and dead poultry	Auctioneering, valuing
Spirits and wines	Cattle, sheep, pigs
Tobacco	Confectioneries
Building materials	Hawking and street selling
Milk and dairy products	Groceries and provisions
Drugs	

Work, however, is not one's only distinguishing feature. The
town is too small and leisurely to make life such that one's employment tells one's whole story. There are many other things
to do besides work. These many other things also give one a
role in the town and place one in a group there. Those census
makers who were demographers give us an account of them.

The young and the old, the married and the single, the fecund
and the childless are variously represented in the town's occupations and on the farms of its hinterland. The figures of vital
statistics and residence yield up a picture of the course that life
takes for each of these groups, and the many problems that beset
the nation and its people show themselves in Ennis no less
than elsewhere in the country.

Townsmen live long. They marry late. They have many children. Country people live longer, marry later, and have more
children than do the people of the towns. Ireland, as we have
seen, has slightly more men than women, but in the towns the
women are a bit more numerous. Men stay on the farms,
women leave, to give this slight overbalance.

Birth control has made practically no inroads as yet, and a family of five is the average in both the town and its hinterland. Some countries, like France and the Scandinavian lands, decline in population or barely hold their own because families are now very small indeed. But that is not the Catholic Puritan way of Ireland. Ireland adopts another restriction on her growth, restricting not birth but marriage. In Ennis, no less than elsewhere in the country, many factors conspire to make the age of marriage generally the latest in the civilized world and to leave unmarried a large proportion of the men and women of both countryside and town. The small farm sets the fashion in this regard, and although not all classes follow that fashion, as we shall see, even in the towns marriage is long delayed and bachelors and spinsters are numerous.

The country boys and girls still flock into the town or pass through it to the world of cities and overseas. (England is the lodestone now, rather than America or Australia, in a day of worldwide restrictions upon immigration.) Boys and girls still wait long and unmarried at home on the farms or in the shops of the town. Marriage does not come to all of them by any means. We shall have occasion to see the pattern such lives have.

But such "problems" as these are no sign of decay or death or economic hopelessness. It is a mistake to read them entirely as signs of poverty and frustration. They are marks of habits and adjustments of long standing. They are no overtones of disintegration and collapse. They must be read for what they reflect of local life, not for what they illuminate about our ideas of the general health or welfare. The good citizens of Ennis and its county lead reasonably happy, useful lives, moderately full like those of other men, and moderately chafing, too. Theirs is an enduring, working, and reasonably successful polity.

But all these possible counts of work and age and sex and parentage, of residence and exile, are incomplete if we cannot fit them into the picture of the physical entity of Ennis that we have drawn. The houses, the shops, the huddled back-street cottages, the new rows of stuccoed blocks are home to these groups and shield their lives from our eyes. The small units in which life so often moves both on the farm and in the town, the families that keep the young unmarried with them or take pride in an old-fashioned fecundity, are housed in them. The physical appearance of the town is no more than a clothing in stone and mortar of the lives within. Stone and mortar, huddled confusion and open space, take on meaning when the kinds of people who make use of them are named.

Ennis houses its citizens in much the same way as all urban agglomerations nowadays; in general, the larger and poorer the family, the smaller its space. On the farm, in general, the small farm means a small house, and many human beings in it. In town, space is at a premium, and only the well-to-do learn privacy or divide a dwelling into many parts, for ceremony, for work, for sleep, for eating, by sex, or by age and state. In the back streets, a kitchen and a sleeping loft are often enough for everyone concerned. But in either case, the town is small, and green fields are never far away, as they are from a city.

The work one does has much to do with the kind of house one lives in and the section of the town in which it stands. Correlation of housing and occupation figures makes a formal picture of the differences. Ennis is only an instance of the general conditions of the nation. If one works with one's hands at manual labor, one has little chance for more space than one or two rooms shared with three or four other persons. If one's work is skilled, one's chances are considerably better. If one is a shop-keeper, one has a greatly better chance for space. Two-thirds of one's peers will have as many as five rooms. But until one has a profession like doctoring, the law, or a Protestant curé, one does not hope for a spacious house, not even one in which there are fewer inhabitants than rooms inside. There are scales in the matter, occupation and wealth, space and good housing, and, of course, they overlap.

In Ennis, small as it is, all such differences are present. The back streets are no urban slum, but they have the role of slum in the town. The peripherally situated clusters of better houses, like the outlying bigger residences with a touch of the manor house about them, few as they are, make a sort of suburban greenbelt. The town is a city in miniature. As in a city, one can judge the role and standing of the inhabitants by their dwellings. Size, architecture, location, use, ornament — all are telltale marks. A census is a very dull canvas for such a painting.

Those who live in the great houses at the town's edge or in the countryside and those who stand by the half door under the rain-drip from the cottage thatch are different. But the difference tells us nothing till we see them act together, separate from one another, segregate themselves as they segregated the houses they have built. Only then do we get a feeling for the kinds that the people of Ennis count. Likes cluster to likes. Differences may be great, but it is similarity that yields us an acquaintance with the real divisions.

Still, likeness is no single trait. Those who cluster together to make the real divisions in Ennis cannot be counted by a single attribute. It is not a matter only of occupation and work and position, or only of things, of possessions, wealth, the houses and their trappings. It is a matter as well of manners, folkways, attitudes, a customary outlook upon life. It is a matter, too, of activities, of recreation, of sport and play, of culture and education, even, we shall see, of religion and belief. Likeness is a matter of social class in Ennis. Class is a master key to the structure of the town.

The people of Ennis know their "places." They are for the most part keenly aware of social standing, position, and class. As in any community, "appearances" must be kept up. Class does not make for aloofness as it does in metropolitan regions, for everyone lives more or less in sight of everyone else. Nor do the folkways demand as in America that a pretense of social democracy be kept up. Each man knows fairly well what to expect of the other and respects the difference. Superiority and inferiority are relative matters. There are infinite gradations. But there are broad outlines none the less, and a man knows the "station" that is his. Ordinarily it is much the same as the one his father had, and in both town and country it is fixed "in the blood." There are always men who have "made their own way," it is true, particularly in the town. There are always those who, others will tell you, have "come down in the world." But everybody is agreed on the directions, on "up" and on "down."

Ennis is clearer about the top and the bottom of the social ladder than it is about the rungs between. Educated persons sometimes adopt the three classes of European convention, hesitating over the myth of English tradition that only a title turns the bourgeois into the aristocrat, or American confusion between wealth and position. Less ambitious or thoughtful persons are content with the equally traditional and very simple opposites of rich and poor, or cultured and ignorant, or respectable and disreputable. In Ennis, as elsewhere, the subject is matter not for generalization but for action and emotion.

Most often specific reference brings forth an occupational name. The convention is that one's occupation stands for one's pattern of life and one's place among one's fellows. On this convention, the great groups, traditionally established, into which the townsfolk and the hinterlanders fall, are those that mark their role in local industry. In the country, there are farmers big and small; there are gentlemen, for in Ireland the word has a social, not a moral, connotation; there are laborers, herdsmen, and fishermen. Others somehow fit themselves in at various points in the hierarchy. In the towns the professional "classes," the "big fellows," the shopkeepers, the "tradesmen" (who in an Irish town are the artisans), and the laborers make a like hierarchy. "Interests" like these are offered in discussion of all kinds as comprehensive explanations of the habits and the aspirations of the folk of the town and its countryside.

323

A man in the town is many things, to judge him by his occupations. He is a dentist, a professional man, but practice is not large and he has a chemist's shop as well. His friends have shops. His clubs are those to which they go. His wife, like theirs, works behind the counter, and his children play with theirs. Yet his income, from many sources, is greater than some others of his colleagues of medicine, who nevertheless account themselves better born, more fashionable, and more accomplished by far than he. They belong to another group than he, whatever the indices may tell us, and the groups have special places in the town.

Such places are made by the habit of people; and they live in the eyes of others than themselves. The bridge crowd is the same as the tennis crowd. This or that big farmer was blackballed at the Gentlemen's Club, although he maintains a rich estate. This doctor's wife is never accepted in the upper circles of the town. On a back street a railwayman's wife berates a daughter who threatens to marry beneath her. A shopkeeper will not drink with a shop assistant. The corner boys deride the golfer in plus fours. Butchering is less respectable than green-grocering, and feathermongering earns even the petty cotter's scorn. The landed peasant disowns a marriage with a herdsman and looks down even on the tradesman with a skill. The lines cross and recross, and values change for each man's views. But in it all there can be seen a nebulous but constant scale of things that are high and things that are low. The places of the groups of all kinds within the town and in the countryside are somehow strung along this scale.

The classification that we erected grouped together those that have common features in the eyes of the people of the town. Three great groups, laborers, artisans ("tradesmen"), white-collar men (those who "took the pen" but are not officials of government), divide up all those who do not belong to the three great activities that the town recognizes as its three functions for the countryside upon which it lives: government, trade, and the professions. The officials divide broadly into those who have office posts and those who work out of doors. The shopkeepers divide into the two large divisions that all townsmen recognize, the "big fellows" and the "little fellows." Shop assistants go in the category of their employers, whom one day they will succeed. Professional workers are those who hold degrees and practice law or medicine, high ranking officers, architects, engineers, and the managers of banks. Clergymen and nuns are grouped here, but not teachers or nurses, who are white-collar technicians.

The schedule that counted out for us the information accumulated on each person's card in the file on Ennis had much to tell, too, of aspects of social life other than those concerning occupation. One's education, religion, politics, sports, clubs, crimes and peccadilloes, and the broad age group to which one belongs were all filled out and counted through. Each of these counts could tell us something more of the pattern of lives in Ennis.

When all these counts were done and each man's attributes stood out on his schedule, the search for a master key went on. We sought a master key that would configure all the social places and divisions in the town at which the schedules pointed. As elsewhere, class is not merely a matter of occupation. Perhaps it might be got at through a correlation of many attributes. Could we proceed by process of elimination and find the ideal types? Could we find the men in the town who made the average man, not of Ennis, but of its classes? What would he look like and what would his attributes be if he were the lower-class ideal, the upper-class ideal, or the middle fellow just halfway between?

One method of finding such persons out was quite easy to use: correlations of occupation with the other counts on which we had sufficient information and the residual numbers that emerged. The counts on which we had the fullest information were, in order, residence, father's occupation, the type of house one lived in. These things we knew for nearly everybody.

Should we put the followers of each occupation through a correlation of these things, in the order named, and have a number of them with us still after the last step, we might congratulate ourselves on having located a group with at least four salient characteristics distinct from others such within the town. The largest number left within an occupation after these three progressive eliminations of minorities could represent an ideal type, a nucleus of uniformity.

The laborers of our files, for instance, survived four-way correlation and yielded up a large residual number to represent the ideal laboring man. Thus, they give us one configured point of fixity within the social scale. One kind of laborer turned up more often than any other: He was a laborer and the son of a laborer. He lived in the huddle of slum in the back lanes of the town, and he lived there in a house condemned as a hovel by the sanitary authority. He was the objective, statistical record of the man in cap and muffler that the town knows.

The artisans or skilled workers, those whom the town calls "tradesmen," did not emerge from correlation quite so quickly, perhaps, but emerge they did. Just as Ennis knows that the tradesmen are a cut above the laborers, so did their ideal type emerge. The composite tradesman, here in the files, was a tradesman, the son of a tradesman (though not necessarily following his father's trade). He lived in the back streets, and he lived in an "artisan's" house, in one of the smaller, newer houses not condemned (though by a narrow margin, for almost as many of his group lived in the houses now condemned).

On the other hand, those grouped together as white-collar workers did not yield up an ideal type out of correlation. There is no such configuration of social places in Ennis; there is no such class. No significant ideal number gives us a key to a history distinct from the laborers and the tradesmen. Residence, origin, house type, for these people, are too widely scattered. They have too little in common to make a class of the occupational bond.

The same is true of the officials of the bureaus of local administration and central government and the railway system. No ideal official type emerges; heredity is too various. But the employees of officialdom, those who work not by the pen but at duties out of doors, yield a clear emergence. Within this group the ideal public employee is a laborer, the son of a laborer, living in the back streets in a house condemned. We have met him before, and he is a "laborer," whoever his employer may be. There are exceptions, and they too emerge, but less importantly. In a smaller category of ideal public employee is a farmer's son, living in the residential periphery in a slightly better house. He may be a civic guard or a railroad man. He is not a townsman, and his stay is not long.

But when we turn to those who make their living by the shops, a clear configuration of social place emerges. The owners and their assistants in the small shops of the town present us with the ideal shopkeeper, a type that townsmen know immediately. He lives in the shop district, along the main streets, lives, indeed, in the small shop he works. He had a shopkeeper for a father. If it was not a shopkeeper he had for a father, then it was a farmer, for only in the case of the few shops in the back-streets area does he ever come from either of the laboring classes of the town, and then but rarely. Townsmen rightly feel that the small shopkeepers mark a configuration of social place that makes a class. They mark the fourth place up the scale of social ranking on which the lowly tinker, outcast wanderer of Irish life, makes the bottom.

The big shopkeepers, wholesalers and merchants, "big fellows" in town, also emerge out of the four-way cross-correlation. The ideal type differs only a little from the small shopkeeper's. He lives in his shop, or (when he lives outside the commercial district at all) in the residential periphery of the town, not, like the little fellow, in the back streets. He is a shopkeeper's son or, if not that, a farmer's son.

From the file, an ideal professional man also emerges, telling us of a condition that has marked Ireland since the days

327

when the professions and the universities were first thrown open to the Catholics, when the Protestant monopoly of the professional fields of law and medicine was overturned. The ideal professional man in Ennis today lives in the greenbelt periphery. He is a farmer's son. Or else he comes out of a big shop. He is characteristically not a townsman at all, but a man who has "made his own way." Or he is a merchant's son deserting trade for a profession in a growing affluence.

These ideal types are artificial, but they are significant. They show us in a measure how right the townsmen are when they give occupational names to social classes. The classes as they designate them for the town are always given names that configure both social place and ideal type. They are always these: the professional people, the big fellows, and then the small shopkeepers, the tradesmen, and the laborers. The five occupational designations are not accurate. They are not correct. They leave many, many men and women aside, but they are symbols nonetheless of the groups into which the town divides. In Ennis, with the Ascendancy (that is, remnants of the landed upper class so recently dispossessed in Ireland) and the tinkers, they mark the seven classes that together make the structure of the town.

Other information shows us once again the place that Ennis has in the countryside it serves. There has been an immense migration townward, and many indeed of today's townfolk look back a single generation to farming forebears. In Ennis today about one-fifth of all the population was born in the hinterland round about. Many are the country people who have flocked into the town. Of these the members of the upper and middle classes are most numerous. The "respectable poor" are about as often townsmen born as their proportion of the population warrants, but despite the influx of "runaways" and landless boys or servant girls from country regions, the "laborers" are townsmen born. The true townfolk, those of several generations' residence, are strangely enough not the merchant burgher families, not even the long-established families of substance. The truest town folk are the laborers, the urban proletariat of the back lanes. These men of the back streets and their women bear names in many cases that go back on the town's rolls to the sixteenth century. They are the one truly fixed class in the town.

The well-to-do of Ennis, the "professional people" and the "big fellows," are more often country born than their share of the total warrants. To an even greater degree, the landlord Ascendancy are more often country born than townsfolk. In an agricultural country, lately feudal, where almost without exception land is a central value for every class, ownership of land and the possession of an estate are still criterial of high prestige. The movement is still strong: the mark of the "big fellow," emergent from the shopkeepers' ranks in town, is the possession of a country house. This is not the whole story, because the success of those who make their own way also contains a chapter on country birth and migration into town. One in every four men of the professional and upper-middle classes comes from outside the county altogether, as does nearly one in every three members of the top. The only others who come from outside the county are to be found among the civic guards, railway men, and the like whose years of residence are not many.

If we push inquiry back a generation, the townward flow from the countryside comes out much stronger still. Forty per cent of the fathers of Ennis residents alive today and scheduled in our files were countrymen. Almost exactly half their mothers were countrywomen. These fathers and mothers, many of them, of course, now dead, brought their country blood and country ways into highways and byways of the town and left a heritage that forms their sons today. The population of the town, like that of all Irish towns, was larger then, and a good deal larger not long before that. But even then it is these transplanted countryfolk who have left descendants in the town. The townsmen have "died out of it," except in the lowest class of all.

Coming in from the countryside is a characteristic of the upper and the middle classes of the town. The fathers and the mothers

329

of the "tradesmen" and the "laborers" are more often townsmen born. Here once again we read the history of the town and its people and the classes they make. The urban poor have always bulked large, a huge and stationary mass within the population. And always over them, their numbers cut, and their pride and skill shorn and oftentimes destroyed by years of unemployment and outside competition, stood the skilled craftsmen of an earlier economic age. The last century has seen the destruction of this class, its complete transformation, in both town and country. Many a descendant of a tradesman once highly skilled continues life today looking for place in a newer occupation and either sinking toward the level of his unskilled neighbors or seeking refuge in a petty official berth or a tiny shop.

If one is a townsman bred in Ennis and if one stays on in the town to make one's life within it, residence, like occupation and the circle of choice of a wife, is fixed by heredity and class. One's residence is no matter of choice; it is in the section of town filled by other members of one's class, a house of the same kind and magnitude in general as the houses of the others of one's position. And so was one's father's house before.

The custom of staying at home in one's parents' house — of living with father or living on in his house after he dies — is widely spread. Two-fifths of the persons scheduled in the town lived so, all of them, it should be noted, past their teens. Where the small shopkeepers prevail, and in the Ascendancy, where there is considerable property to be inherited, the custom is a little more strongly entrenched than elsewhere, but it is general. But in all the classes, fathers' residences were spread through the sections of the town in the same way as are the residences of the present people of the town.

On Bindon Street, where the stately houses are, people are upper-middle or above. If the upper-class people of the town had fathers in the town, their fathers lived there too. The upper-middle-class burghers of the town live in the shop district or in the greenbelt round about. Their fathers, also townsmen, lived there too. The members of the lower-middle class live along the lines of shops that make the main streets of the town. So did those of their fathers who were not farmers.

But the back lanes, the back-streets area, and the back-streets periphery contain no members of the upper-middle or the upper classes at all. Even the lower-middle-class residents are few. And nearly all the townsmen fathers of the laboring class lived there, where still their children live. The scale of class is fixed in Ennis — and fixed in the geography as well.

This then concludes our broad, over-all sketch of the town, its inhabitants, and its history. In it we have presented the background for the following description of shopkeeping and shopkeepers, in which we shall be concerned with two major problems: the nature of the relationships between town and country, and the connections between family and social class in the town. We shall learn how the shopkeepers occupy a strategic place in both.

16

Shopkeepers and Shop Assistants

No aspect of Irish life stands free of the influence of the family. There are those who might persuade us to believe otherwise when they speak in the language of economic theory about trade balances or the statistics of production and consumption. Still others may cite universal historical processes to explain the rise of Irish nationalism and the function of the modern Irish state with its proliferation of bureaucracy. One should not forget, however, that the contemporary versions of organized commerce and government stretch back into an ancient past; they have reached their present form through a long, slow process of response both to internal events and to the ebb and flow of world influences. It should also be remembered, however, that eventually these external forces were all transformed and incorporated into Irish life so as to serve its people in the ways they chose.

Town living, originally an alien way of human grouping and life behavior, has undergone a similar transformation on Irish soil. Today it stands for ways which are distinctly Irish even though its specializations and internal social divisions may seem only remotely similar to an ancient past. When one looks behind the facade of formal institutions and observes the activities of government, religion, education, or commerce, one finds individuals who are products of that past and whose ultimate referral is to the forms of familism that have come in uninterrupted succession from it.

There is no monolithic sameness in the forms of contemporary family groupings (nor was there in the past), and the variety that one encounters is a consequence of both historical process and new influences. In the social distinctions which separate those designated as laborers, shopkeepers, or professional men we can observe differences in family organization and the associated style of life. But to assume that occupation and type of family join in a deterministic union, however great the observed correspondences may be, is to ignore other variations that negate such a causality.

The effort to disentangle the many threads which weave such a rich design of family in its social setting must begin with some point of reference. We have chosen to begin with the system of shopkeeping. If we were to restrict ourselves to an economic perspective, we would be primarily concerned with the conventions which surround the distributive function. Although no one can deny the crucial importance of such activities in any modern nation, these economic conventions are not to be our focus. Instead, we shall concentrate upon familial aspects because, as will become clearer with the unfolding of the analysis, in them lies the key to understanding much of the urban way of life as it finds expression in an Irish town.

Our search will inevitably lead us to the description of the family's natural history: its formation, structure, and transformation. Nor should we ignore its varieties and the place it holds in the full range of social class and institutional complexity. All these aspects and others will engage our attention and although this choice of emphasis leaves aside much that is germane to a full exposition of Irish urban life, the immediate considerations permit no other course.

The selection of shopkeepers as our central focus may, however, be justified on strategic grounds. In their dominance of the geographic heart of the town and the streets which radiate from this center, they occupy the principal arteries of human movement which connect them with all sections of the town and of the surrounding countryside. As suppliers of food and goods their importance extends to all classes and kinds of men. Through descent and marriage they are linked by familial obligations with the countryside. Their children often achieve professional goals and, in their social rise, connect those of common background but diverse social standing. In such ways the social centrality of the shopkeepers is revealed.

Our objective now is to make explicit the nature of the characteristics of those who are engaged in shopkeeping. First the census tells us of variations based on age, sex, and marital status for both of the two occupational categories, shopkeepers and shop assistants, which constitute this group. Unfortunately, we lack specific data on these matters for Ennis, but those of County Clare and the nation will yield the necessary generalities.[1]

Shopkeeping in Ireland is almost exclusively a family enterprise, attracting both men and women, though not in equal proportions. It counts very few under thirty years of age. Most of the men and a goodly proportion of the women are either married or widowed, although widows exceed the widowers by three to one. Entry into the occupation and into the married state are almost simultaneous. Almost all those who become shopkeepers have previously served as shop assistants while they were single. The census counts for the entire nation and for County Clare reveal a remarkable correspondence in almost every de-

[1] All figures based on census of 1926.

tail, and we shall now let these data inform us of the quantitative measure of the generalities.

County Clare counts a few over nine hundred persons as shopkeepers, of whom something under a fifth are found in Ennis. Males outnumber females in the ratio of five to three, the figures being 574 and 341. Shop assistants numbered somewhat fewer in their total than shopkeepers, counting a total of 651 persons divided in more nearly equal sex proportions, with 378 males and 273 females. Of particular interest to us is the proportion of shops which are purely family operations and no one other than family members is utilized. Nearly two-thirds of the shops in County Clare are thus categorized. The remaining third provided the employment for those classified as assistants, an average of slightly over two for each such employer. This distribution also gives us a rough approximation of those locally called either small or big shopkeepers.

The age distribution of male shopkeepers provides further insights. For the nation, practically no one becomes a full-fledged member of the occupational group before the age of twenty-five, but during the next ten years the rate of entry accelerates although those under thirty-five still number only about one-fifth of the total. Over half are between thirty-five and fifty-four, and after that age the absolute and relative numbers decline slowly. The differences between Clare and the nation are slight, but should be mentioned. Clare men enter shopkeeping at a slightly later age and remain in it somewhat longer than do the men of the entire country, although relatively the ages are distributed in the same manner. Seventeen per cent of the Clare men are under thirty-five years of age, whereas in the entire country, 23 per cent are under that age. Both the Free State and Clare have approximately 50 per cent of their shopkeepers grouped between thirty-five and fifty-five. The older ages have proportionately more in Clare, for there 35 per cent of the total are over fifty-five years, and only 27 per cent in the whole country.

The figures on marriage also show some slight variations. Clare male shopkeepers are more likely to get married than their brethren elsewhere. Only one-fifth of Clare men as against one-quarter in the Free State are unmarried. The progression is much the same for each group. It is here that we can observe the remarkably close coincidence between age at time of entry into

Table 10

Male Shopkeepers by Age Distribution and Conjugal Status

| Age Group | County Clare | | Free State | Clare — Single Shopkeepers | |
	Number	Per Cent	Per Cent	Number	Per Cent
14–15	0			0	
16–17	0		.2	0	
18–19	1	.2	.5	1	100.0
20–24	10	1.7	2.8	8	80.0
25–34	85	14.8	18.9	47	55.3
35–44	122	21.2	25.9	25	20.5
45–54	153	26.7	25.4	13	8.5
55–64	98	17.1	15.5	10	10.2
65 and over	105	18.3	10.8	12	11.4
Total	574	100.0	100.0	116	20.2

shopkeeping and assumption of the marital state. We note a rapid increase in the total numbers up to the age of thirty-five, but the total of married males climbs more rapidly than that of bachelors. For example, there are 60 per cent more shopkeepers in the thirty to thirty-four age bracket than in the preceding five year period. The increase in single males, however, was only 4 per cent, while whereas the number of those who were married jumped 147 per cent. In the succeeding ten year period married males increased by 42 per cent, and single males suffered a one-third decline. The total of those who were married obviously drew from both the single group and the newcomers to the occupation. Entry into marriage or the occupation practically ceases among those in the forty-five to fifty-four age span. We find an increase of 8 per cent in the number who are married, and a one-third decrease in the unmarried category, figures that suggest a departure of some single men out of the occupation entirely.

Shopkeeping is one of the rare occupations that is fully open to both sexes, although it attracts men in somewhat larger proportions. In this sense it contrasts with the unwritten but nevertheless real restrictions which prevent women from becoming laborers or artisans, and from entering some of the professions, as well as with their specific exclusion from the clergy. That either sex can fill the role of shopkeeper equally well suggests that this occupation possesses some qualities which permit the condition. The statistical evidence supports this observation in a most unusual way, for when we turn to examine the rates and progressions which the census establishes for females, we find an almost exact correspondence with those which characterize males. Of the two exceptions of any importance the first arises from differences in life expectancy and age differential at time

Table 11

Female Shopkeepers by Age Distribution and Conjugal Status

| | County Clare | | Free State | Clare—Single Shopkeepers | |
Age Group	Number	Per Cent	Per Cent	Number	Per Cent
14–15	0		0.1	0	
16–17	0		0.2	0	
18–19	1	.3	0.5	1	100.0
20–24	7	2.0	2.9	6	85.7
25–34	35	10.3	14.0	16	45.7
35–44	75	22.0	20.8	30	40.0
45–54	76	22.3	24.1	25	32.9
55–64	73	21.4	20.1	15	20.6
65 and over	74	21.7	17.3	13	17.6
Total	341	100.0	100.0	106	31.1

of marriage: specifically, in the country as a whole 35 per cent of all female shopkeepers are widows. The second exception is related to the internal dynamics of the Irish family: shopkeeping fathers sometimes establish unmarried daughters in small businesses of their own, and this fact may help to account for the 44 per cent of female shopkeepers who are spinsters. Otherwise, there are no sexual differences.

Men and women enter shopkeeping at about the same age; they remain in the occupation for about the same span of years; and they decrease in number at about the same rate with advancing age. In County Clare, the females resemble in remarkable fashion their shopkeeping sisters elsewhere. They follow Clare men in entering the occupation slightly later and in approximately the same proportions, but the figure of 31 per cent who remain single falls sharply below the nation's average of 44 per cent. Actually, if we exclude the widows, the married females count for only about one-fifth of the total. What proportion of this fifth may result from the practice of some shopkeepers' setting their wives up in a second shop we do not know, but it seems almost certain that in such eventualities the husbands will also be employed. Here is another example of the social reality that stands behind these counts and illustrates the linkage between shopkeeping and family.

This central fact is less clearly apparent in the age and sex distributions and marital condition among the shop assistants, but like our count for the shopkeepers, quantitative measures serve to frame the questions which lead us to the social dynamics. Shop assisting is primarily an occupation of the young and the unmarried. For the entire country, three-quarters of all the male assistants, and an even larger proportion of females, are under the age of thirty-five; in fact, half the males are under twenty-five and only 5 per cent are forty-five or older. They tend not to marry, but if they do, it is at a later age. Only 16 per cent of the males and 4 per cent of the females take spouses; and of those under thirty years of age, only 5 per cent of the males and 1 per cent of the females are married.

The distributions of male and female shop assistants for Clare are almost identical with those of the nation. In fact, they accentuate the tendencies already noted. Both males and females

Table 12

Male Shop Assistants by Age Distribution and Conjugal Status

Age Group	County Clare		Free State	Clare—Single Shop Assistants	
	Number	Per Cent	Per Cent	Number	Per Cent
12–13	0		.1		
14–15	12	3.2	2.9	12	100.0
16–17	25	6.6	10.2	25	100.0
18–19	53	14.0	13.6	53	100.0
20–24	96	25.4	24.3	95	99.0
25–34	105	27.8	26.8	98	93.3
35–44	44	11.9	12.1	30	66.7
45–54	25	6.6	6.3	13	52.0
55–64	9	2.4	2.6	7	77.8
65 and over	8	2.1	1.1	6	75.0
Total	378	100.0	100.0	339	89.7

enter their occupation at a slightly later age, reach a somewhat higher peak more quickly, and fall away from this more rapidly. The single state is also somewhat more common. Ninety per cent of the males and 95 per cent of the females remain unmarried.

All these series reveal the internal consistencies in distribu-

Table 13

Female Shop Assistants by Age Distribution and Conjugal Status

Age Group	County Clare		Free State	Clare—Single Shop Assistants	
	Number	Per Cent	Per Cent	Number	Per Cent
12–13	0		0.1	0	
14–15	4	1.5	2.2	4	100.0
16–17	27	10.3	9.7	27	100.0
18–19	34	12.9	15.1	34	100.0
20–24	87	33.1	32.1	87	100.0
25–34	64	24.3	26.4	61	95.3
35–44	32	12.3	8.3	27	84.4
45–54	10	3.7	4.0	8	80.0
55–64	4	1.5	1.5	2	50.0
65 and over	1	.4	.6	1	100.0
Total	263	100.0	100.0	251	95.4

Family and Community in Ireland

Figure 14

Age Distribution and Marital Status of Shopkeepers and Shop Assistants: A Comparison of Irish Free State and County Clare

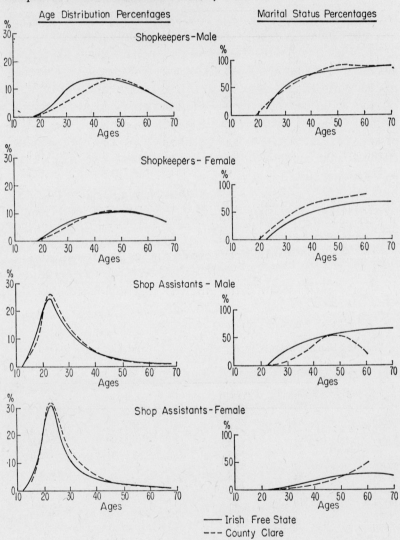

tion for males and females in each of the occupations, and the contrast between the two occupations. Shopkeepers and shop assistants are strikingly dissimilar in their age distributions and in marriage tendencies. Most male shopkeepers are over thirty-five years of age and are married. Most male shop assistants, on the other hand, are under thirty and are unmarried.

No other two occupational groups delay marriage to such an advanced age. Even the small farmers of Ireland, who are unique in the world in this respect, do not approximate the degree of celibacy exhibited here by the shop assistants. In fact, only the Roman Catholic clergy, with its enforced celibacy, offers a rate of near comparability. When we understand, however, that the status of shop assistant is for most a transitory one, preparatory to becoming the fully accredited owner of a shop and entering into full adulthood through marriage, then the statistical measures take on new meaning. Shop assisting and shopkeeping must be viewed as two connected steps in a social process rather than as two unrelated industrial groupings. It is to the description and analysis of this process that we now turn.

17

Induction and Transformation

Townsmen and countrymen are separated from each other in many ways. In the particulars of dress, speech, and manner, either or both declare their origin and their identity. Yet when we look more closely we can also see the marks of cultural similarity within the contrasts as they have been described for us by George Birmingham with such clarity and wit in his *Irishmen All*. How may we explain these divergencies and commonalities? It is easy enough to attribute them to the variable backgrounds from which men come to maturity, and few would dispute the validity of such an assertion. Our question would still await an answer, however, because only as we are able to specify the detail of the process which produces such varying consequences should we be allowed to believe that full comprehension is ours.

In one sense it is to this problem that we now turn. It is a problem of transformation: of youth into adult, and of the countryborn into townsman. Even though the passage is marked by clearly distinguishable stages, the double metamorphosis is both connected and simultaneous. We seek to trace the route of the

342

country youth (usually a young man but not all) whose career, first as apprentice, later as shop assistant, and finally as owner and operator of his own shop with newly acquired spouse, is brought to such a successful stage. The natural history of his movement is no exclusive prerogative of the country youth, however. Sons and daughters born to the family of a town shopkeeper may use the same path, although for most to do so successfully requires that they renew those ties which earlier gave their own parents a foothold.

In addition, we must admit to other purposes which we believe to be as fundamental as those already mentioned. Divergencies and commonalities are no mere listing of identifying characteristics, but an intimate aspect of the patterns which guide man's behavior and of the relationships which join him with others in all his cooperative endeavors. Thus, in the particulars of individual lives we are seeking to understand how the social diversities of town and country are joined and in this union give to Ireland the strength which makes its people into one, though yet separate among themselves. Then, too, we want to learn what we can of the complexities of town life, the structure of its social classes and institutional divisions which organizes the specialization of activities. Somehow, the viability of community life rests upon a constructive balance of tensions among its separate aspects, and the specification of this balance must be extrapolated from individual behavior as it occurs in the course of events. The shopkeepers, with their central position in the life of the town, serve as the reference from which our quest for pattern and structure is directed. Our first step is to examine the relationship between shop owner and shop assistant.

The great majority of the assistants who staff the shops of Irish towns — and of Ennis — are drawn from country families. Shopkeepers will explain their preferences for country lads on the grounds that they are not afraid of work, are amenable to suggestion, and show respect for authority. These are

343

qualities which they believe are less to be expected if a youth is town born. But adaptability and the willingness to work for the benefit of one's employer are not the only qualities which weigh heavily in the choice. The shopkeeper, himself of country stock, knows full well the strength of obligations which bind rural folk and which follow them into town and even beyond in the larger world. We have already learned how rural custom requires that one "go" with family and friends. Neither space nor activity can extinguish such ties, and the assistant in the town's shop carries these with him. And although the employer may rationalize the consequences in economic terms of "good business" the fact remains that they originate in familial considerations. The generalities are succinctly put in a brief excerpt from one informant: "It is expected that the shop assistants' people will give their trade where the boy is employed and that his folks will canvass their friends to support the House. In other words, it's better business to get in the country lad."

Our informant added that because townspeople acted differently, the town boy could not be expected to bring as much business with him. In this contrast we learn something of the differing expectations of family and community ties in town and country, but we must also comment upon the sociological significance of our evidence. From the shopkeeper's perspective he gains through his employees' connections with the folk in the countryside, but this relationship is no one-sided arrangement. In the countrymen's eyes and in his response to their requests for favors, the shopkeeper becomes an intermediary through which they make contact with individuals in the town who in other circumstances would not be directly available to them. Thus the relationship becomes a fully reciprocal one within the definition which both shopkeeper and countryman understand and which extends far beyond either shop or farm family. These lines of communication and their potential extensions should not be visualized as a stabilized network. Instead, they represent extensions of certain obligations embedded in the familial pat-

344

tern to individuals tangential to the shopkeeper-assistant relationship. In the aggregate, the potential reach and magnitude of this system is enormous, and for this reason we have stressed the crucial role of the shopkeeper in providing the channels through which town and country are joined.

Turning to the rural terminus of this relationship we can add further to our understanding of the process. Upon the farm father rests the responsibility for the placement of his children. One son will be selected to succeed him on the land, and, hopefully, a match will be arranged between one daughter and a near-by farmer's son. But the father must also make appropriate provision for the other children. Some will be sent out to aunts and uncles in other parts of the world, but one of the preferred avenues is placing a son or daughter as an apprentice in a shop. Thus, the family extends its connections through one of its members to the town.

There is an additional advantage: apprenticeship is viewed as only the first step in a series of progressions which will carry the young man into shop ownership. In the eyes of the countryman shopkeeping is a dignified and honorable occupation, and the gentility which it bestows makes of one a gentleman. We can find no better statement of the case than that provided by George Birmingham who wrote:

The real attraction of "business" lies in its gentility. The farmer is a man. The carpenter is a working man. A draper's assistant is a gentleman . . . For the Irish still use the word "gentlemen" to describe only those of a certain social position: draper's assistants, for instance, bank clerks, military officers, and landed proprietors. We still draw a line between those who are gentlemen and ladies and those who are not. The attractive thing about "business" as a profession is that it is above the line.[1]

Actually, the father who apprentices a child is motivated by a combination of factors of which social ambition must be reck-

[1] George A. Birmingham, *Irishmen All* (London and Edinburgh: T. N. Foulis, 1913), pp. 215–216.

345

oned as only one. Yet all are related to the family and its senti-ments, and the rise in the world of any individual member adds to the luster of the whole. In any event the arrangement is a mutual one. As the shopkeeper finds it to his advantage to bring in a country lad, so the farm father feels it is to his to send a son into the shop ranks of the town. At each end of the channel of movement individuals cooperate to send and to receive.

Apprenticeship is a time of transition, of separation from fam-ily and locality, and of gradual incorporation into a new world of activity and relationships. It is also a probationary period, of training and learning not only the techniques of shopkeeping, but also urban styles of speech, dress, and mannerisms. If the youth is successful in adaptation he then graduates to a new posi-tion, that of shop assistant, which is itself an intermediate step along the path to an even greater goal.

The process is fully developed in the legal and social prac-tices of Irish society. Each new stage follows the preceding one in exact order. First there is a period of negotiation and investi-gation by both the youth's father and his prospective master. If both parties are satisfied with their findings they sign a contract which indentures the youth and in which the mutual obligations of each party are stipulated. The boy then enters into service and over a period of time completes his training. Finally, upon termination of indentureship he receives a certificate attesting his qualifications and readiness for employment. Such is the out-line of sequences; now let us turn to the substance of each.

Many of the preliminaries remind one of matchmaking, where every precaution is taken to reduce the possibilities of failure or dispute. If the farmer is not already acquainted with the shop and its owner, he makes a thorough investigation. He makes inquiries among his friends in town and country and from the available facts arrives at a decision. He wants to assure him-self that the shop is in a prosperous condition and that his son will receive the training for which he bargains. The personal characteristics of the owner are considered. A shopkeeper who might ill-treat his son or who has objectionable moral or ethical habits is to be avoided. If the father already knows the owner and has full confidence in him, he informs the shopkeeper about the qualities of his son and the advantages to be derived from taking him on. The shopkeeper, who also stands to gain or lose, will be equally careful in his inquiries. The position and background of the family are usually indicative of the type of lad he is to get.

If each one is satisfied, a contract in the form of an indenture is made between the father and the shopkeeper. The specific obligations of the shopkeeper, the apprentice, and the father are listed in the indenture. The shopkeeper agrees to take the youth into his house for a two- to three-year period of training and to instruct him "to the best of his power, knowledge and ability." Covenants also provided for the amount of wages to be paid. According to one shopkeeper, the apprentice was usually paid five shillings weekly the first year, six to ten shillings the second year, and fifteen shillings the third year. Practices vary; one draper said he paid the apprentice nothing until the third year, when he gave him five shillings, but that some shopkeepers gave nothing. The father is also responsible in case of his son's sickness, and if the latter returns home he receives no wages for the time he is absent.

In return for these considerations the father pays indenture money to the shopkeeper. That varies with the type of trade from thirty to sixty pounds sterling. The son agrees to "place and bind" himself as an apprentice to the shopkeeper for the stated period. The contract also stipulates:

. . . that the said Apprentice shall during the said term faithfully honestly and diligently serve [the shopkeeper] and attend to the said trade or business carried on by [him] as aforesaid and shall obey the lawful commands of [him] or [his] representatives or such person or persons engaged in [his] business as [he] shall specify and shall keep the secrets of the said business And shall not absent himself from the

347

service of [the shopkeeper] without [his] consent And shall attend such classes in Technical or other Schools as [he] desire And shall not at any time injure destroy spoil obliterate cancel waste embezzle spend lend or make away with any of the machinery effects books papers writings moneys stamps or other property of [the shopkeeper] but shall in all things conduct and acquit himself as an honest and faithful Apprentice ought to do and shall not join or become a member of any Trade-Union Society or Combination during the existence of this Indenture without the consent in writing of the said [shopkeeper].

The father agrees to make good any loss which the shopkeeper suffers by reason of the "misbehaviour neglect or improper conduct of the said Apprentice." The protection accorded the shopkeeper is seen in this provision:

. . . if the said Apprentice shall divulge any of the secrets of the said business or shall be willfully disobedient to the lawful and reasonable commands of the said [shopkeeper] . . . or shall in any way seriously misconduct himself or shall be so inefficient as to give no promise of becoming a competent workman [of which disobedience, misconduct, or incompetence the said (shopkeeper) shall be the sole judge] after one month's notice of [his] intention so to do to discharge the Apprentice from such apprenticeship and to cancel this Indenture and thereupon the said apprenticeship shall be at an end and this Indenture shall at once cease and be absolutely determined.

Although ostensibly the indenture is for the protection of the shopkeeper, the father and his son also secure certain rights and privileges. The failure of shopkeepers to live up to the spirit of the contract leads to results as unhappy as those which follow its violation on the part of the apprentice. The advantages of spelling out the obligations and the necessity for providing control over those who are no longer under direct parental supervision are stated by one shopkeeper as follows:

The principal reason that a boy is apprenticed is to see that he spends a reasonable length of time in learning the business. If he were not strictly regulated in his actions he might run away and join the army or become a cornerboy. It is designed to prevent him from returning home where he may not be wanted. If the boy does run away the employer can have him brought back by force. I have known cases where boys got imprisonment for breaking their indentureship. The system is very old and it would have died out years ago only it is good for the boy.

The shopkeeper assumes moral as well as contractual duties. He is obligated to look out for the welfare of the young man outside the shop. He prohibits smoking or drinking and has the authority to punish him for any actions to which he objects. He makes sure the young lad says his prayers and attends mass regularly.

Apprenticeship begins with the entry of the country youth into the household of his new master. Although the faces and surroundings he encounters there may appear strange at first, he soon discovers a basic similarity in the pattern of family life to what he already knows. The authority of the shopkeeper is not unlike that which he experienced under the supervision of his father. He joins the family members in their meals and in their prayers and may come to share their joys and sorrows. But in other ways the adjustment may be much more demanding. Separation from the protecting intimacy of one's own family can lead to deep loneliness, as some have reported to us. Even the opportunity to return home on Sunday or holidays does not erase the hurt that comes with knowledge of the finality of his father's decision. Only rarely does an apprentice break his indenture by running away. The majority are hardier. They know they must accept difficult conditions, because there is no place for them on the farm, and they are expected to make good on their own. Resentments against the master and dissatisfaction with the position are subordinated to the demand that they continue. As one shopkeeper phrased it: "On the whole the system is a very good one. When parents bind their child down they encourage him to learn all he can by impressing on him that his future is in his own hands and that when he is out of his time the world is his to live in. He can't go home a failure."

349

For each one, however, there is always the promise of the future, and the varied urban world offers new experiences, which gradually transform the parochial character of his earlier life. But his immediate objective is to learn the practices of his trade, and under the careful tutelage of the shopkeeper the process begins. As one of the masters described it:

When a lad comes in he is bound to serve me for three years and is kept inside. He is taken to a certain counter where he is taught to cut goods, wrap up packages, and in general to do the tedious work around the shop. From this one counter he is transferred to the other departments in the shop, there being six. Some men in training will leave the young fellow in the same place but it is my idea to give him a chance in all the departments. The first two years I don't pay him anything but after that time I will give him five bob a week and then he gets two pounds a week when he has served his time of three years. During the first year the fellow is really an expense to you and he takes up your time in teaching him. He doesn't know how to cut things properly and it may be that you will have to make good some of his mistakes.

The apprentice graduates from the performance of simple and menial tasks to more responsible duties. He acquires a thorough acquaintance with the shop, its arrangements, goods, prices, and customers before he is granted the chance to make a sale. When the apprentice first enters the shop he imagines that selling is the simplest part of the merchandising. The owner soon disabuses him of this belief. The long wait before getting a free hand and the careful preparation he receives impress on the boy's mind the important refinements of selling tactics. His first sales are always to his friends and relatives.[2] The shopkeeper

[2] Practice varies with different types of shops. In any shop where there are a large number of staples with fixed prices, the apprentice would be initiated into selling earlier. The assumption of responsibility comes later in drapery and departmental shops. The practice in chemists' shops is imposed by statute. Here, no apprentice is allowed to fill a prescription until completing a minimum four-year training requirement, except under the supervision of a doctor. Individual temperament of shopkeeper and assistant determines to a large extent practices within any one of these types of shops.

feels that relatives will be more charitable about his mistakes, and the experience thus gained can be applied elsewhere in due course. Once the knack of selling has been acquired, the apprentice makes the transition from serving acquaintances to waiting upon strangers. Ordinarily this step does not occur until the last year. Only then is a fuller measure of responsibility granted.

The evaluation of the position and status of the customer comes only with long experience. Once acquired the salesman will make no mistake in the treatment of the customer or in the quality and type of goods to be shown. His fellow workers point out to him differences in dress, speech, and manners, the criteria on which one bases this judgment. Slight differences have significance for the trained observer. One draper claimed that on the basis of dress he could distinguish the ten-acre farmer from the twenty-acre farmer.

The development of competent judgment extends beyond the evaluation of a person's social position. The understanding of a customer's evaluations in terms of himself and his position in the society is also necessary. This fact is illustrated by a draper who recounted one of his experiences as an apprentice. The older person, his father in this case, used a situation to impress on his son the necessity for such understanding.

One day three men were coming up the street and before they reached the shop door his father asked the son which of the three would buy a new suit. Casey picked out the shabbiest, whereupon his father laughed. When the men came up he [the father] went out in the street to them and addressed them by name, falling into conversation with them. Finally, he turned to the best dressed one and told him it was about time to get a new suit of clothes as he was getting a little shabby. In a few more minutes he had him in the shop and had sold him a suit.

The apprentice does not become a competent salesman until he has learned to move easily and freely in the varied situations he meets. The first demand is that one sell. The rule that no customer should be allowed to leave the shop without making a purchase is equally exigent. If the article he wants is not in stock, then sell him something else. If he objects to the price, make an adjustment. It is believed that once a man has begun to trade with you he will not go elsewhere, but, as a corollary, if he is allowed to leave the shop to make his purchase elsewhere he may never come again. The story told by a draper of an experience in his training period illustrates the point.

I remember several incidents which show the type of training I was subjected to. One day a fellow came in and asked for some brown socks. I couldn't supply them and the fellow went out the door again. The owner saw him and saw what was happening, and as he did he called him back and in the end sold him several pairs of black socks instead. The owner said that the type of person he wanted in business could sell a man black when it was brown socks he wanted.

Even abuse from customers must be taken in good humor, and the apprentice and assistant as well as the owner may often be subject to it. If an apprentice or employee offends a customer, the matter is smoothed over by the owner, who then impresses the seriousness of the mistake on the culprit.

The transition from indentured apprenticeship to accredited shop assistant produces none of the dislocations which accompanied his original entry into the shop world. True enough, he is now emancipated from the strict supervision of his personal life which he experienced as a resident in the house of his master. In his new "digs" in some one of the town's boarding houses he joins others who are like himself in age and status. The new freedom also permits him to seek employment where he will, but more likely than not he will continue on in the shop in which he was trained. Such an arrangement is of advantage to him and to his employer. He knows the shop, its goods, and its customers, and he and the owner are adjusted to each other's personal idiosyncrasies. If he were employed elsewhere in the city he might carry valuable trade secrets with him and, of even greater worth, the trade of his family and friends. If the apprentice has not proved satisfactory, the owner will give him six months' notice, during which time he can look for an opening elsewhere.

The readjustment in the relations with his family which the earlier separation required has long since been accomplished. The social bonds which connect him with family and friends are continually renewed by their frequent visits to the shop. These, together with his infrequent visits to the home farm, redefine and reaffirm the familial and community sentiments. Nevertheless, the subtle influences of town and job have begun their work, and he and his family soon become conscious of changes wrought by new experiences and his coming of age. He is proud of his new status, and his position gives him a feeling of importance and responsibility. He has begun to carve for himself a niche in an urban world which as a country youngster he half feared and half respected.

Changes in personal behavior and appearance now set the erstwhile apprentice apart from those with whom he grew up. As he feels the confidence born of his new achievement he no longer makes such frequent excursions to his home. Still, although their relationships are no longer so intimate, both he and his family feel that they are still one with each other. Family and community ties have not become weakened, but they have acquired a new definition from the shifts in relative positions. The town is now claiming him as one of its own.

Leaving aside the male apprentices for the moment, let us turn to the females. Here conditions are rather different; nonetheless, they offer a valuable contrast with the generalities of custom surrounding the apprenticeship training of males. Practice permits much wider variation in the formalities of recruitment and training of females. Formal indenturing is usually reserved for those who become dressmakers, milliners, and sales ladies. Job requirement is more often seen in the light of skill and performance rather than relationships which bring trade. This fact may account, in part, for a large proportion of shop girls drawn from town-living artisan families. But daughters of small farmers also flock into the towns, sometimes under formal apprenticeship arrangements, sometimes not to become shop assistants. A bar maid may be in from the country and live with the family that employs her, but the training required for adequate performance is not great.

Many of the shopgirls who are town born are employed in small shops where no attempt is made at formal training. Shopkeepers who sell sweets, vegetables, tobacco, stationery, glass, and other miscellaneous items of small value usually hire untrained helpers. As soon as the girl leaves school she is employed at a very nominal rate and given a minimum of instruction. She remains until she marries, when she is replaced by girls of similar background.

The relatively large number of female shopkeepers may be accounted for by adding those who have inherited their shops from fathers or husbands to those few whose businesses cater exclusively to female trade.

For most young men who have just won the new standing of shop assistant a full decade or more will pass before they encounter the last great crisis in their transition to the status of shopowner. The intervening years, however, may well be viewed as part of the full cycle of transformation from youth to adulthood and from countryman to townsman. During the final period the continuous accumulation of experience and capacity for responsibility slowly advances the young man toward the fateful day when he must strike out on his own. Only then comes the dramatic flare-up which signals the sharp break with his employer.

In the meantime the round of duties within the shop does not vary much from day to day. The more menial and routine tasks are performed by messengers or apprentices. The assistant is responsible for the goods on the shelves, which he keeps covered and clean. He marks prices and arranges the display of items sold at his counter. These are duties learned during his apprenticeship. The competent assistant, however, constantly adds to his knowledge as new situations demanding resourceful action arise in the lively and interesting art of salesmanship.

The owner, meanwhile, continues to direct, suggest, and criticize his employees, thus preserving shop discipline and ensuring the continuation of amicable relations with his customers.

The pressure exerted by the shopkeeper to keep his assistants within a prescribed course of behavior also impresses on them their subordinate position in the shop. These restraints extend beyond the shop; elsewhere he is also expected to observe the standards of public decency. If the assistant should offend against the approved canons of behavior, either within or outside the shop, the employer may punish him or threaten dismissal. Such a relationship may command respect, but it also engenders antagonism. There is nothing distinctive about the psychological content of relationships between superiors and inferiors. Admiration or hostility may be found anywhere. Tension can be diminished if established rules are followed and distance maintained. The shopkeeper feels this to be his responsibility. Should an assistant attempt a degree of equality with his employer, he will be rebuffed. There can be no intimacies, and in the enforcement of respect for his position bitterness may arise.

Employers are careful to make no statements about their employees where such remarks may be heard and repeated. They consider it good business practice to avoid discussing personal or shop affairs in front of them. They also say that the immaturity of the shop assistants makes it undesirable for them to know more than is necessary for them to fill their jobs. The assistant who has learned enough to make him a good clerk may still remain ignorant of "trade secrets" which are essential for the conduct of business. Thus the buying of goods, the fixing of prices, profit and loss, total sales, expenses, and similar facts and practices are held solely by the owner. One draper described the general practice when he said:

It is the strict policy of the man who runs a shop never to tell any of his trade secrets and he is especially careful not to say anything in front of one of his shop assistants. The shopboy doesn't have sufficient responsibility to respect their importance. He may, in the presence of other shop assistants, give away that his employer buys his goods for such a price, or that his total profits come to some amount.

Accounts of the irresponsible behavior and disloyalty of assistants form part of the lore of each shopkeeper. Each new incident evokes old ones and makes the owner increasingly cautious and watchful. For example, instances are cited of assistants who have gone to distant cities to purchase what they wanted when they could have been supplied in the shop in which they worked.

The positional distinction which separates owner from assistant within the shop is also found in their mutual exclusivity in community life. Each has different interests, belongs to different clubs, and has his own group of friends. In this respect their patterns resemble the distinctions which other groups draw among themselves. One of the wealthier merchants, in commenting about this, said: "There is the Abbey club, which is the businessman's club. It is a nice little place in winter but we don't use it much in the summer. The Odd Fellows is the shop assistants' club and all the staff of Kennedy's and O'Deas and other places are in it."

He named other clubs and distinguished them by occupational activities — the "gentlemen's club," the "professional man's club," the "courthouse club," the "better class artisans' club," and the "laborers' club." He added:

The reason that there are so many is that there are these different classes even in this little town, which is really laughable. But you couldn't have the employers drinking with the assistants for then they would lose all their respect for you. The clerks and artisans have nothing in common and an entirely different outlook on life so naturally they have a different club.

The commonalty which joins shopkeepers or professional men in specific clubs excludes those of other social ranks. In the life outside the shop an assistant associates with those whose status is similar to his own. His friends are other shop assistants with common interests which set them apart. But their separateness is something other than that which characterizes the divisions between laborer, artisan, and professional man; these are fixed categories of age and status. Shop assistants do not constitute a true social class in the same way, because theirs is an intermediate age position, one from which its members may and are expected to climb to still another rung on the ladder of occupation and status. Their position is one level in a progression which encompasses both geographical and social mobility.

Although the shopkeeper knows that some day his assistants may strike out for themselves, when the time arrives the transition often brings recriminations. This is illustrated in the incident of a draper who had taken a fancy to one of his young men and helped him along. He showed him how to invest his money and in general treated him as a friend, until one day the assistant set up in competition to his benefactor. The older man's objection might not have been so great if he had not also used his position as an assistant to get customers for his own new shop. As the informant expressed it:

To show you how an assistant can violate your confidence I will tell you a story of what this Burke did. There was a man in town who had been trading with O'Casey for years and always gotten what he wanted. He went in to buy a suit and the young man didn't show the customer anything that suited, although he had the stuff and knew what this man's taste was like. He said that we have a new order of goods coming in in two weeks and if you come in then it will mean that we have exactly what you want. The customer said all right. In two weeks he came back and he again showed him the same type of stuff that he didn't want, until he had gotten him, he thought,

357

into a circle, and then he said, "I'm going to open up for myself in a couple of weeks and if you come into my place then I will have exactly what you want!" That is the reason why a shop owner should never tell his assistant too much or do too much for him because he will have a feeling of disgust for his employer.

This case illustrates one of the ways in which the assistant who intends to set up for himself may plan ahead. In another instance he may ask for concessions; ungranted, they create a situation that gives him an excuse to resign. One particular instance of just this sort was described by Collins, a boot merchant, who had set up for himself after a clash with his employer:

I used to work for Tyson and I received 35 bob a week. I asked for another 5 bob and they refused me, so I quit. Tyson from England came here to see me and he offered me any shop I wanted in Ireland and I was to name my own figure, but I told him that when I asked for a raise they wouldn't give it to me and that it was too late now. Then he said it was the fault of the office and not him, but I told him no. He then asked what about my agreement that I wouldn't start a shoe shop here for twenty years. I told him to take his agreement to law, and I would be glad if he did because I would show the people just what sort of a concern he had, and what he paid those who worked for him, and within two weeks he would have to leave Ennis or his shop would be blown sky-high. He asked if I meant it and I said I did, that if he didn't believe it to try and find out and he wouldn't have a shoe shop in Ennis and would never have one again. I then told him to get out of my shop and quit giving me this line of guff and if he didn't I would smash his brains out. It finally ended by his saying, "Will you shake hands?" and I did.

Collins went on to say that he had had it in mind to start out on his own all along, but that if they had agreed to pay him more he would have stayed with the firm. When they refused, it was a good chance for him to clear out and make his own start, as he did.

The most interesting part of this situation comes after Tyson, an Englishman, reminds Collins of the contract provisions about not starting a shop in the same town for twenty years. This additional attempt to resubordinate a former employee met with the bitter challenge "to go ahead and try to enforce that provision but be expected to take the consequence." Tyson did not attempt to enforce the provision, and Collins was not disturbed in the conduct of the shop which he had by this time set up. Not even the offer of superior position and additional pay could induce Collins to return to the pattern from which he had freed himself.

A similar crisis arose out of the bankruptcy of another employer. Three assistants were thrown out of work and thus found a favorable occasion to start on their own. The difficulties confronting them and the manner in which they surmounted these are told in the following account:

The three assistants put their heads together and decided they would start a business of their own. The other two had 125 pounds and Murphy had 35 he had saved. But his father had left him 100 pounds in a will which he was to receive when he was 35. He went out to see his brother Stephen in Ballycorick about this, but he would give him nothing. So he went to a solicitor and got a writ out against him and finally got the money from him.

Now they had a little capital, but they could get no place in Ennis to start their business. In those days it took six or eight months to evict a person so they took forcible possession of a shop; the one where O'Reilly, the chemist, is now, and the landlord could do nothing against them for a time. They got stock through travelers they knew who took their word for it, and they went ahead. The shop did well.

Such problems confront everyone who starts on his own. The first and most important thing to have is money. Without it nothing can be done, and the assistant must often save for years before he has enough to make a start. Although it is uncommon for two or three to join in a partnership, financial aid from families is not unusual.

A place of business must be found, and vacancies in desirable locations or even undesirable ones are rare. Not often is a prospective landlord willing to let his property when he is not too sure that he will ever receive any rent at all, and property rented to a newcomer may possibly go two years without producing income. But Murphy and his partners cut this Gordian knot when they boldly appropriated a building. Ordinarily, however, the assistant acquires tenure not from the landlord but from some person already an occupant.

The cost of securing a shop and making it ready for business often consumes most of the newcomer's ready cash. He must then look to the commercial traveler to sell him goods on credit, meeting the obligation when he can. Such practice is widespread, and wholesalers are in the habit of carrying large accounts and quite ready to accept new ones on credit. In this way they monopolize a man's business by dictating that he buy only from them because of his indebtedness. If the shopkeeper fails to do so, the wholesaler can close him out by the issuance of writs for unpaid accounts.

Once a shop is established, the new shopkeeper knows he can count on the support of his family. Here again the strength of family sentiments helps to make a success of the new enterprise. In the same way that the shopkeeper benefited from the family trade of his apprentice and assistant, so the person starting out for himself expects to receive the custom of his far flung relatives.

Thus we see that among the shop assistants, the personal ties which bind town and country through the shopkeeping system do not die away as the country lads grow older. On the contrary their advance in status gives them an added importance in their relations with the countryside and their own kindred within it. The town's shopkeeping group is constantly being recruited from the rural areas. The channel through which this movement takes place is firmly fixed in both the social system and the legal system of Irish society. Its strength arises from the adaptation of the deeply ingrained patterns of kinship obligation to the economic level, thus transforming that level and converting it into a truly social one.

360

18

Marriage and Family

Before our analysis of the conventions surrounding the formation of the shop family and its subsequent natural history, something should be said of the physical setting which provides the stage for the drama of its life. This excursion will illuminate for us, among other things, the categories of relationships as they are expressed in events and the spatial distributions that accompany them. Within the family distinctions based on sex, age, and status are paramount; but the sale of goods also brings its members into contact with the clientele of purchasers, and the relationships with this group are ordered in spatial ways.

The commercial district of the town is dominated by two- and three-story buildings tightly packed along both sides of streets that stretch from the town's hub toward its outer limits. The activities of this area include much more than just retailing, because these buildings also house the families of the shop owners. In the spatial linkage of economic with familial functions we encounter a pattern similar to that found among the farmers.

361

So also is the identification of property and family much the same.

Among the shops the similarity in external physical appearance and in internal arrangement is great. Above the entryway but stretching the full width of each building is a sign which, with rare exceptions, informs us of the name of the owner and occupants. The type of business conducted within receives no such emphasis, nor is it needed. The identification of name, location, and business is already deeply fixed in the minds of most residents. When one speaks of "Garry's," everyone knows that the reference is to the middle-aged publican who lives on lower Parnell Street. This knowledge may also include his life history — where he came from, whom he married, his children — and a general estimation of his character and standing in the community. If, by chance, there are two men with the same name, then there are other means of identifying them. Location or particular trade are the most frequently used. Thus one speaks of one "Foley" as being at the "height of the street" while the other is on lower Abbey Street, or simply as "Foley the publican." Such a qualification quickly dispels any doubt about whom the speaker is referring to.

In almost all of these shops the threshold is a step up from the front walk. A centrally placed door is flanked by display windows. Smaller shops often show one of each item that is stocked, for the information of the passer-by. Larger shops usually attempt an aesthetically devised display.

Each weekday, winter and summer, the door stands open to welcome all who enter, except perhaps the begging tinker woman. Inside, that portion of the ground floor fronting on the street is given over to commercial activities. Here are the counters, the shelves, and the display cases, on and in which are kept the merchandise offered for sale. The arrangement of the shop emphasizes the ordered relations between the proprietor and his customers. Counters and cases separate him and his help from those who buy.

362

Entrance to the upstairs living quarters is either directly from the street, by a door to one side of the shop front leading to a hall and stairs giving the family access to their quarters, or by an internal staircase which connects the two floors. In smaller shops kitchen and scullery may be on the ground floor in the rear.

The upstairs residential portion of the shop presents a uniformity which is easily described. The room fronting on the street is used as a combined living room and parlor. In area it is the largest room in the house, usually extending the full width of the shop and an equal distance toward the rear, being in shape nearly square. It is furnished with inexpensive oak furniture, upholstered chairs, and oftentimes a valued mahogany sideboard and table which have come down in the family or been bought at an auction. On one side is a fireplace with a small iron grate, beside which stand coal box and brass fire tongs. On the mantel above the fireplace is a variety of objects, bric-a-brac of brass or china which are mementos of some holiday or presents received in celebration of some event. Scattered in among these items are family photographs portraying the bridal couple in their wedding finery and the children at the time of first communion or confirmation and others preserving the memory of some special occasion. In some instances enlarged and tinted photographs of the couple's parents hang in a place of honor above the mantel. Brightly colored lithographs may adorn the walls.

The heirlooms, photographs, and furnishings are symbols which embody and reflect family status. Here the secular rituals of social class and of life crises are acted out. When clergy or special guests call, they are received here. At marriage and death, kin and friends gather here as one. On occasions other than these, it is seldom used.

In some of the larger shops a dining room is on the same floor toward the rear. It is furnished with simple oak chairs, a large dining table, and a dresser filled with china. Pictures of food or of animals hang on the walls. A coal grate is along one wall.

The kitchen is always located at the rear, and in most shops it is the center of family life. The kitchen is the province of the woman as she discharges her never ceasing domestic duties, but it gathers other members of the family at mealtime and for evening activities. Here too is found the family shrine. On the wall hangs a brightly colored print of the Sacred Heart of Jesus, which is illuminated by the glow from a small red lamp placed beneath, and near-by a framed plaque announces the dedication of the family to His Sacred Heart. Each night in a final act of piety and communal unity the family recites the Rosary. Although our description is a sincere statement of the ideal, all too often a husband does not return from the conviviality of the club until long after the children have finished their home work and hopped into bed.

Other rooms on this floor and on the one above are smallish cubicles used for sleeping quarters, allocated on the basis of sex, age, and status. The parental couple may share a room with small children, but sons and daughters, after the first communion, have separate rooms. In the attic is the room of the shop apprentice or the maid, if living in. Bedroom furnishings are of the simplest kind. They include bedstead, a dressing table, clothes cabinet, and a washstand and mirror. Over the bed hangs a crucifix and in the owner's room there is frequently a large religious effigy. The remoteness of the parental room is broken only at times of the stress of sickness or death. Then, priest, doctor, or nurse is granted admission. The exclusion and separateness extends even to the children, who after a certain age may not enter the bedchamber of their parents.

Some aspects of the connection between social relationships and the use of space are quite clear. The division of the shop into its business and residential portions reflects the different uses to which each is put. But this separation may also be seen as based on the categorization, in space, of types of relationships. We have made progress in understanding how pattern as behavior and relationships as structure are joined, but this understanding will be further amplified when we look at the family in greater detail.

Examining the genesis and internal structure of the shopkeeping family, the observer is immediately impressed by its resemblance to the country family. There need be no surprise at such similarities, however, now that we understand the process by which the youth of the countryside are recruited for and incorporated into the system of shopkeeping. The consequences of this extension to the town of the rural loyalties and obligations that unite kinsmen are evident in all other institutions. In particular, through ties of blood and marriage the urban and rural worlds are intimately and permanently joined, and the violent antipathy which once was expressed in open hostility is now contained.

Entrance into the status of shopkeeper and entrance into marriage are almost always coincident. The avenue to marriage, closed to the young man as shop assistant, opens wide when he sets up for himself. Because the possession of property is one of the essentials for getting a wife, the young shop assistant can begin to think seriously of marriage only as he prepares to strike out for himself. With a shop of his own, however, not only is marriage a possibility; a wife becomes an asset to his business.

The period when a shop assistant establishes himself in a shop is a crucial one. With his own, usually meager savings, what he can borrow, and the credit provided by suppliers he can get a place for business and a stock of goods. But to be successful he must also gather in customers, and although he expects his own kin to support him in the new venture, their trade alone is not sufficient. Through marriage, he gains additional capital in his wife's dowry and automatically adds the patronage which his wife's family and its connections will bring to him.

Kinship obligations follow the woman to the shop of her husband in exactly the same way that they followed the young man as apprentice and assistant to the shop of his master or employer. The man ordinarily seeks his wife in the rural areas for the same reasons that the established owner prefers the country lad as a helper. A mature shopkeeper, whose wife had been born on a farm, explained the advantages of the country girl as a wife in the following way:

> When a shopkeeper marries he must get a wife who can help him in the shop. He doesn't want one who has grand ideas about what a fine lady she is, because then she is no good in the house and will only drive the customers away. That is why he must go to the country to find a wife. The country girl has been reared alongside of her mother. She knows how to cook, sew, and to keep house, and she hasn't a lot of grand ideas in her head that the town girls have. When she comes to town she feels that she has made a real advance in the world and she appreciates the things she gets, while the town girl who has always had these things will only be wanting more than her husband can give her and will be careless and won't do her share.

The similarity between the pattern of the rural family and that of the shopkeeping family makes it comparatively easy for the country girl to assume her role as the wife of a shopkeeper. The same values which are stressed in the one type of household have their counterpart in the other. Within the family each girl learns the responsibilities of wife and mother, and she can discharge these equally well in either farm or shop. Although a subordinate in her husband's sphere, she is fully competent in her own. In addition, she assists her husband in his work as well as caring for the family and household.

The town-born shopkeeper is equally conscious of the advantages which accrue from selecting a country girl to be his wife. One young shopkeeper whose country-born father had left him a good business declared: "If you want to get married there is nothing to do about it, but to look out for a country girl. Most shopkeepers make out through their family trade. The only thing to do is to marry a rich woman in from the country and then all her friends will come in to you to trade."

If we examine the method by which the shopkeeper in the town secures a wife from the country, we encounter customs that are also deeply imbedded in rural society. Their observance ensures the continuity of property and family effectively in the rural setting as well as in the town. The customary practices surrounding "getting married" are embodied in a system of matchmaking very similar to the one we saw the farmers use. The match is a contractual arrangement between the parents of the marrying parties and involves the transfer of property. But it also involves much more. Each family must be certain that its prestige does not suffer through an ill-advised marriage. Social position and future prospects are ingredients as important as personal taste and compatibility.

The preliminary investigations and negotiations which establish the suitability of the match and which ensure against the contingency of misrepresentation are usually conducted by the families of the proposed groom and bride. The father of the boy inquires among his friends if they know of a girl with family and "fortune" suitable for his son. When a family with a likely girl is found, representatives of the two families begin the preliminary period of investigation. The boy's father, if he is unacquainted with the girl's family, makes inquiries about its "character." He makes sure that its members have been free from the taint of insanity or crime and that the proposed girl has the capabilities which make a good wife.

The girl's father makes similar inquiries about the boy's family and the condition of the shop. He wants to know the amount of its trade, stock, and furnishings and whether or not it is free of indebtedness. The negotiations may be broken off immediately by the discovery of any single objectionable feature. One shopkeeper summarizes the precautions which are taken when he says:

If a man is marrying a daughter into a shop and giving her a dowry, he wants to protect her against the possibility that her husband or the shop will turn out to be a lemon. He finds out if the proposed groom is a gambler, drunkard, spendthrift, or a damn fool, or if he is an invalid or has insanity in his family. He also wants to protect her from marrying into a business that has gone down the hill or is heavily indebted.

The man and his family are equally interested in the personal characteristics of his proposed bride. One shopkeeper, who commissioned a friend of his to be on the lookout for a girl to bring into his shop as a wife, cautioned his emissary: "If she bobs her hair, goes to the cinema, or wears silk stockings, I don't want to have anything to do with her." The friend explained: "He wanted a woman that would live the simple sort of life that he was accustomed to."

During the period of mutual investigation there takes place the practice locally called "walking the shop." The girl's father and his friends go to the shop of the prospective groom and inspect it thoroughly. They determine its location and size, the state of repair, the quantity and quality of the goods, its furnishings, and they count and step off the rooms. The owner sometimes resorts to deception, and on the day appointed for "shopwalking" his shop may be stocked with furniture and goods borrowed from his friends. He hopes to get a larger dowry because of his apparently prosperous condition. If the girl's people are satisfied that the shop is a good one and the young man desirable as a husband for their daughter, the next step is to decide the amount of the dowry.

The size of a girl's dowry is arrived at through bargaining between the representatives of the two families. Offers and counteroffers are made and rejected until a satisfactory settlement is reached. The size of the "fortune" is roughly equal in value to the value of the shop. Family prestige also plays a part, because the sum decided upon reflects in some degree the family's status in the community. One young unmarried shopkeeper who was looking for a wife expressed himself as follows:

You depend on the size of your shop and your prospects alone to get the girl and her family. The value of your shop has to be roughly about the same as the fortune. It is just the same as the bargaining between two farmers who make sure that the fortune the one receives or the other gets is neither too big nor too small for the size and quality of the farm and the position of either family.

When the contract is finally drawn, it has three principal provisions: a statement of the amount of the dowry to be paid by the bride's father; the stipulation that the groom's father retain no proprietary interest in the shop; and the provision that in the eventuality of the death of the husband, his wife becomes the heir-at-law. In this way, the shop is secured for the wife and her children, and their future is safeguarded.

One shopkeeper with four daughters for whom he had to provide spoke of his responsibility in this way:

Shop marriages are as much a contract as marrying on the land. If I am to place my daughter in marriage, it is my duty to protect her in every possible way. Take it this way, I become a party to a marriage and I am giving five hundred pounds to her future husband. It's my duty to see that my girl is protected in law. Should her husband die, we'll say within a year or two [after their marriage] or anything else extraordinary happen, my job is to see that she is as much the owner of the property as the husband.

It is common knowledge that even the most meticulously observed precautions in matchmaking cannot always guarantee a good marriage or future economic security. Accounts of misadventures become a part of the lore, and their details provide guides and cautions. The instance we shall report as example also illustrates a variant practice, in that it was the male who "bought" into a shop. A shopkeeper, well versed in the ways of his fellows, is our informant:

369

In Ireland as well as in every other part of the world you have the human shark who is out to fleece his neighbor. I remember a man who brought fifteen years' savings home from New York in 1912, probably a thousand pounds or more. He wished to get married at home. His folk made inquiries in Ennis and found a suitable shop and girl and the match was made; innocent country people dealing with clever wits.

There was a man and his wife running a business with the help of a sister-in-law. They had another house in the town, an idle shop in good repair on the lower end of Parnell Street. The match was made for the sister-in-law with the Yank, who paid over, I believe eight hundred pounds for their good-will of the house and business, and marrying the sister-in-law in the bargain.

While the happy couple were on their honeymoon a lot of the good furniture was removed to the other house and the stock in trade [liquor] was much reduced also by substituting nicely labeled bottles of colored water. You see, he took no inventory of furniture and stock and his greatest mistake of all, he left his people-at-law, strangers to him, to mind the business. The result has been stated. He should have put in one of his own family until he came home.

Although the pattern we have described is the fundamental one, certain exceptions should be noted. Murphy, a large shop-keeper in the town who had three sons and two daughters, took one of the sons into the shop. This son had kept company with a girl, the daughter of a less prosperous shop owner, for a number of years, but parental opposition was such that the father refused to sanction the marriage. Finally the son took matters into his hands and married the girl regardless of his father's wishes, much to the chagrin of his father, who expressed the opinion "that it was a bad match," as he explained it, because the shop which the girl had was practically bankrupt. In this instance there was no monetary consideration; the deviance from custom lay in the fact that the son refused to follow the father's wishes and did not accept the usual pattern of behavior.

In another instance the father died before he had made provision for the marriage of his son or daughter, with the result that the two, now both over fifty, live with their mother over their shop, and with little possibility that any match will be made. In another case, three sisters whose parents had died could make no decision about which one should get the shop. The three of them run the shop, but they are of such an advanced age, there is scant likelihood that any one of them will ever marry.

Situations like these have also been reported among country families. The precipitate action of some strong-headed youth marrying outside his proper sphere and without observance of customary procedures threatens both security and status of the family. Equally serious is the premature death of parents or their negligence in selecting a successor. Because a child must await parental decision, there is little he or she can do in such circumstances except exercise patience. Although conventions prescribe proper behavior, they carry no power of coercive enforcement, but failure to observe them can adversely affect the fortunes and future of all those directly affected.

Shopkeeping in the towns of Ireland is a family affair. Husband, wife, and children join together in cooperative labor in order to meet both economic and domestic requirements of the family and of their joint enterprise. To understand the relationships between the members of a shop family we must look to the internal division of labor and to the roles of husband and wife within the shop, as well as considering their participation beyond its walls in the affairs of community. From such description emerges a basic pattern which can stand as representative for most shop families. But we must also look to the variations within the pattern, because in these exceptions we find the elaborations which reflect other factors. A typological array would establish, for example, differences based upon size of shop and type of goods sold or service rendered. The partial family of spinster, bachelor, or widow introduces another complexity. Frequently the merchant — a designation which fits the big operator — no longer lives on his premises. These and other variations, when examined within the original context of familism, yield further insights into the processes of formation, growth, and change.

The shop system is organized primarily around the male, the husband and father, and he plays a more active and important part in the family and the larger society than does his wife. It is his name over the door that identifies the shop for the outside world. His wife is no less important in her own sphere, although like the shop she and her children bear his name.

The wife's activities are limited almost entirely to the confines of the dwelling and to the family. In fact, her only regular contact with affairs beyond the house results from the fulfillment of her religious obligations. Church-going is almost never a family affair; that is, husband and wife attend mass separately. Such separation is one part of the rigid separation in public of males and females, and this fact together with the limited opportunity for female association beyond church and family deserves special note. Only when we reach the upper-middle classes do we encounter any relaxing of these restrictions.

It is easy enough to attempt to explain this state of affairs by repeating the prevalent Irish belief that a woman's natural interest is in family. Let one of our informants, speaking in reference to the wives of shopkeepers, give his version:

> The women in this country never form clubs because they are so mean that they can't get along with each other. The reason for this is that the women in this country never pull together. After the school-going age, they never have friends with other girls. Their one ambition in life is to get married, get a home and children, and that will be their sphere and they don't want to get out of it. They want to work in the kitchen, sit in the living room, and sleep in the bedroom, take care of the children, and have nothing to do with the other women. In fact, they often don't even wish to go outside to take a walk. The women here will have nothing to do with each other. On the streets you never see two women together unless they are members of the same family. In that case they do go together and work together, but otherwise they do not.

372

The fact is explicit. House and family are the central interest for the woman. In this setting female associates are mother, daughter, sister — none other. In her own rearing in a farm family or in a townsman's shop, she has been carefully schooled in all that it is necessary to learn and to do, and to do well, with a minimum of complaint. Preparation of food, care of clothes, washing, cleaning, tending the needs of children and husband are the tasks that fall to the woman. That she might have occasional help from a hired girl or growing daughter does not negate the learning or the responsibility.

Shop life, however, puts additional demands on her time beyond those of strictly family activity. She assists her husband in many of his routine affairs. During the noon dinner hour and on those occasions when he is absent for any length of time, his wife takes care of the business. Some women do shop accounts and handle finances, and in a few cases the husband has established a second shop elsewhere in the town and put his wife in charge. In these and other ways, the conduct of the shop may be viewed as a family enterprise, and much of its success depends upon the assistance of the wife. In this arrangement, not unlike a partnership, a man and his wife seek agreement before decisions are made.

Although in fact the wife plays an important part in the management of the shop, in the affairs of the town it is her husband who stands as representative for his family. Her conventional role in this regard is a subordinate one. No matter how much the man may rely on the judgment of his wife, he will remain the responsible head of the family and the shop in the eyes of the community. In fact, in the case which follows we see the extension of this role to the widows of former close business associates.

At one time in the past the Master Bakers of Ennis met regularly to discuss their various problems. At these meetings they decided on the price to be charged for bread and the wages of their employees and discussed those customers who had recently changed their trade from one bakery to another. Our informant,

373

one of this group, said that everything went well until most of the owners died, leaving their widows in charge. It then became difficult either to get the widows together or to get them to decide upon common policies. Because of this situation and the need for concerted action, he said that in a short time he found that he was running every bakery business in town. He told the women when to raise or lower the price of bread or wages. He complained, however, that the arrangement was not very satisfactory because the widows had the idea that the more bread they sold the more money they made, although actually it was easy to acquire a list of insolvent customers and soon go bankrupt.

This case illuminates for us several aspects of the familial nature of shopkeeping in addition to the managerial role of the male. The identification of the shop with a particular family is continued by the widow's succession. Hers is only a temporary responsibility, however, and ends when she passes control to one of her children. In the period of transition, the widow is supported by the same social and legal mechanisms which led to the formation of the family originally. The perpetuation of the identity of shop and family also requires the observance of those principles which makes Irish familism such a powerful force.

Several aspects of the contrasting roles of males and females have already been suggested. The managerial aspects belong primarily to the husband, his skills having been acquired through the directed training of apprenticeship and the subsequent knowledge gained as assistant and eventual owner. This technical background is, of course, a prerequisite for success in business. But financial acumen is only one of the measures by which a shopkeeper and his family are judged. The worth he holds in the eyes of others, beyond his business, comes from his participation with them in religious, civic, political, sporting, or club affairs. The freedom of movement accorded to him, as a male, is virtually as complete in its way as are the restrictions placed upon his wife, as a female. In this counterpoise of family and community each sex has its appointed place and accepted activities.

The freedom is in no sense an absolute one, though, for values and factors other than maleness enter to limit the range of movement and association. The sociability provided in the nightly gatherings at the men's clubs is restricted to contacts with those of comparable manners and social position. In this reckoning there is a subtle but effective classification of the ranking which each man holds in the eyes of those who pass judgment on his merits by admitting him to their midst or by rejecting him.

No such formal procedure bars his admission to the ranks of workers in religious and political affairs. But his choice of field and the part he plays are also subtle reminders of where he stands in his own opinion and in the estimation of his peers. In their whole, these differentials locate the family and its relative standings with others. It is the male as representative of his family who must contend with others to win or lose a place in the sun. The specifics will become more sharply apparent as we proceed.

Among those who fall in their upper or lower ranks, some variation may be observed but such differences are of degree only. The customs surrounding marriage are much the same, although the more polite term "property settlement" is substituted for "fortune" and haggling over details passes from direct confrontation to negotiation in the solicitor's office. In this upper group, young people have slightly more freedom in choice of mates, although social ranking still restricts the range of marriage partners and considerations of family outweigh those of personal preference.

The pattern of those owning large shops shows its most striking differences in the physical and familial separation of business and domestic arrangements. No longer does the wife need to stand alongside her husband, tending to the needs of customers. Shop assistants take over these duties. Living arrangements are now entirely on the second floor, or, in some few instances, shop and residence are physically separated. Domestic responsibilities of the wife have not been altered, but her performance of them has. She now uses hired help for the more onerous of the household duties. The freedom she gains permits her to intensify her religious and familial activities, but does not bring extension into leisure-time social or cultural affairs. Her restrictions to house and family are like those of other women of the shopkeeping class.

Nor are there substantial changes in the behavior of the male as proprietor and family head. We associate the greater prestige which accompanies his affluence with club memberships and the male intimates of his leisure hours. The lessening of his direct involvement in domestic affairs follows upon the greater attention he bestows upon his business affairs. In all these matters the already sharply differentiated roles of male and female become even more marked, although parents join a heightened concern with their status aspirations for their children.

In the education, training, and disposition of the children, the differences in standards of values and conduct between big and small shopkeepers begin to show themselves. Such differences reflect an increasing acceptance of urban values and behavior and the weakening of the ties to one's rural origin. In one sense we are witness to the process of acculturation through incorporation. Parental choices about the education of their children — and the responsibility and decisions are completely theirs — have a profound effect on the future careers of their sons and the marriage prospects of their daughters. Social aspirations for the family are to be won or lost in what happens to their children.

Children have usually begun their school careers by the time they are six. In Ennis, the girls are sent to the Convent and the boys to the Christian Brothers. There is also a national or public school with lay teachers, but very few of the shopkeepers send their children there, preferring the more genteel atmosphere of the "Brothers" or the "Convent." These are the separations which, even among the young, give testimony to the reality of social class. One young bank clerk in Ennis, whose father had been a shopkeeper in an adjacent county, described his school days as follows:

I went to the national school until I was about ten. The master was a fine person with a distinguished bearing. You can always tell breeding when you see it. The town of Cahir hasn't the type of poor people nor so many of them as has Ennis, and there were quite a number of boys of nice families in the school. There were quite a lot of roughs, too, but you didn't associate with them. The difference wasn't noticeable and the schoolmaster had a great deal of tact and didn't bring it home to us in the school. In the playground you would be on one side with your friends and the others off to the other side. After you go away to school, or grew up, you never see them again.

The validation of social position begins early, and the school is not exempt from social distinctions. On the playground or in the classroom each child learns how he is similar to or different from others. The separation can be complete, as in the case of our informant who was sent off to a private Jesuit school at the age of ten.

The fashionable religious schools in Ireland and England draw as pupils the children of the few wealthy shopkeepers in each town, together with the children of the professional men. Afterward many of them are sent on to the university to prepare for the professions.

The training which formal education provides carries many shopkeeping sons and daughters beyond the confines of their fathers' occupation. They enter diverse occupations, the selection of which is largely dependent upon the decision of the father. The big shopkeeper hopes to hand the management of the shop to one son and to educate the others to become solicitors, doctors, or bank clerks or to enter some governmental post. His daughters acquire the manners which prepare them to become the wives of professional men or persons of equal status.

The smaller shopkeeper hopes that his son will graduate from the Christian Brothers and his daughter from the Convent. Some of the boys may be sent to the local diocesan college for an additional two, three, or four years, and a few enter the priesthood. Some may train for clerical jobs, but for most there is always the expectation to return to their father's shop. After graduation from the Convent, the girl may be given additional training to prepare her for becoming a teacher or a nurse, or she may take her portion and become a nun. Most of the daughters, however, remain in the shop waiting for an opportunity to marry.

In those families where education does not continue beyond late adolescence, the sons and daughters enter actively into shop life as soon as they have finished their schooling. They are then between fifteen and eighteen years of age. In order to preserve the identity of shop and family, the father must select one of the children as his ultimate successor. The favored son begins a new period of training under the tutelage of his father, or as an apprentice elsewhere, in which he prepares for his life career.

There is little difference between the training which the father offers and that which his son might receive as an apprentice. One baker said that he had served his time under his father and that he, in turn, was now training his son to take his place. He explained that he had started the boy with the simplest techniques and had gradually taught him more and more until he felt that his son had thoroughly mastered the trade. When the boy had finished his training, he was to be given a formal document testifying to his proficiency as a Master Baker. Not many shopkeepers formalize the training of their sons to this extent, when the son remains within the family shop.

The training which the young man receives prepares him for

the eventual management and full control of the shop. As he gains experience in the details of its operation further responsibility is extended to him. In one instance, the father took his son with him on buying expeditions and there instructed him. In a few years the son had been given complete control of the business, and the father, who by then had practically withdrawn from active management, only inquired of prices and profits and occasionally offered a few suggestions. Soon afterward the old man died, and the son inherited control of the business. Under such careful direction, the transition from one generation to the next had been made easy.

The training period is only one step toward a further and final induction of the son into the shopkeeping world. In that final step the son acquires a wife and assumes near-full control. Once again it is the father whose position requires that he assume the responsibility for initiating this last transition. Here the customs surrounding marriage and matchmaking offer the conventional guidelines, not only for the young couple, but for the parents as well. The formal contract which seals the agreement contains provisions that protect certain rights of the couple now retiring from their business. According to one solicitor who had drawn many such contracts, they all follow a well-known pattern. The father gives to his son the shop and all its assets, but reserves for himself and his wife the use of a portion of the house during the period of their natural life. The son must also provide them with food and fuel and an annual cash payment. The younger children of the family are to be allowed to live at home until they come of age, at which time they are to be paid a stipulated sum by the owner (their elder brother), the payment of which causes their interest in the shop to be forfeit.

Unmarried adult daughters still living at home must also be provided for. Ordinarily, they are given their portion at this time and must leave the house to make way for the new couple. If the father owns other shop property in the town, he will in some instances start these daughters in business in a small way.

379

Many of the spinsters who tend small shops are shopkeepers' daughters for whom provision was made at the time of the marriage of their brothers. Their possession, however, is a contingent one, ending with their death, when the shop reverts to the brother or to his heirs.

The preparation of the son for shop management, the marriage contract, his marriage to a country girl whose kinship ties reassert the connections with the countryside, the dispersal of siblings, the semiretirement of the elderly couple are all parts of a succession which is customarily prescribed and ensures perpetuation of the family. But this natural history of family succession in perpetuity may also be threatened by the failure of some to fulfill their obligations or by the injection of some unanticipated event which upsets the normal procedures. Here again custom provides the means by which resolution of the difficulties may be sought. A childless couple utilizes the obligations of kinship to bring a nephew from the country to be their heir. The legitimate familial successors whose rightful claims are threatened through the remarriage of a widowed parent press their case in the courts. The silent sanction of boycott may be utilized against other aggressors. Even the power of the church may be brought into play. Whatever their source — religious, legal, economic, or social — these are the sanctions which support or correct individual frailty in its misdeeds or mischance. In the summarizations which follow we report some of these happenings as illustrative of the problems and of their resolution.

The facts of the first case are paraphrased from an account published in the local newspaper. A Mr. John Keane had married the widow of a shopkeeper. She had had five sons by the previous marriage. Her first husband, in his will, had devised his property in trust to his wife for the use and education of his children. Keane had brought a hundred pounds with him into the shop and had five children by his wife, three of whom were living. The children of his wife by her first marriage were educated out of their joint earnings. One became a priest, two were chemists, and two had migrated to America. One of the sons had married and lived with his step-father and mother in the house.

The relations between the step-father and the step-son became strained after the mother's death. Through the intercession of the son who had become a priest, Father Flaherty, it was agreed that Keane would leave the house if the step-son, the brother of Father Flaherty, would assume all indebtedness of the shop. He agreed to this, but failed to meet the obligations, and the step-father was processed in law for the debts. Keane then brought suit against his step-son for his failure to observe the agreement.

Keane protested in his testimony that it was not until after the death of his wife that he learned that he and his children had no claims to the property. He had thought that the hundred pounds he had brought with him into the shop entitled him to become owner on the death of his wife.

The court decided that Flaherty, who was in possession of the shop, must pay the debts. Since Keane had waived his claim to the shop he was not liable under Law for the obligations which he and Flaherty's mother, acting together as husband and wife and joint owners of the shop, had contracted.

In Ireland, it is not customary for shop widows to remarry. They are expected to hold the shop into which they were married in trust for the children. In this instance, the wise provision in the will of the first husband protected the rights of his offspring in the family shop.

In another instance we can see the application of legal and social pressure in order to restore to a family a shop which had passed from its hands through extraordinary circumstances. The judge, in his decision, wisely acquiesced to the dictates of the situation. A shopkeeper who had no sons married one of his daughters to a man named Fogarty, who brought a fortune with him to the shop. It was agreed in the marriage settlement that two of Fogarty's sisters-in-law had the right to remain in residence with him and his wife. Trouble soon developed between the man and his wife's sisters, so they moved out.

Everything remained calm until the daughter of the original owner, Fogarty's wife, died leaving no heirs. The other two sisters were resentful that the valuable shop had been lost to the family and the community sympathized with them. A quiet boycott was started against Fogarty, who lost most of his customers. Business dwindled until the pressure brought by creditors forced the shop into bankruptcy and it was put up for sale by court order.

The sister of Fogarty's dead wife was the only bidder at the auction. She purchased the premises for one hundred pounds, a sum considerably under the true value of the shop. Fogarty's solicitor protested at the low sale price, which did not half meet the encumbrances. At the court hearing held to confirm the sale the judge stated: "He [the judge] relied on the affidavit of Mr. Blood-Smythe [counsel for the woman] who stated that the one hundred pounds was the best price to be obtained under all the circumstances of the case."

Fogarty protested that one hundred pounds was not a suitable price and said that the house would be cheap at two hundred and fifty pounds and that it would realize more if it had been put up locally. His complaint was of no avail. The judge pointed out that even if a larger sum had been realized, he, Fogarty, would still receive nothing as the encumbrancers had first claims and that he must confirm the sale. He also added his certain belief that the presiding auctioneer was capable of extracting the last shilling from the pockets of anyone willing to buy property.

Fogarty's offense was that when his wife died without offspring he possessed property that custom prescribed should revert to the family of the original owners. The law made no provision for such eventuality, and neither did the marriage settlement, as it was supposed that children would be forthcoming. The boycott that drove him into bankruptcy and the forced sale which restored the property to members of the original family were as effective as any device could be.

In these two examples, we see the mutual reinforcement of custom and law to maintain or restore the identity of shop and family. Even in those situations where the customary arrangements do not provide an easy and immediate method of meeting every contingency, there are inherent in the system other mechanisms to restore the disturbed equilibrium.

An eventuality which threatens one family might equally well extend to all. In addition, because it is the familial base of shopkeeping on which town and country are linked, the effects of a threatened disruption of these relationships can extend to other segments of the society. This is prevented first by the customs which prescribe behavior within the system and second by the extension of its values to other institutions.

19

Mobility and Continuity

Within the paradox of seeming timelessness and unceasing change, the life of an Irish town moves through the days of recurring routine, the more broadly spaced rhythms of heightened activity marked by fair day, festival, or holiday, and on across the generations and centuries. The certainties are more than just those of taxes and death; they also encompass those patterns of behavior and the social forms whose persistence is attested by a search of the past.

But transformation is also evident. There are those for whom the derelict buildings that once housed thriving industry or garrisoned British troops evoke memories of other times. Recall brings a deeper poignancy, however, rising from a much more intimate and personal base. It is believed that town life is revitalized by the steady recruitment of country youth to whom its attractions are so enticing, but that their children or their children's children must suffer the tragic fate of familial extinction. The belief is partially supported by fact. Only the town's laborers, the people of the back streets, seem exempt from the consequences of the process which works with such inexorable precision for others. Excluded as they are by heritage and position from seeking other social levels, they endure generation after generation in their tradition of deprivation.

As we come to understand the natural history of individual and family within the context of custom and group, we shall see how renewal and transition are part of the same process. Shopkeeping families do die out of the town in a literal sense if there is no renewal, through marriage, of connections with the countryside. But families also disappear from the town for other reasons. Social aspirations carry the members of a family into professional, governmental, and religious careers and thence into orbits beyond the locality of birth. These generational transitions reflect the response to the more fully developed institutional forms of the urban world and to patterns and values which accompany them. But in the striving for enhanced social position, there is no break with the already deeply embedded status aspirations of the country family. We have discussed the background; now description and biography will give us the fact and flavor of the process we seek to understand.

Although we lack a detailed count of movement into and out of shopkeeping we do have some idea of the magnitude. About half the shopkeepers in Ennis gained their businesses through inheritance, and of these only one-fifth were second-generation town born. Thus, half the shops were held by those having fathers in other occupations. When we consider the great emphasis placed upon identity of shop and family and the conventions that support each family, the rate of replacement seems quite high. The small, spinster-operated shops which change operators each generation could account for some portion of the total. Bankruptcy was uncommon and hence not important as a factor. In all the many cases which came to our attention, the failure to maintain or renew the reciprocities which flow from kinship and friendship appeared time and again to explain the disappearance of shop families from the town. The following accounts show the range of specifics.

Rynne, a small farmer who lived about ten miles west of Ennis, apprenticed one of his sons as a smith. The son moved into Ennis, where he established himself in his trade and started a small shop in which he sold buckets. From this beginning he expanded until he owned a hardware shop, became wealthy, and bought a great deal of property. The son who inherited the shop married the daughter of a prominent shopkeeper of Limerick. His children included a son who became a writer, a son who went into law and is now an important government official, a daughter who married a local solicitor, and a son who never married but remained in the shop and "like all those whose fathers had made money he assumed the attitude of a gentleman business man." The brother-in-law solicitor handled the legal affairs of the family and looked after the extensive property holdings which the elder Rynne had accumulated. The sister had no children, and when her brother in the business died, the property was sold. No member of the Rynne family remained connected with the shop.

The rise to wealth and subsequent departure from the community that is reported in the account above is a common three-generational cycle. For other families the generational sequence has yet to be completed, as we learn from a local physician's account of his father and of his own career. Patrick Mangan's father had been born on a farm and as a young man had been apprenticed in a draper's shop, where he later became an assistant. When he was about thirty-five he started a shop on his own and soon afterward married. His wife brought a fortune of three hundred pounds from her country family. One son and daughter were the only children.

Dr. Mangan reports his early years as follows: He attended the diocesan college until he was about fifteen years old, but because he had not been doing too well, his father decided that he should come into the business. Mangan was perfectly willing

386

to go into the shop, and for five years his father taught him the techniques of shopkeeping. Then Patrick began to feel dissatisfied in the shop and decided that he wanted to do better in the world. He told his father, but the elder Mangan just laughed and thought it was a joke. Their relations became strained, and two or three incidents within the shop made the situation worse. One day young Mangan became annoyed with a customer and landed a swinging upper-cut to his jaw, laying him out. "My father thought I had killed the man and came rushing up and shouted, 'Here you, get out, you've no place in this business.' I yelled I would get out and that my father was right and I could do better elsewhere."

Mangan resumed his interrupted studies and went to the National University where he "prepared for a doctor." During this period his father died, but his sister returned home from her studies and ran the business until Mangan got his degree. When he returned to Ennis, it was necessary for him to assume control of the business for a few months, but soon he began to look for a house in the residential section, and when one became available he hung out his professional shingle. Soon afterward he married.

During the course of the next few years Mangan established himself as a doctor in the community. As his practice consumed more of his time, he gradually withdrew from the family business. At the present time it is under the management of one of his assistants, and although he does the buying and his wife does the accounts, he has no other formal connection with the shop. He realizes himself that very soon he will probably divorce himself completely from the shop world.

The history of the Mangan family reiterates for us the linkage of family and shop system in Ireland. But movement from country to town is only one phase of a double mobility. The other is realized in fulfillment of aspirations which bring social advancement. Hopefully, one or more sons are educated for the professions, and convent-trained daughters marry upward socially.

387

Not all such hopes are realized, however, and many a young man suffers in bitterness at the fate which denied his dreams of glory. The demands of family proved more powerful than those of career in the case we now present. Patrick O'Casey, a publican-provision-dealer-politician, had come in from the country areas and established a shop in Ennis. Michael, his only son, who provided us with the facts of his history, had been sent first to St. Flannan's, then to Rockwell, the fashionable Jesuit school, and finally to a commercial school in Dublin. He was gradually heading toward a professional career when the untimely death of his father and the crippling of his mother by paralysis brought him quickly home, where he was forced to assume the responsibility of the family business. He objected violently to this fate, because he had had visions of arriving in Ennis as a fully accredited solicitor.

His thwarted desire for social recognition found outlet in the utilization of other means to gain recognition. There was in Ennis a person called "Moran the Millionaire," who had acquired wealth in America and had returned to Ireland hoping to be accepted in "county" society, but without success. Young O'Casey often referred to his association with Moran and the good times they had together. The intimacy was mostly imaginary, as the private social functions of the Morans did not include O'Casey, who probably would have been uncomfortable had he been present.

O'Casey was instrumental in organizing a tennis club which became known locally as the "shop assistants' club." He complained of other members on the grounds that they did not dress properly for the game. In a burst of bitterness he once said: "If you want to know what is wrong with Ireland, I will tell you. We are all misfits, we are all in jobs that we loathe. Successful men counsel work, but that is because they are in occupations they like. There is something glamorous about being a solicitor, and having everybody come to you. I would like to have been one."

Young O'Casey's behavior was the subject of comment in the town. His resentment at being forced back into the pattern from which he had nearly escaped often took the form of violent verbal outbursts. It was reported that he had said, "They tell us that God is found in every house. The other night I looked in every nook and cranny and I couldn't find him, so he must have passed me by," bringing him a visit and a severe reprimand from the priest. This story became current in the town and caused such comments as "the drunken puppy" and rumors that he had lost his trade and the money he had got from his father.

The frustrated aspirations of O'Casey contrast with the realized professional career of Dr. Mangan. Both faced severe family crises, and although the solution for each was different, we are again reminded that the obligations which family duty imposes exceed all others.

In still another instance the movement of one member of a family brought disaster to those who remained as shopkeepers.

The first O'Brien came into town about eighty years ago. He saw his chance and made some money. They had a very refined hardware shop, nicely kept and arranged. They were very nice people. One of the sons, Louis, was a young barrister. An heiress from San Francisco, a Miss Danaher, came over and was touring around the country and fell in love with and married Louis. He got all the money, gave up his practice, and took a big country house where he kept a pack of hounds and moved about and was accepted in the county society. This went to the heads of the rest of the family and they would hardly look at anyone and they began to fail, and finally had to sell out, as they wouldn't speak to the people they did business with. You can't run a shop like that.

The upward movement out of shopkeeping does not always carry one into the professions. Wealthy shopkeepers whose children are not disposed to continue the business may sell it and, with the proceeds, move to some metropolitan center to live. One informant said that the wealthy Scanlons would have taken their money and gone to Dublin if it had not been for a shrewd

389

old uncle who thought that if the business was good enough for their father it was good enough for their children.

A local doctor, in talking about the disappearance of shop-keeping families, said that when the father or grandfather have made a lot of money in business, the children seldom concern themselves with the business afterward. They turn it over to a manager and live on the income. The fortune slips away from them, bit by bit; pretty soon there is nothing left, and the family disappears. When we look for factors which explain the disinclination of the children to continue as active managers of a family business, we discover that the education they receive explains much. The effects of advanced formal schooling are sufficiently obvious to make one merchant generalize the process:

> One of the troubles with shopkeepers is that their children become so well educated that they can't do anything. No shopkeeper in this town ever has the shop in his family more than three generations. This is because the son is sent off to college and is given a good education and when he comes back the father puts him into the business, but he doesn't know how to treat with the common people. They like to be spoken to, and when he wraps up their packages and won't speak to them pretty soon they won't be coming around to him any longer to do business.

The informant particularized his generalization when he predicted that young Houlihan, who had just returned from college to conduct his father's business, would be unable to do so for this very reason. Formal education may be a necessary ingredient for upward movement, but it may also disrupt the family and impair its position in the shop world. The father who brings his son into the shop after giving him an advanced education may find it is impossible for his boy to adapt his behavior to meet customers in an acceptable manner. The purely personal basis of the trader's relations requires that he meet customers on an equal footing. Academic training does not provide such an orientation. Only through the specific learning that comes with apprenticeship can there be a reasonable guarantee that both technical skills and appropriate values are incorporated.

In these and the other accounts of the disappearance of shop-keeping families from the town, poor financial management was never advanced as a reason. Perhaps an accountant or banker would have seen it otherwise. But the phrasing we encountered was always in the context of the renewal and perpetuation of obligation and reciprocities. These could be expressed more fully and freely in an atmosphere of social equality engendered by family and friendship. The snobbery of wealth, education, or elevated social position could be as fatal to the preservation of relationships as the failure of a father to provide for family succession through matchmaking.

There still remains, however, an additional behavioral realm to be explored. Irish behavior is deeply influenced by beliefs in the inevitability of supernatural rewards and punishments. An individual who is dishonest, breaks the taboos surrounding sex and family, or comes into conflict with the church lays himself open not only to community condemnation but also to heavenly punishment. Such a mode of thought provides a reference from which all events may be judged. Thus, business failures are sometimes thought to be acts of divine retribution. The greedy publican who impoverishes his customers by encouraging them to drink or lets them gamble on his premises can bring suffering to the families dependent on the earnings thus squandered.[1] The penalties are believed to be great, and one publican attributed to the immoral behavior of members of his trade

[1] The publican's role in the community is rigidly defined by law and social custom. His business is licensed, regulated, and supervised by the state, which prescribes the hours and days on which he can or cannot open for business, specifies the quality of the liquor which he can sell, and denies him the right to sell on credit or to minors. Custom also places restrictions on his behavior. No attempt is made to stipulate the number of drinks to be sold to one man at a time, but the publican who endeavors to inveigle his customers into spending all their earnings with him is censured by public opinion.

391

the explanation for their disappearance from the life of the town:

It is a fact that I can prove and can mention a lot of people we know, but who I don't want to name, that a publican lasts only one generation and that the family has the public house only during the lifetime of the owner. It is that way with almost all the public houses in town and I am about the only exception, my father having a public house before me. It is because they open card rooms and the publicans who have cardrooms always come to a fall [which he thought well deserved]. The trouble is they are brought down by the prayers of [aggrieved] wives and mothers and sisters. I never would have a card-room on my premises. It keeps the men and boys away from their families and they lose a great deal of money that should be going to household expenses. I could make a lot of money that way, by keeping a room open for card playing, but I wouldn't do that.

Death by violence is also offered as an explanation for the decline of certain businesses. For example, a quarrel between a publican and his wife led to her suicide, and within a very short time he left the community a bankrupt. Another story reports that during the "troubled times" some Republicans went to a public house where they knew that some of the Black and Tans were carousing with some women. They opened the door and fired into the interior, killing one soldier and wounding one woman. The spirit of the murdered man was supposed to walk about. Soon afterward the house was deserted, and today it stands in ruins.

Even those who helped the enemies of Ireland are thought to have suffered retribution. Those who aided the Black and Tans during the Anglo-Irish war are believed to have been punished for this. Cases are cited of shopkeepers who grew wealthy from their trade with the enemy but eventually lost it all. Even the public house where they drank or were billeted did not escape the blight. One woman, an intense nationalist, who had a public house, said:

I never took any of them [the Black and Tans] in and refused to do it and told them to fill up the public houses first. Isn't it a funny thing but all the houses that took them in have gone down since. Quinns, Shaughnessys, and Nonos. Nonos had only a little shop, not a pub at all, but she took them in and they have all gone down since.

Transgression against the religious sanctions also brings disaster in its wake. For a person to be lax in his religious duties is to invite disaster. Frank Moroney, a bookkeeper with a religious turn of mind, recounted the story of a neighbor of his who drank all the time, and although he didn't neglect his church duties, he was away before the mass was half over. "He had a good job and his wife had a shop and before long he lost his job and just last week they were evicted out of their house." He continued:

O'Donnell in the shop next to the Abbey suffered the same fate. He was prosperous and his wife had a good practice as a maternity nurse in town here. I was scandalized and I often said to my wife that they made me very angry because though they ran to mass every day, the hypocrites, they stayed only a short time, paying not much attention, and going down only on one knee, which is a mark of disrespect and a sign of ignorance on the part of one who does it. They did this for a long time until finally they lost their trade for some reason that nobody knows and the wife found herself out of employment, and then they both left town.

The hard-headed economist might have difficulty in assessing a system which responds to ghosts, curses, or prayers. Not so the Irish townsman. For him supernatural forces are as real as, and far more potent than, a balance sheet. His is a perspective which accounts for success or failure within the direct context of behavior. The significant accounting may be a spiritual one, or it may be a tally of observed or neglected favors received and given. The supernatural, legal, or social categories are not fully separate from each other, they become such only in the mind of the analyst. Our accounting, in contrast, is from the perspective of the town and couched in its distinctive language. Our concern has been to seek those connections which join town and country and to relate these to the movements, demographic and social, of individuals and classes.

20

Reciprocals of Family and Credit

Examining the patterns and mechanisms which define and stabilize the position of the family in the shop system, we have found that the shopkeeping system is basically familial and that in form and behavior the shop family resembles the farm family from which it is recruited. We have also seen that Irish society gains additional cohesiveness through familial type connections which extend into and from the town. When we seek the means by which this integration is effected, we encounter the practices surrounding the giving and receiving of "credit."

The credit system provides linkages other than the purely familial. True, its practices strengthen the relationship that arise from kinship, but in addition it joins the immediate family circle of a shopkeeper to the urban world.

At first glance the use of credit would appear to be chiefly an economic convenience gladly extended by the shopkeeper to his customers. A closer study, however, reveals that in Ireland

394

credit is much more than a commercial practice; it is a social mechanism performing an important function for the society — that of stabilizing the relations between the shopkeeper and his customers.

Examination of the credit system shows how the values and practices surrounding credit bring the inhabitants of the rural areas into permanent relations with the shopkeepers of the towns. In many instances the credit system is complementary to the kinship ties which connect the farm and shop families; in other cases it stands in its own right as a mechanism linking the two. The relations founded on credit can be as lasting as those which have their origin in the obligations of family. Trade relations based on family connections are merely an extension of the sentiments binding the family together; they are capable of surviving many disrupting factors. Those based on credit may be viewed as an extension of the sentiments surrounding the reciprocal familial relations.

Custom prescribes the behavior of each individual in a credit relationship. The establishment and continuation of this relation is dependent upon the existence of a debt for unpaid goods or, more rarely, for money loaned. An unpaid debt gives the shopkeeper a monopoly of his debtor's purchases. (The shopkeeper may also charge interest on an overdue account.) The debtor acknowledges the obligation by payment of a portion of the account at stated intervals. He seldom clears the account, however, for when he does it is tantamount to a complete severance of the ties between customer and shopkeeper, a thing that both parties attempt to prevent because the customer also receives practical benefits under this plan. Thus, through the combination of family and credit patterns in the shopkeeping system, a permanent and stable relationship between the residents of town and country is maintained.

The practices which surround the giving and receiving of credit are not localized in Ennis or County Clare. Direct investigation and the available literature demonstrate that they are widespread. One of the principal officials of the Congested Districts Board attested the universality of the credit system when in 1908 he appeared before the Devon Commission on Congestion in Ireland and said: "Most small landholders keep a running account with a shopkeeper, because there are certain portions of the year when they have no cash, and the shopkeeper does not expect payment except at periods of the year when he knows that the farmer is in funds."[1]

The term "running account" is descriptive of the practice whereby a farmer continues to buy from the same shopkeeper over a period of years, occasionally paying installments on his debt. He ordinarily makes a partial settlement with the shopkeeper after the sale of his agricultural produce, but, except in unusual circumstances, never makes a final settlement. It should be noted that even those who may be able to clear their accounts do not do so. Not only is this true among the small farmers; the wealthier farmer who is not dependent upon the shopkeeper to carry him through the period when his stock or crops are not ready for market follows substantially identical practices. He too keeps a "running account" with a shopkeeper, upon which he makes payments at stated intervals, and which he never closes. That he is thus linked with the shopkeepers of the town through the observance of the customary practices surrounding the use of credit adds further significance to the credit system.

This perpetual indebtedness has not always been viewed favorably by those interested in the welfare of Irish farmers and the improvement of Irish agriculture. During the early part of this century the shopkeeping system, and particularly the credit relations between shopkeepers and farmers, aroused a good deal of concern. The movement, under the aegis of Sir Horace Plunkett, R. A. Anderson, and Lord Monteagle, had its inception in

[1] *Parliamentary Report,* Royal Commission on Congestion in Ireland, vol. XXXII, p. 129 (Mr. H. Doran).

1889.[2] In 1894 the Irish Agricultural Organization Society, Ltd. (I.A.O.S.) was inaugurated to further the work.

At first, the promoters were eager to form cooperative societies among the farmers for purposes of production and marketing and were interested also in the establishment of cooperaive creameries. In their efforts at reform, they came face to face with the knotty problem of credit. They considered the shopkeeper a parasite on the farmer and felt that he was claiming more than his share for the services he performed for the farmer, one of which was giving credit. The establishment of cooperative agricultural banks was proposed to give the farmer credit on easy terms and thus permit him to escape the yoke which they felt had been placed upon him by the shopkeeper. Cooperative stores were to allow the farmer to buy his necessities without paying the exorbitant profits which they thought the shopkeepers were exacting. George Russell (A.E.), who became associated with this movement, was particularly interested in the shopkeeper-farmer relations and vehement in his condemnation of certain practices he had observed, writing as follows in a tract first published in 1916:

The first thing which strikes one who travels through rural Ireland is the immense number of little shops . . . What are all these little shops doing? They are supplying the farmers with domestic requirements: with tea, sugar, flour, oil, implements, vessels, clothing, and generally with drink . . . Nobody has tried to amalgamate them, or to economize human effort or cheapen the distribution of the necessaries of life. This work of distribution is carried on by all kinds of little traders competing with each other, pulling the devil by the tail; doing the work economically, so far as they themselves are concerned, because they must, but doing it expensively for the district because they can not help it. They do not serve Ireland well. The genius of amalgamation and organization can not afford to pass by these shops, which spring up in haphazard fashion, not because the country needs them, but because farmers or traders have children to be provided for. To the ignorant this is the easiest form of trade,

2 Sir Horace Plunkett, *Ireland in the New Century* (London, 1905).

and so many are started in life in one of these little shops after an apprenticeship in another like it. These numerous competitors of each other do not keep down prices. They increase them rather by the unavoidable multiplication of expenses; and many of them, taking advantage of the countryman's irregularity of income and his need for credit, allow credit to a point where the small farmer becomes a tied customer, who can not pay all he owes, and who therefore dares not deal elsewhere.[3]

And as he testified in his appearance before the Devon Commission:

Another result, and in my opinion the worst result of the lack of cheap money has been that the farmers run up long bills with their traders, and where they can not pay cash they get their requirements at what are called "long prices," and in many cases the prices merit the adjective.

. . . but I do say that high prices and his interest added in the books for goods given on credit are frequent enough to make the introduction of a new system desirable, if only through competition, to make a more equitable system of trading prevail.[4]

He then gives an example of three Mayo farmers who bought fertilizer, one of whom bought on credit and paid twice the price for "the privilege of deferring payment for seven or eight months. This was, I think, exceptional, but 25 per cent added on for six months' credit was not uncommon." [5]

It is a fact, as Russell pointed out, that as long as a person is indebted to a shopkeeper, he does not take his trade elsewhere. The additional fact that those able to clear their debts seldom do so makes it apparent, however, that the advantages to an individual who maintains credit relations with a shopkeeper outweigh disadvantages which might arise from his "tied position." The farmer undoubtedly pays more when he buys on credit, and frequently shopkeepers charge interest on overdue accounts.

[3] A. E. (George Russell), *The National Being* (New York, 1930), pp. 21-22.
[4] *Parliamentary Report,* vol. XXXV, p. 53.
[5] *Parliamentary Report,* p. 53.

Thus, from the standpoint of shillings and pence, the farmer who maintains a credit account pays more for his goods.

The shopkeeper, too, may stand to lose by this arrangement, for there is always the possibility that his customer may be unable or unwilling to pay. David Talbot-Crosbie, in his testimony before the Devon Commission, stressed this fact and condemned the "economic impracticability" of the system, but in his denial of the abuse of the credit system by shopkeepers, he demonstrated another aspect:

I want to say as regards the system practiced by small farmers of living on credit instead of paying cash, that it is extravagant for the customer and unsatisfactory for the shopkeepers, as they are kept so long out of their money, and therefore, can not work on the principle of small profits and quick returns. Credit is the most expensive system to live on. Tenants go into a shop where they have a pass-book. They never settle their account. They do not care what prices are put down so long as they get the things. They just pay the highest possible prices, and they never know how they stand. It is very bad for the tenants and it is very bad for the shopkeepers, who are a tremendously long time out of their money.

At this point in his testimony he was queried as follows:

The difficulty, I suppose, is that nearly all these people are very much in debt to the shopkeeper, and that unless there was some means by which they could pay off their debts, they can not get away from the screw the shopkeeper would put on if they tried to go somewhere else.

His reply was:

That is it; although I must say, as regards the shopkeepers, I have never found them acting harshly or with unkindness to the people.[6]

The customary practices surrounding the credit system carry penalties only for the failure to recognize the obligations that

---

[6] *Parliamentary Report,* vol. XXVI, p. 218.

the credit relation entails. One of the obligations which a shopkeeper assumes when he enters such a relationship is to supply goods to his customer, expecting payment only when the customer has the money. The position of the shopkeeper allows him to put the "screw" on his debtor, as the interrogator suggested, but unless the debtor fails in his obligations, the creditor ordinarily does not do so. The shopkeeper is constrained from the use of harsh measures by fear of condemnation. He too carries obligations. Mr. Doran, the land commissioner, testified as follows on this point:

It would be very bad policy on his [the trader's] part to pursue that man [the debtor] and come down on him straight away for his debt. A shopkeeper is not quite exempt from local odium if he does an unreasonable thing.

He would try to prevent the man who owed him money [from going away], but I know many cases where the head of a family owed a debt to the shopkeeper, and the shopkeeper would lend him part of the passage money to help to send his daughter to America in the hope of getting the debt paid from her earnings. That is quite common.[7]

The assistance rendered by the shopkeeper to his client assumes many forms, but it should not be interpreted as charity on his part. He profits from the goods he sells, and he also expects return for favors he gives. We interpret his action as an attempt to preserve the relation with his client. Even the threat of a customer's insolvency is a contingency he must meet. The shopkeeper who assists the daughter of a debtor to emigrate in the hope that she will remit the money to cover her father's indebtedness relies on the sentiments of family cohesion.

Only in the most drastic circumstances are the credit relations between shopkeeper and customer ever severed. Even in those cases where the farmer is definitely insolvent and the possibilities of his meeting his debt are small, the relation already established usually is continued. The shopkeeper goes on supply-

[7] *Parliamentary Report*, vol. XXXII, p. 129.

ing goods to the man although he thinks it is unlikely that the account can ever be cleared. Should he refuse his debtor further credit he will alienate him, and the customer is then free to seek credit and goods elsewhere. In such an eventuality the shopkeeper loses not only trade but also the chance of payment, however slight, for the individual is soon indebted to a rival.

One shopkeeper, asked how he calculated the amount of credit he would give to any one man and whether his decision was based upon the value of the man's farm, replied: "No, I simply give it to them according to the man's wants."

Questioned further about his policy toward an individual who was deeply indebted and wished to increase the debt, he answered: "I might refuse, and before he would starve I might give in more or less to tide him over the time."

The investigator suggested that there must be some limit because "no man can carry on business that way." The reply was: "We have no limit. When they earn it they are very honest in paying it, and when they can not pay it we have nothing to get." [8]

There are legal and social practices by which the shopkeeper may force the debtor to pay his account, but only in exceptional cases are these used, because they mean the certain disruption of the credit relation. There is, however, an extension of the credit system through which the shopkeeper can obtain the money without disrupting the credit relationship and the farmer can postpone the necessity of immediate payment of his debt. This is the banking system.

The banks in Ennis and other market towns meet the credit needs of local shopkeepers. Bank credit is not, however, ordinarily available to small farmers. They look to the shopkeeper for credit and sometimes for small loans. In such instances the shopkeeper acts as a kind of private bank as well as a credit manager. Even wealthy farmers who borrow directly from banks will request shopkeepers to sign their notes as security.

In Ennis, one shopkeeper who was reported to have over five

[8] *Parliamentary Report,* vol. XLII (Mr. Joseph Cloherty).

thousand pounds due him from goods sold and loans said of this practice: "You don't know whether you will have to pay the note at the bank or not, but it is better to keep the account alive in the hope that some time in the future the individual will be able to pay." Thus the credit relation may sometimes be threatened, but there are methods for resolving the crisis, as we shall see. Their application is decided upon by the shopkeeper, who occupies the commanding position in these relations, although the cooperation of the debtor is also a necessity.

In the majority of credit relationships the contingency of insolvency seldom arises. The farmer meets his obligations regularly according to the dictates of custom. One large draper in Ennis describes the practice of buying and paying as follows:

It is usual that the man and his wife will come in at the same time and make their purchases together. He may buy fifteen or twenty pounds worth of goods and have it put on account. When he comes in again just before Christmas he will make a payment of ten or twelve pounds on his bill and buy another lot of goods of equal value, but it is seldom that he will pay the entire bill, or that he will pay as much on his bill as he will buy when he comes in to make a purchase.

Rare indeed is the case in which the debtor does not make every attempt to fulfill his obligations toward his creditor. The shopkeeper has no legal security that his debt will be paid. His security lies in the observance of customs and the obligations imposed by reciprocity. The money owed the shopkeeper is more than a debt, it is a personal obligation. In most cases it has arisen from a relationship of long standing, perhaps even one that originated in a previous generation.

The following story by a merchant in Ennis illustrates the binding nature of the relation which those who contract debts feel toward the shopkeeper. A small farmer near town left instructions in his will that certain debts were to be paid, but the heir fell on hard times and was unable to meet them. He in turn died and the debts were passed on to the grandson of the original debtor.

One day he came into Boylan's down on Market and said to Miss Boylan there, "I owe you for my father's coffin, for my grandfather's and for his father's and I want to pay you for them. I don't want the debts on my conscience any longer as I am going to get married." Miss Boylan said that she no longer had the books and she didn't know what the debt was, and she thought that he was not beholden to her any longer for it was over sixty years that the debt had stood. But he insisted on paying so they worked out a reasonable amount for the coffins of those days and he paid her. She wanted him to pay her only half but he insisted on paying in full and she gave him back half of it as a present.

These several examples give us some notion of the range and depth of mutual responsibilities associated with the distribution of goods and the payment for them. When we add to these obligations those based on ties of kinship we encounter a system of reciprocities by which townsmen and countrymen are joined in a stable system of relationships extending from the past into the future. The mutual obligations recognized as part of these familial and economic patterns need not be restricted to these areas of behavior alone; they may be readily extended to others, including the areas of politics and religion. It matters little whether the ties that bind men are derived from blood or debt; the obligations associated with them are usually carefully observed.

The responsibility for the smooth working of the system belongs to both shopkeeper and customer. Each must recognize his part in the customary arrangements, although the resolution of crises threatening the relation falls more squarely on the shopkeeper because of his usually strategic position. Insolvency of the debtor may require the lending of money or recourse to the banking system, as we have seen. But if the debtor evades his obligations, either by refusing to pay a debt or by trading elsewhere, the shopkeeper can take steps to force him to fulfill his obligations.

The methods which the shopkeeper uses to achieve his end are also rooted in custom. One small farmer near Ennis describes the consequence of not trading with one's creditors. He says:

I am dealing with say Malones. I could be dealing there for years. There was a bill of five pounds on me there. I used [would] pay two pounds [and] raise [buy] a couple of bags [of flour]. The bill was [would be] up again to five. Another day I would pay the five. I wanted stuff [that day and] they would give me stuff. That would raise the bill again and so on. I was never clear. They wanted me to leave them my whole year's produce and why not when I was not clear if I went to town for a half sack flour and got it a shilling cheaper at any other house and they [were] to find it out I would have an attorney's letter before a week when I did not leave the money to themselves [trade with them].

The "attorney's letter" warns the individual that he has an outstanding account which should be paid immediately or court action will ensue. The mere threat of court proceedings stirs the average countryman to action because of his desire to avoid the disgrace that such publicity brings on his family. The fear of unfavorable publicity is the strongest weapon the shopkeeper has to enforce adherence to the obligations of the credit system and although he can threaten legal action he seldom resorts to it. Court proceedings are frequently costly, and in the end the shopkeeper often gains nothing for his expense save perhaps some unfavorable publicity of his own. One shopkeeper in Ennis explained why the legal system is seldom used to collect old debts:

If you go to court and have the sheriff process the man, the sheriff will probably tell you he already has several to serve on this man and that he isn't able to serve any of them and to serve another will only cost you money and do you no good. Annuities and rates have precedence over other bills, and so you put the bill in your pocket and forget about it.

The shopkeeper has another and more subtle means by which he can enforce payment. He secures the necessary unfavorable publicity for his debtor without incurring either expense or social liability to himself. One shopkeeper explained that if an account is overdue you mail the man a statement using a two-penny stamp. If he pays no attention to you, another is mailed, and still another. If, after a time, there is still no answer, you mail him a statement using a half-penny stamp, in which case you do not seal the envelope. The shopkeeper knows that the postmaster where the debtor gets his mail will be certain to open the unsealed envelope and read the contents. Because the postmaster is always a source of news for the countryside, the information that so and so owes an unpaid account is certain to be passed on. Both shopkeeper and debtor are aware that he will be the subject of conversation in every household in the locality. The shopkeeper expects that the debtor will pay rather than have another half-penny statement mailed. But such drastic measures are used only as a last resort for the certainty is great that the action will bring a severance to the relationship.

We had the opportunity to observe the profound effect of this practice on one individual. A young doctor from a neighboring town was in the habit of spending his nights in an Ennis hotel, drinking with his friends. Through an oversight (according to him), he had failed to pay his bar bill and received his statement in a half-penny envelope. A few days later he appeared in a rival hotel, where he condemned the other hotel owner for his unwarranted action. His principal complaint was that the bill had been mailed to him with a half-penny stamp, and he was certain that everyone in his home town would be talking about him behind his back, saying that he did not pay his bills and that he was drinking away all his money and spending his nights carousing. He vowed that he would never buy another drink in that hotel.

Through the application of the controls or sanctions similar to the ones we have sketched above, the reciprocal character of the credit relationship is regulated and maintained. Not only does custom prescribe the arrangements by which the credit system operates and is maintained, but it also prescribes the penalties for their infraction. Whenever the smooth working of the system is jeopardized custom also provides the guidelines within which solutions are sought.

There is another context, however, in which the long-standing relationships between shopkeepers and farmers should be viewed: the stereotype that most farmers hold of the town and its inhabitants. For the average small farmer, the town is a strange and unfriendly place. Even in the countryside his security is rooted in his own locality and those living only a few miles away will be strangers to him. The countryman is sensitive to the patronizing treatment that he sometimes receives in the town, and he is fearful that he will be cheated, even robbed by those of the back streets if he should become drunk. Town-dwelling kinsman or shopkeeper-friend provides him with a haven and, to the extent that obligations are honored, a source of assistance in times of need. Even these relationships, however, are not free of potential tension. The farmer's position is usually a dependent one, and his manners, speech, and dress are different from those of the shopkeeper. He believes the shopkeeper to be a very intelligent fellow because he does not have to work hard, he makes a great deal of money, and he is able to travel about and meet people.

The shopkeeper, in turn, has a variety of ideas about the countryman. If he has been born and reared in the town, he finds the farmer something of an enigma. He may refer to him as a tricky fellow who would cheat you if he had the chance, and in the next breath he tells you that it is practically impossible to understand him. In his opinion, farmers are very deep, and you never know what is going on in their heads. Often he will recount with laughing indulgence tales of rural buffoonery. Customs surrounding marriage, birth, or death are considered either amusing or barbarous, and certainly there is little sympathetic understanding of the purposes they serve. On the other hand, the shopkeeper openly recognized that the farmer is the basis of his prosperity. He will tell you that when the farmers are having bad times, the shopkeepers will also, because shopkeepers depend upon farmers for business.

The antagonism that the farmers (and the town's laborers as well) feel toward the shopkeeper are not without some basis in fact. In an earlier day the "gombeen" shopkeeper charged exorbitant prices and interest on unpaid debts and even took over the holdings of his customers as payment, sometimes resorting to eviction. Such are the remembered evils of the past.

Even today shopkeepers have been noted for sharp practices in their dealings — watering the whiskey, putting cheaper brands in more expensive bottles, selling substitutes, using scales which give short measure, and selling inferior products as first-quality goods. These unscrupulous practices may be found out soon enough, but the farmer is never certain of receiving what he counts as fair treatment. Another charge leveled against the shopkeeper, particularly the publican, is that of putting the "screws" to those whom he has got into debt. One Ennis publican said that if a man came into his shop and needed a pound or so for a week or two he would gladly give it to him, and he always kept a supply of money on hand just for that purpose. He did so as part of his policy of doing good turns for people, a policy that actually amounted to putting the person under obligation to him. He explained that when the man returned to make payment he would buy a drink or groceries. In appreciation for the help, he would be willing to trade there. The publican saw nothing wrong in this behavior; in fact he considered himself a benefactor who helped people over a slim period, providing a service for which he thought he ought to be repaid.

A still more serious charge is political favoritism. Publicans are thought to seek out public office for the benefit of themselves and that of their customers. Indeed, one publican, also a member of the County Council, authorized official relief only for those who would trade with him.

Neither statute nor custom can prevent deviation from approved behavior by those who are so minded. Although unethical practices are recognized as such and condemned, those who are confronted with the need to meet obligations toward kin and friend feel no deep moral ambivalence about the fact that law or custom will be violated in so doing. It is an inexorable rule that one stands with one's own, and there is none more despicable than the turncoat or the informer. Although the credit relation seldom evokes such extreme displays of courage or cowardice, its reciprocities take the same distinctive form as those found in the interpersonal relations among small farmers.

In its simplest form the credit relation may be viewed as a creditor-debtor relation involving only goods and money. But neither shopkeeper or client limits it to such a narrow definition. The system imposes a much wider set of obligations on both parties and in some circumstances extends beyond the two principals. In particular, the shopkeeper is expected to act, when requested, as intermediary on behalf of his client. The request may concern the placement of a son or daughter in employment; it may involve putting in a good word to a Land Commission official to influence him in the assignment of land; it may require a visit to a county official; or it may be only a request for advice.

It is easy to interpret such behavior as the utilization of already established lines of communication. But such an interpretation does not account for the potential extension of relations to include a wide range of people who are not ordinarily in contact with each other. Once such new relations have been established through requests made and favors granted, a debt has been created for which payment can be requested at some future date. Although there may be reluctance or inability to extend the pattern of obligation beyond the orbit of day-to-day activities, the potential of such an extension is always present. Those who have learned how to use this form of ordered relationships in business, politics, and other endeavors have acquired the key to success.

With a system of this kind it is easy to understand that, whatever it may be in other parts of the world, bureaucratic practice in Ireland is no equal and impersonal application of rules to problems. Likewise, the rigidities of an accounting system may cast up figures which express profit and loss, but shopkeeping in the towns of Ireland cannot be understood from such statistics.

The conceptual representation of the structure of the pattern of the shopkeeper-client relationship poses an interesting problem. Each shopkeeper can be visualized as the central point in a series of balanced but unequal reciprocals; there is an expected quid pro quo in the discharge of mutual obligations but no equivalence in the specifics. The debt itself can be counted as the concrete evidence of the obligation, but either individual is free to extinguish it at any time, the debtor by clearing his account, and the shopkeeper by demanding payment.

The shopkeeper-debtor relationship may also be viewed as a point from which either party may establish new connections with people that the other party already has some kind of relation with. Such tangent use of one relationship to reach others, either directly or indirectly, is exemplified in the case of the apprentice or shop assistant whose relatives trade at his place of employment.

It is easier to understand how kin obligations and cooperation follow a family member beyond his immediate community than it is to account for their appearance in non-familial relations. But there it is, and Irish society cannot be understood except as we recognize the fact. In a general sense we can explain strength, persistence, and inclusiveness of these relations as the result of habituation in space and over time which carries appropriate customary modes of action. The extension of the family-like reciprocals to other relationships is of immense help in explaining persistence and change. For example in any enumeration of social forms the Irish family may be counted as the only one which is truly Celtic in origin. Yet Ireland has received and the Irish have incorporated town living, several land-tenure patterns, exotic religious and governmental systems, and other innovations. Those who brought these new forms of human grouping and practice have brought change to older ways, but it has been a gradual change within already existing outlines. Practices are continuously modified, and certain of their specifics may even disappear. Those which persist appear to be the elemental forms of Ireland's interpersonal relationships. They unite family and kin, appear again in the shopkeeper-client relation, and are found in different guises in other institutional arrangements. Perhaps here we have the key to the gaelicizing process, which over generations has converted each wave of foreign cultural imports into a truly Irish form.

Index

Index

Index

243; market areas, 275; calendar of fairs, 276

Cliamhan: special term for son-in-law, 89; in-marrying sons-in-law, 110

Cliques: old men's, in the *cuaird*, 173; young men's in Rynamona, 186; intermediate and transitional cliques, 191; incorporation of local craftsmen into, 263

Cóir, a traditional obligation, 73, 75

Col: as blood-relationship, 80; comparison with civil law degrees of consanguinity, 81

Comhair, see Cooring

Community: norms about age, 163; bestows nicknames, 168; role of old men, 171; the old men's *cuaird,* 173; seat of public opinion, 186; structure of cliques, 190; place of local craftsmen, 264; relations of farmers and non-farmers, 265–271; geographical basis, 274

Congested districts, proportions of farmers on each size holdings, 14

Conjugal status: of shopkeepers, 335–338; of shop assistants, 338–339

Consumption, of farm produce, 19

Cooperation, *see* Cooring

Cooring: as agricultural cooperation, 72–74; as ceremonial assistance, 73; as social obligation, 74; with local craftsmen, 254; compared with *meitheal,* 255

Corn: value of produce, 4; harvest, 43

"Country divorce," as means of assuring heir, 132

Country people, *see* Farmers

Cousins, reckoning of, 82–83

Crafts: former local, 226; surviving rural, 244; local specialization and "handymen," 245; development, 250; differences in remuneration, 251; process of emergence and disappearance, 261; community organization, 263

Creameries: in Limerick, 8; recent introduction of, 227

Credit: social function of, 394–395; as "running account," 396; and "tied account," 398; and banking, 401; re-

payment of, 402–403; as communication system, 408–410

Crime, provenance in social situation, 112

Cuaird: hospitality, 75; age status behavior, 126; old men of the community, 173; as controlling old men's clique, 174; Rynamona example, 176–186; women in, 196

Customers: and family obligations, 344; adjustment to, 351–352

Dancing: as young people's pursuit, 189

Daughter-in-law: term for, 89; introduction of, 122

Demography: decline of population, 94; unique statistics of marriage, 99; high fertility, 102; interpretation in light of family system, 150; old age statistics, 153–161; sex ratio, 195

De Valera: "economic war" during regime of, 29; program of industrialization, 224

Devon Commission on Congestion, 396, 399–401

Distribution, *see* Trade

Dominance, parental, 54

Dowry, *see* Fortune

"Economic war," effect of on small farmers, 29

Education: facilities in Ennis, 313; of shopkeeper's children, 376–378; and effect on son's success, 390

Eggs: value of produce, 4; home consumption, 20

Éire, see Irish Free State

Emigrant remittances, in family dispersal, 144

Emigration: flow since famine, 95; causes, 96; effect of changes in agriculture, 97; remittances, 144; as mechanism of family reformation, 147

Ennis: history of, 309–311; hinterland of, 311–312; as market center, 312–314; physical appearance of, 314–15; variations among residents: based on appearances, 316–317; as seen in

414

417